Governing the Child in

D0626645

Governing the Child in the New Millennium

Edited by Kenneth Hultqvist and Gunilla Dahlberg

RoutledgeFalmer

NEW YORK & LONDON

Published in 2001 by
RoutledgeFalmer
29 West 35th Street
New York, NY 10001

Published in Great Britain by
RoutledgeFalmer
11 New Fetter Lane
London EC4P 4EE

RoutledgeFalmer in an imprint of the Taylor & Francis Group.

Copyright © 2001 RoutledgeFalmer

Printed in the United States of America on acid-free paper.

10   9   8   7   6   5   4   3   2   1

Library of Congress Cataloging-in Publication Data is available from the
Library of Congress.

Hultqvist, Kenneth and Dahlberg, Gunilla
    Governing the child in the new millennium / edited by Kenneth Hultqvist
        and Gunilla Dahlberg
            p.   cm
    Includes bibliographical references (p.) and index.
    ISBN: 0-415-92830-3 (hbk.)—ISBN: 0-415-92831-1 (pbk.)

To Morrison

Contents

Foreword

This book is the result of a joint effort to rethink current ways of thought and practices about the child and childhood, especially as these "entities" appear within the field of childhood education. "Education" or "educative processes" will be used in the broad sense of the words, covering also forms of immanent pedagogy or "silent" ways of governing/organizing the lives of children.

Our work started with a series of seminars in Copenhagen in August 1998. The seminars were loosely framed, and the task we put to ourselves was simply this: *To think about the status and character of childhood at the end of the twentieth century.* From this rather loose beginning there emerged a collection of issues and arguments that we felt were important in today's context of change. These were about liberalism and liberal ideas about the child's self-governance, the universals of traditional childhood thought, relations of power and knowledge, and the national/global dimension of childhood.

The authors of this book are concerned with childhood as an invention and particularly with childhood in this historical conjuncture of ours. The themes, issues, and arguments that we present do not cohere in a single conceptual structure or way of theorizing, but we share the conviction that much of the twentieth century's ways of reasoning and theorizing about the child and childhood have to come to an end. Some of us would say that it is modernism's rationalism that has come to an end, while others would argue that we are still anchored in modernist ways of reasoning. Notwithstanding, modernist thought in the beginning of the third millennium is different from that of the first half of the twentieth century. To complicate matters, there is no *the* modernity, shared by each and all. The European and American version of Enlightenment and liberal thought have spread around the globe, but the meanings and the symbols that are attached to modernity vary from one country to another. Modernity is much like what some of the authors of this volume would call a "floating signifier," an empty sign that carries various political strategies and national imaginaries. Also, it would be Eurocentric not to acknowledge the existence of other ways of organizing the lives of children. As the South American contributions to this volume show, childhood is also inscribed in clearly illiberal and anti-Enlightenment traditions.

Childhood is about to change, and there is no general formula of change. However, there is the possibility of developing languages that are open enough to account for variations and that also pay due respect to the singularity of change. This volume is a modest effort in such a direction.

Finally, we want to thank Sten Petersson, Annika Thelin, and Gunnar Åsen at the Swedish Agency for School for their intellectual support and for providing us with the financial opportunities to arrange the seminars in Copenhagen.

Our seminars were part of the Organisation Mondiale pour l'Éducation Préscolaire (OMEP) Congress in Copenhagen in August 1998, and we would like to thank the OMEP Committee for its kind support and for letting us share the facilities of the Congress.

Stockholm, June 1, 2000   Kenneth Hultqvist and Gunilla Dahlberg

Governing the Child in the New Millennium

Kenneth Hultqvist and Gunilla Dahlberg

Introduction

In a lecture held in 1983 at the college de France, Michel Foucault made a beautiful response to an article written two hundred years earlier by Immanuel Kant (1784). In Foucault's view, Kant was the first philosopher who raised issues about the difference between the past and the present. For Kant this difference lay in a certain self-reflectiveness of the Enlightenment and modernity, introduced by the events of the French Revolution. Using his reason, Kant argued, Man could liberate himself from self-imposed constraints on his freedom.

In his work, Foucault historicized Kant's conceptions of "man," "reason," and "liberty," and for him, the presence of these concepts was intimately related to new patterns of governing human beings (Foucault, 1980, 1991). Man emerged with the decentralization of sovereign authority and with the new liberal constraints on the exercise of power. From the French Revolution on, power was not so much about the use of violence and restrictions as about knowledge and the administrative resources of the state to promote the well-being and health of the population. Kant's formula of self-governance in the name of autonomy and freedom is in Foucault's view part of this shift in the exercise of power.

Slightly transposed, the birth of man led to the construction of the modern child in the childhood discourse of the nineteenth and twentieth centuries. The new view of the child became institutionalized in areas such as welfare for children, schools, social policy, social work, child psychiatry, and other public institutions (Rose, 1990).

It is broadly acknowledged today, both in academic and public debate, that childhood is about to change: in the way that social and educational research is constituted, in the new decentralized strategies of government, in the image production of media, and in the images of the lifelong learning conceptions and globalization produced by national governments and international organizations such as WHO, OECD, and UNICEF. For the most part, however, the discussion is either on the structural changes in the economy or the social conditions that influence childhood from the outside, or change is treated as an evolutionary process. In these and other forums of discussion, there is seldom any mention of the productive effects of knowledge, which is treated as an epiphenomena of the structural changes in economy and society (Popkewitz, 2000).

The authors of this book will offer another vantage point to the understanding of the current changes in childhood. We subscribe to the Foucauldian ideas that man/child is an invention of thought and that discourse and knowledge are productive aspects of current changes. There is no natural or evolutionary child, only the historically produced discourses and power relations that constitute the child as an object and subject of knowledge, practice, and political intervention. As does Kant, we acknowledge the value of a presentism approach to the understanding of actuality; but as Foucault, we favor a certain historicism in our dealing with the present. The historical forces and discourses that once produced the child/man as an object and subject of discourse are still with us and their presence is felt through the way we interrogate our actuality. This assumption is part of the minimal framework of this book.

Our concern with the present is diagnostic, which we define as the exploration of significant shifts in the regimes of knowledge and power that guide and govern the conception of the child in such various fields as education, media, and popular culture. The issues we raise include the following: (1) how historical discourses and practices that are mobilized today in education, popular culture, the media, and social policy construct the child differently from the past; (2) how historical relations of power reinscribe issues of inclusion and exclusion; (3) how the child is mobilized in different local and national contexts; and (4) how national differences in the way the child is conceived of can be used to explore the relationship between the local/national and global.

The Natural Man/Child

Until quite recently, in the prevailing view childhood was the culmination of evolutionary processes, the origin of which lay in the civilizing processes of Western societies and the hereditary endowment of human beings. It was the work of Ariès (1962) and others that questioned this assumption. Ariès argued that childhood and our modern conception of the child emerged with the bourgeoisie society and especially with the division between public and private space that relocated the child and segregated him or her from the worldly affairs of the adults. Ariès's work is important and has rightly been celebrated as a landmark in the study of childhood. However, his functionalist analysis tended to underestimate the inventive character of childhood. Childhood did not emerge solely as an effect of structural changes in society but was an invention of thought. Before childhood became a "structure," the child, as we conceive of it today, had to be invested with the needs and the capacities that we assume are part of the child's nature. Without the intervention of such thought we would not even know what to look for, nor would we be able to invent the necessary strategies and techniques to safeguard the child's development.

Jean-Jacques Rousseau is a paramount figure in this context. Rousseau did not invent the modern child, but he spoke from a position that was not easily available for his contemporaries. He had three key ideas. The first of these ideas was that the child had a vulnerable mind that needed to be protected from the influence of—as he saw it—a depraved adult world. His second idea was about liberty, the goal of the educative process being a life of freedom to be self-governed and autonomous. His third idea concerned the source of educational authority, which for Rousseau was not man made but resided in the nature of the child. It was nature that guided both the child and the educator through the educative process. To be free, then, would be to act in accordance with nature: the site of freedom and the great master of the order of things (Rousseau, 1877, 1977). Through these and similar ways of reasoning, a space was inaugurated that prepared the ground for educative processes as well as for other interventions in the lives of children.

Rousseau's ideas were rehearsed, changed, and displaced in different national and social contexts during the nineteenth and twentieth centuries. Drawing on Darwinist notions about the development of the species, G. Stanley Hall and his collaborators inaugurated the child study movement in the United States. Using the cultural recapitulation theory as a framework for his studies, Hall argued that the child's development recapitulates the development of man (Hall, 1888). As for Rousseau, the study of the child was essential for Hall, as it provided the governing authorities, practitioners, and parents with the knowledge they needed to arrange practices and institutions for the rearing and education of children. Moving ahead in time, this heritage was further developed by, for example, Maria Montessori, Arnold Gesell, Jean Piaget, and Pierre Janet. Similar patterns of thought were repeated in the other sciences of the child. In sociology, nature was socialized and historicized (Ariès's study is part of that tradition), but the child was as thoroughly inscribed in the universals as was the child of pedagogy or psychology. The focus had shifted from nature to society, but the reification[1] of "society" by Emile Durkheim and the other pioneers of sociological thought (Jenks, 1996) made the child look as natural as the child in developmental psychology.

Childhood as a Problematic of Governing

The narrative of childhood thought, then, is about the child's natural route to self-governance and reason. This liberal framework is recognizable in the various versions of the child from Rousseau on. Childhood has been about the formation of the self-guiding child and citizen, and the overarching concern of the project of childhood is with the emancipation of the child from the restraints of traditions and the dark forces of the old world. When liberated, the child would guide him or herself by the rational thought inscribed in psychology and the other social and human sciences. Knowledge, in this narrative, is just the servant of the emancipation of the child's natural self-governing capacities; it represents and orders the visible and nonvisible features of the child.

We view the subject matter differently. The ordering of knowledge is not about representation but about the production of historical truths that govern and guide the conduct of the child. This view of the productivity of knowledge is absent from childhood thought. Absent also are the links and connections that once made the modern view of the child and childhood possible. Historically, the liberal construction of the children is linked with the construction of capitalist economies, industrialization, and the formation of the nation-states of the eighteenth and nineteenth centuries. It also wears the marks of colonialism and the early processes of globalization (Baker, 1998). During this period, new ways of reasoning about the exercise of power emerged that would link human beings in new and unexpected ways with the emerging new world order of nation-states (Anderson, 1991). The principle of sovereignty and the methods of inflicting pain on bodies became increasingly obsolete. Instead, sovereignty was replaced with decentralized regimes of ruling that sought to promote the self-governance of individuals and collectives by acting on their conduct, the subject's actions upon him or herself (Foucault, 1991). The new identities that came into existence this way were not of a natural order, but the product of inventions of thought that brought unity to diverse groups of people that happened to inhabit the same geographical territory. The way this belonging was constructed transcended previous local face-to-face relationships of small communities and enabled the abstract patterns of communications that are typical of the modern national and transnational orders. Individuals were to carry their homes[2] inside themselves as they moved beyond the realms of the local to the national and the global (Popkewitz, 2000). Knowledge became the essential intellectual technology in this social administration of the self, as it inscribed the prevailing national imaginaries and the liberal mentalities about human conduct through schools and in the other institutions and practices of childhood. Early childhood thought emerged within these new parameters of political thought and it spoke the new language of power when reasoning about the child.

Historically, the self-governing individual coincided with modernity and the two master discourses of liberal freedom and autonomy (e.g., Foucault, 1991; Habermas [see Bernstein, 1992]; Wagner, 1994). Early childhood thought inscribed a certain understanding of modernity that separated issues of power from issues of freedom and produced a rather one-sided version of liberty and individualism. Contingent historical processes—forces that related to problems of governance in modern societies—became reified and as a result the child was "made up" as the container of natural progress.

Maria Montessori's work in Italy is a good example of the dilemmas that haunted early childhood thought. In a series of books and articles (e.g., Montessori, 1912, 1936), Montessori argued that the child's natural tendencies toward freedom and autonomy were arrested due to the forces of tradition (premodern societies). She also argued that the construction of new and liberal institutions (e.g., preschools) was a prerequisite for the development of the child's inborn tendencies. She even argued that the freedom of the child was necessary for the establishment of the science of psychology. Otherwise, she claimed, the psychological and pedagogical gazes were unable to detect and visualize the secrets of nature; nature was obscured as long as the traditional practices reigned (Hultqvist, 1997, 1998; Walkerdine, 1984; see also Dahlberg, Moss, & Pence, 1999). The historical act of combining psychological thought with pedagogy produced the image of a self-regulating child; a child when set free would regulate or steer him or herself with the slight guidance of the professional pedagogues.

Montessori's work points to the inherent contradictions in childhood thought. If children are governed by nature, why, in the first place, do we need to nurture and educate our children? Why do we need experts to guide and govern the child? Why not rely on the authority of nature itself? The nineteenth- and twentieth-century thought on the child was tormented by such internal contradictions. Barry Hindess (1993) has pointed out that liberal thought traditionally moved in two directions: to conceive of freedom and autonomy as natural states or as historical constructions with a telos. Both of these perspectives were present in early childhood thought. On the one hand, childhood was a natural process; on the other, it was to be realized through the practices of educators and others who sought to save the child's soul from the same uncertainties that made childhood possible as a historical project.

As we have tried to point out, the one-sidedness of childhood thought is not simply the result of intellectual mistakes, nor is it solely the pioneering efforts of Rousseau, Montessori, Gesell, Piaget, and others. The child of childhood thought shares the destiny of the anthropological version of man in Kant's philosophy. Both Kant's man and Montessori's child are supposed to emancipate themselves from past traditions and authorities. Kant's story, which has been told ever since by the Western liberal political rationalities, is a salvation story about progress and reason.[3] The story is reminiscent of previous religious discourse. Man's gaze is undoubtedly focused on the modern secular order, but his self-reflections draw on the confessional practices of Christianity.[4] When moving outside of himself, he found "that religious thought was transferred to the field of politics . . . concepts of salvation and perfection were moved from the heavens to earth" (Popkewitz & Pitzman, 1986, p. 13). The emancipation of man in Kant's philosophy can be read in the light of this transition from religious to secular discourses on man/child. The man/child is a hybrid, as it is constructed from heterogeneous historical forces and discourses.

The contradictions of childhood thought were not ever resolved but have been with us since the days of the pioneers. They led to the construction of the normal child with a normal way of reasoning and emotional and aesthetic experience, but they also produced their opposites: otherness and the fears and anxieties that surrounded the figures of the nonnormal child, the racially "inferior" child, the proletarian boy and girl—characters that would, should these threats not be counteracted, disrupt the sanitary logic of the child's nature. In the memories that we now make of the past, it is increasingly recognized that the knowledge of developmental psychology, sociology of childhood, and child pedagogy was not universal. This knowledge emerged in local sites to deal with problems and possibilities that appeared urgent at the time, for example, to create the images of a nation or to build popular education, preschool institutions, parents' education, and other arrangements for the welfare of children. Neither was this universal/local language neutral; rather it was the effect of and inscribed relations of power. A growing body of research demonstrates that early developmental discourse relied on racist thought that excluded all but those children with the right signs: being white, middle class, and living under orderly conditions, preferably in small towns on the U.S. east coast (Baker, 1998; see also Hennon, 2000). It also inscribed differences that related to social class and gender (Walkerdine, 1995).

The Reinvented Child of Liberal Thought

The previous discussion points to the need for a continual critical scrutiny of the past, not for the sake of the past but for the sake of the present. The historical forces and discourses that once produced the child and childhood are still with us and their presence is felt through the way we interrogate the present. However, today's discourses on the child reassemble past discourses in new patterns and inscribe different assumptions about the child. The child of the twenty-first century is neither the subject of classical modernity of the eighteenth and nineteenth centuries nor the subject that emerged with the construction of the welfare states of the post-World War II period. The welfare idea of governing individuals in the name of society has lost much of its naturalness, and in the prevailing rationalities of administration the assumption seems to be that society can be ruled in the name of free and autonomous individuals (Rose, 1996a). Using a different conceptual apparatus, Wagner (1994) argues that current changes are signs of an ongoing deconventionalization of the language and sign systems of modernity. For Wagner, this process is due to the inability of the national welfare states to keep their previous closure, which was a precondition for a stable and naturalized sign system. Most notably, this transition, whether it is called postmodernity or late modernity, entails the withering away of previous categories and explanatory systems of childhood.

Current deconventionalization processes reveal, as in chapters by Valerie Walkerdine (Chapter 2) and Nancy Lesko (Chapter 3), the contingency of the ways of reasoning and practice that constructed childhood (in Lesko's case adolescence) as space and time. The space of childhood is no longer the euclidean space of previous developmental thought (e.g., Piaget) but the multidimensional space of cyberspace that revolves around concepts like energy and flow. Walkerdine and Lesko interrogate the present with reference to the historical relationships of power that constructed the gendered child (Walkerdine) and the adolescent (Lesko), and they also explore how these relations of power are mobilized in the twenty-first century.

The temporal dimension of childhood is also explored by Chris Jenks (Chapter 4). In his piece, Jenks shows how the practices in schools inscribe the temporal dimensions in the child's body. The normalizing practices or procedures teach the child implicitly (and sometimes very explicitly) that time is a valuable property and that one has to care for one's use of time to become a successful child. Jenks's chapter is a dialogue with the modernist themes of liberty and discipline and how these themes coincide in various versions of sociology and developmental psychology to produce the child's bodily experience.

While it may be wise not to exaggerate statements of the current destabilization processes of modernity (Rose, 1999, and Wagner, 1994, both refer to the tendency to treat society as a fiction rather than as a solid fact à la Durkheim), such changes are easily recognizable both within and beyond the educational field. Welfare and the caring for the self have become a lifelong involvement; the concept of "lifelong learning" is an indication of this development. The move toward an ethic of one's self (Rose, 1996b) also implies a more active stance toward community. Community is no longer just national community or society, but communities grounded in individual choice. And if we look around, in education and in other social practices, efforts are made to empower the child. Curricula constructs the child not as a passive recipient but as an active producer of knowledge, engaged in interaction with the adult world at all levels. Children (and teachers and parents) are participatory and interactive subjects, engaged in interactions with a world that lacks inherent stability and coherence. These themes are developed in several chapters.

Thomas S. Popkewitz and Marianne N. Bloch (Chapter 5) use the parent/child relationship to engage in issues concerning the social administration of the child's freedom. The reinvented formula of social administration in today's context, they argue, prepares the child for an extended journey beyond the imaginary space of the nation-states of the nineteenth and twentieth centuries. The child of the twenty-first century is no longer bound by the previous imaginaries that constructed nationhood and citizenship, but carries a home within him or herself that extends beyond the imaginaries of the cosmopolitan citizen of the first half of the twentieth century

These and similar changes do not necessarily imply that the project of modernity has come to an end (i.e., it has been replaced with postmodernity), but they do suggest that there is a change in the overall pattern of the processes of modernity.[5] The centered subject, inscribed in the theories of psychology and pedagogy and enacted in children's institutions, is replaced by the "flexible self," a self that is willing and capable to respond and act in a constantly changing environment. In the context of education, we see the emergence of new technologies that order and conduct the child's actions in new ways. The educated subject in Lynn Fendler's piece (Chapter 6) is produced at three levels: through a recent epistemological mutation that focuses on the whole child, that is, all of the child's intellectual and nonintellectual abilities; and through the reinvention and establishment of new connections between the twentieth-century discourse of development and interactionism. Theoretically, this indicates a new paradigm of exercising power, or what Fendler calls the "control society," which depends on the continuous and never-ending examination of the whole child.

The deconventionalization (and denaturalization) of previous categories of thought are acknowledged broadly in today's social and natural science language. In the simple and straightforward economy of this language we are what we can say of ourselves and what we can do with ourselves and others. And what we can say about ourselves is dependent upon the tools, techniques, and technologies that we use to investigate and govern ourselves. Biotechnology and genetic engineering prove the point well. Biotechnology is not the study of biology (or nature), it is a study in the name of biology. As it turns out, nature and biology today look considerably less natural (and biological) than just a few decades ago. They have become open to the acts of choice and manipulation (Rose, 2000). This connection is made by Kenneth Hultqvist in Chapter 7, which is about the recent change of discourse on the child in the Swedish educational context. Education in Sweden in the late twentieth century reintroduced the child of Bildung, a European continental conception that flourished in Sweden and elsewhere in the nineteenth and twentieth centuries. Bildung is not about education, as in the Anglo-American context, but about the cultivation of one's mind and soul. Today's Bildung is reminiscent of the nineteenth- and early twentieth-century conception of it in, for example, ideas about the child's nature. But the epistemology that constructs this child has more in common with the advanced epistemology of (for example) biotechnology than with the humanist subject of past centuries.

Global Patterns of Childhood

As Wagner (1994) and Rose (1999) suggest, in slightly different ways, the changing terrain of the subject/child is a global phenomenon. While globalization is not an altogether recent event (see Chapter 5 of this book), current changes seem to be more encompassing than in any other previous period of time. Current discourses about the efficient, autonomous, and flexible child are distributed on a global scale, in formal education and schooling and by means of discourses and images that are transmitted by the global media. However, this homogenization of discourses does not necessarily imply, as is suggested in current discussion of globalization (e.g., Castel, 1996), that childhood or other social phenomena become disconnected from their local/national context. The "global" does not refer to an autonomous sphere of influence that exists beyond the level of nation-states and countries. It is rather the terminal point of signs about the child and childhood that are produced in local contexts (see Chapter 5). When such signs are removed from their local sites, they become naturalized and seemingly disconnected from their local context. Popkewitz has introduced the concept of the "indigenous foreigner" to account for such local/global exchange of signs (Popkewitz, 2000). The indigenous foreigners—for example, international heroes such as John Dewey, Michel Foucault, and Lev Vygotskij—are empty signifiers, homeless figures of thought that circulate freely in the global distributive apparatuses of research and education. When these figures are temporarily arrested in a local context, they take on the characteristics of that context before they move on to other contexts and become the target of further interpretations and reinterpretations.

The South American contributions in this book prove the point well. The European and U.S. versions of modernity spread globally, but their impact is restricted by the presence of local traditions, some of which are counterdiscourses to Enlightenment and liberalism.[6] Historical differences (e.g., in the national imaginaries, the role of the state in governing the child, and the power relations that organize the discourse on the child and its childhood) condition the way that the dominant global discourses are received in different national contexts. The widely spread educational discourse about flexibility, autonomy, and efficiency, for example, will be received differently and produce different effects in Europe and the United States[7] than in Argentina, Brazil, or Mexico.

Mirian Jorge Warde provides a good case in Chapter 8. In her piece, Warde shows how the reasoning about the state and the family in Brazil historically produced a conception of childhood that made the family and the school the naturalized site of childhood. The normality of childhood was achieved by ways of reasoning that made the family the sole responsible agent of normality and also the cause and the blame for the production of abnormal children that were unfit for school. The fluent production of normality was organized by the combination of school and family, while abnormality, outside the reason of the school/family, became the concern of the state that managed these children in special institutions for the excluded. This historical divide is reproduced in current reception of global discourses of national and individual efficiency. Efficiency, in today's Brazilian context, is produced as the cognitive child of psychology (which is a very different child than in, e.g., the U.S. and Swedish contexts, where the child is conceived of as a whole child. See Chapters 6 and 7), while the rest of the children are outside of childhood and beyond hope and salvation.

Inés Dussel (Chapter 9) continues Warde's discussion about inclusion and exclusion in the national context of Argentina. While Warde points to the lack of hope among the excluded, Dussel's chapter is about the possibility of such hope and the continuous struggle for justice. Empirically, Dussel's chapter deals with a group of adults who are reclaiming their names and their right to an identity that was taken from them when they were small children. The military removed them from their parents by force, adopted them, and gave them new names. Using the framework of a Foucauldian analysis and Derrida's notion of justice, Dussel argues that these children, who are now adults, produce memories of a lost childhood that is part of an ongoing struggle about justice and injustice, exclusion and inclusion. Interestingly, this struggle for identity and justice is not, as in previous struggles in Argentina, pursued at the level of the formal institutions of childhood but on "the street level" (the streets that were formally excluded from childhood, not only in the South American context but also in the U.S. and European contexts). Dussel uses this observation to argue for the eventlike character of childhood. Childhood is not a structure but an event that is made and continuously remade.

The chapters in this book point to the diversity of childhood. The European child is different from both the American and the South American versions. Not even the South American child is homogenous. As analyzed by Rosa Nidia Buenfil (Chapter 10), the Mexican child is produced within an amalgam of discourses that tied anti-Enlightenment discourse with the European Enlightenment traditions and a nationally produced heroic popular mythology that Buenfil calls the Mexican revolutionary mystique. Drawing on different educational documents from the 1930s to the 1990s, Buenfil makes a detailed analysis of the shifting relations of power that produced the child as an object and subject of educational concern in the Mexican historical context.

A History of the Present of the History of the Present

A few decades ago, not many scholars paid attention to the discourses that are now called postmodernism or poststructuralism. Not even Michel Foucault, today conceived of as one of the major contributors to this field of thought, knows the character of postmodern thought, and Foucault declared his ignorance of it in an interview from the beginning of the 1980s. The interviewer asked him: "Are you a post-modernist?" and Foucault replied: "I am not informed." After being told, he said to the interviewer: "I do not understand the kind of problems that this term refers to, or how it can be a common denominator of people who in fact deal with quite different problems" (Raulet, 1985, p. 68). Foucault's response is open to interpretation, but it is probably safe to argue that the discourses that today travel globally as postmodernism and poststructuralism carry Foucault's name. It is also both conceivable and probable that poststructuralism now has reached a level of influence that will have an impact on the discourses and practices that organize childhood. Poststructuralism, then, is not only an intellectual tool for doing histories of the present but is part of the current production of governmentalities. It is therefore, as Julie McLeod argues (Chapter 11), important to analyze the impact of poststructuralist thought on the child and childhood. McLeod's chapter is about the effects of feminist poststructuralist discourse on the production of childhood in the Australian national context. She convincingly argues that poststructuralist feminist thought is involved in the production of new governmentalities in the Australian context. McLeod's chapter also shows that any evaluation, whether it is about poststructuralism or other intellectual currents, must take into account national influences on the reception of "foreign" theories. The Foucault in France is not necessarily the Foucault in Australia, Sweden, the United States, or South America.

Conclusion

The concern of this book is with the diagnosis of current changes in the conceptions and practices of childhood. Our ambition, however, is not to be conclusive but to be tentative and exploring. Such a general attitude or ethos does not necessarily result in a singular theoretical orientation, but it might produce a certain commonality in views on method. The issues and arguments that we explore and try to diagnose are tied to specific fields of problematizations in local contexts; for example, in educational research, government programs, popular culture, and media in different national or local contexts. While such an approach is concerned with the singular and eventlike character of social and historical phenomena, it does produce a certain generality in that it might inspire research that goes beyond the local points of application, both within and beyond the area of childhood. The reader will also note— and this corresponds with our method/ethos—that there is no singular chapter on "globalization." Rather, the global and the national appear through the way the book is organized. One way or another, each of the chapters pursues the global while dealing with the local and the national.

As we stated in the foreword, our project started with a very open question about the status and character of current childhood. In hindsight, however, we could not but, as the late Michel Foucault would have put it, relate to our own archive, that is, the project(s) of modernity. This dependency on a common historical bias probably adds to the theoretical coherence of the book.

Notes

[1] It may be true that Emile Durkheim and the early sociologists inaugurated the study of society, but we agree with Thomas Osborne and Nikolas Rose (1997) that the groundwork for this discovery was prepared by the medical men or the doctors who invented the social domain as one of governing. They did so in the name of preventive medicine. The social was invented, then, well before sociology discovered the abstract notion of society.

[2] The idea of a home (the People's Home) was deliberately used in the Swedish context during the postwar years to construct an individuality that would fit industrialized society (see Chapter 7).

[3] It is well documented that reason in childhood thought was a salvation discourse and a way out of the dilemmas and crises that faced modern societies. See Walkerdine (1995).

[4] On the relation between self-reflexivity and confessional practices, see Foucault (1980).

[5] To some observers such as Foucault and Deleuze this process of change not only is about the death of God and the God-centered universe (Nietzsche) but about the vanishing of the human subject as it has been conceived since the Enlightenment: the sacred object of religion and classical modernity. To others (e.g., Wagner, 1994) change is less dramatic and is conceived of as the historical outcome of a renewal of the processes of modernization.

[6] Popkewitz pointed out to us that even the anti-Enlightenment discourses in Latin American countries are of European origin. We agree, but our argument is that

the inscription of Enlightenment and anti-Enlightenment discourses is different in Latin America than in the United States and Europe.
[7] There are also differences between the U.S. and European versions of Enlightenment and modernity. See, for example, Fergusson (1997) and Wagner (1994).

References

Anderson, B. (1991). *Imagined communities: Reflections on the origin and spread of nationalism.* London: Verso.

Ariès, P. (1962). *Centuries of childhood: A social history of family life.* New York: Vintage Books.

Baker, B. (1998). "Childhood" in the emergence and spread of U.S. public schools. In T. S. Popkewitz & M. Brennan (Eds.), *Foucault's challenge: Discourse, knowledge, and power in education* (pp. 117–43). New York: Teachers College Press.

Bernstein, R. J. (Ed.) (1992). *Habermas and modernity.* Cambridge, MA: MIT Press.

Castel, M. (1996). *The information age: Economy, society and culture. Volume I: The rise of the network society.* Oxford, UK: Blackwell.

Dahlberg, G., Moss, P., & Pence, A. (1999). *Beyond quality in early childhood education and care.* London: Falmer Press.

Fergusson, R. L. (1997). *The American Enlightenment 1750–1820.* London: Harvard University Press.

Foucault, M. (1980). The confession of the flesh. In C. Gordon (Ed.), *Michel Foucault: Power/Knowledge* (pp. 194–228). London: Harvester Wheatsheaf.

Foucault, M. (1991). Governmentality. In G. Burchel, C. Gordon, & P. Miller, *The Foucault effect: Studies in governmentality* (pp. 87–104). London: Harvester Wheatsheaf.

Hall, G. S. (1888). *The contents of children's minds on entering schools.* New York: Kellogg.

Hennon, L. (2000). The construction of discursive space as patterns of inclusion/exclusion; Governmentality and urbanism in the United States. In T. S. Popkewitz (Ed.), *Educational knowledge: Changing relationships between the state, civil society and the educational community* (pp. 243–61). New York: State University of New York Press.

Hindess, B. (1993). Liberalism, socialism and democracy: Variations of a governmental theme. In A. Barry, T. Osborne, & N. Rose (Eds.), *Foucault and political reason, liberalism, neo-liberalism and governmentality, economy and society,* pp. 65–80. London: UCL Press.

Hultqvist, K. (1997). Changing rationales for governing the child: A historical perspective on the construction of the child in two institutional contexts—the school and the pre-school. *Childhood, 4,* pp. 405–24.

Hultqvist, K. (1998). A history of the present on children's welfare in Sweden. From Fröbel to present-day decentralization projects. In T. S. Popkewitz & M. Brennan (Eds.), *Foucault's challenge: Discourse, knowledge, and power in education* (pp. 91–116). New York: Teachers College Press.

Jenks, C. (1996). *Childhood.* London: Routledge.

Kant, I. (1784). *Beautwortung der Frage: Was ist Aufklärung.* Berlinische Monatschrift.

Montessori, M. (1912). *The Montessori method.* London: Heineman.

Montessori, M. (1936). *The secrets of childhood.* Bombay: Orient Longman.

Osborne, T., & Rose, N. (1997). In the name of society, or three theses on the history of social thought. *History of the Human Sciences, 10* (3), 87–104.

Popkewitz, T. S. (2000). Globalization/regionalization, knowledge, and the educational practices: Some notes on comparative strategies for educational research. In T. S. Popkewitz (Ed.), *Educational knowledge: Changing relationships between the state, civil society and the educational community* (pp. 3–24). New York: State University of New York Press.

Popkewitz, T. S. (2000). National imaginaries, the indigenous foreigner and power: Comparative educational research In J. Schriever (Ed.), *Discourse formation in comparative education* (pp. 261–94). Berlin: Peter Lang Verlag.

Popkewitz, T. S., & Pitman, A (1986). The idea of progress and the legitimation of state agendas: American proposals for school reform. *Curriculum and Teaching, 1* (1–2), 11–24.

Raulet, G. (1985). Michel Foucault interviewed by G. Raulet. *Structuralism and poststructuralism, Res Publica,* vol. 3. Lund: Symposium.

Rose, N. (1990). *Governing the soul: The shaping of the private self.* London: Routledge.

Rose, N. (1996a). The death of the social: Refiguring the territory of government. *Economy and Society, 25,* 327–66.

Rose, N. (1996b). *Inventing ourselves: Psychology, power and personhood.* New York: Cambridge University Press.

Rose, N. (1999). *Powers of freedom: Reframing political thought.* Cambridge, UK: Cambridge University Press.

Rose, N. (2000, February 8). The politics of life itself: Biosociality, genetics and the government of the human vital order. Paper presented at an open lecture at the Stockholm Institute of Education.

Rousseau, J. J. (1877). *La nouvelle Héloise.* Paris: Firmin-Didot.

Rousseau, J. J. (1977). *Emile, eller om uppfostran,* del I och II. Göteborg: Stegelands förlag.

Wagner, P. (1994). *A sociology of modernity: Liberty and discipline.* London: Routledge.

Walkerdine, V. (1995): Utvecklingspsykologi och den barncentrerade pedagogiken: införandet av Piaget i tidig undervisning In K. Hultqvist & K. Petersson (Eds.), *Foucault, namnet på en modern vetenskaplig och filosofisk problematik* (pp. 124–71). Stockholm: HLS förlag.

2

Safety and Danger

Childhood, Sexuality, and Space at the End of the Millennium

Valerie Walkerdine

Introduction

In recent years a number of major concerns have been raised regarding the safety of children in public and private spaces, both in relation to their vulnerability to dangerous adults but also the problem of dangerous children who prey on others. British examples of incidents leading to these concerns include the James Bulger case, where two ten-year-old boys murdered a two-year-old boy, and the Dunblane massacre, in which children in a primary school were shot by a gunman. American examples include the spate of recent school killings by boys and the murder of the child beauty queen JonBenet Ramsey. We might also include the recent furor in Belgium over the discovery of pedophile rings. In all of these examples there is one of two features: the dangerous adult (almost exclusively male) who is violent and/or sexually predatory on young children, or the protoviolent boy or protosexual girl, as in the cases of James Bulger and JonBenet Ramsey, respectively. As one British judge put it in a case of child sexual abuse, the girl involved was understood to be "no angel."

Anxieties about the safety of children in public and private space and the specter of dangerous children, in particular boys who commit murder, feed anxieties about a world out of control and in which it is no longer possible to protect children. I want to look at this in two ways. The first involves the need to rethink concepts of what childhood means in postmodernity and childhood's relation to a concept of space that can no longer be contained within traditional developmental discourses. The second is to think about how adult anxiety about child protection in public and private space relates to complex issues about adult sexuality, what Jacqueline Rose (1985) called "the desire of adults for children."

This anxiety manifests itself not only in the well-known examples given but also in fears that there is no longer any place or space in which children are safe—certainly not school with its crazy lone killers or teenage gunmen; not home with the threat of child abuse; and not the street, park, or playground with its lurking strangers. I make this contrast because, as we will see, thirty years ago, within educational practices, the home and school were often envisaged as safe havens in which children could develop normally and naturally. What then has happened to our idea of childhood and development within this context in which sex and violence feature so prominently?

I want to explore the way in which this huge anxiety about children and the status of childhood has erupted at the end of the twentieth century. It is understood in terms, on the one hand, of pathological adults who sully the otherwise sound barrel so that it is not necessary to ask questions about masculine sexuality. On the other hand, I want to argue that indeed such issues raise profound questions about the status of adult sexuality and its object. In particular I want to raise some issues about the easy separation of normality and pathology. In addition to this, I want to think about the way in which models of childhood from within developmental theory also privilege a particular model of normality, to the extent that it is certain children, children who are Othered, who become the object of pathologization discourses. Normal, and hence natural, boys are naughty and playful, not violent. Normal girls are well behaved, hardworking, and asexual (Walkerdine, 1989, for example).

What is the relation between the changes in the understanding of public and private space and the constitution of the subjectivities of children within those spaces? Traditionally, within the discourses of modernity, it has been developmental theory that has been marshaled to tell the truth about a naturally developing child within a natural environment. That environment was meant to protect children from the dangers understood as inherent in an industrialized urban landscape. Now in a context of a postindustrial and postmodern landscape there is no longer taken to be any safe haven, no environment safe for natural development.

Anxieties about Children in Public Space

So much has changed since the individualist developmentalism of earlier decades in which children's exploration of physical space was seen as basic to development. Now there are increasing fears about the safety of children in any kind of public space. For example, we have moved from the idea of the primary school as a safe environment in which the right kind of development might be accomplished through the easy exploration of concrete physical space—as in the applications of Piaget, with the school being understood as a safe and nurturing environment in which development can occur naturally in contrast to sometimes difficult environments outside (see in particular the government report "Children and their Primary Schools," 1967, discussed in Walkerdine, 1984)—to the primary school as a site of danger. The concern about safety is less a worry about environmental danger (though that certainly plays a part) and more about the threat posed by the violence and sexuality of adults. In this sense then, a great deal has changed, from even the 1960s and 1970s, as the idea of development as unhindered play in a natural environment is less and less on the agenda. This is very significant in terms of our approach to the assumptions about space made within developmental theory.

Most work on space from within traditional developmental theory depends upon distinctions made by Piaget in 1967 between topological and euclidean space, arguing that children acquired spatial concepts through their active manipulation of objects within the physical world, recognizing first that there were two dimensions and later three. However, this model of solid space fits neither subatomic physics nor cyberspace. Piaget argued that children cannot master three dimensions before two, suggesting also that young children had difficulty with the abstract, needing first to experience the concrete. Cyberspace requires a conception of space as flow and energy, not as fixed, solid, and geographical. Quite young children playing computer games handle with ease the complex relation of two to three dimensions, the n dimensional space of levels in platformers (accomplishments that concretely they should not be able to do), for example, with its intricate relation of movement in virtual space and reaction time, suggesting the necessity of a different conception not only of the space that children inhabit but of the processes of acquisition of modes of understanding of that space itself. If the spaces in which children grow up have changed fundamentally from those of previous generations, in terms of the anxieties and possibilities that surround them, and if a space of flows and energies replaces that of solids, then the time has come for us to rethink the concepts of childhood and of space as well as the relationship between them.

In addition to this, adults are presented as not only part of the problem (especially of course adult men) but also as unable to put a stop to what is happening to children and indeed to the destruction of the environment: children are left to their own devices, as is graphically illustrated in television series like *Teenage Mutant Ninja Turtles* (Urwin, 1995) and *Rugrats*. In this context, a new space is often put forward as being outside these concerns, one in which rational play may be offered, without the fears attached to public space and indeed without undue interference from adults: cyberspace is adult-free, unknown, and unsupervised. To the technophile, it is a new frontier, an untamed and anarchic space in which transformation might still be possible (Fuller &

Jenkins, 1998). However, this is crosscut by technophobia, in terms of discourses about media effects, which play upon the dangers of new technologies to the vulnerable minds of the children of the masses as the producer of addiction on the one hand and violence on the other. In particular, in Britain at least, two forms have been singled out for concern: videos (movies) and computer and video games. The murder of James Bulger in Liverpool by two young boys brought to the surface not only the danger to children in public space but the danger wrought by children themselves. The children in danger have to be saved from dangerous children, but those dangerous children have minds made vulnerable and oversuggestible by their environment (these are, of course, the children of the poor) and the effects of the media are most marked upon them, thus both videos and games are blamed for addiction and for violence. Actually, then, in effect, we have at the end of the twentieth century the twin poles that were there at its birth: the vulnerable-minded protoviolent masses and the superrational explorers of the unknown (in this case, the information superhighway). In relation to this, femininity is still constituted as Other and girls rarely figure as either murderers or superrational explorers, though those categories are constantly challenged.

Children and New Technologies

I will summarize the major conditions of possibility (Henriques, Hollway, Urwin, Venn, & Walkerdine, 1998) for the discursive constitution of the present concern with children and new technologies. The emergence of social psychology at the end of the nineteenth century, with its emphasis on the group as a crowd (Le Bon, 1895; Tarde, 1890), built on earlier concerns about the irrationality, vulnerability, suggestibility, and absence of morality of the "dangerous classes." These characteristics paved the way for the understanding of poor peoples as psychologically lacking and pathological and can be related directly to the kind of assumptions that became taken for granted in work on children of the poor in general and children and the media in particular. That is, that certain children had minds that were vulnerable to outside influences, hence concerns about violence and addiction. These become very clear in the debates surrounding the James Bulger case and video nasties, for example. This generated strategies of population management in relation to psychopathology on the one hand and popular entertainment and crowd control on the other.

The ready use of existing concepts in the emergent pre- and postwar traditions of mass media and communication studies, principally in the United States, and the use of, for example, theories of vulnerable masses and social psychology, in the work of the Frankfurt school, helped to cement this discursive apparatus. American social psychology made moves in the 1950s to make psychoanalytic insights amenable to scientific inquiry. One of the kinds of work on children to emerge from this was Bandura's work on social learning theory, producing a number of key studies, highlighting the role of imitation in the production of antisocial behavior and signaling the way in which children could be understood as aggressively and violently imitating what they saw on television. In Britain, the 1956 study by Himmelweit, Openheim, and Vince argued that children could be addicted to television, with the worst addicts being working-class children whose viewing habits were less likely to be supervised by their parents.

Moral concern about violence and addiction was generated at this time, building upon the moral technologies from the nineteenth century (and indeed before this). Concern about violence and addiction were two of the major concerns addressed by research on video games, as was previously also the case with the arrival of video technology. In the United States in particular, such research appears to have developed in tandem with the anxiety about the loss and disappearance of childhood itself, with figures such as Neil Postman (1994) arguing that television signaled the erosion of childhood, to arguments about addiction and abuse (for example, Best, 1990; Ivy, 1995; Jenkins, 1992), which suggested that 95 percent of American adults are addicted and/or had abused childhoods, presenting this as one of the major American anxieties of the late twentieth century. This can be put together with the fact that almost all research on violence and the media comes from the United States. In Britain too, however, there has been a sharp increase in anxiety about children as victims of abuse and perpetrators of crime, with a number of psychologists lining up behind Elizabeth Newson (1994) to argue, controversially, that the only thing to have accounted for the change in children's behavior (pace the Bulger case) is violent videos. British media and cultural studies have tended to use notions of media literacy to counter notions of passively imitating children (Buckingham, 1991). However, this tends to build upon preexisting strategies and technologies that stress rationality as a counter to the irrationality of the dangerous classes.

Discourses of Modernity

Grand metanarratives of modernity elide the specificities of childhoods. In order to understand these metanarratives it is necessary to work not with a general theory but with an approach that understands the discourses and practices through which particular subjectivities are produced. This means that childhood is understood not as a natural state best described through developmental accounts but that these very accounts can be understood as historically specific "regimes of truth" that constitute what it means to be a child at a particular time and place (Walkerdine, 1998).

The theoretical framework underlying this approach has been articulated in a number of publications (for example, Foucault, 1977; Henriques et al., 1998). In brief, what is particularly important is the concept of subjectivity, that is, that the human subject is produced in the discursive practices that make up the social world (as opposed to a pregiven psychological subject who is made social or socialized). This means that we need an understanding of how what Foucault (1977) called the microphysics of power actually works to form the discourses that produce and regulate what it means to be a subject within different social practices. In this analysis, the subject is produced through the discursive relations of the practices themselves and is not coterminous with the actual embodied and lived experience of being a subject. To understand the relation between subjectification (the condition of being a subject) and subjectivity (the lived experience of being a subject), it is necessary to examine what subject-positions are created within specific practices and how actual subjects are both created in and live those diverse positions. The reason that I am laboring this point is that to understand subjectivity is not the same as understanding "learning" or "cognition"; rather, the issue becomes how to examine both how social and cultural practices work and how they create what it means to be a subject inside those practices. Thus, the understanding of how practices operate and how subjects are formed inside them becomes one and the same activity. For Foucault, power/knowledge is a central component of the current social order. To examine what counts as childhood, therefore—as well as the relation of children to popular culture—we need to examine how that relation is formed inside the discourses that constitute the technologies of the social (Foucault, 1977).

Understanding the Historical Dimension

In Foucault's approach to the "history of the present," it is necessary to examine how the present is constituted through the historical production of power/knowledge relations. In relation to children and popular culture, we need to look at least to the post-Enlightenment concern about the oversuggestible, irrational poor (Blackman, 1996). Work on the suggestibility of crowds (for example, Le Bon, 1895; Tarde, 1890) paves the way for the later emergence of social psychology and of mass communications research. The important twin issues of the mass medium and the vulnerable and suggestible mind cohere to produce a social psychology and a psychopathology of groups in which mass irrationality and suggestibility have a central place (Walkerdine, 1997). I want to argue that the concern about the regulation of the masses through their mass suggestibility and irrationality became one of the central aspects of the technologies through which they were regulated.

In brief, concern about rationality and irrationality and the vulnerability of the minds of certain children to the media finds its antecedence within the emergence of these discourses and technologies. We can trace the surveillance of children's viewing, for example, in and through the technologies of the regulation both of what counts as childhood and what was shown to children (films, television, video games). This intersected with concerns about children and rationality that also tied in with the production of the rational government of the masses and the bourgeois order, in which to be civilized was to be understood as ultimately rational, with women, the masses, and colonial peoples being defined as dangerously outside rationality. To produce the individual in the image of reason, therefore, was to produce a subject who would accept the moral and political order of a liberal democracy apparently according to their own free will and not rebel (Walkerdine, 1984). It is out of these intersecting discourses and claims to truth that we can find the current concerns about children and the new media and technologies. Indeed, if we are to examine current concerns we can find that they cohere largely around concerns about the vulnerability and suggestibility of young minds, with those being understood as most at risk being the children of the masses, the poor. Alongside that, however, we can also find a utopian discourse of the new information superhighway as a new frontier, a new space for the production of a new, and perhaps super, rationality. In this way, the concerns about children and space split into an opposition between cyberspace as a new space for the production of a new rationality (which replaces a traditional developmentalism) and the pathologized others—the children of the poor, who may be subject to the breakdown of these other spaces.

The Eroticization of Little Girls

While we can identify boys as a target for discourses about the relation of dangers to children to dangerous children, we also need to examine the issue of what is often taken to be the intrusion of adult sexuality into the lives of young girls. How can little girls be safe if adult men take them as sexual objects, as in concerns about pedophilia and child sexual abuse? Nevertheless, young girls themselves, especially working-class girls, are often understood as being part of the problem, which raises the difficult issue of the relation of childhood to adult sexuality. The topic of popular portrayals of little girls as eroticized, little girls and sexuality, is an issue that touches on a number of very difficult and often taboo areas. Feminism has had little to say about little girls, except through studies of socialization and sex-role stereotyping. With regard to sexuality, almost all attention has been focused on adult women. Little girls enter debates about women's memories of their own girlhood in the main: discussions of little girls' fantasies of sex with their fathers or adult men, as in Freud's Dora case, the debate surrounding Masson's claim that Freud had suppressed the evidence that many of his female patients had been sexually abused as children, and, of course, the discourse of abuse itself. The topic of little girls and sexuality has come to be seen as being about the problem of the sexual abuse of innocent and vulnerable girls by bad adult men, or conversely, less politically correct but no less present, the idea of little girls as little seductresses. I want to open up a set of issues that I believe are occluded by such debates— the ubiquitous eroticization of little girls in the popular media and the just as ubiquitous ignorance and denial of this phenomenon. In the rest of the chapter, I want to concentrate on this issue in particular.

Childhood Innocence and Little Lolitas

Janie is six. In the classroom she sits almost silently well behaved, the epitome of the hardworking girl, so often scorned as uninteresting in the educational literature on girls' attainment (Walkerdine, 1989). She says very little and appears to be constantly aware of being watched. She herself watches the model that she presents to her teacher, classmates, and me, seated in a corner of the classroom making an audio recording. She always presents immaculate work and is used to getting very high marks. She asks to go to the toilet and leaves the classroom. Since she is wearing a radio microphone I hear her cross the hall in which a class is doing music and movement to a radio program. The teacher tells them to pretend to be bunnies. She leaves the hall and enters the silence of the toilets, and in there alone she sings loudly to herself. I imagine her swaying in front of the mirror. The song that she sings is one on the lips of many of the girls at the time I was making the recordings: Toni Basil's "Mickey" (see Walkerdine, 1997).

"Mickey" is a song sung by a woman dressed as a teenager. In the promotional video for the song she wears a cheerleader's outfit complete with a very short skirt and is surrounded by large, butch-looking women cheerleaders who conspire to make her look both smaller and more feminine. "Oh Mickey, you're so fine, you're so fine, you blow my mind," she sings. "Give it to me, give it to me, any way you can, give it to me, give it to me, I'll take it like a man." What does it mean for a six-year-old girl to sing these highly erotic lyrics? It could be argued that what we have here is the intrusion of adult sexuality into the innocent world of childhood. Or indeed, that because she is only six, such lyrics do not count because she is incapable of understanding them. I shall explore the issue of childhood innocence in more detail, and rather than attempting to dismiss the issue of the meaning of the lyrics as irrelevant, I shall try to place these meanings in the overall study of little girls and sexuality. In moving out of the public and highly surveilled space of the classroom, where she is a good, well-behaved girl, to the private space of the toilets she enters a quite different discursive space, the space of the little Lolita, the sexual little girl, who cannot be revealed to the cozy sanitized classroom. She shifts in this move from innocent to sexual, from virgin to whore, from child to little woman, from good to bad. The public surveilled space of the classroom is still understood as a space in which sexuality is left out or kept at bay. It is in the unsurveilled private space that the child-woman can be manifest and which therefore presents problems within educational discourse. Of course, what is also pointed up by the research on Janie is that by the use of new technology (she wears a radio microphone) the public/private space dichotomy becomes blurred because the very act of recording her brings that space to the public attention. Such a shift is also central to many practices of "real people" television (see Pini & Walkerdine, forthcoming) and popularized in such Hollywood films as *EdTV*.

Children and the Popular

I want to explore some of the "gazes" at the little girl, the ways that she is inscribed in a number of competing discourses. I will concentrate on the figure of the little girl as an object of psychopedagogic discourse and as the eroticized child-woman of popular culture. I have argued in previous work that the nature of the child is not discovered but produced in regimes of truth created in those very practices that proclaim the child in all his naturalness. I write "his" advisedly, because a central plank of my argument has been that although this child is taken to be gender-neutral, actually he is always figured as a boy, a boy who is playful, creative, naughty, rule breaking, rational. The figure of the girl, by contrast, suggests an unnatural pathology: she works to the child's play; she follows rules to his breaking of them; she is good, well behaved, and irrational. Femininity becomes the Other of rational childhood. If she is everything that the child is not supposed to be, it follows that her presence, where it displays the above attributes, may be considered to demonstrate a pathological development, an improper childhood, a danger or threat to what is normal and natural. However, attempts (and they are legion) to transform her into the model playful child often come up against a set of discursive barriers: a playful and assertive girl may be understood as forward, uppity, overmature, too precocious (in one study a primary school teacher called such a ten-year-old girl a "madam"; see Walkerdine, 1989). Empirically then, "girls," like "children," are not discovered in a natural state. What is found to be the case by teachers, parents, and others is the result of complex processes of subjectification (Henriques et al., 1984). Yet, while this model of girlhood is at once pathologized, it is also needed: the good and hardworking girl who follows the rules prefigures the nurturant mother figure, who uses her irrationality to safeguard rationality, to allow it to develop (Walkerdine & Lucey, 1989). Consider then the threat to the natural child posed by the eroticized child, the little Lolita, the girl who presents as a little woman, not of the nurturant kind, but rather the seductress, the unsanitized whore to the good girl's virgin. It is my contention that popular culture lets this figure into the sanitized space of natural childhood, a space from which it must be guarded and kept at all costs. What is being kept out and what is safe inside this fictional space?

The discourse of natural childhood builds upon a model of naturally occurring rationality, itself echoing the idea of childhood as an unsullied and innocent state, free from the interference of adults. The very cognitivism of most models of childhood as they have been incorporated into educational practices leaves both emotionality and sexuality to one side. Although Freud posited a notion of childhood sexuality that has been very pervasive, it was concepts like repression and the problems of adult interference in development that became incorporated into educational practices rather than any notion of sexuality in children as a given or natural phenomena. Indeed, it is precisely the idea that sexuality is an adult notion that sullies the safe innocence of a childhood free to emerge inside the primary school classroom that is most important. Adult sexuality interferes with the uniqueness of childhood, its stages of development. Popular culture then, insofar as it presents the intrusion of adult sexuality into the sanitized space of childhood, is understood as very harmful.

Visually these positions can be distinguished by a number of gazes at the little girl. Psychopedagogic images are presented in two ways: the fly on the wall documentary photograph in which the young girl is seen always engaged in some educational activity and is never shown looking at the camera, and the cartoon-type book illustration in which she appears as a smiley face, rounded (but certainly not curvy) unisex figure. If we begin to explore popular images of little girls they present a stark contrast. I do not have room in this piece to explore this issue in detail, but simply let me make reference to newspaper and magazine fashion shots and recent television advertisements—for example, ads for Volkswagen cars, Yoplait yogurt, and Kodak Gold film. All present the highly eroticized alluring little girl, often (at least in all three TV ads) with fair hair and ringlets, usually made up and with a look that seductively returns the gaze of the camera. Indeed, such shots bear far more similarity to images taken from child pornography than they do to psychoeducational images. However, the popular advertisement and fashion images are ubiquitous: they are an everyday part of our culture and have certainly not been equated with child pornography.

It would not be difficult to make a case that such images are the soft porn of child pornography and that they exploit childhood by introducing adult sexuality into childhood innocence. In that sense they could be understood as the precursor to child sexual abuse in the way that pornography has been understood by some feminists as the precursor to rape. However, I feel that such an interpretation is oversimplistic. The eroticization of little girls is a complex phenomenon, one in which a certain aspect of feminine sexuality and childhood sexuality is understood as corrupting of an innocent state. The blame is laid both on abuse—and therefore pathological and bad men who enter and sully the terrain of childhood innocence—and on the little Lolitas who lead men on. But popular images of little girls as alluring and seductive, at once innocent and highly erotic, are contained in the most respectable and mundane of locations: broadsheet newspapers, women's magazines, television advertisements. The phenomenon that we are talking about therefore has to be far more pervasive than the approach that some men are rotten apples, pathological and abusive. This is not about a few perverts but about the complex construction of the highly contradictory gaze at little girls, one that places them as at once threatening and sustaining rationality, little virgins that might be whores, to be protected yet to be constantly alluring. The complexity of this phenomenon, in terms of both the cultural production of little girls as these ambivalent objects and the way in which little girls themselves as well as adults live this complexity, how it produces their subjectivity, has not begun to be explored.

Eroticized Femininity and the Working-Class Girl

Let us return to Janie and her clandestine singing. I have been at some pains to point out that Janie presents to the public world of the classroom the face of hardworking diligent femininity, which, while pathologized, is still desired. She reserves the less-acceptable face of femininity for more private spaces. I imagine her dancing as she sings in front of the mirror, which can be understood as an acting out, a fantasizing of the possibility of being someone and something else. I want to draw attention to the contradictions in the way in which the eroticized child-woman is a position presented publicly for the little girl to enter but simultaneously treated as a position that removes childhood innocence, allows entry of the whore, and makes the girl vulnerable to abuse. The entry of popular culture into the educational and family life of the little girl is therefore to be viewed with suspicion, as a threat posed by the lowering of standards, of the intrusion of the low against the superior high culture. It is the consumption of popular culture that is taken as making the little working-class girl understood as potentially more at risk of being victim and perpetrator. Janie's fantasy dirties the sanitary space of the classroom. But what is Janie's fantasy and at the intersection of which complex fantasies is she inscribed? I want to explore some of the popular fictions about the little working-class girl and to present the way in which the eroticization presents for her the possibility of a different and better life, of which she is often presented as the carrier. The keeping at bay of sexuality as intruding upon innocent childhood is in sharp contrast to this.

There have been a number of cinematic depictions of young girls as capable of producing a transformation in their own and others' lives, from Judy Garland in *The Wizard of Oz*, through Shirley Temple, *Gigi*, and *My Fair Lady*, to (orphan) *Annie*. In the majority of these films the transformation effected relates to class and to money through the intervention of a lovable little girl. Charles Eckert (1991) argued that Shirley Temple was often portrayed as an orphan in the depression whose role was to soften the hearts of the wealthy such that they would identify her as one of the poor, not dirty and radical, but lovable, to become the object of charity through their donations. In a similar way, Annie is presented as an orphan for whom being working class is the isolation of a poor little girl, with no home, no parents, no community. She too has to soften the heart of the armaments millionaire, Daddy Warbucks, making him soften at the edges, as well as find her own happiness through dint of her lovable personality. It is by this means that she secures for herself a future in a wealthy family, which she creates by bringing Daddy Warbucks and his secretary, Grace, together. By concentrating on these two characters alone it is possible to envisage that the little working-class girl is the object of massive projections. She is a figure of immense transformative power who can make the rich love, thereby solving huge social and political problems, and she can immeasurably improve her own life in the process. At the same time she presents the face of a class turned underclass, ragged, disorganized, orphaned, for whom there is only one way out: embourgeoisement. Thus she becomes the epitome of the feminized and therefore emasculated, less threatening, proletariat. In addition to this, Graham Greene pointed to something unmentioned in the tales of innocent allure: the sexual coquettishness of Shirley Temple. His pointing to her pedophilic eroticization led to the closure of *Night and Day*, the magazine he edited, after it was sued for libel.

What does the current figure of the eroticized little girl hold? What fantasies are projected onto her and how do these fantasies interact with the fantasy scenarios little working-class girls create for themselves and their lives? If she is simultaneously holding so much that is understood as both good and bad, no wonder actual little girls might find their situation overwhelming. It would be easy to classify Janie and other girls' private eroticization as resistance to the position accorded to her at school and in high culture, but I hope that I have demonstrated that this would be hopelessly simplistic.

Fantasies of Seduction

Let us see then what psychoanalysis has had to say about seduction and the eroticization of little girls. It is easy to pinpoint Freud's seduction theory and his account of an autoerotic childhood sexuality. We might also point to the place of the critiques of the seduction theory in the accusation that psychoanalysis has ignored child abuse, the raising of the specter of abuse, as a widespread phenomenon and the recent attacks on therapists for producing false memories of abuses that never happened in their clients. In this sense then, the issue of little girls and sexuality can be seen as a minefield of claim and counterclaim focusing on the issue of fantasy, memory, and reality. If one wants therefore to examine sexuality and little girls as a cultural phenomenon, one is confronted by a denial of cultural processes: either little girls have a sexuality that is derived from their fantasies of seduction by their fathers or they are innocent of sexuality, which is imposed upon them from the outside by pathological or evil men who seduce, abuse, and rape them. Culturally, we are left with a stark choice: sexuality in little girls is natural, universal, and inevitable; or, a kind of male gaze is at work in which the little girl is produced as object of an adult male gaze. She has no fantasies of her own, and to paraphrase Lacan we could say that "the little girl does not exist except as symptom and myth of the masculine imaginary." Or, in the mold of the Women Against Violence Against Women approach of "porn is the theory, rape is the practice," we might conclude that popular representations of eroticized little girls is the theory and child sexual abuse is the practice. Girls' fantasies prove a problem in all these accounts because only Freud credited them with any of their own, although he made it clear that, like others working on psychopathology at the time, feminine sexuality was the central enigma. Indeed his main question was, What does the woman, the little girl, want? A question to which Jacqueline Rose in her introduction to Lacanian writing on feminine sexuality (1985) asserts that "all answers, including the mother are false: she simply wants." So little girls have a desire without an object, a desire that must float in space, unable to find an object, indeed to be colonized by masculine fantasies, which create female desire in their own image. Of course, Laura Mulvey's original 1974 work on the male cinematic gaze has been much revised and criticized (e.g., Screen, 1992), but critics have tended to ignore the complex production of subjectivity.

Let us return to the psychoanalytic arguments about sexuality. Laplanche and Pontalis (1985) discuss seduction in terms of "seduction into the fantasies of the parents." Those fantasies can be understood in terms of the complex intertwining of parental histories and the regimes of truth, the cultural fantasies that circulate in the social. This may sound like a theory of socialization, but socialization implies the learning of roles and the taking on of stereotypes. What we have here is a complex interweaving of the many kinds of fantasy, both "social" in the terms of Geraghty (1991) and others and psychic, as phantasy in the classic psychoanalytic sense (in psychoanalysis it is spelled with a "ph"). Lacan, of course, argued that the symbolic system carried social fantasies that were psychic in origin, an argument he made by recourse to structuralist principles from de Saussure and Lévi-Strauss. However, it is possible to understand the complexity in terms that conceive of the psychic/social relation as produced not in ahistorical and universal categories but in historically specific regimes of meaning and truth (Henriques et al., 1998).

However, what Freud did argue for was what he called a "childhood sexuality." What he meant was that the bodily sensations experienced by the baby could be very pleasurable but this pleasure was, of course, always crosscut by pain, a presence marked by the absence of the caregiver, usually the mother. In this context little children could learn in an omnipotent way that they too could give these pleasurable sensations to themselves, just as they learned, according to Freud's famous example of the cotton reel game, that in fantasy they could control the presence and absence of the mother. So for Freud there is no tabula rasa, no innocent child. The child's first senses of pleasure are already marked by the phantasies inherent in the presence and absence of the Other. However, as Laplanche and Pontalis (1985) point out, the infantile sexuality, marked by an "infantile language of tenderness," is crosscut by the introduction of an adult "language," the language of passion. "This is the language of desire, necessarily marked by prohibition, a language of guilt and hatred, including the sense of orgastic pleasure" (p. 226). How far does this view take us down the road of sorting out the problems associated with models of childhood innocence?

The model suggests that there are two kinds of sexuality: an infant one about bodily pleasures and an adult one that imposes a series of other meanings upon those pleasures. We should note here that Laplanche and Pontalis do go as far as implying that not all of the fantasy is on the side of the child but that the parents impose some of their own. The sexuality would then develop in terms of the admixture of the two, in all its psychic complexity. Let me illustrate that briefly by making reference to a previous study of mine (Walkerdine, 1985) in which I discussed my own father's nickname for me: Tinky, short for Tinkerbell. I was reminded of my nickname by a father, Mr. Cole, whose nickname for his six-year-old daughter, Joanne, was Dodo. I argued that Tinky and Dodo were fathers' fantasies about their daughters: a fairy with diminutive size but incredible powers on the one hand and a preserved baby name (Dodo, as a childish mispronunciation of JoJo) on the other. But a dodo is also an extinct bird, or for Mr. Cole, that aspect of extinction that is preserved in his fantasy relationship with his daughter as a baby. Joanne is no longer a baby; babyhood—like the dodo—has gone, but it is preserved in the fantasy of Mr. Cole's special nickname for his daughter, and in so designating her, he structures the relationship between them: she remains his baby.

In the case of my own father's fantasy, Tinky signified for me the most potent aspect of my specialness for him. I associated it with a photograph of myself aged three winning a local fancy dress competition, dressed as a bluebell fairy. This is where I won and "won him over": my fairy charms reciprocated his fantasy of me, designating me "his girl" and fueling my oedipal fantasies. But I am trying to demonstrate that those fantasies are not one-sided on either the parent's or the little girl's side but, as the Tinky example illustrates, that the "language of adult desire" is entirely cultural. Tinkerbell and bluebell fairies are cultural phenomena that can be examined in terms of their semiotics and their historical emergence as well as their production and consumption. My father did not invent Tinkerbell or the bluebell fairy; rather he used what were available cultural fantasies to name something about his deep and complex feelings for his daughter. In return, I, his daughter, took those fantasies to my heart and my unconscious, making them my own. Of course it could be argued that this sails very close to Laura Mulvey's original position, following Lacan, that woman (the little girl) does not exist (or have fantasies that originate with her) except as symptom and myth of male fantasy. But I am attempting to demonstrate that a position that suggests that fantasies come only from the adult male is far too simplistic. My father might have imposed Tinkerbell on me but my own feelings for my father had their own role to play.

I want to argue that the culture carries these adult fantasies, creates vehicles for them. It carries the transformation of this into a projection onto children of the adult language of desire. In this view the little seductress is a complex phenomenon that carries adult sexual desire but also hooks into the equally complex fantasies carried by the little girl herself. The idea of a sanitized natural childhood in which such things are kept at bay, having no place in childhood, becomes not the guarantor of the safety of children from the perversity of adult desires for them but a huge defense against the acknowledgement of dangerous desires on the part of adults. In this analysis, "child protection" begins to look more like adult protection.

It is here then that I want to make a distinction between seduction and abuse. Fantasies of Tinky and Dodo were enticing, seductive, but they were not abuse. To argue that they were is to make something very simplistic out of something immensely complex.

As long as seduction is subsumed under a discourse of abuse, issues of "seduction into the fantasies of the parents" are hidden under a view that suggests that adult sexual fantasies about children are held only by perverts who can be kept at bay by keeping children safe and childhood innocent. But if childhood innocence is really an adult defense, adult fantasies about children and the eroticization of little girls is not a problem about a minority of perverts from whom the normal general public should be protected. It is about massive fantasies carried in the culture, fantasies that are equally massively defended against by other cultural practices, in the form of the psychopedagogic and social welfare practices incorporating discourses of childhood innocence. This is not to suggest that children are not to be protected. Far from it. Rather, my argument is that a central issue of adult sexual projections onto children is not being addressed.

So the issue of fantasy and the eroticization of little girls within popular culture becomes a complex phenomenon in which cultural fantasies, fantasies of the parents, and little girls' oedipal fantasies mix and are given a cultural form that shapes them. Laplanche and Pontalis (1985) argue that fantasy is the setting for desire, "but as for knowing who is responsible for the setting, it is not enough for the psychoanalyst to rely on the resources of his (sic) science, nor on the support of myth. He (sic) must become a philosopher!" (p. 17). In poststructuralist terms this would take us into the domain of the production of knowledges about children and the production of the ethical subject. I want to explore lastly this latter connection by suggesting several courses of action and to examine briefly the issue through a specific example of a "moral panic" about popular culture and the eroticization of children.

Minipops

I want to end by examining briefly the case of *Minipops,* a series transmitted on Channel Four television in 1983. The series presented young children, boys and girls, white and black, singing current pop songs, dressed up and heavily made up. This series became the object of what was described as a moral panic. The stated intention of the director was to present a showcase of new talent, the idea having come from his daughter, who liked to dress up and sing pop songs at home. The furor caused by the programs was entirely voiced by the middle classes. The broadsheet papers demanded the axing of the series on the grounds that it presented a sexuality that spoiled and intruded into an innocent childhood. One critic wrote of "lashings of lipstick on mini mouths" (*Sunday Times,* 1983). By contrast, the tabloids loved the series. For them, the programs represented a chance for young children to be talent spotted, to find fame. There was no mention of the erosion of innocence. Why this difference?

It would be easy to imagine that the tabloids were more exploitative, less concerned with issues of sexual exploitation so rampant in their own pages, with the broadsheets as upholders of everything that is morally good. However, I think that this conclusion would be erroneous. While I deal with this argument in more detail elsewhere (Walkerdine, 1997), let me point out here that I have argued that the eroticized little girl presents a fantasy of Otherness to the little working-class girl. She is inscribed as one who can make a transformation, which is also a self-transformation, which is also a seductive allure. It is not surprising therefore that the tabloid discourse is about talent, discovery, fame: all the elements of the necessary transformation from rags to riches, from flower girl to princess, so to speak. Such a transformation is necessarily no part of middle-class discourse, fantasy, and aspiration. Rather, childhood for the middle class is a state to be preserved, free from economic intrusion and producing the possibility of the rational and playful child who will become a rational, educated professional, a member of the "new middle class."

Seduction and the eroticization of little girls are complex cultural phenomena. I have tried to demonstrate that the place of the little working-class girl is important because her seductiveness has an important role to play in terms of both a social and personal transformation, a transformation that is glimpsed in the fantasies of fame embodied in series like *Minipops*. The figure of the little working-class girl then simultaneously holds transformation of an emasculated working class into lovable citizens and the fear against which the fantasy defends. This is the little Lolita: the whore, the contagion of the masses that will endanger the safety of the bourgeois order. On the other hand, child protection as the outlawing of perversion and preservation of a safe space for innocent childhood can also be viewed as class specific and is indeed the fantasy of the safe space that has not been invaded by the evil masses.

I have tried to place an understanding of unconscious processes inside of all of this because, as I hope that I have demonstrated, psychic processes form a central component of how social and cultural fantasies work. Some may argue that my recourse to psychoanalysis presents such psychic processes as universal and inevitable but I have tried to show the social and the psychic merge together to form any particular fantasies at a specific moment. This is only a very small beginning that may help to sort out how we might approach a hugely important topic that has been badly neglected.

Conclusion

Let us return then to the notion of public and private space. How are the current imaginaries about the child and the adult related to a regeneration of childhood and the positions of children in postmodernity? With the example of the eroticization of young girls, I have tried to show just what might be at stake inside the concerns about child safety in public and private spaces, that is, questions about adult male sexuality and the place of that desire. It is clear that we need to rethink our approach to the study of childhood to encompass an understanding of the specificity through which children become subjected in the practices of postmodernity, in which we can understand a post-Enlightenment discourse of nature and natural rationality as one of the current fictions that functions in truth. The threat posed by the breaking apart of this fiction becomes a different problem than the one envisaged as simply about moving to a new space—in this case, cyberspace—in which development may still be properly accomplished by the isolated protorational boy. Might we therefore begin to examine what kinds of subjects and subjectivities are created in relation to popular media? What are the ways in which such discourses and practices prepare children for the world beyond the screen? The male figures of the rational middle-class explorer and the protoviolent and addicted working-class boy, the well-behaved protomother and the little working-class seductress certainly exist not only as subject positions but are constantly created as modes of subjectivity within the practices of game playing. These are neither ahistorical nor transcultural figures but quite specific to the time and place that produces them. They are also replete with the fears, phobias, and fetishes of late twentieth-century Western cities. How might we begin to explore the situated production of all subjectivities of the world's children as they face the huge differences confronting the new millennium? It is not only our approach to the understanding of space, of popular culture that must change but our approach to the issue of childhood itself.

Rationality and its Others—irrationality, madness, criminality, sexual perversion—are popularly understood as the effects of success or failure of sexual perversion or similarly the result of simplistic ideas about the effects of the media upon that socialization. If we are to begin to construct both alternative kinds of accounts and to intervene differently in work with children, we must take seriously the simple pathologization that is rooted in the long-established practices of regulation of the poor and the masses. In these modes of regulation, adult pathology is expressed mostly by those who were poorly socialized as children. This prohibits our gaze toward something else, that is, the way in which the practices of pathologization sit so neatly alongside those very discourses and practices in which the eroticization of little girls is commonplace and the Internet explorer one of today's anarcho-heroes. If we begin to interrogate both what is spoken and the way it sits so neatly alongside that which receives no comment, we may be able to approach the complexities of explanation and intervention in childhood in a different kind of way.

References

Best, J. (1990). Threatened children: Rhetoric and concern about child victims. Chicago: University of Chicago Press.

Bhabha, H. (1984). The other question: The stereotype in colonial discourse. *Screen, 24*, pp. 18–36.

Blackman, L. (1996). The masses: Retelling the psychiatric story, *Feminism and Psychology, 6*, (3), pp. 361–79. Special Issue on Class.

Buckingham, D. (1991). *Intruder in the house.* Fourth International Television Studies Conference, London.

Cole, M. et al (1971). *The cultural context of learning and thinking.* New York: Basic Books.

Deleuze, G., & Guattari, F. (1987). *A thousand plateaux.* Minneapolis: University of Minnesota Press.

Eckert, C. (1991). Shirley Temple and the house of Rockefeller. In C. Gledhill (Ed.), *Stardom* (pp. 39–50). London: Routledge.

Foucault, M. (1977). *Discipline and punish.* Harmondsworth: Penguin.

Fuller, M., & Jenkins, H. (1998). Nintendo and new world travel writing. In S. Jones (Ed.), *Cybersociety* (pp. 55–70). Thousand Oaks, CA: Sage.

Geraghty, C. (1991). *Women and soap opera.* Oxford, UK: Polity.

Greene, G. (1980). *The pleasure dome: The collected film criticism, 1935–40, (of) Graham Greene.* J. R. Taylor (Ed.), Oxford: Oxford University Press.

Henriques, J., Hollway, W., Urwin, C., Venn, C., & Walkerdine, V. (1998). *Changing the subject: Psychology, social regulation and subjectivity.* London: Routledge.

Himmelweit, H., Oppenheim, A., and Vince, P. (1958). *Television and the Child.* London: Oxford University Press.

Jenkins, P. (1992). *Intimate enemies: Moral panics in contemporary Great Britain.* New York: Aldine de Gruyter.

Laplanche, J., & Pontalis, J. B. (1985). Fantasy and the origins of sexuality. In V. Burgin, J. Donald, & C. Kaplan, *Formations of fantasy* (pp. 76–95). London: Routledge.

Le Bon, G. (1895/1968). *The crowd.* Dunwoody, GA: N. S. Berg.

McRobbie, A. (1979). Settling accounts with subcultures. *Screen Education, 34*, pp. 17–28.

Mulvey, L. (1974). Visual pleasure and narrative cinema. *Screen, 16* (3), pp. 55–68.

Newson, E. (1994). Video violence and the protection of children. University of Nottingham Child Development Research Unit.

Piaget, J. (1967). *The child's conception of space.* New York: W. W. Norton.

Pini, N., & Walkerdine, V. (forthcoming). *Girls on film: New visible fictions of femininity.*

Postman, N. (1994). *The disappearance of childhood.* New York: Vintage Books.

Rose, J. (1985). *Peter Pan or the impossibility of children's fiction.* London: Macmillan.

Rose, J. (1985). Introduction. In J. Mitchell & J. Rose (Eds.), *Jacques Lacan and the Ecole Freudienne Feminine Sexuality* (pp. 1–58). London: Macmillan.

Screen (1992). *The sexual subject.* London: Routledge.

Sunday Times (1983, March 13). P. 36.

Tarde, G. (1890). *La Criminalité.* Paris: F. Alcan.

Urwin, C. (1995). Teenage mutant ninja turtles. In C. Bazalgette & D. Buckingham (Eds.), *Not in front of the children* (pp. 35–51). London: BFI.

Walkerdine, V. (1984/1998). Developmental psychology and the child centred pedagogy. In J. Henriques, W. Hollway, C. Urwin, C. Venn, & V. Walkerdine, *Changing the subject: Psychology, social regulation and subjectivity* (pp. 153–202). London: Routledge.

Walkerdine, V. (1985). Video replay. In V. Burgin, J. Donald, & C. Kaplan, *Formations of fantasy* (pp. 105–47). London: Routledge.

Walkerdine, V. (1988/1990). *The mastery of reason*. London: Routledge.

Walkerdine, V. (1989). *Counting girls out*. London: Virago.

Walkerdine, V. (1992). *Reasoning in a post-modern age*. Fifth International Conference on Thinking, Townsville, Australia.

Walkerdine, V. (1993). Beyond developmentalism. *Theory and Psychology*, 3, 4, 451–69.

Walkerdine, V. (1997). *Young girls and popular culture*. London: Macmillan; Cambridge, MA: Harvard University Press.

Walkerdine, V., & Lucey, H. (1989). *Democracy in the kitchen: Regulating mothers and socialising daughters*. London: Virago.

3

Time Matters in Adolescence

Nancy Lesko

The modern age is defined by time, by a temporalization of experience, that is, an understanding that events and change are meaningful in their occurrence in and through time. Millennial, evolutionary, and individual life narratives share such temporalizations with an emphasis on the endings. But not all times are the same, as debates at the turn of the century and today, for example, over daylight saving time, indicate. There remain public and private times, slower and faster times, and more and less rationalized times.

I examine conceptions of adolescence as partaking of panoptical time, a condensed, commodified time built upon global hierarchies of gender, race, and class and understood at a glance as natural. Panoptical time emphasizes the endings toward which youth are to progress and places individual adolescents into a sociocultural narrative that demands "mastery" without movement or effect. In these ways I interrogate the development-in-time episteme through which adolescents are known, consumed, and governed. I conclude by considering contemporary challenges to the slow, linear time of adolescent development.

Modern Time

Although the steam engine appears in U.S. history textbooks as the marker of modernism,

> *[t]he clock*, not the steam engine, *is the key-machine of the modern industrial age* . . . in its relationship to determinable quantities of energy, to standardization, to automatic action, and . . . to accurate timing. . . . The clock is not merely a means of keeping track of the hours, but of synchronizing the actions of men [*sic*]. (Mumford cited in Landes, 1983, p. xix, emphasis added)

Reinhart Koselleck argues that the *temporalization of experience* (the view that all change occurs in and through time) *"is the defining quality of the modern world"* (cited in Bender & Wellbery, 1991, p. 1, emphasis added). The temporalization of experience utilized clock time, standardized world time, active measurement, and counting of time. Time was tracked in order to use it. "The mechanical clock made possible . . . a civilization attentive to the passage of time, hence to productivity and performance" (Landes, 1983, p. 7). And productive use of time became a central measure of better, more valuable individuals and groups. E. P. Thompson describes how the new time-discipline was imposed across a range of social devices and practices: bells and clocks, the division of labor, the supervision of labor, money incentives, preachings and schoolings, and the suppression of fairs and sports. He summarizes, "In mature capitalist society all time must be consumed, marketed, put to use; it is offensive for the labour force merely to 'pass the time' " (Thompson, 1993, pp. 394–95). Clock time and productivity fell into step with an existing American emphasis on progress (Popkewitz & Pitman, 1986).

This temporalization of human life and growth occurred with and through numerous social processes and events. The railroads, for example, were central to the adoption of world standard time because their profits were intertwined with schedules, with being on time. The Prime Meridian Conference in 1884 hosted representatives of twenty-five countries who agreed to establish Greenwich, England, as the zero meridian and "determined the exact length of the day, divided the earth into twenty-four time zones one hour apart, and fixed a precise beginning of the universal day" (Kern, 1983, p. 12). Prior to this coordination, a railroad traveler from Washington, D.C., to San Francisco would have set her watch to 200 different local times. Accurate train schedules were, in turn, dependent upon the telegraph, which made possible the uniform method of determining and maintaining accurate time signals and transmitting them around the world. Even such a brief introduction to the making of standard universal time provides a sense of modern temporalization and standardization, which otherwise appear natural and inevitable.

Sciences and Time

The sciences were also active in modern temporalization. Foucault locates the cutting edge of scientific temporalization in the development of natural history with its central task of classifying according to structure and taxonomic character. While medieval scientists and citizens had conceptualized the cosmos as comprised of static laws and regularities, natural historians began to describe change and growth over time. The French paleontologist Lamarck, along with competitors Cuvier and Smith, pieced together fossil remains of extinct organisms and placed them in a chronological order. This was the beginning of a theory of evolution, an altogether original conception of development in and through time. In 1809 Lamarck published the first evolutionary family tree, showing the branched series by which the complex organisms of the present day were related back to earlier, simpler forms of life and so to the hypothetical point of the "first beginnings of organization" (Toulmin & Goodfield, 1965, p. 179). Toulmin and Goodfield argue that it was in this scientific quest for the "origin," which Darwin linked to his work with the title *The Origin of Species*, that time consciousness was produced:

> *The new epistemic order was development-in-time* and underlay such new conceptualizations as the evolution of species, the ages of human life, and the development of society. (Lowe, 1982, p. 49, emphasis added)

Johannes Fabian (1983) augments this history of science by examining how the discipline of anthropology spatialized time through concepts of "development" and "civilization." Fabian argues that a defining practice of anthropological research is the locating of primitive others in another time (and space) and that this temporal distance, termed "developmental" or "cultural," rests upon more advanced and less advanced positions on the evolutionary scale. Accordingly, to designate a people as occupying "a different time" was to label them as wholly other, inferior, and occupying a less-evolved position.

> Constructions of otherness do not begin with evolutionism and other schemes of distancing whose ideological character we now recognize; they are already built into our very presentations of identity/sameness as an exclusive "here and now," which we accept without much questioning. One trick especially, which we seem to play again and again— the trick of denying coevalness, same time, to those whom we perceive as distant and different—works as a "construction with time." (Fabian, 1991, p. 190)

Narratives of cultural evolution and of individual adolescent development prioritize the ending; they are primarily narratives of fulfillment: "the important thing in tales of evolution remains their ending" (Fabian, 1991, p. 193). This fact links these narratives with Christian millennialist ones (Haraway, 1997; Popkewitz & Pitman, 1986). Much of the import of cultural evolutionism, claims Fabian, is that it allows us to read events as omens of things to come. The theory of cultural evolution makes otherness ominous by construing it as "past future" (Fabian, 1991, p. 195). For example, moral panics around youth regularly call up a sense of "past future"—that the future will be diminished, dragged down by teenagers' failures to act in civilized or responsible ways. The discourse on teenage pregnancy portrays young mothers as signifying decline into an immoral and economically backward society, another "past future" (Lesko, 1994, 1997).

Awareness of changing temporalities was not confined to scientists. Stephen Kern portrays a dense, vital network of discussion, protest, and theorization of time among artists and philosophers at the turn of the twentieth century as further evidence of the "primariness of time" (1983, p. 50). Common, daily experiences of inventions such as the telephone, the high-speed rotary press, and the cinema sparked debate about time, and, more precisely, about the past, the present, and the future. Kern portrays debates about public versus private time and whether time was reversible or irreversible, heterogeneous or homogeneous, and continuous or atomistic. Kern juxtaposes Ibsen's and Kafka's plays with Cubist painting and the philosophy of Bergson to promote a strong sense of the new temporal consciousness as abiding, though decidedly nonunitary. The introduction of world standard time created greater uniformity of shared public time and simultaneously triggered theorizing about a multiplicity of private times.

Adolescence and Development-in-Time

Closely on the heels of world standard time, adolescence was reformulated in psychological and sociological terms as "the promise of individual or collective regeneration" (Passerini, 1997, p. 281). During the decade 1895 to 1905 the new adolescent was invented as turbulent, as the "seed of new wealth for the future" (Passerini, 1997, p. 281), and as the source of progress for the race. The conceptions of adolescence went hand in hand with new social sites and practices: longer stays in school, organized leisure in scouting and in urban playgrounds, juvenile justice policies aimed at prevention, and the outlawing of child labor. Overall, such practices helped define an adolescence that demanded a slow, steady movement toward maturity; reformers were especially wary of peaks of emotional intensity, which were linked with precocity. Precocity, especially masturbation, was a direct path to degeneracy. Protected adolescence needed to become bland, sanitized of even religious conversion experiences, which could be too tumultuous. Youth were defined as always "becoming," a situation that provoked endless watching, monitoring, and evaluating. As time was made and marked in public, standardized ways, the modern, scientific adolescent became a multifaceted social site for talk about the productive use of time, the glorious future, and, sometimes, the inglorious past. Slow, careful development-in-time was identified as the safest path.

Adolescent development-in-time was similar to the development of the child and distinct from it. The developing child is both in and out of time (James & Prout, 1990), measured by time but not in the adult/present. The development of adolescents was, like that of child saving, grounded in racial and class differences; development was synonymous with becoming civilized, that is, becoming white, middle class, and, preferably, male (Baker, 1998). The developing child is also closely watched so that its learning proceeds according to its nature, neither too fast nor too slow (Walkerdine, 1984). The developing child, if coached well, will avoid juvenile delinquency and other growth disorders (Walkerdine, 1984). Thus, many of the same political rationalities were operative in forging the developing child and the adolescent. However, while the developing child can be sanitized as innocent, the knowledge of sexuality relentlessly stalks adolescent development. The incitement to worry over teenagers is largely sexual anxiety—sexuality that invokes animality, self-abuse, loss of male energy, and antisocial attitudes. Sexual precocity, especially masturbation, was the gateway to degeneration because of its serious consequences for the development of individuals, the nation, and the race. The normative slow pace of proper development has been about curbing precocity and channeling emotions toward games and team loyalty.

The child and the adolescent are dissimilar in the importance of cognitive growth, which occurred later and was de-emphasized in adolescence (Walkerdine, 1984). Adolescent maturation was overwhelmingly about raising masculine boys to lead and to follow orders, while the gendered politics of childhood were different (Walkerdine, 1990). The temporal ordering of children's development enlisted women as teachers and mothers, while adolescent development was primarily about boys and men. Finally, I think that adolescent development-in-time is more Janus-faced; the more that adolescent development is invoked, the harder it is to find the teenager in the present moment. Adolescent development concentrates on "futures past"—on the past (other times and nonmodern practices) and on possible replications of the past in the future. It looks away from the messy, sexualized adolescent in the present, while always referring to the raging hormones. Child development seems to invoke real children in the present, however romanticized and sanitized; however, Jenks's (Chapter 4 of this volume) examination of time in British elementary school classrooms describes how the future's claim on the children's present actions is established. Finally, child development and adolescent development seem to invoke different uses of individualism. "The child" is a unique individual. "Adolescence" calls forth the group first, then only later, with Erikson and Piaget, the individual teenager.

Panoptical Time

In order to further explore the interrelations of adolescence with the development-in-time episteme, I introduce "panoptical time," a particular rationalization of time that was condensed into quickly perceived images. These easily understood and utilized images created the ways that youth were understood and experienced and the ways they, in turn, experienced their teenaged years. Just as Foucault's reading of the panopticon promoted an understanding of its totalized mode of surveillance, with both prisoner and guard subjectivities affected, so too can linear, historical time moving toward "progress" be examined for how it disciplines subjectivities and objective knowledge. As already established, terms such as "civilization" and "development" spatialized time and the least civilized peoples were represented as most remote in time from the present (Fabian, 1983). McClintock builds upon Fabian's ideas with her concept of panoptical time, an understanding of development through time that incorporated the assumed superiority of Western civilizations and could then be utilized by individuals in governing others and themselves:

> By panoptical time, I mean the image of global history consumed—at a glance—in a single spectacle from a point of privileged invisibility. . . . To meet the "scientific" standards set by the natural historians and empiricists of the eighteenth century, a visual paradigm was needed to display evolutionary progress as a measurable spectacle. The exemplary figure that emerged was the evolutionary family Tree of Man. (McClintock, 1995, p. 37)

The tree offered a simple classificatory scheme that easily switched between evolutionary hierarchies within nature and evolutionary progress across human cultures. The Tree of Man portrayed a "natural genealogy of power" (McClintock, 1995, p. 37), a unified world history according to the colonizers. Thus, panoptical time is colonial time, although it was as useful at home as in imperial efforts. Diagrams of evolutionary family trees (see Figure 1) mapped "natural" social difference through time. The most developed men were white middle-class European males in the present: "Aryans" are located at the tips of both trees. The viewer of the Tree of Man has a privileged invisibility and an appetite, an incitement, to understand and classify others in this spatialized time. The Tree of Man provides classification "at a glance" and, with equal efficiency, a panoptical view of human groups through time.

Psychologists who constructed the stages of individual human development followed the evolutionary tree model and utilized colonial time. Younger children and arrested youth were analogous to older and more primitive peoples (lower branches), and each individual child had to climb her own evolutionary tree (Gould, 1977). Adolescence actively participated in this reenactment of global history through the theory of recapitulation—the belief that each individual human's growth recapitulates the stages of evolution of the race—and through the weighting of adolescence as a racial swing point,

MORPHOLOGICAL TREE OF THE HUMAN RACE.   ÆSTHETIC TREE OF THE HUMAN RACE.

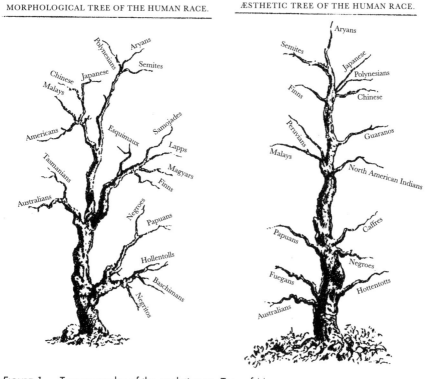

FIGURE 1.   Two examples of the evolutionary Tree of Man.

Copyright © 1995. From IMPERIAL LEATHER by Anne McClintock. Reproduced by permission of Taylor & Francis, Inc./Routledge, Inc., http://www.routledge-ny.com

a time when an evolutionary leap forward was accomplished or missed (Lesko, 1996). According to G. Stanley Hall, adolescence marked the boundary between civilized and savage, a time when an individual and his race remained "arrested" or moved toward a higher ranked position, termed civilized. Since adolescence was identified as the cusp, the turning point, the teenager regularly called forth the underbelly of the colonizers' evolutionary narrative: worries over degeneration, contamination, and the anxious scrutiny of physical characteristics, behavior, and morals for signs of decay (Stoler, 1995).

I suggest that a dominant aspect of the discourse on adolescence is its location within panoptical time, within a time framework that compels us—scholars, educators, parents, and teenagers—to attend to progress, precocity, arrest, or decline. Adolescence both makes and marks time. The developmental framework is simultaneously colonial (with privileged, invisible viewers and hypervisible, temporalized, and embodied others) and administrative (ranking, judging, making efficient and productive). I develop this idea of the panoptical time of adolescence by examining three images that regularly represent teenagers: physical "stigmata" and delinquency at the turn of the century; pubertal processes and "budding" bodies in adolescent medicine; and psychosocial growth in Erikson's eight stages. Adolescence is not mapped via a tree, but by tables and charts of physical regularities, rates of pubertal change, and psychosocial steps. These all function to rank individuals according to their placement in time (Foucault, 1979, p. 146), a process which will facilitate their placement and processing by institutions. In other words, I interrogate the development-in-time episteme of adolescence by focusing on three schemas that lay out growth, arrest, and decay. Within each image the privileged, knowledgeable reader (who resides in the adult "here and now") may discern problems of atavism, developmental delays, or precocity.

Adolescent Physical "Stigmata"

In 1896 an article on degenerate youth in the *Pedagogical Seminary*, one of the journals founded by G. Stanley Hall, interpreted deviations from normal growth or progress as ominous for the future and offered an early panoptical view of adolescence. The physical and psychical traits of fifty-two "delinquent" youth (twenty-six boys from the Lyman School for Boys at Westboro, Massachusetts, and twenty-six girls from the State Industrial School for Girls at Lancaster, Massachusetts) were compared to those of "normal" men and women. George Dawson, the author, described delinquent youth according to facial, bodily, and behavioral peculiarities. In one table (see Figure 2) the delinquent girls and boys were compared to normal women and men in incidence of webfeet, protruding ears, large birthmarks, and other "stigmata." Throughout the text, Dawson states that criminals and decadent races have round heads, large lower jaws, and asymmetrical faces. Thus, delinquent youth were placed with "past types," that is, degenerate peoples, who were neither growing nor in balance, the other two states for organisms. The categorizing of civilized and savage peoples by deviations in general proportions of the body; in asymmetries of face and skull; in oddly formed jaw, palate, or eyes; in developmental irregularities in speech or walk; and in psychical problems (including sexual activeness, explosive activity, and egotism) were common across evolutionary and racial sciences and known as the "stigmata of degeneration" (Fausto-Sterling, 1995; Gilman, 1985; Horn, 1995; McClintock, 1995).

Youth with degenerate stigmata were referred to as "atavistic," as throwbacks to primitive people, in body and conduct "a reemergence of the historical and evolutionary pasts in the present" (Horn, 1995, p. 112). The criminal was linked by abnormal anatomy and physiology to the insane person and to the epileptic, as well as to those "others," including "the ape, the child,

TABLE III

Showing Stigmata according to types of Delinquency; also in comparison with Normal Standards.[2]

	Theft		Unchastity		Assault		Incendiarism		General Incorrigibility		Totals for Boys	Totals for Girls	Per cent of Delinquent Boys having Stigmata	Per cent of Normal Men having Stigmata	Per cent of Delinquent Girls having Stigmata	Per cent of Normal Women having Stigmata
	Boys	Girls	Boys	Girls	Boys	Girls	Boys	Girls	Boys	Girls						
No. of Observations,	10	4	5	10	2	0	3	0	6	12	26	26				
Plagiocephali,	3	1	1	1	0		0		2	3	6	5	23.0	20.0	19.2	17.2
Platycephali,	1	0	1	2	0		0		0	0	2	2	7.7	15.0	7.7	0.1
Scaphocephali,	1	0	0	0	0		0		0	0	1	0	3.8	6.0	0.0	0.0
Hydrocephali,	1	0	0	0	0		0		0	0	1	0	3.8		0.0	
Asymmetrical Face,	3	1	1	6	0		2		2	4	8	11	30.8	6.0	42.3	0.1
Prognathous Jaws,	1	0	1	3	0		1		0	5	3	8	11.5	34.0	30.8	10.0
Large Lower Jaw,	2	1	2	1	2		0		1	2	7	4	26.9	29.0	15.4	6.5
Precocious Wrinkles,	1	0	1	0	0		0		0	0	2	0	7.7		0.0	
Bad Eruptions,	0	0	3	0	1		0		0	0	4	0	15.4		0.0	
Large Birth-marks,	1	0	0	0	0		0		0	0	1	0	3.8		0.0	
Asymmetrical Ears,	3	0	0	2	0		2		2	1	7	3	26.9		11.5	
Protruding Ears,	4	0	3	0	0		0		2	0	9	0	34.6		0.0	
Deformed Palate,	4	1	2	4	1		0		3	4	10	9	38.6	19.0[3]	34.6	19.0[3]
Asymmetrical Arms,	4	1	2	5	1		1		2	5	10	11	38.6		42.3	
Web-feet,	0	0	0	0	0		0		1	0	1	0	3.8		0.0	
"Pigeon-breast,"	0	–	0	–	0		1		2	–	3	–	11.5		–	
Total Stigmata,	29	5	17	24	5	0	6	0	17	24	74	53				
No. per Child,	2.9	1.2	3.4	2.4	2.5	0	2	0	2.8	2	29	2				

[1] *Nervous Diseases of Children:* p. 12.
[2] Lombroso: *DHomme Criminel,* 2d French Ed., p. 170.
[3] Clouston: *Neuroses of Development.*

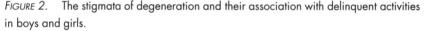

FIGURE 2. The stigmata of degeneration and their association with delinquent activities in boys and girls.

From George Dawson, 1896, A study in youthful degeneracy, The Pedagogical Seminary 4(2), 237.

woman, prehistoric man, and the contemporary savage" (Horn, 1995, p. 112). Homosexuals were also understood as primitive throwbacks (Terry, 1995). Dawson (1896) provides an early version of the development-in-time episteme applied to adolescence, one that focuses more on degenerative traits than on markers of normal growth or progress. Dawson located degenerate youth in an earlier time and simultaneously extrapolated its effects on the future health of society. Dawson's categories evoked and would have been understood within an evolutionary chain of being, one in which development was becoming normative, and stasis and degeneration were deviant and threatening. We may imagine readers of Dawson's study operating upon an explicit evolutionary history—as portrayed in the following image—"progress consumed at a glance." Atavistic youth were located in panoptical time in both Dawson's chart and in the hierarchy of heads (see Figure 3). Progress and degeneration were inextricably linked (Bederman, 1995; Nye, 1985) and consumed at a glance in both illustrations. Dawson utilized panoptical time in his analysis of delinquent physical "stigmata" and in his administrative incitements to cure and prevent such degeneracy.

Pubertal Processes

Two effects of the always imminent atavism of youth were especially important for education, social work, juvenile justice, and related fields. First, the potential atavism of youth incited ever finer surveillance of youth and their timely development. Both physical and psychosocial traits had to be carefully mapped, a process that continues in contemporary scholarship, for example, on young adolescents or social-emotional learning. Second, schools instituted strict time schedules to minimize tendencies toward degeneracy, with age-grading, daily timetables, and control over clothing and appearance as central techniques.

Panoptical Time Charted on Developing Bodies

In an anthology of state-of-the-art scholarship on adolescence in the early 1990s (Feldman & Elliott, 1990), drawings of the "pubertal processes" utilize panoptical time. Figures 4 and 5 show breast and pubic hair growth stages in girls and penile and pubic hair growth in boys.

These charts emphasize the development-in-time perspective, as well as the erotic dimension of looking at adolescent bodies, a scientific scopophilia (Terry, 1995). Although not as comprehensive as evolutionary trees, they do call forth a sense of panoptic time—the privileged, invisible observer consumes scientific realities of adolescent development-in-time at a glance. McClintock argues that any modern fetishized object must be able to be consumed at a glance. Such charts incite looking, provide knowledge to be consumed, as well as confirm the reality of adolescent physicality. Adolescent immaturity/development relies upon knowing-by-looking, an "optics of truth" (McClintock, 1995, p. 50). This optics of truth has a long history and Dawson's empirical observations of physical characteristics also privileged the embodied and the visible as indicators of moral and social health.

Panoptical Time Charted on Developing Psyches

A vivid illustration of the panoptical time of adolescence is Erik Erikson's influential step diagram. Erikson's theoretical schema, "Eight Ages of Man,"

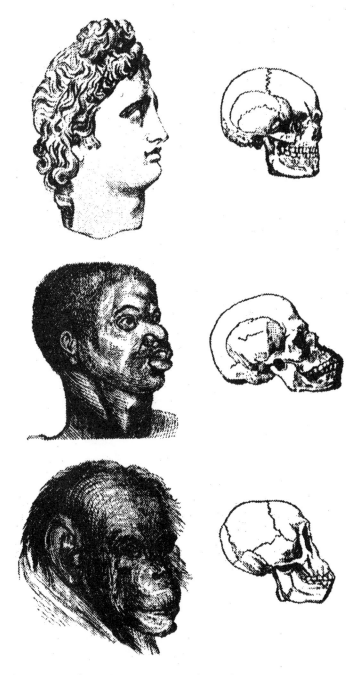

FIGURE 3.   Panoptical time: Progress consumed at a glance.
Copyright © 1995. From IMPERIAL LEATHER by Anne McClintock. Reproduced by permission of Taylor & Francis, Inc./Routledge, Inc., http://www.routledge-ny.com

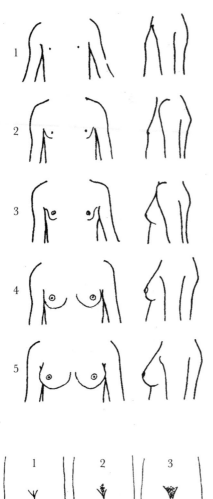

BREASTS

1. No breast development.
2. The first sign of breast development has appeared. This stage is sometimes referred to as the breast budding stage. Some palpable breast tissue under the nipple, the flat area of the nipple (areola) may be somewhat enlarged.
3. The breast is more distinct although there is no separation between contours of the two breasts.
4. The breast is further enlarged and there is greater contour distinction. The nipple including the areola forms a secondary mound on the breast.
5. Mature Stage Size may vary in the mature stage. The breast is fully developed. The contours are distinct and the areola has receded into the general contrur of the breast.

PUBIC HAIR

1. No pubic hair.
2. There is a small amount of long pubic hair chiefly along vaginal lips.
3. Hair is darker, coarser, and curlier and spreads sparsely over skin around vaginal lips.
4. Hair is now adult in type, but area covered is smaller than in most adults. There is no pubic hair on the inside of the thighs.
5. Hair is adult in type, distributed as an inverse triangle. There may be hair on the inside of the thighs.

FIGURE 4.   Pubertal processes at a glance.

From W. A. Marshall & J. M. Tanner, 1969, *Variations in the pattern of pubertal changes in girls*, Archives of Disease in Childhood *44*, 291. Reprinted with permission.

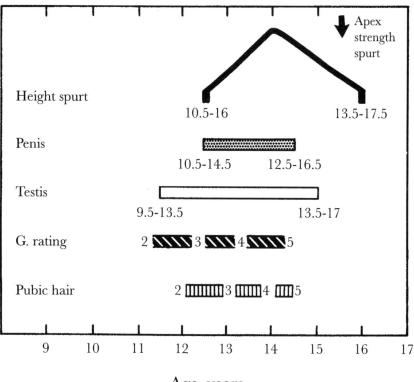

FIGURE 5.   Pubertal processes at a glance.
From J. M. Tanner, 1962, Growth at Adolescence, Oxford: Blackwell Scientific. Reprinted with permission.

was intended to be a "global form of thinking" about childhood, adolescence, and adulthood portrayed as a series of crises or periods of enhanced vulnerability and potential (Erikson, 1950/1985, p. 273). Panoptical time is explicitly depicted by Erikson in words and in Figure 6:

> An epigenetic diagram thus lists a system of stages dependent on each other; and while individual stages may have been explored more or less thoroughly or named more or less fittingly, *the diagram suggests that their study be pursued always with the total configuration of stages in mind.* (1950/1985, p. 272, emphasis added)

Erikson's diagram, like the Tree of Man, allows the unnamed observer to consume the human life course and adolescence at a glance. This diagram beckons us to locate and evaluate adolescents, as well as children and adults, by their progress toward the higher stages. Are they in the right box? What evidence of that stage conflict can we discern? Is "resolution" in sight? Erik-

Eight Ages of Man

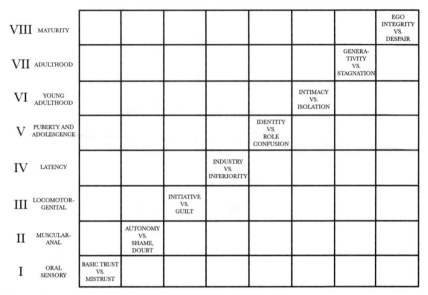

VIII MATURITY							EGO INTEGRITY VS. DESPAIR
VII ADULTHOOD						GENERA-TIVITY VS. STAGNATION	
VI YOUNG ADULTHOOD					INTIMACY VS. ISOLATION		
V PUBERTY AND ADOLESCENCE				IDENTITY VS. ROLE CONFUSION			
IV LATENCY			INDUSTRY VS. INFERIORITY				
III LOCOMOTOR-GENITAL		INITIATIVE VS. GUILT					
II MUSCULAR-ANAL	AUTONOMY VS. SHAME, DOUBT						
I ORAL SENSORY	BASIC TRUST VS. MISTRUST						

FIGURE 6.

From Erik H. Erikson, 1950/1985, Childhood and Society, New York: W. W. Norton & Co., 273. Reprinted with permission.

son's characterization of the adolescent crisis as Identity vs. Role Confusion has become synonymous with modern adolescence, as he proposed that it should be: "We may, in fact, speak of the identity crisis as the psychosocial aspect of adolescing" (1968, p. 91). The categorization and placement of the adolescent in psychosocial developmental time defines youth in the United States and to some degree around the world. Erikson's psychosocial stages place adolescence in another time—"there and then"—a lower step, a younger age, a different crisis. The privileged viewer of Erikson's chart understands the full trajectory as well as the imperative to proceed to the top step. We privileged viewers likewise understand our administrative imperatives to aid those others who are progressing normally as well as those who move too slowly or too quickly. Age-graded and morally sensitive educators are especially attuned to timely progress.

Similarly, Piaget provides a panoptical view of cognitive growth from prelogical to abstract thought. According to Walkerdine, "It is the empirical apparatus of stages of development which of all Piaget's work has been most utilized in education" (1984, p. 190). Piaget's developmental stages helped teachers to naturalize individual development and thus to turn away from regimentation and control, which could go awry and produce childhood aggression that might spawn juvenile delinquency. Walkerdine claims that Piaget's empirical studies convinced psychologists and educators that these stages did exist and charted a path toward the modern, democratically inclined, reasoning adult. Piaget's stages emphasized the individual's natural path toward reason and the teacher's constant watchfulness to provide the appropriate materials, stimuli, and tasks. Teachers who either pushed too fast or lagged behind their students' developmental needs were faulted. Piaget's cognitive developmental stages regularly appear in courses and textbooks in secondary education, although adolescents' emotionality is often seen to undercut their abilities to reason. Nevertheless, Piaget provides another example of the development-in-time episteme, for he laid out a panoptical map of cognitive development that simultaneously offers educational practices. Just as with Erikson's psychosocial stages, Piaget's cognitive stages can be consumed at a glance and utilized by privileged viewers of children and youth.

School Times

By the 1870s, age-graded schools were entrenched across the United States. Age-grading was a preeminent structure of schooling and was rationalized as efficient and effective. Joseph Kett traced the beginnings of age-graded curriculum in evangelical Protestant Sunday schools; from there they spread to private and public schools, promoting a systematization of schooling. It had been the norm for one-room schoolhouses, secondary academies, and even colleges to enroll students across a wide age range; it was common for academies (secondary schools) to have male students as young as twelve up through their early twenties. Age heterogeneity had been unremarkable, but the reform efforts of 1830–1850 included greater standardization according to age and achievement, working toward a school that was increasingly a controlled environment for children and youth (Kett, 1974, 1977).

Age-graded schools were part of an intensification of age and related norms. The establishment of graded schools not only concentrated children of the same age together in a stage-based, factory-like setting but also eliminated incidences and tolerances of precocity (Chudacoff, 1989, p. 36). Four-year-olds were no longer allowed to enter elementary school, nor were ten-year-olds tolerated in high school. This "compressing of age ranges and decreased tolerance of precocity" occurred in American and British secondary schools and also in universities (Chudacoff, 1989, p. 37). Textbook writers and publishers accepted and perpetuated age-graded developmental schemes. "Statistical laws" were established primarily upon predictions according to age. Not only could predictions about national population and consumption be based upon age census data but every aspect of life could be mapped and modeled, including morality, crime, full-time employment, prostitution, divorces, birth of children, and hygiene. "In an era that prized efficiency and scientific data, age statistics were the most convenient criteria for measuring and evaluating social standards" (Chudacoff, 1989, p. 91).

Leonard Ayres fashioned a high-profile educational career by calculating the percentages of over-age students in American schools. His *Laggards in Our Schools* (1909) demonstrated that U.S. schools were filled with retarded—that is, over-age—children. He calculated that 33 per cent of students were over-aged (that is, not at the proper grade for their age) and argued for greater educational efficiency and a curriculum more in line with average students (Callahan, 1962). Statistics, such as Ayres's 33 percent of over-age students, became "part of the technology of power in a modern state" (Hacking, 1991, p. 181). Proceeding through the grades (not being held back) became normative. Today we automatically anticipate problems if students are held back or if they skip a grade and are out of step with their age peers. Statistical age-based norms became the basis for bureaucratic practices but also became the "classifications within which people must think of themselves and of the actions that are open to them" (Hacking, 1991, p. 194), a topic taken up later in this chapter.

Schools not only became more age-homogeneous but they utilized close supervision of students' time to enforce timely development. Schools for African-American and American Indian students, who were perceived as less civilized, demonstrated hypervigilance over time (Anderson, 1988; Lomawaima, 1995). The "exacting demands of a uniform schedule" were expected to teach the necessity and "the habitual practice of orderly, meek existence" (Schlossman, 1977, p. 30), at least for certain youths. The "regulation of time" aimed to create a disciplined habitus in criminal tribespeople (Tolen, 1995, p. 95), as it did in reformatories in the United States (Schlossman, 1977). According to Foucault, "Time penetrates the body and with it all the meticulous controls of power" (1979, p. 152). Then and now adolescents regularly incite moral panics by their failure to embody an "orderly, meek existence."

I have found little evidence of debates over the nature of institutional time in schools and other youth organizations around the turn of the century. Teachers and other youth reformers seemed to accept clock time and its demand for homogeneous, public, irreversible, and fragmented time (Kern, 1983). Such a view of time supported the belief that youth in public and private schools should be learning and behaving on identical timetables; this view of time helped establish slow children as hopelessly other. Timely development was always interwoven with strict surveillance of the body. Success could be established and displayed convincingly via "normal" dress and deportment (Alexander, 1995; Schlossman & Wallach, 1978) and by students moving up at the normal rate, one grade per year. Precocity—in appearance and in age—were signs of deviance and educators learned vigilance over development on time.

Moratorium Experiences, or Growing Up in "Expectant Time"

The concept of adolescence as a *moratorium* is part of Erikson's significant impact on popular and scholarly conceptions of youth and adolescence. Although the concept of a youthful moratorium of responsibility may seem quite uncontroversial, when historicized as part of an interrogation of modern temporality, we may consider it differently. The concept of an adolescent moratorium is a specific example of panoptical time, with its invisible observer and contradictory imperatives. In this section, I focus on some experiential dimensions of panoptical time. What are some aspects of living within panoptical time? How does the time of a moratorium effect youth? How can we conceptualize teenaged time experiences within such a modernist temporal order?

Stephen Kern explores how modern emphasis on productive time was experienced by persons in different social positions. Kern coins the term "expectant time" to describe how "the assembly line and Taylorism diminished the factory worker's active control over the immediate future in the productive process and relegated him to an *expectant mode,* waiting for the future to come along the line" (1983, p. 92, emphasis added). Kern argues that this passive temporal mode, oriented toward the future, has material effects on people. "Individuals behave in distinctive ways when they feel cut off from the flow of time, excessively attached to the past, isolated in the present, without a future, or rushing toward one" (Kern, 1983, p. 3). This section explores how the moratorium of adolescence may have material effects on youth.

Children and youth are positioned like Kern's factory workers—waiting passively for the future. According to James and Prout (1990) children and youth are both imprisoned in their time (age) and out of time (abstracted), and they are thereby denied power over decisions or resources. Teenagers cannot go backward to childhood nor forward to adulthood "before their time" without incurring derogatory labels—for example, immature, loose, or precocious. The dominant concepts regarding youth's position in the Western societies, "development" and "socialization," make it impossible for youth to exercise power over life events or to represent themselves, since they are not fully developed or socialized (Prout & James, 1990). Kern's historical analysis of "expectant time" pushes us to consider the experiences of being caught in age and time.

Despite the passivity of the adolescent moratorium, Erikson's norms for a healthy personality demand an active mastery of one's environment, a unified personality, and accurate perceptions of oneself and the world (Erikson,

1968, p. 92). I want to call attention to the difficulties of actively mastering one's environment and securing "identity" when youth are simultaneously contained within an "expectant mode." In the sections below, I explore the conflicted experiences of "becoming but not being." Because the naturalized discourse of youth is so powerful, it is difficult to conceive of how the normative age-grading, vigilance over precocity, and incitement to activeness might affect youths' experiences of being teenaged, and how these powerful pulls and pushes help produce the knowable and known adolescent. In order to denaturalize adolescent "identity conflicts," I juxtapose postcolonial theory with sociological studies of Norwegian childhood and life history accounts of American college students. This bricollage portrays some aspects of "expectant time" and suggests the regularized, material production of youth crises.

Describing the Colonized

> The most formidable ally of economic and political control had long been the business of "knowing" other peoples because this knowing underpinned imperial dominance and became the mode by which they were increasingly persuaded to know themselves: that is, as subordinate to Europe. (Ashcroft, Griffiths, & Tiffin, 1995, p. 1)

Knowledges that portray the colonized as inferior influence both the colonized and the colonizer. Frantz Fanon (1952/1986) first documented the devastating psychological effects of colonialism on the "natives." The institutionalization of colonialism kept social structural inequalities muted, while the colonized and their psychologized "dependency complex" became hyper-visible (Cesaire, 1972, p. 40). As economic and political constraints fade from view, colonized people appear as the rational source of a colonial order because they "need, crave, demand dependency." In Bhabha's (1994) theoretical terms, colonial discourse involves a splitting: it obscures the relationships of institutions and apparatuses of power while it emphasizes the inadequacies of the colonized.

Postcolonial scholarship offers broad, incisive, and useful critiques of Western knowledges. Postcolonial work offers a particular understanding of portraits of adolescents as emotional, confused, controlled by hormones, unstable, and looking for identity, all of which are popular attributions. When we look at these attributions as a set of relations, rather than as the natural qualities of people between the ages of twelve and nineteen, postcolonial analyses emphasize the processes of producing and consuming certain knowledges about the inferiority of youth (Memmi, 1965). The next sections provide examples of knowledge of adolescents that split off power apparatuses and leave emotional responses that prove the immaturity of youth.

Big and Little Twelve-Year-Olds: Critiquing Age-Based Norms

Anne Solberg (1990), a Norwegian sociologist, has documented how different sets of family relationships make children "big" or keep them "little." She contrasted a twelve-year-old girl in a family that distributed both household responsibilities (cooking, cleaning, laundry) and household resources (private time and discretionary spending) among two adults and two children with a twelve-year-old boy in a family that expected little from him (occasionally he was asked to help out with a particular task) and also accorded him few rights (no regular discretionary income, for example). Solberg found that in the first family both the adults and the girl considered the twelve-year-old as big, responsible, and capable. The second family tended to view the son as little and childlike. Solberg's point is to suggest that chronological age must be supplemented by a concept of social age, that is, of age as socially produced through material practices. Of course, Solberg's study is on a small scale, but it suggests the usefulness of interrogating the relationships between knowledge about youth nature and sets of material practices.

The variability documented by Solberg in "big" and "little" twelve-year-olds is vigilantly absent in schooling, which enforces rigid age-graded expectations:

> By the early 1900s, passage from elementary school to junior high school and from junior high school to senior high school marked important transitions for youths and nurtured precise expectations and norms for each age-bounded grade and type of school. A fourteen-year-old who was still in the sixth grade was keenly aware of being out of step with peers, as were boys who did not switch from knickers to long pants at thirteen. Equally important, these peer groups and accompanying age expectations were bolstered by new scientific standards for physical and intellectual attainment. (Chudacoff, 1989, p. 72)

"Feeling Your Age"

My interviews with U.S. college undergraduates preparing to become teachers provide sharp images and feelings of being teenaged that suggest an unsettledness from dimly perceived power relations and from heightened competition with one's age-mates. Renee, a midwestern daughter of a veterinarian, described adolescence as a growing consciousness of herself as a social being:

> You begin to actually become conscious of who you are. When your body goes through . . . puberty. . . . You really become concerned about what you look like or how you present yourself. I think that's when you start becoming aware of your effect on the world and your place in it. In adolescence you realize that this is the place you're going to have to live in. *You start feeling your age.* (Int. 1, 1993, p. 10, emphasis added)

But what is "feeling your age"? Renee discusses a consciousness of her pubertal body and becoming concerned with how she looked and how others perceived her. She began to manage herself in line with how others responded to her. In Foucault's terms, the disciplinary gaze, or biopower, began to operate in more explicit ways on and through her body and social relationships. Renee provided clues to other aspects of feeling her age. Her middle-class background, niceness, and Christian values seemed to prevent her from directly critiquing her parents, but over the seven months of the study, she talked more openly about their conflicts. At the beginning of the study in the autumn of 1991, Renee described the conflict as awkwardness:

> If I'm looking at my middle school years . . . you wanted to be somebody so big yet you were still this kid that was under your parents' control. You didn't know what to do. I mean, if you tried to act big, you could get in trouble, and yet if you acted like a baby then people would make fun of you. . . . I just felt it was a very awkward in-between time, to make those decisions for yourself, yet your parents are still in control of you. So, *are those decisions really yours?* (Int. 1, 1993, pp. 16–17, emphasis added)

Here Renee questioned one premise of the discourse of adolescence—she had been informed that middle school youth should act big and make decisions, yet she also knew that the decisions weren't really hers; that is, if she chose wrongly, it would be held against her. Here was a shaky performance of autonomy in which the audience, her parents, were like puppeteers controlling her actions via encouragement and enthusiasm.

Renee provided a specific example to illustrate her "awkwardness" around decision making:

> I have an older sister who plays soccer and she was actually an All-American, and I remember when I was little I just started playing soccer because she was. Then as time went on, I don't know if I was actually making a decision to play soccer or it was just, that was what I should be doing according to my parents . . . 'cause I remember at times I wanted to do other things and yet I was afraid to say something. I thought

I'd hurt their feelings, yet I wanted to be the big person to say, I want to do other things. . . . If I would have had enough courage to say something, I might have . . . [voice trailed off]. (Int. 1, 1993, pp. 19–20)

Here Renee described power struggles with her parents over who made decisions. Expressing only frustration, not anger, as she recounted it, Renee termed the experience "awkward," a minimizing term for what seemed vivid and troublesome memories.

Two months later in a group interview with three other undergraduates, however, she dramatically rewrote the story, omitting the power struggle and calling it her identity crisis:

I think you need to have them [identity problems]. I had an identity problem in high school . . . I played soccer because my sister played soccer and. . . . [pause] I didn't really like it, but I played it. So I think that was an identity problem. But *looking back on it, I wouldn't have had it any other way because I met so many of my friends through soccer and I wouldn't have been in shape or anything like that. I don't know where I would have been without it, so I think you have to go through the identity crisis to continue to develop* (Focus Group 2, 1993, pp. 25–26, emphasis added)

In this revision, Renee adopted an instrumentalist position that soccer helped her find friends, get in shape, and find a place in the world. She concluded that this "identity problem" was necessary in order to develop. Only when we look at both versions of the story can we see that an "identity crisis" was a conflict with parents over use of leisure time. Conflicts with her parents were rewritten as her identity crisis, an example of the splitting off of context and power relations and the psychologizing of youth. The second version affirmed the necessity of adult control of youth. "I don't know where I would have been," she summarized, if her parents' perspective had not dominated. In order to develop, she needed dependency. Fanon identifies how in a colonial society that proclaims the superiority of one race, others must "turn white or disappear," that is, become like the dominators or face erasure or censure (1952/1986, p. 100). Similarly, in a society that proclaims the superiority of adults, children and youth must become like adults or face censure. Renee's acceptance of her parents' perspective on her middle school activities was a process of legitimizing adult power, recoded via the psychological concept of an identity crisis and her need for others to make decisions. To paraphrase Fanon, she had to have an identity crisis or disappear.

I have used Renee's statements to argue that the discourse on adolescence, like colonial discourse, omits material conditions of existence and focuses solely on the psychological state of youth to position the psychological traits as the logical source of the social structural inequities, or the reasons adolescents have to be controlled. In this example, I emphasized Renee's readiness to interpret power struggles in terms of psychological problems of the youth and to simultaneously drop any attention to the structuring conditions that effect the problem. Homi Bhabha (1994) argues that the colonial space is agonistic: the relationship between the colonized and colonizer is one of constant, if implicit, contestation and opposition. Most often when conflict between adolescents and adults is described, teenagers are defined as rebellious, that is, the source of the conflict is within them, their hormones, emotionality, and inability to see beyond the present moment. The concrete interactions of rebellious youth with adults are seldom made visible, so that the simple, unitary description of teenagers as rebellious stands. In this way, the discourse on adolescents tends to produce a fixed opposition between adults and youth, approaching the permanent opposition of the colonizer and the colonized.

For Renee, feeling her age involved doubting her decisions, distancing from her own desires, and accepting her parents' decisions as "in her best interest." In this view, feeling one's age was learning to accept a form of manipulation over decisions and to see oneself as others see you, thereby creating a doubled self. In my analysis, the adolescent "identity crisis" has a social origin and is materially produced in the passive and expectant mode of "growing up."

For Melanie, another undergraduate, feeling one's age meant competition and always coming up second best:

> There is just something about being a teenager that makes you think that you're not very good . . . no matter how hard you try, there is always someone in the classroom that gets better grades than you. Or no matter how hard you try there's always . . . some other girl gets to go out with the guy you wanted to go out with since the beginning of the school year. No matter how hard you try, the other team always wins or the other girl can always run faster than I can. Or, my best friend wants to talk to her brother instead of talking to me. Or there is always something there . . . or no matter how hard you try, your boyfriend still breaks up with you. But there is always something there, that once you get out, once you get up a step, you get knocked back down one. (Int. 3, 1993, p. 10)

Melanie felt her age in enhanced competition for social status and self-worth. Chudacoff (1989, pp. 126–32) confirms that narrow age-groupings force continuous comparisons among age-mates, and meeting those well-defined expectations for life accomplishments confers social status. In my view, the expectant time modality and the psychosocial emphasis on active mastery of one's environment, staged within the corporate model of U.S. high schools (Eckert, 1989), contribute to an intensified search for self and social status. This effect of power relations, in which adolescents are defined as irresponsible and rightly without much power, is what is often referred to as "peer pressure." As in colonial discourse, the colonized are declared naturally unfit to be in any other situation. Youth, like colonized peoples, "need, crave, demand dependency" (Cesaire, 1972, p. 40).

Thus, the position of youth is multiply inferior. They are expected to measure up to finely tuned assessments of productivity, learning, morality, and achievement while remaining in a social position that is dependent and watched over not only by adults but by their age-peers as well. Their dependence communicates their inequality, and their "becoming" status appears to legitimate it. Being fourteen or sixteen is measured by peers and by adults within a system where adolescents' position remains one of lack or absence. Adults are people who *are*, adolescents *will be* in the future (Morss, 1996). In these ways, adolescents, like the natives portrayed in ethnographic accounts, are imprisoned in their age as absence and suspended outside of historical time.

Holocaust Dreams

Reinhart Koselleck provides another dimension of living in "expectant time" in his interpretation of dreams from concentration camp inmates as an inversion of temporal experience.

> In the camp, conditions prevailed that made a mockery of all previous experience; conditions that appeared unreal but were real all the same. The compulsion to derealize oneself in order to become paralyzed at the final stage of existence led also to an inversion of temporal experience. *Past, present, and future ceased to be a framework for orienting behavior.* (Koselleck, 1985, p. 224, emphasis added)

In "utopian camp dreams" the inmates dreamed along the lines of daytime fantasies, that is, about life beyond the electric fence. The past was transferred into wishes for the future; however, "such dreams were the harbingers of death" (Koselleck, 1985, p. 224) since within the camp system, courage and perseverance could lead to destruction. The "salvational dreams" ceased to try to "anchor the person of the dreamer in reality and thus became, apparently paradoxically, the sign of a chance for survival" (Koselleck, 1985, p. 224). Koselleck argues that salvational dreams corresponded to the experience of the camp and were devoid of both images and action; that is, they were without a modern, temporal order. This destruction of the person's self-constructed world, which usually heralds schizophrenia, is an inversion that had some effectiveness in a concentration camp confinement.

The timelessness to which the inmates were condemned assumed in the salvational dreams a redeeming significance, more precisely, a redeeming power. *Estrangement from the empirical self* became a silent weapon against the system of terror that ran through both inmates and overseers in the concentration camp. The diabolic inversion, that death appeared to be a better life and life a worse death, was what had to be confronted. Only in salvational dreams did the inferno find its fictive termination "outside" of time and at the same time offer the inmate a grasp of reality. (Koselleck, 1985, p. 224, emphasis added)

I read Koselleck's analysis to suggest that under extreme conditions of terror, when no self-confirming or self-making action is possible, time—any sense of past or present or future—also ceases. The empirical self separates from the unspeakable horror of the camp internment by splitting from the self via dreams that reject a time consciousness and the possibilities of action related to past, present, or future events. Here the "mastering" of one's environment totally ceases as indicator of the self. I am using the shock of an analogy between adolescence and concentration camp inmates to highlight the possible disorientation and self-estrangement that could be effects of stringently patrolled confinement in expectant time. In extreme conditions, those dwelling in expectant time lose the connection with temporalness altogether and with a purposive sense of past, present, and future. Confinement in the seemingly interminable present, the waiting for something to happen, the sense that others know your past and future while you remain in the dark— all of these characteristics of youths' times do not add up to the Holocaust. However, I draw on Koselleck's work to dramatize the sense of *confinement in temporality and its possible connections to disorientation and self-estrangement* that are possible in adolescence.

I am suggesting that we consider the powerful effects of teenagers being condemned to an "expectant time"—a moratorium of responsibility and of power. Expectant time is supported by theories that tell us that youth need dependency because they are confused about their identities. Solberg's (1990) work points out that twelve-year-olds can be big or little in relation to the facts of variable material practices. My interviews with Renee and Melanie suggest that in adolescence they felt both a youthful lack of power and strong pressures to "master their environments." Koselleck's analysis of Holocaust dreams suggests that within a confinement of total passivity, the suspension of temporal identity and ability to act and master one's environment can be "salvational." This means that youth's refusal to consider the consequences of their actions (a familiar refrain in secondary schools) could be considered as salvational rather than as evidence of immaturity. For me, these pieces suggest that youth's passive temporal position, always "becoming," waiting for the future to arrive may effect the identity crises that, in turn, prove adolescents' need to be kept with little power and few decisions. This section has examined the seemingly insurmountable "tasks" and the sometimes surreal experiences of "expectant time" in order to cast a different light upon commonsense meanings of "peer pressure," "conformity," and "rebellion." Extreme experiences of expectant time may produce a withdrawal from modern temporality, from a sense of past, present, and future; and teenagers may hang on to atemporality as a psychic salvational dream, while many of their teachers offer the timeless axiom that the high school years are the "best years" of their lives.

Chronotopes of Adolescence

This section offers a Bahktinian perspective on the construction of adolescence with and through time. Bahktin's ideas about distinctive chronotopes within novel genres may help distill some conclusions about time and the discourse of adolescence. He analyzed different novel genres on the basis of how they create identifiable relations between time and event. He follows Einstein in defining a chronotope as a particular relation between time and event. There is no such thing as time-in-itself. And Bakhtin believed that "time in real life is no less organized by convention that it is in a literary text" (Holquist, 1990, p. 115). The chronotope of adolescence suggested in this chapter has several characteristics. First, like many novels, adolescent discourse is set in abstract adventure time, that is, time appears to have a chronology, but the characters do not age and remain unaffected by time and events. Television series like *Dawson's Creek* and *My So-Called Life* occur in abstract adventure time, where changes do not register on the characters; for example, their minds do not develop. "It is as if the hands on the clock in Einstein's exemplary railroad station moved, but the trains all remained stationary on their tracks" (Holquist, 1990, p. 117). This abstract adventure time produces narratives that are ahistorical and decontextualized and makes it notoriously hard to paste on context.

Second, because of the panoptical gaze, the institutional frame around the discourse on adolescence, nothing much is supposed to happen. Avoiding precocity through slow development means that the present is emptied of meaningful events; the past may have significance but really only the future matters. Having been constructed from turn of the century millennial and evolutionary narratives with a focus on fulfillment, the end of the adolescence story remains primary. Adolescence is usually understood to end when a person finishes school, gets a full-time job, marries, and has children (Buchmann, 1989).

Third, since the end of the story matters, and adults know what the correct and happy ending is (increasing maturity and responsibility, school achievement, full-time employment, marriage and children, property ownership, in that order), only deviations or pitfalls along the prescribed plot merit attention. The panoptical gaze makes youth into cartoonlike, or clownish, figures. Although youth themselves are expected to take each moment seriously, we, the adult audience, know that these things are relatively trivial. Since we know the panoptical sequencing, we may watch and comment on adolescence with detachment and humor. Thus, the characters in the narrative of adolescence may easily loose their humanity and become stereotypes.

Finally, to put adolescence into this narrative framework is to consider the "readers" of the stories as well. We consumers of adolescent narratives are bound emotionally to the story. We are happy, satisfied, and comforted by narratives of fulfillment (conventional adolescent development); we are disturbed and alarmed by precocity and risk. We may blame families, bad schools, uncaring governments, lack of economic opportunities, and crazy kids, all of which may be, in part, accurate. But what is generally absent from view is the narrative structure and conventions of the discourse on adolescence, in which we are emotionally and professionally invested (in both the problems and the successes).

My analysis calls into question conventional findings from sociologists, psychologists, and educators that youth and the social niches they occupy are temporally out of sync, that is, there is a mismatch between developmental needs and youth circumstances. For example, Csikszentmihalyi & Schmidt (1998) utilize a sociobiological view to argue that the evolutionary traits of youth (e.g., to challenge boundaries) are mismatched to the school and social environment, which are either too constraining or too dangerous. Cote and Allahar (1996, p. 82) utilize an Eriksonian perspective to ask how youth can "formulate a viable and stable identity under uncertain and even hostile circumstances." With relatively few rights and economic resources, youth are denied possibilities to act, which means they cannot develop a "sense of temporal and spatial continuity" (Cote and Allahar, 1996, p. 82). Because they cannot take up meaningful roles that connect them to a future, argue Cote and Allahar, they suffer identity confusion which "incapacitate[s] them or lead[s] them to high levels of risk-taking and gratuitous violence" (p. 83). These scholars offer a critique of adolescence that utilizes a sense of temporality, but one that accepts the modern development-in-time episteme that I have questioned.

This familiar out-of-sync temporal analysis accepts the expectant temporal mode that is foundational to the modern, scientific discourse on adolescence. I agree that there is a tension between the private times of youth (as well as of adults and children) and public institutional standardized time; but

I have also argued that basic ideas of adolescence were formed within that "world standard time," not in conflict with it. What these critiques fail to acknowledge is how adolescence is profoundly a construction with time, not just empirical objects that can be placed in one temporal sequencing or another. I have suggested that this is a panoptical time and an expectant time, which require youth-as-subjects to actively use time, not just pass time.

In this chapter, I have explored three dimensions of the discourse on adolescence—the teenaged years as panoptical time, as expectant time, and as abstract adventure time. My aim has been to understand how adolescence remains so resistant to deconstruction and reconstruction. By foregrounding the modern development in time episteme and then examining the ways adolescence is made with and through time, I have pursued how adolescence is naturalized via objective, commodified knowledge-at-a-glance and subjective experiences of expectant time, with its constructed anomie and rebellion. Taking up both the objective and subjective pieces, the narrative chronotope of adolescence located in abstract adventure time, where events occur but nothing really changes, cobbles the pieces together. Adults patch together their subjective experiences through the panoptical concept of identity and the developing pubertal body; but the chronotope of adolescence works to trivialize the intensity of the expectant time, while simultaneously reinforcing it by endless retellings (in social science research, but also in popular culture, say in television, novels, and documentary films). With these various pushes and pulls, I think adolescence has become a comic figure, serious yet trivialized, institutionally ordained and reduced to stereotypes, commodified and malleable as a sign of futures, pasts, fears, and hopes. So viewed, the adolescent is endearing, frightening, unavoidable, and exploitable.

Other Times?

Might adolescence have a future that is different from the past that I have sketched above? In the larger work that this chapter is part of (Lesko, forthcoming), I argue that adolescent development was a shorthand way to worry about and strategize for a familiar, controlled order within remarkably unstable landscapes at home and abroad at the turn of the twentieth century. Thus, adolescent development (this includes theories, empirical studies, institutionalization, and therapeutic interventions) was, in part, an answer to certain problems presented by economic, international, and familial change. Specifically, adolescence helped identify and create a vision of the modern citizen, who would be equipped for the challenges of the new social, economic, and world arrangements (Popkewitz, 1998). This historically situated analysis suggests that we might anticipate new conceptions of adolescence along with the articulation and popularization of different problems.

Just as at the turn of the twentieth century, there are now challenges to modern economic, intellectual, global, and familial arrangements. Citizenship and nation-states are likewise under revision (Shafir, 1998). Adolescence and children are likely to be redefined in the process, as the global economy expands and discards unproductive processes and people (Stephens, 1995). I want to consider how global forces may intensify, modulate, adapt, and disrupt panoptical time, the development in time episteme, expectant time, and the chronotope of adolescence. What indications suggest a shift in modern temporal arrangements?

David Harvey describes an accelerating compression of time and space accompanying global capitalism. There is now a "schizophrenic rush of time" central to postmodern life and a fluidity across space that matches instantaneous global communications (1990, p. 309; see also Greider, 1997). Postman (1982) links technological growth with the speedup of time and a resulting disappearance of childhood. Since childhood was based upon sequential learning, which was slow and demanding, the revolutions in electronic literacies make that slowness intolerable and obsolete. Thus the slow development in time of the modern panoptical adolescence is under pressure exerted by global capitalism and technology.

Other scholars document different kinds of revisions to the development-in-time episteme. For example, Field portrays childhood in contemporary Japan as undermined by "a new continuity between childhood and adulthood through technocratically ordered labor" (1995, p. 51). Taking a life course perspective, Buchmann (1989) argues that differences between youth and adults are eroding because of the fluidity of life scripts, especially in western Europe and the United States. The formerly stable order of schooling, employment, marriage, and child rearing in many middle-class and working-class lives has been changed by economic downsizing, as well as by changing values around cohabitation and children. Although Harvey, Postman, Field, and Buchmann posit different scenarios, each presents evidence that the slow temporal pace of the developing child and the identity-seeking adolescent are changing. It is tempting to reduce complex changes in temporal ordering and pace to an inversion of generations, with youth leading adults into the brave new world of technology (e.g., Rushkoff, 1996), but I find the dynamics more complicated.

Certainly, time and history have begun to be theorized in nonlinear ways; for example, time is imaged as a sieve or as folds (Serres & Latour, 1995), and models of recursiveness in science and mathematics threaten the dominance of linear historical time (Stewart, 1998; Thompson, 1996). However, I think that such theorizings, apart from the widespread popularization of new social and economic problems, are unlikely to stir enough dissatisfaction with the development-in-time episteme for a major reconstruction of time and history.

I think the time and space compression that Harvey describes further erodes political support for meeting adolescents' (and children's) needs. The era of child saving in the United States ended with welfare reform in 1997. The resources once committed to education, health, and social welfare programs of panoptically viewed youth and children are now utilized to build prisons, install metal detectors in schools, and criminalize younger children as adults. As children below ten years of age have become erotic, spectacular, and marketable, the teenager's market share has sunk. Slow development in time may no longer be functional, and quick leaps from childhood to adulthood may be called for by virtual workplaces and education provided on-line. Such a view is in keeping with interpretations that emphasize greater flexibility—of organisms, welfare systems, and individual potential (Hultqvist, 1998). Flexibility may distinguish up-and-coming life course theories, as schooling becomes lifelong learning. The clear boundary between adolescence and adulthood is blurred, as everyone needs to keep becoming.

Even if adolescence becomes a recursive state, rather than a life stage left behind once and for all, the superiority of the here and now seems likely to remain privileged and dominant. Despite changes associated with virtual time, flexible bodies, and lifelong learning, the episteme of development-in-time appears likely to prevail. The heralding of the new millennium seems to provide further support for the dogma that the present always surpasses the past, the core idea of progress: "Through progress, we never cease to be at the summit, on the cutting edge, at the state-of-the-art development. It follows that we are always right, for the simple, banal, and naïve reason that we are living in the present moment" (Serres & Latour, 1995, p. 48–49). Nevertheless, an appreciation of this modern temporal reasoning may help us think and act in untimely ways, that is, "counter to our time and thereby on our time and . . . for the benefit of a time to come" (Nietzsche quoted in Rose, 1999, p. 13).

References

Alexander, R. M. (1995). *The "girl problem": Female sexual delinquency in New York, 1900–1930.* Ithaca, NY: Cornell University Press.

Anderson, J. D. (1988). *The education of blacks in the south, 1860–1935.* Chapel Hill: University of North Carolina Press.

Ashcroft, B., Griffiths, G., & Tiffin, H. (1995). Introduction. In B. Ashcroft, G. Griffiths, & H. Tiffin (Eds.), *The post-colonial studies reader* (pp. 1–20). London: Routledge.

Ayres, L. P. (1909). *Laggards in our schools: A study of retardation and elimination in city school systems.* New York: Charities Publication Committee.

Baker, B. (1998). "Childhood" in the emergence and spread of U.S. public schools. In T. S. Popkewitz & M. Brennan (Eds.), *Foucault's challenge: Discourse, knowledge, and power in education* (pp. 117–43). New York: Teachers College Press.

Bederman, G. (1995). *Manliness and civilization: A cultural history of gender and race in the United States, 1880–1917.* Chicago: University of Chicago Press.

Bender, J., & Wellbery, D. E. (1991). Introduction. In J. Bender & D. E. Wellbery (Eds.), *Chronotypes: The construction of time* (pp. 1–18). Stanford, CA: Stanford University Press.

Bhabha, H. (1994). *The location of culture.* New York: Routledge.

Buchmann, M. (1989). *The script of life in modern society.* Chicago: University of Chicago Press.

Callahan, R. E. (1962). *Education and the cult of efficiency.* Chicago: University of Chicago Press.

Cesaire, A. (1972). *Discourse on colonialism.* Trans. Joan Pinkham. New York: Monthly Review Press.

Chudacoff, H. P. (1989). *How old are you? Age consciousness in American culture.* Princeton, NJ: Princeton University Press.

Cote, J. E., & Allahar, A. L. (1996). *Generation on hold: Coming of age in the late twentieth century.* New York: New York University Press.

Csikszentmihalyi, M., & Schmidt, J. (1998). Stress and resilience in adolescence: An evolutionary perspective. In K. Borman & B. Schneider (Eds.), *The adolescent years: Social influences and educational challenges* (pp. 1–17). Ninety-seventh Yearbook of the National Society for the Study of Education. Chicago: University of Chicago Press.

Dawson, George E. (1896). A study in youthful degeneracy. *Pedagogical Seminary, 4* (2). 221–58.

Eckert, P. (1989). *Jocks and burnouts: Social categories and identity in high school.* New York: Teachers College Press.

Erikson, E. H. (1950/1985). *Childhood and society.* New York: W. W. Norton.

Erikson, E. H. (1968). *Identity: Youth and crisis.* New York: W. W. Norton.

Fabian, J. (1983). *Time and the other: How anthropology makes its object.* New York: Columbia University Press.

Fabian, J. (1991). Of dogs alive, birds dead, and time to tell a story. In J. Bender & D. E. Wellbery (Eds.), *Chronotypes: The construction of time* (pp. 185–204). Stanford, CA: Stanford University Press.

Fanon, F. (1952/1986). *Black skin, white masks.* Trans. Charles Lam Markmann. London: Pluto Press.

Fausto-Sterling, A. (1995). Gender, race, and nation: The comparative anatomy of "Hottentot" women in Europe, 1815–1817. In J. Urla & J. Terry (Eds.), *Deviant bodies: Critical perspectives on difference in science and popular culture* (pp. 19–48). Bloomington: Indiana University Press.

Feldman, S. S., & Elliott, G. R. (1990). *At the threshold: The developing adolescent.* Cambridge, MA: Harvard University Press.

Field, N. (1995). The child as laborer and consumer: The disappearance of childhood in contemporary Japan. In S. Stephens (Ed.), *Children and the politics of culture* (pp. 51–78). Princeton, NJ: Princeton University Press.

Foucault, M. (1973). *The order of things: An archaeology of the human sciences.* New York: Vintage Books.

Foucault, M. (1979). *Discipline and punish: The birth of the prison.* Trans. A. Sheridan. New York: Vintage Books.

Gilman, S. L. (1985). *Difference and pathology: Stereotypes of sexuality, race, and madness.* Ithaca, NY: Cornell University Press.

Gould, S. J. (1977). *Ontogeny and phylogeny.* Cambridge, MA: Belknap Press.

Greider, W. (1997). *One world, ready or not: The manic logic of global capitalism.* New York: Touchstone Books.

Hacking, I. (1991). How should we do the history of statistics? In G. Burchell, C. Gordon, & P. Miller (Eds.), *The Foucault effect: Studies in governmentality* (pp. 181–96). Chicago: University of Chicago Press.

Haraway, D. (1997). *Modest_witness @ second_millennium.* New York: Routledge.

Harvey, D. (1990). *The condition of postmodernity.* Cambridge, MA: Blackwell.

Holquist, M. (1990). *Dialogism: Bakhtin and his world.* London: Routledge.

Horn, D. G. (1995). This norm which is not one: Reading the female body in Lombroso's anthropology. In J. Terry & J. Urla (Eds.), *Deviant bodies: Critical perspectives on difference in science and popular culture* (pp. 109–28). Bloomington: Indiana University Press.

Hultqvist, K. (1998). A history of the present on children's welfare in Sweden: From Froebel to present-day decentralization projects. In T. Popkewitz & M. Brennan (Eds.), *Foucault's challenge: Discourse, knowledge, and power in education* (pp. 91–116). New York: Teachers College Press.

James, A., & Prout, A. (1990). Re-presenting childhood: Time and transition in the study of childhood. In A. James & A. Prout (Eds.), *Constructing and reconstructing childhood: Contemporary issues in the sociological study of childhood* (pp. 216–38). London: Falmer Press.

Kern, S. (1983). *The culture of time and space, 1880–1918.* Cambridge, MA: Harvard University Press.

Kett, J. F. (1974). History of age grouping in America. In J. S. Coleman (Ed.), *Youth: Transition to adulthood* (pp. 9–28). Chicago: University of Chicago Press.

Kett, J. F. (1977). *Rites of passage: Adolescence in America 1790 to the present.* New York: Basic Books.

Koselleck, R. (1985). *Futures past: On the semantics of historical time.* Trans. Keith Tribe. Cambridge, MA: MIT Press.

Landes, D. (1983). *Revolution in time: Clocks and the making of the modern world.* Cambridge, MA: Belknap Press.

Lesko, N. (1994). The social construction of "the problem of teenage pregnancy." In R. A. Martusewicz & W. M. Reynolds (Eds.), *Inside/out: Contemporary critical perspectives in education* (pp. 139–50). New York: St. Martin's Press.

Lesko, N. (1996). Past, present, and future conceptions of adolescents. *Educational Theory, 46* (4), 453–72.

Lesko, N. (1997). Before their time: Social age, reproductive rights, and school-aged mothers. In S. Books (Ed.), *Neither seen nor heard: Invisible children in the society and its schools* (pp. 101–31). Mahwah, NJ: Lawrence Erlbaum Publishers.

Lesko, N. (forthcoming). *Act your age! Generational politics in the discourse of adolescence.* New York: Routledge.

Lomawaima, K. T. (1995). Domesticity in federal Indian schools: The power of authority over mind and body. In J. Terry & J. Urla (Eds.), *Deviant bodies: Critical perspectives on difference in science and popular culture* (pp. 197–218). Bloomington: Indiana University Press.

Lowe, D. M. (1982). *History of bourgeois perception.* Chicago: University of Chicago Press.

McClintock, A. (1995). *Imperial leather: Race, gender and sexuality in the colonial contest.* New York: Routledge.

Memmi, A. (1965). *The colonizer and the colonized.* Trans. Howard Greenfield. New York: Beacon Press.

Morss, J. R. (1996). *Growing critical: Alternatives to developmental psychology.* London: Routledge.

Nye, R. A. (1985). Sociology and degeneration: The irony of progress. In J. E. Chamberlin & S. L. Gilman (Eds.), *Degeneration: The dark side of progress* (pp. 49–71). New York: Columbia University Press.

Passerini, L. (1997). Youth as a metaphor for social change: Fascist Italy and America in the 1950s. In G. Levi & J. Schmitt (Eds.), *A history of young people in the west.* Vol. 2 (pp. 281–342). Cambridge, MA: Belknap Press.

Popkewitz, T. S. (1998). Dewey, Vygotsky, and the social administration of the individual: Constructivist pedagogy as systems of ideas in historical spaces. *American Educational Research Journal, 35* (4), 535–70.

Popkewitz, T. S., & Pitman, A. (1986). The idea of progress and the legitimation of state agendas: American proposals for school reform. *Curriculum & Teaching, 1* (1–2), 11–24.

Postman, N. (1982). *The disappearance of childhood.* New York: Delacorte.

Prout, A., & James, A. (1990). A new paradigm for the sociology of childhood? In A. James & J. Prout (Eds.), *Constructing and reconstructing childhood: Contemporary issues in the sociological study of childhood* (pp. 7–34). London: Falmer Press.

Rose, N. (1999). *Powers of freedom: Reframing political thought.* Cambridge, UK: Cambridge University Press.

Rousmaniere, K. (1997). *City teachers: Teaching and school reform in historical perspective.* New York: Teachers College Press.

Rushkoff, D. (1996). *Playing the future: What we can learn from digital kids.* New York: Riverhead Books.

Schlossman, S. (1977). *Love and the American delinquent: The theory and practice of "progressive" juvenile justice, 1825–1920.* Chicago: University of Chicago Press.

Schlossman, S., & Wallach, S. (1978). The crime of precocious sexuality: Female juvenile delinquency in the Progressive Era. *Harvard Educational Review, 48* (1), 65–94.

Serres, M., & Latour, B. (1995). *Conversations on science, culture, and time.* Trans. Roxanne Lapidus. Ann Arbor: University of Michigan Press.

Shafir, G. (Ed.). (1998). *The citizenship debates.* Minneapolis: University of Minnesota Press.

Solberg, A. (1990). Negotiating childhood: Changing constructions of age for Norwegian children. In A. James & A. Prout (Eds.). *Constructing and reconstructing childhood: Contemporary issues in the sociological study of childhood* (pp. 118–37). London: Falmer Press.

Stephens, S. (Ed.). (1995). *Children and the politics of culture.* Princeton, NJ: Princeton University Press.

Stewart, I. (1998). *Life's other secret: The new mathematics of the living world.* New York: John Wiley & Sons.

Stoler, A. L. (1995). *Race and the education of desire: Foucault's "History of Sexuality" and the colonial order of things.* Durham, NC: Duke University Press.

Terry, J. (1995). Anxious slippages between "us" and "them": A brief history of the scientific search for homosexual bodies. In J. Terry & J. Urla (Eds.), *Deviant bodies: Critical perspectives on difference in science and popular culture* (pp. 129–69). Bloomington: Indiana University Press.

Thompson, E. P. (1993). *Customs in common.* New York: The New Press.

Thompson, W. I. (1996). *Coming into being: Artifacts and texts in the evolution of consciousness.* New York: St. Martin's Press.

Tolen, R. J. (1995). Colonizing and transforming the criminal tribesman: The Salvation Army in British India. In J. Terry & J. Urla (Eds.), *Deviant bodies: Critical perspectives on difference in science and popular culture* (pp. 78–108). Bloomington: Indiana University Press.

Toulmin, S., & Goodfield, J. (1965). *The discovery of time.* New York: Harper & Row.

Waksler, F. C. (1991). The hard times of childhood and children's strategies for dealing with them. In F. C. Waksler (Ed.), *Studying the social worlds of children: Sociological readings* (pp. 216–34). London: Falmer Press.

Walkerdine, V. (1984). Developmental psychology and the child-centred pedagogy: The insertion of Piaget into early education. In J. Henriques, W. Hollway, C. Urwin, C. Venn, & V. Walkerdine (Eds.), *Changing the subject: Psychology, social regulation, and subjectivity* (pp. 153–202). London: Methuen.

Walkerdine, V. (1990). *Schoolgirl fictions.* London: Verso.

4

The Pacing and Timing of Children's Bodies

Chris Jenks

Introduction

In December 1997 the pupils of Northwich School performed Charles Dickens's *A Christmas Carol* as a show for their parents, teachers, and school governors. This is not an uncommon choice of school play and, no doubt, pupils in many other schools in England were, at the same time, also acting out this classic tale. *A Christmas Carol* is, in essence, a moral tale about the importance of generosity for the maintenance of social relations—generosity of spirit, pleasure, compassion, and money—but it is through the metaphorical play around the themes of time itself that the transformation of miserly, vicious Scrooge is achieved. The end of the play sees Scrooge rescued from the compulsions of his character through the literal embodiment of time past, present, and future. Via frightening, bodily encounters with the different ghosts of Christmas, Scrooge begins to see the part the passing of time and past experiences have played in the shaping of his own biography and, finally, he is shown a vision of the future that, if he does not mend his ways, will prove tragic. In sum, therefore, the moral causality of *A Christmas Carol* lies in its espousal of the Protestant Ethic—that "time is money"—linked to the demands of the biological clock—that "time is short". Thus, the play acts as a reminder that social action is temporalized through its location in individual biographies and that, in this sense, its consequences reverberate across the life course through the lived, bodily experiences of individuals.

That children are so frequently involved in acting out such a temporal and moral tale at school is perhaps not surprising for, as this chapter will argue, in their everyday lives it is precisely this embodiment of time passing that children learn. They do so in two interlinked ways. First, children are, as we shall show, defined through their bodies, bodies that are seen to develop and mature in relation to externally derived conceptions of their social, intellectual, physical, and moral competencies. Second, through a temporal disciplining of the body in the everyday social practices of the classroom—a discipline wrought upon the body by the self or by others—time becomes understood by children as a commodity that is subject to an exchange relationship based on both discipline and/or liberation. Children are taught, and some of them more painfully learn, that present behavior shapes future outcomes and that pleasurable futures may be denied on account of present misdemeanors. Presented in this way it was made clear to each child actor in *A Christmas Carol*, for example, that if they did not concentrate on their school work, including behaving well in class (see later), they could envisage being forbidden to attend the very show that, for such a long time, they had invested so much of their time and efforts in.

But what is, perhaps, of more import is that such misbehaviors are themselves temporally circumscribed. As Corrigan (1979) has noted, classifications of bad behavior are, often and principally, the result of disputes between staff and pupils over time use. In this chapter we distinguish therefore between "curriculum time"—time that is controlled by teachers—and those times, such as playtime, that are seen by children as being under their control, showing how the paramouncy of curriculum time is achieved and sustained in the classroom through the controls and demands placed upon children's bodies by staff. However, as we also explore, through the adoption of particular bodily styles some children manage to extend their control over time at school and wrest free from the restrictive demands that curriculum time places upon their bodies and behaviors.

The Study

This chapter draws on data from an ongoing ethnographic study of children's understanding and use of time. The study focuses on ten- to twelve-year-olds and their experiences of the transition from primary school to secondary school. It is taking place in schools in an urban and a rural setting in the north of England. We worked in a small village primary school that has fifty-seven pupils, six of whom are in the present Year 6. The two other primary schools comprise one in the city center of a large town and another in a bigger village. These are comparable in size, with about 225 pupils, thirty-five of whom in each school are in Year 6. The study followed a self-selected group of these children into their secondary schools. It uses a wide range of methods to capture children's conceptions and practices of the time and temporality, exploring the following aspects of children's time: everyday time at home and at school, social relations and time, the transitional time at school, time values and social organization, and biographical time including issues of age and development. We use a variety of methods, such as individual and peer group interviews and participant observation at school, but have also developed some particular research tools. These are enabling us to explore some more specific aspects of time and temporality through allowing both us and the children to make the abstract notions of time concrete in our conversations.

Childhood, Bodies, and Time

Children's experience of time (as a social category) is mediated through a series of cultural narratives that are focused upon the self and body as appearance and behavioral practices. The narratives we focus on in this chapter are derived from the historical progress of modern cultures and in particular from both conceptualizations of time passing and understandings of the self as embodied and placeable. Time as understood in contemporary society is known through a mechanistic and quantitative model provided initially by Kant and his immanent categories of understanding. This philosophical perspective has become writ large within European and North American cultures through conspiring with scientific notions of linear causality, with moral imperatives of progress and improvement, and with elements of a pressing political economy. Through the capitalist requirement of costing all being and therefore all bodies, time itself was rendered a significant variable in the productive process and a cost in relation to space and labor. Bodies were thus rendered a mobile resource in the logistics of productivity. We propose in this chapter that, as children and in growing up, we gradually come to know that time is tangible and valuable and that our bodies owe an obedience to temporal constraint. Time is a scarce resource—it is not to be wasted and indeed should be invested, and thus, significantly, we come to understand that time lays out the ground rules for present and future behaviors. And in this childhood learning, as we set out later, the body plays a central part.

These understandings are further impressed onto our consciousness by another determining moral imperative of modernity, that of mortality (the very interface of time and embodiment). We cannot afford to compromise on life—indeed, it is in notions of time passing that we can measure and evaluate our time spent. However, it was not until Bergson in the nineteenth century that the topic was approached through the conception of time as *duree*. That is, time is to be seen as duration, a series of qualitative changes interweaving and permeating one another. *Duree* is the very essence of reality; it is a constant becoming, never a static achievement. Time seen merely in this latter form, Bergson believed, as something made in the mathematical Kantian way, is actually to conceive of another kind of space, not a passage of being. This shift has meant that the narrative experience of time for childhood, and indeed a major part of our child-rearing ideologies, has now become focused on the temporal texture and the quality of being and embodiment, rather than simply being understood as the quantity of time passing, which is registered and sequenced as the "aging" body. As we shall go on to show through a series of ethnographic examples, this perspective can be seen to predominate in children's everyday lives at school such that time and being provide a fixed and inflexible juxtaposition through which children come to grips with the sometimes painful experience (though increasingly less corporal) that bad deeds in the present may produce bad consequences in the future. More importantly, such a perspective represents cultural conceptions of "continuity" to children. This entails the understanding that mastery in "shaping one's own future" takes place through attending to past and present behavior. This process, in many senses, involves the successful development of an acceptable vocabulary of bodily placement, both as the locus of self but also as the normalizing symbol of incorporation, that is, of being "in one's place."

Within sociology, these spatiotemporal divisions are understood through two competitive traditions that here we term "liberating" and "controlling" in relation to the ways in which time is seen to act upon and empower or constrain the individual and the body. The former is located within the Durkheimian tradition and arises from Durkheim's concern to delineate the basic "categories of understanding," the ultimate principles that underlie all our knowledge and that give order and arrangement to our perceptions and sensations—including, for example, the concept of time. Reviewing the dominant epistemological explanations Durkheim dismisses the types of idealism that depict the ultimate reality behind the world as being spiritual, informed by an Absolute; or those that account for the categories as being inherent in the nature of human consciousness. Such an "a priorist" position, he says, is refuted by the incessant variability of the categories of human thought from society to society; and further it lacks experimental control, it is not empirically verifiable. In thus rejecting a Kantian position that demands that such categories exist somehow beyond the individual consciousness, as prior conditions of experience, Durkheim prefers to constitute time as a representation, rather than as something that is immutable and universal:

> Men frequently speak of space and time as if they were only concrete extent and duration, such as the individual consciousness can feel, but enfeebled by abstraction. In reality, they are representations of a wholly different sort, made out of other elements, according to a different plan, and with equally different ends in view. (Durkheim, 1915, p. 441)

Thus, although the categories of thought vary from society to society, within any one society, they are characterized by universality and necessity. In relation to concepts of time, therefore, he writes:

It is not my time that is thus arranged; it is time in general, such as it is objectively thought of by everybody in a single civilization. (Durkheim, 1915, p. 10)

For Durkheim, therefore, society is the fundamental and primary reality; without it there is no humankind—but this is a reciprocal dependency. Society can only become realized, can only become conscious of itself and thus make its influence felt through the collective behavior of its members—that is, through their capacity to communicate symbolically. Out of this concerted conduct springs the collective representations and sentiments of society and further, the fundamental categories of thought—including, of course, that of time. So for Durkheim the classifications of time are social in origin. They arise from and reflect the patterns and rhythms of social life. Such a soft determinism, or what has been called a social Kantianism, implies that sociality itself proceeds both mind and matter and the latter two realms are shaped according to the ways of the social. Seasons reflect sociotemporal dispositions; calendars are manifestations of symbolic and ritualistic patterns; all appearance of fixity and naturalness is derived, historical, and ultimately conventional.

The divisions into days, weeks, months, years etc., correspond to the periodical recurrence of rites, feasts, and public ceremonies. A calendar expresses the rhythm of the collective activities, while at the same time its function is to assure their regularity. (Durkheim, 1915, pp. 10–11)

Such a view of time implies, therefore, an almost symbiotic, if not sympathetic, relationship between the individual and time and certainty. In relation to the child, such a view implies a temporal context that is liberal if not liberating in as much as it enables the child to become at one with the meter of the historical process. The child's body, and indeed the child's identity, become microcosmically analogous to the total body of the social (an idea later taken to cybernetic hyperbole by Talcott Parsons through the "stable unitary isomorphism" of his social system). In the following sections we show how such a "liberating" temporal narrative is inscribed upon children's bodies during their experience of schooling.

Our second perspective is somewhat different in the gloss it places on children's embodiment of time, and we have termed this as "controlling"; time is seen and experienced as a disciplining constraint. And here the work of Foucault stands out as emblematic. For Foucault, just as he regards knowledge as power, so too he understands time as a primary device and strategy in the exercise of modernity's power. Foucault inevitably fits temporality into his thesis on disciplinary regimes and the constraint of the free will with the most singular time-power device of modernity being the timetable—its object being the body. Indeed, the timetable can be regarded as a metaphor for modernity itself. Rather than an instance of social rhythms expressing themselves in regularized patterns à la Durkheim, timetables are, for Foucault, combinations of moves within the politics of experience. Specifically, Foucault speaks of the history of the timetable as follows:

> The time-table is an old inheritance. The strict model was no doubt suggested by the monastic communities. It soon spread. Its three great methods—establish rhythms, impose particular occupations, regulate the cycles of repetition—were soon to be found in schools, workshops and hospitals. The new disciplines had no difficulty in taking up their place in the old forms; the schools and poorhouses extended the life and the regularity of the monastic communities to which they were often attached. The rigors of the industrial period long retained a religious air; in the seventeenth century, the regulations of the great manufactories laid down the exercises that would divide up the working day . . . but even in the nineteenth century, when the rural populations were needed in industry, they were sometimes formed into "congregations," in an attempt to inure them to work in the workshops; the framework of the "factory-monastery" was imposed upon the workers. (Foucault, 1977, pp.149–50)

Discipline, it would seem, involves the control of a body, or more specifically an activity, and does so, most effectively, through a timetable. This device, for Foucault, is of monastic origin and relates to the regular divisions in the monk's day, which was organized around the seven canonical hours. Through the systematic extension of this fundamental device—the timetable—a regularity and a rhythm became instilled in all activities and tasks; productivity and predictability were assured. Such rhythms became applied to the individual and individual's body, and were thus eventually integral to the individual's performance of duty and style of life. So, for example, soldiers are drilled persistently even beyond basic training, and children are required to eat, sleep, wash, and excrete, mostly at specific and regular times. For the child then even the most elementary bodily functions are scheduled and play, which we superficially regard as free and perhaps creative, occurs in designated spaces within the curriculum.

Within the modern conditions for discipline there is a further internal temporal segmentation for each activity. That is to say, each activity is periodized and subdivided into steps or stages and, for the individual, the learning of tasks is similarly subject to a spatial and temporal division of labor. Just as an appropriate combination of exercises makes for the fit and healthy body, so also a series of component activities contributes to a more specialized and efficient function in relation to task, a fact well known to Adam Smith in his theory of the division of labor. Foucault uses the example of children and their mastery of handwriting, and here some of us (those old enough) might recall the achievement of a "perfect page" of handwriting, the laborious process of breaking each letter of the alphabet down into a series of technical strokes with the hand/pen. The symbolic reward for such technical perfection would be the issue of personal exercise books; thus inability to disport such books would signify a predisciplined body. What such bodily conditioning instills at a different level are life-governing imperatives such as "being on time" or "always being in the right place at the right time"!

What Foucault's discussion of the conditions of discipline brings us to, therefore, is a realization that such control functions through a combination of devices; what he refers to as "tactics." The whole premise of adult inter-action with the child, even often in pleasure, is control and instruction. All conditions combine and conspire to that end. The individual, it appears, emerges therefore through the modern form of control, exercised through regimes of discipline as Sheridan describes:

> This power is not triumphant, excessive, omnipotent, but modest, sus-picious, calculating. It operates through hierarchical observation, nor-malizing judgment, and their combination in the examination. (Sheri-dan, 1980, p. 152)

Foucault's time is thus no benign medium in which to be and grow. This "time" is always intended and planned, it governs and it manages, and, most serious of all, it is internalized to become the regulator and arbiter of all experience (all the time we think that we are exercising free will). Foucault's child is therefore captured through time and captured by it and, in a radical interpretation, the body becomes the very instrument of time. Later in this chapter we detail such temporal body management through empirical ac-counts of children's everyday experiences in the classroom.

The two perspectives we elect here are set within the tradition, but they must not be read as being all that is the case; otherwise we will be in danger of constituting the classroom as an austere political arena. The dichotomy between freedom and constraint is informative but not exhaustive of our need to understand (Jenks, 1998).

Developmental Time

These liberating and controlling perspectives on time use represent, therefore, two points of departure for us in exploring children's embodiment of time. However, these perspectives are themselves subject to and have to engage with a more dominant perspective on childhood that derives from the very temporality of children's bodies. Both everyday and, to a large extent, professional conceptions of the child are dominated by an almost hegemonic grasp of the child's aged body in relation to developmental theories. Most seriously crystallized in the work of Piaget, but others also, the child has come to be understood as an unfolding project, a natural trajectory, a staged becoming, and an inevitably incremental progress into adulthood. Such understandings have received more recent challenge (Burman, 1994; Jenks, 1982; Morss, 1990) and deconstruction but the roots of such a belief run deep and integrate seamlessly with the physiological demands of medicine and the logistical demands of a society based on hierarchical stratification and hierarchical distribution of provision. This is a powerful discourse that routinely structures children's experience, their time, and how their bodies are read and managed. Children are, indeed, read as if they were pausing on the path to reason, but their pauses are both determined and determining. And these pauses, suspensions, or interruptions in the developmental journey are marked out for children in terms of the achievement of competence, full adult competence being journey's end—the modernist project writ small! This journey that, in part, we detail later may be experienced by children as alternately liberating and disciplining.

The entrenched status of such developmental models is nowhere better witnessed than in the everyday interactions of the school classroom. Here a stratification and disciplining of the child population is achieved through the marking out of levels and stages of competence and achievements, essentially measured in relation to the steady progress of chronological age and achievement of developmental tasks. In their everyday life at school children are suspended in social groups constituted through an almost taken-for-granted theory about a "natural" concordance between age and maturation. Children's peers, friends, associates, competitors, and playmates are therefore to a large extent determined and assembled according to age cohorts that are meant to equate pragmatically with their interests, achievements, and abilities. Furthermore, even though modern schooling seems to provide some flexibility within this model through horizontal streaming—that is, that children within a single year group work on different levels toward different key stages—this may inadvertently place upon children a greater burden in relation to demonstrating achievements of competence and maturity. The potential liberation that such "levels" and "stages" may bring through its disassociation from the development demands of the aged body may be replaced, instead, by an overemphasis and increasing specificity about the achievement of competencies through a disciplined body. It is difficult enough to achieve normatively, and compete, within an age cohort, for a member of a specialist set assembled because of particular common excellences or techniques of the body there is nowhere to hide.

Significantly, for example, one of the ways in which children's social competence and intellectual "maturity," as opposed to the age of the physical body, is judged by teachers is in relation to children's abilities to manage their time effectively (and that is, we will emphasize, effectively from an adult point of view). And in the everyday social practices of the classroom, these ideas about the use and social organization of time become narrated through and inscribed upon children's bodies. In this sense, we uncover here what Bourdieu (1977, p. 94) has called an embodied memory that is entrusted with "an abbreviated and practical i.e. mnemonic form, the fundamental principles of the arbitrary content of the culture."

Curriculum Time

The insistent demands wrought by the embeddedness of developmental models of childhood have, until recently, meant that children's bodies—seen as aged bodies in terms of years lived through—have been used as the primary ordering principle through which the social organization of the school is achieved. Children enter primary school aged five and leave for secondary school aged eleven, irrespective of the social and educational competencies they may, or may not, have acquired en route. However, while these entries and exits remain for the three primary schools participating in the study, and the children are divided into year groups or age classes, in the daily organization of lessons they may be reorganized and reordered. Instead of using the body's age as a classifier, its competencies and skills are used to cluster children in relation to levels of achievement. Thus children identify themselves not only as being ten or eleven years old but they also use the terminology of "level" and "stage." These levels are defined in relation to the demands of the National Curriculum or, for example, the key stages of a reading scheme. It should be noted that children themselves are highly skilled in using this categorical system to position themselves relative to one another. For most children in the village school their prospective move to secondary school has highlighted, for them, the importance of this system—the children understand that the level they achieve at their final tests at primary school will determine the group they will be placed in at secondary school. These points were illustrated in a conversation with Hannah and Julie, two ten-year-old girls from the village school, Wellthorpe, as they discussed the practices for the SATS tests in May and what it means for them:

HANNAH: When you go to Molton school, I think it tells you what class you have to be in. Like if you are really, really brainy or if you're not that good.

JULIE: In my practices I have got three levels four, one level five, and a level six.

HANNAH: I have got one five and all the rest are fours.

PIA: Why is it important for you, the tests?

HANNAH: I think it's quite good. Because it tells you what class you'll be in and everything like that and the levels tells you what position you are in. Like if you get a five you are in a good level aren't you—and if you get a four—you're alright. The ones that are a bit dumb in our class get like three's and stuff, like Tom, Peter and Lilly.

PIA: But, why is it important to you whether you get a level three or not?

JULIE: Well, my mum would be quite disappointed, because I am quite brainy, aren't I—and if I get a six which is the highest I think, I'll be top class at Molton wouldn't I.

In this manner the children make sense, therefore, of the way the teacher requires them to sit in class during the school year, that is with which group and at which table and, in particular lessons, which color of the books they are working with. Through these clues they are able not only to orient themselves in the present time and space but also to become aware that these tests form an important marker and punctuation of how present behavior and performance can work to shape, and to effect, an ordered disciplining of their prospective futures. In a complex way the tests become understood as embodied practices, not abstract and external exercises. The test, as performance, and the outcome of the test, as competence, both legitimize and justify the placing of bodies and this becomes realized in thought. "Because it tells you what class you'll be in and everything like that," as Hannah said.

In Northwich School, which is a large inner-city school, pupils' ability is in the same vein, seen as highly differentiated (that is, understood as "mixed") in relation to the aged body. At each change of lesson in the mornings the children routinely regroup themselves, moving from classroom to classroom or sitting at different desks in their "form" room, in accordance with their level of attainment in maths or English. It constitutes a well-rehearsed orchestration of "ability," visibly demonstrated by the movement of the bodies. Thus in any teaching group, at any particular point in the day, in the city school children aged nine, ten, and eleven may be receiving tuition alongside one another, a situation magnified in the smallest of the village schools where children aged seven to eleven years old routinely occupy the same classroom for all their lessons. Although their classroom maintains an invisible spatial division of the room into three age groups, curriculum time operates here also in such a way that children throughout the school day are engaged in grouping and regrouping. Thus it would appear that, despite the apparent hegemony of bodily based developmental models of childhood, the age of the body is made a deliberately fragile indicator of children's identities at particular points during the school day. Within the national structuring of educational provision, levels of achievement take precedence over age specifically in relation to the core curriculum subjects of maths and English, which are viewed as fundamental to all other learning. By contrast, in those other subjects that more apparently focus on the techniques and abilities of the body (skills such as manual dexterity, artistic ability, physical agility, even musicality) children find themselves, once more, regrouped according to the chronological age of their bodies. Such a distinction and fluctuation in the use of the aged body as an identifier underlines, we suggest, children's gradual embodiment of the temporal narrative of "time as investment" during their growing up at school. As one child in the city school noted, it is "Maths and English that you will need all your life," rather than subjects like science or art.

But it was not just in relation to the organization of formal teaching that conceptions of the age, maturity, and competence of the body were variously and variably employed to regulate and quite literally time-table children's lives at school. The more casual judgments made by teachers to assess, monitor, and control the behavior of children routinely drew upon these different, external, and temporal ranking systems to assess children's behavior during curriculum time. Thus, as one teacher remarked, observing what she regarded as the "silly" behavior of two girls, that "Year 6 girls should know better"— they should be "sensible," that is, literally use their senses so as to better regulate or discipline the bodies in accordance with some externally set propriety denoted by developmental age. On another occasion a ten-year-old boy was made to attend Key Stage 1 singing lessons—those performed by younger children—as a form of ritualized degradation, the penalty for his age-inappropriate conduct in class on the previous day.

And indeed whole groups of children could also be identified in this manner. One teacher in the city school offered the opinion that her current Year 6 was immature. A long-serving and experienced teacher, she felt this particular class to fall below an implicit behavioral expectation for eleven-year-olds and, by way of explanation, pointed out that a key indicator of this immaturity was the children's failure to use their time properly. They lacked self-discipline over time use and organization. At the start of each school day the attendance and dinner registers were taken, during which time the children were supposed to sit and read. That this group of children needed reminding and reprimanding each day was seen by the teacher as a sure sign of their immaturity. In previous years children of this age would not have needed such close monitoring of their behavior.

That the children themselves may, however, simply be choosing not to comply with this rule was an explanation offered by the teacher for their failure to conform. However, had it been, this would simply have served, in her eyes, to underline their immaturity; noncompliance about time use would inevitably invoke retribution in terms of further constraints being placed on the children's own use of time. And yet close observation of this period of relatively free time in the school day revealed that many children were in fact making an active choice about how to spend their time. They were managing it on their own rather than the teacher's terms and thereby liberating themselves from its discipline. In a day that is heavily structured for children in terms of how their time is spent—indeed finding time to do the research has proved difficult— this thirty-minute period is a valuable breathing space, relatively unstructured and unsupervised, not quite a lesson and yet not playtime. What this time could actually be spent doing was open to multiple interpretations by the children: some children did read; others, however, got out their reading books, opened them, and then sat lost in thought or whispered to their friends; others gathered around the bookshelves in a huddle with their pals, ostensibly to choose a new book but never taking one down from the shelf; others sat and fiddled with their pencil cases or with their hair, their books open in front of them, but never turned a page; still others wandered around the room, looking busy, as they ferreted in their trays or searched the resources table. A small number of children sat at their tables with no books visible or talked openly with their friends. Thus, out of a class of thirty-five maybe only ten children were "sitting and reading" for the whole period of time. But it was only those children who failed to adopt the body posture and style of "sitting and read- ing" who would be daily judged by the teacher to be behaving in an "im- mature" manner. Although the majority were not actually sitting and reading they passed the time as if they were, adopting behaviors that conformed with those associated with the act of reading.

The bodily constraints that curriculum time places on children can also permit them some liberation. Field notes record ten-year-old Gemma, who sat quietly for an hour in a practice test for the SATS. She kept her head down, neither speaking to her classmates nor putting pen to paper. Through such bodily deportment she gained time for herself. Her bodily posture, a body bent over the table with sheets of paper in front of her, reflected a body at work at school—studying—and did not therefore attract the attention of the teacher who oversaw the children's performance. Now, if we address this realm of phenomena too strictly within our models of time passing then we can begin to generate accounts of children's "resistance" through ritual as if they conspired in a subversive political insurgence, albeit through passivity or dumb insolence. But this would be to exaggerate and consciously politicize a situation that although regulatory and constraining is also, at another level, pastoral and benign. That children are controlled is an instance of power and hierarchy, but to stop them running or rocking on their chairs may also be a way of ensuring their safety and exercising a duty of care. That children engage in the form of "passing" displayed by Gemma is a way of gaining control, but also of "getting by" or what de Certeau refers to as "making do." He argues that

> The operational modes of popular culture . . . exist in the heart of the strongholds of the contemporary economy (see here the school). Take, for example, what in France is called la perruque, "the wig." La perruque is the worker's own work designed as work for his employer. It differs from pilfering in that nothing of material value is stolen. It differs from absenteeism in that the worker is officially on the job. La perruque may be as simple as a secretary's writing a love letter on "company time" or as complex as a cabinetmaker's "borrowing" a lathe to make a piece of furniture for his living room . . . this phenomenon is becoming more and more general, even if managers penalize it or "turn a blind eye" on it in order not to know about it. (de Certeau, 1984. p. 25)

Gemma's device is a control mechanism and an "artistic trick" through which she conspires and manages with and in the situation and that, according to de Certeau, helps to:

> . . . traverse the frontiers dividing time, place and types of action . . . these transverse tactics do not obey the law of the place, for they are not defined or identified by it. In this respect, they are not any more local-izable than the technocratic (and scriptural) strategies that seek to create places in conformity with abstract models. (1984, p. 29)

It is therefore children's knowing attention to bodily posture and appearance that may enable them to strategically take control over their own time at school, as they pass leisure as work.

A common practice among the teachers at all the schools is to let those children leave the classroom first who present an organized and tidy exterior appearance. Therefore those children who wish to be first to go out to play or to leave school in the afternoon learn quickly to sit up straight, silently, with their arms folded on the clear desk space so that their group might be picked as the first to escape from the classroom. The importance of such body style in relation to children's learning has been noted by Bourdieu in his account of the workings of the "habitus":

> The principles [of culture] em-bodied in this way are placed beyond the grasp of consciousness, and hence cannot be touched by voluntary, de-liberate transformation, cannot even be made explicit; nothing seems more ineffable, more incommunicable, more inimitable, and therefore more precious than the values given body, made body by the tran-substantiation achieved by a hidden persuasion of an implicit pedagogy,

capable of instilling a whole cosmology, an ethic, a metaphysic, a political philosophy, through injunctions as insignificant as "stand up straight" or "don't hold your knife in your left hand" . . . The whole trick of pedagogic reason lies precisely in the way it extorts the essential while seeming to demand the insignificant. (Bourdieu, 1977, pp. 94–95)

In the day-to-day encounters that children have in school with pedagogical practices it is clear that it is the body that is the primary medium through which cultural essentials such as effective time use—"time is money," "time is short" and must not therefore be wasted—are experienced. Teachers both discipline and empower or, as it were, liberate, children through temporal narratives focused on the minutiae of the body's behavior and, as noted in the following examples, it is often disputes about effective or correct time use that provoke such temporal lessons.

At two of the schools in particular, the children are required to keep relatively quiet and to work consistently throughout the lessons. However, if the level of noise and talk among the children rises or if the teacher wants the children to attend better to their work the children are temporarily halted in their progress with the demand: "Hands on your heads." Up go thirty-five pair of hands to land on the head. Or the children may hear the order: "Sit up straight, fold your arms on the table." In this way, although children's activities are momentarily punctuated in time—they are made to stop work and sit still—the intention of such commands is to instruct them about the way to proceed more effectively and to make more efficient use of their time through adopting more disciplined behaviors. It is thus, through punctualizing children's time by imposing a particular bodily order, that the connections and continuity of curriculum time are restored and enabled.

Time-Shifting and Body Discipline

A further embodied temporal practice to which children become subject is that which teaches children that time is a commodity. Through systems of both reward and punishment, children learn that present behavior has consequences for the future and in teaching children such lessons the daily school assembly is an eloquent vehicle.

Thus, for example, in Northwich School a pupil's past academic achievement is publicly acknowledged in the weekly "Curly Wurly assembly." Each pupil has a record-of-achievement card and, throughout the weeks at school, may collect a star for good work. These stars are recorded on the card and once a child has amassed fifteen stars this achievement is made public in the Curly Wurly assembly. The whole school is gathered together for this event and the children in each year group are asked, in turn, who has achieved fifteen merits. Children with fifteen stamps on their cards must then go to the front of the hall and stand before their peers. They are then given a Curly Wurly (a chocolate candy bar) and a sticker to wear upon their bodies, and they shake hands with the deputy head of school—a ritual focused on the individual body of the child. Rarely, a child might manage thirty stars. In this case the child will receive two chocolate bars. This whole ritual is very corporeal; the body is paraded, decorated, and awarded with titillating food. Through a very public exposure of the body, therefore, past behavior is visibly rewarded in the present.

Bad behavior is also exposed and made visible. If children fidget, talk, or fail to pay attention in assembly they too will be removed from the collective body of children and are made to sit alone, at the front, where the age hierarchy of the school may be most keenly felt. The youngest children always sit at the front, with the eldest lining the back walls of the assembly hall. This means therefore that frequently a ten- or eleven-year-old child will be forced to spend the assembly time sitting isolated in front of a line of four- and five-year-olds, the child's large size contrasting with the smaller bodies of the younger children and thus providing a further visible reminder of the offense. A teacher at one of the village schools uses the same system to temper troublesome pupils during assembly and on one occasion she had moved Martin, one of the boys from Year 5, to sit in the front row as he had been bothering the boys next to him. She accounted for her action as follows: "It means I can keep an eye on him." But the comments from his agemates and those older and slightly younger than himself demonstrate the less explicit consequences of this movement. Eight-year-old Tim said: "Yes, that's good!—let him sit with the babies." Thus time-shifting occurs in two ways: through the temporary reassignment of age achieved via the physical movement of bodies, and through an unwanted public exposure for a moment in time as the penalty for the incorrect use of curriculum time.

Should such public exposure, however, prove insufficient to instill in children the local sense of temporal order that constitutes curriculum time, then further temporal and spatial restrictions may be placed on them. Not infrequently this entails additional demands being made on children's own time at school such that the privilege of playtime (that part of the school day that is relatively free of external constraints) may be withdrawn. In the city school, children who have behaved badly in assembly or in class are told that the next playtime, or the next few playtimes, will have to be spent standing outside the staff room for the duration. The symbolism of this is stark. Bodies that normally at this time of day are running around the playground for pleasure and engaged in activities of their own choice are rendered immobile. Faces are turned to the wall so that they cannot see their friends or participate in games at a distance. All they can hear is the noise of other children running free. Thus their identities are hidden from view except to the teachers who come and go from the staff room; that this disciplining of the body takes place outside the staff room simply serves, for the miscreant, to underscore the gravity of the offense. Time is made literally to stand still for the child—the welcome punctualization of curriculum time that playtime brings is forgone and the child's control of time at school becomes elided, an experience and a lesson narrated through the immobility of the body.

In these ways time-shifting is used by teachers to sanction and control children's behavior through the systematic use of temporal rewards and withdrawals. These are often focused on restrictions to be placed upon the child's body; not in terms of the minutiae of the positioning of hands or folding of legs described in our account of curriculum time but rather in relation to the usage of pleasurable time in the future. Thus it is children's future pleasure that is exchanged for present antisocial behavior: through bodily discipline, then, children learn that time is a valuable commodity.

Conclusion

This chapter has explored the different ways in which children come to understand the qualitative passage of time both in relation to their everyday lives at school and in relation to their growing into adulthood. The central feature of our argument is that in this process of learning the body plays a critical and orienting role. The body does not simply define or locate the child at a particular point in the life course, but through its physical representation of that development stage, it permits the overlay of concepts of social competence and maturity. The competencies and capacities of the body are themselves, in turn, made the focus of the particular temporal regimes associated with the punctuations of curriculum time at school, and thus time comes to be literally embodied by children through the twin processes of discipline and empowerment that shape their everyday relations at school.

This chapter derives from research conducted within the project "Changing Times" as part of the Economic and Social Research Council (ESRC) program "Children 5–16." All three authors have equivalent status in the preparation of work for publication; they are Pia Christensen and Allison James from the Department of Anthropology and Sociology at the University of Hull and Chris Jenks, who presented an earlier version of the work at the Copenhagen symposium.

References

Bourdieu, P. (1977). *Outline of a theory of practice.* Cambridge, UK: Cambridge University Press.

Burman, E. (1994). *Deconstructing developmental psychology.* London: Routledge.

Corrigan, P. (1979). *Schooling the smash street kids.* London: Macmillan.

de Certeau, M. (1984). *The practice of everyday life.* Berkeley: University of California Press.

Durkheim, E. (1915). *Elementary forms of religious life.* London: George Allen & Unwin.

Foucault, M. (1977). *Discipline and punish.* London: Penguin.

Jenks, C. (1982). *The sociology of childhood: Essential readings.* London: Batsford.

Jenks, C. (Ed.) (1998). *Core sociological dichotomies.* London: Sage.

Morss, J. (1990). *The biologising of childhood: Developmental psychology and the Darwinian myth.* London: Lawrence Erlbaum.

Sheridan, A. (1980). *Foucault: The will to truth.* London: Tavistock.

5

Administering Freedom:
A History of the Present

Rescuing the Parent to Rescue the Child for Society

Thomas S. Popkewitz and Marianne N. Bloch

Introduction

When one looks at current U.S. policy and academic discourses about social change and a responsive welfare system, a certain presentism appears. It heralds the bringing of the parent and community into contact with welfare agencies of the child as a new, progressive reform that will bring about a prosperous country and a realization of its commitments to equity and justice. But such rhetorical claims of a progressive evolution toward a utopian vision ignore the historically bounded reason through which action and participation are constructed. Such reveling of the present ignores the ways in which the family, the child, and the community have been objects of concern that circulated in state, public health, moralists', and educators' discourses since at least the nineteenth century.[1]

We will call this concern a register of social administration that connects the child, family, and community. We use the notion of register to consider how different discourses, institutions, and technologies overlap to form a common sense or reason through which action is generated. In the first half of the chapter, we look at the late nineteenth century and early twentieth century to understand the narratives and images that connected the family, child, and community as a register of social administration (Rose, 1999; Wagner, 1994).[2] That administration was related to freedom, new systems of reason to inscribe calculated systems of self-inspection and self-consciousness as the knowledge of the child, parent, and community. The register of social administration embodied an amalgamation of discourses that circulated through different institutions and social agencies—the state, social science, medical clinics, mass media, philanthropy, and welfare institutions.

In the second half of the chapter, we move to present reforms. Here again we suggest that the register of social administration continues to have a focus on connecting the scope and aspirations of public powers with the personal and subjective capabilities of individuals. But the identities fabricated, in the double sense of fictions and "making," to connect the family, childhood, and community are located in a different amalgamation of discourses and social arrangements. Where the reason of the turn of the twentieth century built a universalized citizen whose individuality embodied national salvation narratives and social, collective practices, the present is a self-managed and active individual whose operative networks and interpretive schemes are expressed in metaphors of community as well as a constructivist, entrepreneurial self. In both sections of the chapter, we suggest that these differences in social administration of the past and the present exist within unequal playing fields that have continued to embody changing rules and distinctions that have qualified and disqualified individuals for action and participation.[3]

Our working in a history of the present is a critical engagement of the present by making its production of collective memories open for scrutiny and the possibility of revision (Dean, 1994; also see Popkewitz, Franklin, & Pereyra, 2000).[4] Our strategy is to historicize the present and to disturb "that which forms that groundwork of the present, to make once more strange and to cause us to wonder how it came to appear so natural" (Rose, 1999, p. 58). Our method is to read through multiple social and intellectual histories as well as primary documents. But our purpose is often different from the social and intellectual history that we read, reinterpreting the systems of reason that ordered the objects of scrutiny and reflection. But as we tell this story of reason, we also find that it requires different emphases and ways of privileging concepts at different historical points.

Constructing the Child and Family: Registers of Social Administration and Freedom at the Turn of the Twentieth Century

Writing from this side of the Atlantic, most Europeans would find it difficult to think of the United States as a welfare state engaged in programs of social administration in care of the child and family since the nineteenth century. Individualism, a decentralized political (and educational) system, and the lack of a family policy embody the common mythology about what some commentators call a "nonstate" state. But at a different level, social and political discourses coincide to make caring for citizenry as well as its territory (de Swann, 1988). The conduct by which children, family, and community should be cared for connects the welfare of individuals with the scope and aspiration of public power, although not as a homogeneous discourse to administer the caring. We raise this point to consider the United States as a modern welfare state governing in care of the self.[5]

Provisions of Participation: Displacing and Revisioning Salvation Themes

The governing of the welfare state embodied a disposition that change could be harnessed and progress produced through a reflexivity that made the person as an object of scrutiny and the subject of self-scrutiny (Rose, 1989, 1999). The citizen, the family, and the worker were to be shaped and fashioned around the rationality of freedom in liberalism. The conduct of individuals was to be organized through self-motivation and a sense of individual responsibility and obligation (Hunter, 1994). The joining of the registers of social administration with those of freedom, as Wagner (1994) argues, is one of the hallmarks of modernity.[6] Freedom was an artifact of governing and a politics of life that operated through practices that one brings to bear to act on oneself and others rather than only through a calculus of domination and liberation (Rose, 1999).

Registers of Social Administration and National Imaginaries The projects of social administration were to reconstitute identities. The ideas of a calculated progress shaped the character of the child and the family. New regimes of the body (scientific hygiene), of the intellect (literacy, mathematics), and the inculcation of virtuous habits of childhood were available to manage and discipline and to articulate the character of the child and the family. But the administration of the self was also to reconstitute the poor and immigrants through restoring the child and family. The urban was memorialized as the new cradle of civilization as well as the producer of sin.

Increasingly, the connections between the family and the child became a site of scientific invention (Bloch, 1987; Bloch & Popkewitz, 2000; Silverberg, 1998).[7] From countries as diverse as Finland, Portugal, and the United States, it was believed that science would produce progress through systematic public provision, coherent public policy, and rational government intervention (Haskell, 1977; Rueschemeyer & Skocpol, 1996; Silva & Slaughter, 1984; Wagner, 1994; Wittrock, Wagner, & Wollmann, 1991; also see, e.g., Popkewitz, 1992, 1993; Simola & Popkewitz, 1996).

The patterns of governing traversed what was conceptually made distinct, such as the public and private and that which has been called the social and the cultural. Lasch argues that as rule of force gave way to rule of law, social relations took on increasing importance, and, in the United States, were tied with the notion of civil society as something distinct from the state. But the rise of a concept of civil society mediated a pattern of governing as agencies outside of the family expropriated and reformulated parental functions through an abstract, impersonal, evolutionary process known as the "transfer of functions" (Lasch, 1977, p.25). The legal doctrine of *parens patriae* made the state serve as a surrogate parent in juvenile courts and compulsory schooling (see Grubb & Lazerson, 1982; Richardson, 1989, pp. 77–78).[8] *Parens patriae* overlapped and sanctioned other discursive practices to constitute intervention practices in the family as a sphere of state governing.[9]

The joining of the family and the child were central in reconstituting a national narrative and a concept of the home that could accommodate both changing and contested frontiers and abilities. The image of the Republic's American identity was being threatened through immigration from southern and eastern Europe and migrations of African-Americans from the south after the American Civil War that were coupled with the growth of cities and an unbridled capitalism. The family became the earliest and most immediate place for socialization and the paradigm of the self-abridgment of culture and thus a way of expressing fears and anxiety of the threat to a national identity. The connections between child, family, and community in social policy, health, social science, and schooling joined the metaphorical "American family" of the nation with the family and the child in the construction of identity (Wald, 1995).

For some of the founders of American social science, the school was the central site in which to fabricate the child and the family. Edward Ross, one of the early sociologists, argued in the 1920 book *The Principles of Sociology* that no institution was as important as the school in the taking of diverse populations and making them into one social entity:

> Thoroughly to nationalize a multitudinous people calls for institutions to disseminate certain ideas and ideals. The Tsars relied on the blue-domed Orthodox church in every peasant village to Russify their heterogeneous subjects, while we Americans rely for unity on the "little red school house." (cited in Franklin, 1986, p. 83)

An assemblage of connections produce a relation of the child and family as an object of political rationality and social administration. U.S. social and medical policies, schooling, and day care and nursery schools of the early twentieth century tried to inculcate a universal, healthy child, the good scientific "professional" at-home mother, and a normal family that would be autonomous and responsible for themselves. While not without contradictions, they emerge with a belief that reform was a purposeful intervention to alter and improve social and personal life—in short, the welfare of citizens. The register of administration was to make the family and the child develop, grow, and be nurtured as free individuals. However, the connections were not some natural ordering of primal relations to be nurtured.[10]

The Project of Reform: The Production of the Cosmopolitan "Self"

Three significant elements will be discussed in the formation of the register of social administration that continues to the present, but with important differences today. First, the joining of the social administration with freedom united the betterment of society and the individual as one project. Progress at the turn of the century was focused on a social collective identity aligned with nationhood and the citizen at the turn of the century, the Americanization of immigrants, or the making of a "British subject." The register of social administration was the amalgamation of particular sectors with quite diverse problems—such as epidemic disease, criminality, and dangerous and endangered children in the past century—each addressed and ameliorated discretely through particular institutions and administrative practices. It is significant that the joining of the registers of social administration and freedom was also a collapsing of the distinction between the cultural and the social.

Second, the "soul" was the site of the administration· of freedom. Earlier religious themes of salvation were displaced by secular discourses that made the inner dispositions, sensitivities, and awarenesses of the individual the site of individual salvation. A salvation story was now told in the name of the new, secular citizen in the early twentieth century whose subjectivity embodied the obligations, responsibilities, and personal discipline aligned to liberal democratic ideals.[11] But the freedom to be given to the inner self-directed capabilities, dispositions, and habits of the individual was not "the antithesis of political power, but a key term in its exercise, the more so because most individuals are not merely the subjects of power but play a part in its operations" (Rose & Miller, 1992, p.174).

Third, the fabrication of the soul embodied a modern identity that we will call the "cosmopolitan self." No longer bound to a sense of identity built through geographical location and face-to-face interactions, the liberal freedom inscribed an identity that could move among the new more abstract, anonymous relations that characterized modernity. Individuality embodied a being "at home" in multiple and more anonymous social relations formed through, among others, urbanization, the new capitalist industrialization, a generalized Protestant view of salvation, and liberal political rationalities. Identity was no longer identified solely with place but with gesellschaft, the idea of the organic solidarity of society expressed in the modern notions of careers—roles—as well as theories of child development and family upbringing. Through the constructions and reconstructions of the cosmopolitan self, we can give attention to the historical possibility of the global citizen who has a traveling home through the discourses that connect the child, family, and community.

The idea to administer the development of inner discipline is not a new social strategy; it is found clearly in the Reformation and the Counter-Reformation, particularly in the new Jesuit teaching (see, e.g., Durkheim, 1938/1977). But what is different about modernity is the amalgamation of ideas and institutions that related to the new liberal political philosophies of the eighteenth and nineteenth centuries that universalized and globalized the political rationalities in the fabrications of childhood. The salvation of the soul is inscribed in the register of social administration that made freedom into a calculated technology of law and social science, as well as new institutions designed to care for the family and the child. These themes will be interwoven in exploring the changes in the registers of social administration that connect the child, the family, and the community.

Social Science: Saving the Soul, Fabricating the Citizen, and Reforming the Poor

The sciences of the family and the child inscribed a culture of redemption (Popkewitz, 1998a; also see Napoli, 1981; O'Donnell, 1985). The registers of social administration visioned/revisioned the child as no longer to inculcate obedience in its previous religious sense but to shape and fashion personality through the child's emulation of the teacher, through techniques to encourage self-knowledge and enhance the feeling of sympathetic identification, and by establishing links between virtue, honesty, self-denial, and pleasure (Rose, 1989, p. 223). Religious technologies of the confessional of the church are translated into a secular, psychological domain that struggled for the soul of the earthly city of modern rationality and reason. The discourses of social science refocused a Social Darwinism of the early part of the nineteenth century in which poverty was a consequence of individual sin. By the end of the century, poverty could be understood as a consequence of social conditions—such as of urbanization—and the evils of unbridled capitalism (see, e.g., Haskell, 1984b).

A salvation narrative circulated among multiple institutions to save the soul through connecting the child, family, and community. The family and the home were constructed as an entity to be administered by agencies outside the home that mediated the functions of the home through new rationalizations of childcare and schooling. There was considerable attention to the parent, both good and bad; the gendered assumptions about who was to be targeted by the new expertise were clear, as were the race and class-based discourses. Scientific research that described good child rearing or normal child development also framed the attributes that were disreputable, deleterious, and abnormal (Baker, 1998; Bloch & Popkewitz, 2000; Silverberg, 1998; Sklar, 1998).

The question that confronted reformers and social scientists was how to shape the transition from the "liberal" state of the early nineteenth century to the regulatory "positive" state of the early twentieth century.[12] The school was to replace aspects of the family in the child's upbringing but connected to multiple other welfare institutions concerned with reshaping the family as a unit of socialization. The sciences of the child and the family would not only provide a cognitive knowledge but also discipline the capabilities, values, dispositions, and sensitivities through which individuals problematized their world and individuality.

The registers of social administration embodied gendered discourses. Upheld were the spiritual dignity of marriage and domesticity, in the context of the United States, as mothers' real or normal work. The dignity of marriage and ideals of domesticity inscribed the connection to the idea of childhood itself:

> The new idea of childhood helped to precipitate the new idea of the family. No longer seen simply as a little adult, the child came to be regarded as a person with distinctive attributes—impressionability, vulnerability, innocence—which required a warm, protected, and prolonged period of nurture. Whereas formerly children had mixed freely in adult society, parents now sought to segregate them from premature contact with servants and other corrupting influences. Educators and moralists began to stress the child's need for play, for love and understanding, and for the gradual, gentle unfolding of his nature. Child rearing became more demanding as a result, and emotional ties between parents and children grew more intense at the same time that ties to relatives outside the immediate family weakened. (Lasch, 1977, pp. 5–6)

The Civilizing Practice: The Child, Family, and Community as the Primary Group

The constitution of society at the end of the nineteenth century embodied a cosmopolitan self fabricated in the networks of interpersonal relations structured in the family. The notion of the primary group provided a way to reason about the interpersonal relations through overlapping science, political, and redemptive discourses. Sociology and psychology, in particular, reordered the moral standards to be upheld and reconstituted them through calculated intervention practices. The battles of science against poverty, the evil effects of modernizations, and gender became intertwined in the moral crusades that were embodied in the knowledge systems of social science (Sklar, 1998).

The Primary Group and Fabricating the Cosmopolitan Self The family and the child involve a double image and narrative in the United States. The nation was defined as "the American family," placed in analogy to the family and gender roles as well as to the reproduction of children. To reconstruct a national imaginary was to reconstruct the family. The idea of family at all levels was the notion of kinship, that is, to see the binding of generations by a common training and a national character related to English-Americanism. Embedded in the language of kinship was the impulse to rationalize and calculate the family and the child (Wald, 1995).

The notion of kinship to reason about the child and family was recast in sociology as that of a primary group (Greek, 1992). The primary group reinscribed the importance of interaction and connections but through calculable practices. Working with civil service bureaucracies, the labor movement, state agencies, the new philanthropic agencies, and others on the faculty at the University of Chicago (most notable were George Herbert Mead and John Dewey), such an idea was embodied in the "community studies" of the new department of sociology at the University of Chicago. "Community sociology" made its object of study the connections of the family, marriage, urban conditions, and, in some instances, women's issues related to the feminist movements of the times to consider the new problems of socialization and identity formation.[13]

The idea of the primary group was reformatted and remade through the idea of the family. The new theology of science visualized the family as the cradle from which civilization was produced. The work of Charles Horton Cooley, one of the leaders of the Chicago School of Sociology, for example, saw the family as a primary group where a child learns of civilization through face-to-face interaction—an assumption that persists in various forms in contemporary thought. Cooley thought that the family and the neighborhood provided the proper socialization through which the child could lose the greed, lust, and pride of power that was innate to the infant and thus become fit for civilization. The communication systems of the family would, according to Cooley, establish the family on Christian principles that stressed a moral imperative to life: self-sacrifice for the good of the group. Parents, under the guidance of the new social theories of health, would develop altruistic instincts that expressed self-obligation and self-responsibility in their children (see Lasch, 1977).

Images of the Protestant moral and ethical life were overlaid with science to humanize and personalize individual discipline. The family as a primary group was a moral technology in which God's work was to be done. But the civilizing of the child and the family was a double language connecting to narratives and images of a collective moral order of the nation. The discourse of the primary group universalized and naturalized people of different ethnicity, religion, race, and language so it was possible to think of the self as part of a collective moral order of the nation (for discussion of national imaginaries, see Anderson, 1991; Balibar & Wallerstein, 1991; Bhabha, 1994).

As in sociology, the early theories of psychology embodied the struggle over the soul of the child to produce a citizen who would act wisely and autonomously in the new political and social institutions of the times. Prior to the end of the seventeenth century, the child was perceived as a vessel of evil, tainted with original sin, with physical and emotional efforts to wrest infants from the hands of Satan (Paoletti & Kregloh, 1989). With Locke's 1692 *Thoughts Concerning Education* was a revolutionary vision of the child as a tabula rasa—an unmarked slate in which teachers and parents could inscribe beliefs, behavior, and knowledge. The inscription of the young child embodied the religious faith in "catching children early."

But the child of the late nineteenth century would be developed through conceptions of a calculated nature that scientific theories and experimentation could increasingly administer as a rational, linear progression. Increasingly sophisticated physical and psychological research probed every step of child-hood in the psychological research of the early twentieth century. Scientific technologies of observation, testing, and assessment combined with the statis-tical reasoning of chance and probabilities to fabricate the normal and good child, parent, family, and teacher. Individual children were compared with others of their age to invoke a new meaning to the idea of normal. Freudian psychoanalytic theory placed great emphasis on a child's early experiences and the process of identification with the same-sex parent. According to Ariès (1965), changes in ideas about dress in childhood offered models of children's development to adulthood in which the saintliness of the child needed to be protected against adults.

Strategies of social administration were to aid the evolution to a more equitable and humane society through focusing on the child and the family. Inscribing the naturalism of Darwin, the psychologist G. Stanley Hall, who researched child growth and development, as did other psychologists, com-bined biological descriptions with scientific observations about growth that focused on the middle and upper classes of society as normal. Hall's child study, for example, joined Rousseau's idea of the noble savage with a Dar-winian notion of the survival of the fittest. Stages of childhood and adolescence were reflections of "natural" processes of the recapitulation of the race, if normal conditions prevailed (Richardson, 1989, pp. 25–26).[14]

Parents, especially mothers, were inundated with information and advice on the care and training of children, from prenatal care to the problems of adolescence, all carrying a message of scientific expertise, and knowledge of good, normal childhood/family/parenthood. Thus, the rules of conduct in-corporated important changes:

> psychologists began to discover the extent to which young children and babies were aware of and affected by their surroundings. This led to an increasing emphasis on the role of the mother as her baby's teacher not simply caretaker. Mothers had long been responsible for the moral edu-

cation of children as well as for their early lessons in reading and other skills. But where the eighteenth-century parent believed that a baby boy would become a man by instinct, directed by his masculine nature, the late-nineteenth century parent was being told that masculinity could, and should be taught." (Paoletti & Kregloh, 1989, p. 26)

These different sociological and psychological discourses fabricated a cosmopolitan self through ideas of the primary group, socialization, and later notions of learning. The child and the family are "seen" and to act with only the rules of development, growth, and cognitive formation and thus unencumbered with historical restrictions and human biases. The child who is socialized and learns in school, for example, embodies universal rules related to a collective social mooring that has no temporal dimensions and that, at least at the turn of the twentieth century, seemed independent of ethnicity, race, gender. Thus, the early twentieth-century modern, cosmopolitan self seemed to exist with a continuum of values that seemed independent of social and cultural differentiations and history. Not only was the child and childhood naturalized, it was deployed as a global discourse to understand culture and society.

We can begin to identify shifts in the notion of the individual in the early years of the twentieth century. Wiebe argues that there was a shift to understanding the whole individual as "a play of many characters within a single body" (Wiebe, 1995, p. 185). Through John Dewey—as well as Walter Lippmann, an important social commentor—was a decentered character with the disappearance of a single fixed standard of conduct and moral code. The modern individual was no longer seen as a single personality and wore many hats. The individualism further opened up the vast interior of life for governing. In the nineteenth century, the middle-class Americans visualized character as architecture that was bounded to the whole even if it had strange closets and hidden fissures. In the twentieth century, these impulses were reconstructed "as boundless sources of energy though which individuals discovered who they were: personality flourished only through exploration and growth" (Wiebe, 1995, p. 186). Whereas self-determination was a key word of democratic individualism in the nineteenth century, achievement in the twentieth century depended upon the individual searching for the real self and also for the real relationships with other people.

Pedagogies and Governing the Child

Pedagogy inscribed the registers of social administration with those of freedom through different discourses that overlapped. Concepts of community, family, and home that developed the child (with generalized norms of social cohesiveness and progress) were inscribed in the modern preschool and school; these schools simultaneously sought to make one's individual being social by absorbing the child into the universalized thought and consciousness of the ages (Burke, 1923; Charter, 1923; Rice, 1895; also see Bloch, 1987; Kliebard, 1986).

Freudian and neo-Freudian theories hoped to find the knowable child and adult in the teacher and parent who, when taught, would facilitate the erasure of primitiveness or difference from the universal norms (see Bloch, 1987, for examples of Dewey's subprimary curriculum, *Hill's 1923 Conduct Curriculum*).[15] The child study movement became one of scientific measurement in which the technologies of early behaviorism, represented, for example, by Robert Thorndike's work in the first quarter of the twentieth century at Columbia University, were used to access the knowable, readable child through studies in laboratory schools, through tests and measurements, and through the inscription and acceptance of stages and norms for development (Bloch, 1987; Rose, 1989).

The body, subjectivities, and sexualities were targeted through curricular practices that focused on all children attaining universal social and emotional norms of what was considered good/normal development (Bloch, 1987; Bloch & Popkewitz, 2000). In addition, for Dewey and others at the University of Chicago, science was not the measurement of capacities and growth but how the dispositions of the citizen were bound to community. Dewey was concerned, as were others of his time, with the heterogeneity as a challenge to the integrity of American identity. He spoke about the need to Americanize the new immigrants lest they "foreignize us" (quoted in Wald, 1995, p. 204). Dewey was also concerned about the social disintegration of the immigrant family as children were Americanized too rapidly in the exchange of one family structure for another and one narrative of identity for one radically different.

It is in this context of anxieties in the face of a reconstruction of national identity that we can understand the discourses that linked community, family, and child. Dewey, in his subprimary and primary school curriculum, envisioned the school as a miniature community that was to initiate the child into an effective social membership through a self-directedness of the child (see Bloch, 1987). This self-directedness was, in one of Dewey's most oft-quoted statements, so that "we shall have the deepest and best guarantee of a larger society which is worthy, lovely, and harmonious" (Kliebard, 1986, p. 81). Thus, the manners and morals of conduct that were to remove the child and teacher from local values and ethnic "cultures" were to be brought back to reconstitute the home and local communities.

Pedagogy was the struggle to reconstitute the child, not to teach school subjects. Literature, songs, and "activities" of the different reform projects associated with progressive education, for example, established particular narratives about participation, choice, and self and group understanding as well as problem solving for the new American citizen. The taxonomies of knowledge in science and mathematics were paramount as they represented the verifiable world through which identities would be anchored since one's personal locality was less significant than the more generalized connections in which one participated in society.

The New Expertise: The Teacher and the Governing of the Self

One[16] can think of the turn-of-the-century pedagogical training as taking the parent out of teaching and teacher education by separating them geographically and through separating teachers and their education from other professionals (for example, the "professional mother); but they were brought back together, too, through governing processes that fabricated the cosmopolitan teacher and parent whose dispositions and sensitivities were associated with the new images of Americanization rather than with ethnicity and old European traditions.[17] New classes of people supervised and evaluated the patterns of growth, development, and mental health of the cosmopolitan self—social workers, psychologists, and kindergarten teachers ordered and monitored its creation. The revision of expertise as "civilizing" practices of the child and family also revised the identities of the teacher that are embodied in modern discourses of professionalization and the profession in teaching (Popkewitz & Simola, 1996).

As teacher education in the nineteenth century was becoming formalized along with other autonomous "communities of experts" (Haskell, 1984a), it was to select not only self-motivated and morally devoted candidates but, according to a leading educational reform, to awaken and "to produce morally trained *men* and *women*, rather than, except in special cases, scholars" (Horace Mann in Mattingly, 1977, p. 44, emphasis in original). The teacher was to possess a professional, cosmopolitan self, a person whose own inner sense of self would have the moral and "reasoned" capability to reconstitute the inner capacities and dispositions of the child. William Russell,[18] the first president of Teachers' College and one of the leaders in the development of teacher education in the United States, said, for example, teacher training can provide

> "the most successful methods of imparting knowledge or rather of constituting the mind, as far as possible, its own instructor." The "faithful teacher" possessed a command of subject as well as "the means of operating on conscience and bringing the young mind under an early feeling of the principle of duty, that it may possess the power of self-direction and self government . . . In one word," . . . the teacher must acquire skill

in managing the mind: his must be "the gentle hand that can lead the elephant with a hair." (Russell in Mattingly, 1977, p. 122)

If one looks at learning theories and many of the pedagogical practices of this period, much of the new expertise was legislative. That is, one of the tasks of teaching was to develop a uniform, calculable rational cosmopolitan self who could act and develop naturally as self-responsible as a universal citizen that, at the same time, had prescribed boundaries and tasks to seemingly preserve social harmony and order. This legislative expertise was related to finding the correct rules in which the best, most efficient family and child can be produced. Its most prominent strand was homologous to Taylorism, which redesigned work by redesigning people into mass productive systems through work-time studies (Braverman, 1974; Gee, in press). In the pedagogy of the kindergarten and early primary grades, Taylorism was related to the reform of classroom organization most often associated with discourses of social efficiency, while child development pedagogy appeared to be less related (Kliebard, 1986).

However, what has often been lost in social histories of the curriculum is that both the social efficiency movement in schooling and industrialization as well as child development orientations were possible to consider only in the broader conjuncture that tied the registers of social administration with freedom. Taylor, social efficiency, and child development-oriented educators thought that the new efficiency or the new freedom of, for example, child-centered play would free the worker/child in the realization of a liberal democracy.

The new expertise of the child and family circulated as strategies of early intervention in different institutions and social practices. Psychology, home economics, social welfare, and the educational sciences (educational psychology and teacher education) intersected discursively to inscribe salvation stories through medical models that communicated progressive notions to parents. The Mothers Congress, which later became the Parent Teacher Associations (PTAs) in most American schools, nursing schools, new "parenting" magazines, public clinics, and governmental communications circulated the new medical and scientific discourses. The psychologies of childhood were viewed as a form of preventive medicine to counteract the problems of the parent, particularly to offset the problem mother who appeared to produce the problem child (see discussion of clinical projects in Richardson, 1989). From the doctor's office, to government pamphlets or magazine portrayals of the good parent, to social science and psychology/child development classes, the new middle-class and elite mothers-to-be were also brought into scrutiny. Popular magazines carried articles by psychologists such as G. Stanley Hall about early sexual distinction as essential to correct adult development. Child guidance clinics were organized to provide community-based mental hygiene services that focused on the significance of strong emotional qualities of family inter-action on child socialization.

The new expertism of the calculating, cosmopolitan self was supported not only through state government practices but also through large philan-thropic foundations and university departments in the United States. Philan-thropic leaders (e.g., the Fords, Rockefellers, and Mellons) believed that there was a close identification between the private interests of entrepreneurs, the moral precepts of Protestant salvation, and the public good developed through a scientific philanthropy. The various Rockefeller Foundations, for example, funded child study and parent education research whose effects provided dis-courses about the model family and child development; they also established disciplinary "homes" in universities that supported particular versions of social science that related medical models to moral issues of the family, child rearing, and development (Richardson, 1989; Sears, 1975). Philanthropic reformers of the Progressive era worked directly or indirectly with children and parents (mothers most often) in a variety of institutions. "Charity" or "progressive" kindergarten programs and day nurseries in settlement houses were estab-lished where teachers were to help children learn self-regulated behavior through free play, moral and appropriate social conduct, and, particularly in day nurseries and kindergartens for urban poor, teach parents hygiene and other social behavior in the afternoon.

Pluralism and Social Inclusion/Exclusion

The new expertise was transcribed on an unequal playing field that excluded as it simultaneously sought to include. If we examine the new learning theories and studies of child development, they were to increase individual freedom through the intersecting practices of health, science, and welfare institutions, such as the school. Yet the categories of childhood ascribed particular universal sets of norms that were not universal but historically particular. The child study movement in the United States, for example, embodied particular bi-naries to divide children: whiteness/blackness, male/female, and civility/sav-agery (Baker, 1998). These binaries classified the subjective dispositions of children through norms drawn from a particular Protestant view of individ-uality that was English-speaking, male, and racially/heterosexually charged.

The distinctions and differentiations to order the development of the child and the social health of the family qualified and disqualified individuals for participation through the principles inscribed as the inner characteristics and capabilities of the healthy and normal. The curriculum was to exorcise the Old World norms and culture of the family through foreign language annihilation and inscription of particular sets of manners that would modernize the soul through a self-reflexivity that utilized rational time, the scientific ordering of personal life (such as found in the notions of cleanliness and health), moral scriptures into a health curricula drawn from the medical and psychological notions (Wagener, 1998). The teacher who was increasingly of immigrant background was to be professionally educated in the general, cosmopolitan ideas of the university that universalized a particular liberal rationality that also covered particular ethnic identities and radical socialist ideas being brought from Europe.

It is within this shift in the fabrication of individuality that we can approach the notion of pluralism that circulated at the turn of the twentieth century. In the constructions of the school curriculum, pluralism was ordered to produce a social like-minded person and universal values that would provide for social cohesion (Franklin, 1986). Using ideas about participation and cooperation, the early curriculum theorists, sociologists, and psychologists were concerned with creating the American that would function as an instrument of social control to contain the threat of the growing diversity of the population. For some curriculum theories, the idea of social cohesion was related to the images of cultural homogeneity of rural small towns; for others, cohesion was related to urban life and industrialization that required new ways to think about forming the American.

It is in this joining of a social image of the nation and citizen and the individual that a particular pluralism is constructed (Olneck, 1989). The register of social administration connected the child, family, and community to the nation through particular normalization of diversity. Coinciding historically with a universal, monocultural model of the self in American "nativism" and "America First" movements was another image that constructed a sameness from diversity. The hyphenated American—a German-, Italian-, Norwegian-American—conceptualized community and ethnicity within a continuum of values. If we look at early childhood education, by the 1930s that pluralism represented children from diverse ethnic and class backgrounds as capable of becoming the homogeneous good democratic, autonomous citizen. The ethnicity and community in the settlement house movement and the community sociology were studied to understand how to bring the subjectivities of the child from its ethnic or non-English or northern European habits into the new identities of childhood embodied in the school curricula. The hyphenated identity constructed differences through norms that scaffolded whiteness, Protestantism, and gender.

Before moving to the second section of this chapter—to the present—we would like to revisit an earlier discussion about the registers of social administration and the formation of the modern welfare state. The register of social administration we have argued involved overlapping discourses of state policy, philanthropy, social science, health, medicine, and morality. These discourses overlapped to circulate among multiple institutions and social sites to fabricate the cosmopolitan self with universal characteristics bound to seemingly fixed and externally validated moral and civic obligations. We have thought in this context of the welfare state as a problem of governing in care of the citizen, with the "care" fabricated through dealing with actual conditions of change as well as producing practices that ordered the principles, participation, and actions of the family, the community, the child, and the teacher. Therefore, the "fabricated" identities to make a democratic responsiveness divided and excluded as well.

Reconstituting the Child, Parent, Community, and Teacher: The Turn of the Twenty-First Century and the Reconstituting of Freedom

Our movement now to the present recognizes certain continuities and discontinuities in the registers of social administration to connect the child, family, and community. There is still a concern with freedom that connects the scope and aspirations of public powers with those of the personal and subjective capabilities of individuals. The site of struggle is still with the soul and for a cosmopolitan self who has a traveling home. But these continuities can be misleading, as there are different internments and enclosures in the present, as the universalizing capabilities of the self now embody a particular, collaborative constructivism in which identity is located in an active, entrepreneurial individuality and within intersecting local, communal settings. Socialization is less an issue than representational cultural politics and community identity. The constructivist, cosmopolitan self reconfigures the knowledge of expertise to one of partnership rather than of legislation.

Provisions of Participation: Displacing and Revisioning Salvation Themes

Since at least the end of World War II there has been a shift in the systems of reasoning that, at its most simple level, refers to the concern with how knowledge is socially produced and constructed (see, e.g., Bourdieu & Passeron, 1970/1977; see "education," e.g., Cherryholmes, 1988; Giroux, 1992; Kohli, 1995). The different strands concern how knowledge is socially constructed, in some cases drawing on anthropological and sociological perspectives and in others on psychology (one can compare the sociology of Pierre Bourdieu with the psychology of Howard Gardner). In an analytical sense, the epistemological changes that relate to constructivism have multiple intellectual trajectories and no clear definition (Bloor, 1997). But if we consider the different trajectories of a constructivism as connected in the registers of social administration and freedom, we can explore the different effects of knowledge as a field of cultural practices and cultural reproduction.

Participation and Empowerment as Strategies of Administration We can explore the shift in the notion of the cosmopolitan self in discourse of participation in the post-World War II years in the United States. Salvation is placed in the local community and through cultural/psychological discourse in constructing identity (such as self-esteem related to participation). The complete and successful individual is one whose cultural/psychological "home" is in multiple, local centers. Essential in that home was a particular type of constructivism that was to empower through calculated intervention of the parent and the community (Edelman, 1977; Popkewitz, 1976). The modernist beliefs inherent in the programs of the 1920s and 1930s are replaced by new subjectivities representing the renewed need for individuality and flexibility in the face of anxieties/uncertainties over freedom, democracy, and economic interdependencies in the globalized culture(s) and economy(ies) in the twenty-first century.

The War on Poverty in the 1960s illustrates this shift to a constructivist, participatory identity as the center of political change. Its seemingly commonsensical idea was that bureaucratic mentalities were not efficient, as they removed the people locally involved in the outcomes of institutions from their oversight and involvement.[19] Children, parents, and communities were to make the decisions in institutions that affect their lives. For people of color and of poverty, salvation was to occur through participation in parent advisory boards for low-income, ethnically and linguistically "different" children.

The community-parent-child was placed into a new web of psychological theories about the lack of success—that is, the cause of poverty—being a lack of self-efficacy and/or a lack of self-esteem to affect their own interests. The problem of the social administration was to counter low self-efficacy/self-esteem in the personality of the poor as they sought to redefine their personal and communal life (Popkewitz, 1976). The intervention strategy was to reach parents from different communities in programs in order to teach child upbringing practices. The discourses of psychology targeted exclusively the poor and "different" parents; child development research and experts provided the basic curricula, representing a universal conception of the good child as an integration of social-emotional, (English) language, and cognitive development, the majority of which was determined by developmental milestones derived from the psychologist Gesell, other child development research, or neo-Freudian or Piagetian stages of development. The Head Start program, for example, inscribed patterns of childhood development into mandated parent education programs through the use of television (e.g., *Sesame Street*) and preschools.

The War on Poverty intersected discursively with the civil rights movements and feminist movements that also installed a constructivism but in the name of radical political change. The problem of participation was first related to statistical reasoning—a categorical representation (poor, Spanish-speaking families, etc.)—then to the cultural politics of exclusions, participation, and "voice." During the 1960s and 1970s, the trajectories were also related to a new global politics of anticolonialism (and postcolonialism) that not only affected the construction of new global systems but had a "domestic" influence in the reception of Franz Fanon and Pablo Freire with projects aimed at empowerment, democratization of the self, and the giving of voice to the previously marginalized.

One can think of the turn of the twentieth century pedagogical training as taking the parent out of teaching and teacher education, only to bring them back in the images of the cosmopolitan teacher and parent whose dispositions and sensitivities were associated with the new images of Americanization. The communities, ethnicity, languages, and old European traditions were to be transported to a new cosmopolitan, collaborative, and active self. Now community is inscribed with cultural-psychological characteristics rather than with social capabilities. Parent/community participation is self-responsible and self-motivated, as well as flexible to help the school achieve its mission of administering the child to be free and self-motivated.

The Constructivist as a Field of Cultural Practices

The constructivism of the new cosmopolitan self is an amalgamation of different discourses and technologies directed to develop the freedom of the individual; a set of distinctions, divisions, and rules for action and participation. Pedagogical constructivism is an amalgam of particular cognitive psychologies and symbolic interactionist approaches joined with political discourses of reform.[20] An image is projected of the "new" teacher (and child) as an "empowered," problem-solving individual capable of responding flexibly to problems that have no clear set of boundaries or singular answers. The discursive practices give concrete form to practices of reforms such as in cooperative learning, and group or peer learning.[21]

Embodied in the constructivism is an entrepreneurial self in which the individual is responsible for his or her self-actualization through an active life. The self is the self-constructing subject, a flexible "actor," ready to respond to new eventualities and empowered through self-reflection and self-analysis, including the incorporation of the voices and actions of local communities to construct and reconstruct one's own "practice," participation, and ways of reason. The soul is targeted as no longer the inculcation of an externally validated morality and obligations but a self who is self-managed for the active construction of an ethical life (Rose, 1999).[22] The site of administration is now one of a cultural production of individuals who work on themselves through self-improvement, autonomous and "responsible" life conduct, and lifelong learning. The salvation theme is to empower and to emancipate the child/family through their moral aspirations and desires.

In what might seem contradictory, the constructivist cosmopolitan self involves images of the universal child that intersect scientifically derived age norms with the normalizations of the dispositions and sensitivities of a problem-solving child or person. Developmental knowledge is (still) the mainstay or foundation for best practice in contemporary U.S. educational reforms.[23] Scientifically guided principles, based on "generalizations that are sufficiently reliable," suggest the continuing efforts to find a universal and scientific signpost for who the child is and how to guide his/her progress or development.[24] Thus, at one level, many of the same norms detailed in psychological research studies from the 1940s still guide physicians', social workers', parents', and teachers' practices of today, with few adaptations to broaden norms to include other children.

But the notions of development intersect with a new normality of the child—a child who will be flexible, who is developmentally ready for the uncertainties and opportunities of the twenty-first century. Notions of a universal development overlap with flexibility, problem solving, and uncertainty to provide new salvation themes. Where the child of the late nineteenth century had to begin to prepare for a pluralism whose image was united in a universalized "American," the American child of the twenty-first century must be prepared to be a global citizen/worker, flexible, adaptable, ready for uncertainties in work as well as family. He/she must also be a citizen prepared to recognize and work with diversity, whether in the United States or elsewhere. This joining of a universalism with a pragmatic outline may seem contradictory or even illogical, but as Bourdieu (1984) has argued, the logic of practice and common sense is more complex than the practice of logic.

Being is one of a flexibility and activity, preparing for a society of an as yet undefined type but reflecting universalized ideas of flexibility and activity. The individuality is pragmatic but calculating in a flexible range of situations. Sometimes the constructivism is expressed in political terms of neoliberalism about people maximizing their interests through market analogies, and sometimes in the psychologies of the child that focus on "making knowledge" through maximizing interactions and creating flexible networks for understanding. At this moment we can refer to the new welfare systems in which it becomes the individual who is a job seeker rather than an unemployed person.

As Wagner (1994) suggests, it would be historically incorrect to understand the notion of "entrepreneurial" as an economic metaphor that defines cultural practices; rather it should be understood as a hybrid of discourses in which new patterns of calculative routines are to "make" the citizen who manages his own personal ethics and collective allegiances (also see Rose, 1999).

The new cosmopolitan self that is embodied in constructivist, entrepreneurial being is not a return to a romanticized past but a reconstitution from which we recognize who we are and our sense of being. While not homogenous and with conflicting patterns, the seeming reattachment to the face-to-face patterns of gemeinschaft that sociologists bemoaned as disappearing in the nineteenth century reappears, but in different configurations and connections. While we can say that the cosmopolitan self is being made, it is of a different making, one where identity is a collaborative, participatory individuality whose salvation is the work in communities and with a pluralism whose meanings are different from the turn of the twentieth century (for general discussions, see Boyer & Drache, 1996; Popkewitz, 1998a; Wagner, 1994).

Pluralism and Community

The constructivist self operates from self-interests and with values of self-reliance and autonomy that are accomplished in plural communities and in a self-accounting of oneself as an ethical actor. Narratives of pluralism connect identities in community. The pluralism makes the family and community into the new settlement houses. Whereas settlement houses of the late nineteenth and early twentieth centuries were for urban areas and urban families (including religious immigrants or refugees from Ireland and eastern and southern Europe), the new late-twentieth-century interventions are for racially and linguistically others, the constructed homogeneity of families and communities—the new hyphenations of the African-Americans, Hispanics/Latinos, the new Southeast Asian immigrants, or other political/economic refugees. The new calls for pluralism are coupled with new salvation narratives of multiculturalism, while practices of social administration target the conceptually homogeneous and homogenized group constructed artificially for interventions.

Community and individuality are cast as some pristine, pure quality in the civilizing processes of the new primary group. Community is a universalized place where the parents are involved and coach the child, and where the community collaborates with teachers and schools to empower and give voice to community expertise and interests/experience; this is in opposition to the early part of the century where teachers were to educate the parent to universal rules of national sagas.

The notion of community is a representation of groups that stand by themselves and along with other communities that have no collective social identity except in the collection of different communities themselves. The formation of the citizen is not related to externally validated morals and obligations but as a culture of the self that addresses the self-management of individuality or the active (self-) construction of an ethical life.

Constructivist Sciences and the Expertise of Governing

The new provisions for participation and new salvation themes encompass new pedagogical strategies and expertise. These relate to the constructivism and self-active individuality of the child, family, and community and an expertise to facilitate individual self-actualization as the ethical project of personal self-governing.

The Reason of Pedagogies: The Active Teacher/Child The images and narratives of the professional teacher in education have become enmeshed in the late 1990s with images of the collaborating child and parent. Early educational models of parent involvement from the 1960s that target the parent and the community have been generalized to elementary and secondary teacher education where parent involvement and education, as well as school-home collaboration are considered new, challenging reforms (e.g., Bloch & Tabachnick, 1994; Borman & Colleagues, 1998; Epstein, 1995; McCaleb, 1994; Nieto, 1992). The decentralization of teacher decision making is a reform to enhance teacher voice, reflection, and active and empowered participation in schools and school reform. Standards for teacher education at the early childhood level as well as for primary-level teachers dispose future teachers toward educating all children and diverse populations. They also encourage or reiterate a need to involve parents and collaborate with communities. Finally, teachers are to be flexible and open to cultural diversity as a component of developmentally appropriate teaching practices (Bredekamp & Copple, 1997).

The different trajectories briefly described previously produce new registers of social administration and freedom. Whereas the salvation stories of the turn of the century constructed a universal cosmopolitan self that was applied to all social classes (through, for example, the settlement houses teaching of health in city homes and schools to the problem-solving self of the progressive education of Dewey), the salvation stories of the present are of an active sense of self whose emotional bonds and self-responsibility are circumscribed through networks of other individuals—the family, the locality, and the community. The location of responsibility is no longer traversed through the range of social practices directed toward a single public sphere: the social. The fabrications of the family and the pluralism in community are new connections between political aspiration and individual calculations and events.

Teachers are asked to go into the community, become part of communities to better know their pupils and their families, to become trusted, or to know what should be included from community knowledge (Bloch & Tabachnick, 1995; Borman & Colleagues, 1998; Delpit, 1995; Ladson-Billings, 1994; Swadener & Lubeck, 1995; Tabachnick & Bloch, 1995). Parents are responsible to the child, involved in schools and children's education, and capable of making choices for their children's sake, while at the same time they are full-time workers for society; as in the late nineteenth century, asked in the name of saving the child to teach normal behavior and skills to children.

The Expertise of Partnership The constructivist cosmopolitan self embodies new types of expertise in which to mobilize the individual. The expert is one who engages in partnerships and in pacts with the community and individual to enable the individual to manage better and to be healthier and happier. To teach or to be a social worker is to be an enabler who provides information, lifelong learning, and tutoring that can steer self-development and self-management of the ethical individual. The expert is embodied in today's reforms about the empowerment of teachers and parents through participation in community, calculated as site-based management, home-school collaboration, parent choice, vouchers, and the new charter schools initiated by teachers and parents for diverse reasons.

This new common sense of the expert is reconfigured to administer the parent and community. The new practices of expertism are brought closer to the child through pedagogical theories about learning, administration of schools (classroom management), and assessment techniques that appear more intrusive in the life of teachers, children, and community. The construction of being makes resistance and revolt more distant and less plausible as it is the self's capacities and potentialities that are the site of perpetual intervention (see Boltanski, 1993/1999; Rose, 1999).

The production of the teacher entails new assessment methods to calculate and supervise. The teacher is an action researcher, assessing the child through life histories or portfolios, and the child is one who makes and remakes his or her own biography (the constructivist child). The movements toward qualitative research are embedded in reconstituting patterns of social administration and effects of power that are not merely additive to those patterns at the turn of the twentieth century. These patterns are also embodied in the shift to qualitative research that gave new ordering principles to social and educational research in the 1970s (Popkewitz, 1981).

While moving to an active, empowered, and decision-making society, the decentralization of the active, collaborative teacher and parent is also steered through a mixture of federal, state, and community standards, examinations, and outcome-based educational reforms that embody homogeneous objectives and pedagogy necessary for all to achieve or perform (high standards for everyone). As in the past, the constructivist, cosmopolitan self is not only of schools. The microprocesses of science, teacher education, parents' magazines, and pediatric offices continue to target conduct in subtle ways.

The Cosmopolitan Self and the Inclusion/Exclusion of "Being"

Constructivism is an amalgamation of different discourses and technologies that is not only directed to develop the freedom of the individual; it is a set of distinctions, divisions, and rules for action and participation.[25] The new registers of constructivism universalize particular local dispositions as seemingly natural for all.

The universal and the inclusionary are also simultaneously systems that exclude. The exclusions occur through naturalizing and normalizing the problem-solving abilities as capacities for "making" for the child's success (and failure). The psychological and interactional models of "good teaching" are classifications that divide while pretending to be universal concepts. The ordering and dividing are also brought into the home as distinctions that make for a child's good or poor self-concept, or in the proper or improper family habits for a child to read at home or to do homework.

The inclusion/exclusion of the universalizing effect is brought into efforts, particularly in the contexts of targeted social groups (urban education), to bring more teacher and community voices into school decision making; it carries with it a construction of voice and experience that is seemingly of a pure and homogeneous identity, constructing and highlighting similarity of group and negating difference (see Delpit, 1995, for example). While teachers are taught that they should be active, reflective, and collaborative, and that their experience should be included in curriculum and school decision making, the notion of voice inherent in the involvement of both parents and teachers in educational reform carries the notion of democracy and inclusion while homogenizing voices (e.g., "teacher voice," "Latino" mothers). In addition, the communities whose voice is to be heard are not all communities but only those who need their (homogenized) voice to be heard.

But the concepts of child, family, and expertism are related to particular capabilities drawn from particular groups who have the power to sanctify and consecrate their dispositions as those appropriate for the whole society.[26] The capabilities of the child that Walkerdine (1988) explored empirically with child-centered pedagogies, for example, are a normalized vision of the natural child that is not natural but socially constructed as truth. The emphasis on verbalization and justification in child-centered pedagogies, she argues, relates to particular gendered and bourgeois conceptions. The system of inclusion/

exclusion naturalizes the being of the child as a state of being that orders participation rather than on fixed categories related to structural concepts, such as race, class, or gender. This is not to argue that such structural categories are not important but that they are formed within normalizing and racializing processes that need to be accounted for in the production of power.

The salvation themes to rescue the poor and previously marginalized embody capabilities whose universal qualities cannot be had. The constructivist individuality produces its opposition in the child and family constructed as needy—lacking good self-concept or at risk. This is the dilemma of welfare in care of the self. The systems of reason to care for the child and family place them as outside of normality and as not possible to ever be "the average."

Changing Connections of Governing the Child, Family, and Community

The welfare institutions that care for and educate children are phrased as one of democratizing and making those institutions more responsive to the parent and community. When focusing on the children of the poor and marginalized social groups, the concept of democratization is also phrased as a way to "rescue" the child through rescuing the parent. It is thought that parents, with the proper habits, dispositions, and behaviors, would enable the success of their children as they develop into adults. Discourses of "community" are also attached to this democratization, suggesting that the solution to democratization is localized and flexible strategies, more choice, local collaboration between teachers and parents, and involvement.

Our essay sought to historicize these connections through a problematization of reason. We sought to see connections where others have seen divides. We placed the knowledge of parenting, childhood, community, and the expertism of schools into a historical proximity to each other to consider their configurations. Central was placing the connections within the joining of registers of social administration and freedom that made the family and childhood in the reforming of the home and school. We argued that in the past and the present are overlapping discourses of psychology, community sociology, and medical models of the individual that made the soul the site of struggle. At the turn of the twentieth century, that struggle was given form through intersecting narratives of Americanization and institutional practices of missionaries, philanthropic discourses of salvation, and pedagogy. It imagined a cosmopolitan self that was ordered through universal norms of child development, the family as a primary group, and a legislative expertise. We further argued that these relations and discourses are still present, but within a different amalgamation of ideas and institutional practices through which the cosmopolitan self is being constructed and the soul is the site of struggle. Today's cosmopolitan self is constructivist, active, entrepreneurial, and works for the self's capacity and potentialities through a perpetual intervention in one's life.

The new connections of child, parent, and community are ruled by an expertism that governs communication systems through which desire and striving for self-actualization and individual personal responsibility are constructed. A new form of expertise is a partnership that the professional investigates, maps, classifies, and works on the territories of individuality for a lifelong learning. The enabling professional empowers the individual for self-management of choice and the autonomous conduct of life. These new territories of individual make resistance and revolt, as we argued, more distant and less plausible.

Our historicizing the present is not to argue against participation, community, or salvation themes for seeking a more humane and just world. It is just the opposite as we, the authors, still live with Enlightenment purposes. The new flexible, independent, autonomous, responsible, and problem-solving child/parent/citizen of the turn of the twenty-first century illustrates the ways in which the governing of the soul has shifted, and a globalized cultural and economic future; however, this shift is not a natural progression toward freedoms but a continuation of internments, enclosures, and inclusions/exclusions. These effects of power require a continual critical vigilance.

While we have focused on the particular relations of registers of social administration and freedom in the United States, the construction of the cosmopolitan self also embodies movements to intricately join the individual, the community, the nation, and globalization since at least the colonializations of the sixteenth and seventeenth centuries. The construction of the national imaginary and salvation stories of the American were related to European colonialization. They embodied a hybridity that overlaid English, French, and German images and narratives into a single plane that formed by both distancing and reattachments. At the same time, the fabrication of the cosmopolitan self in the past and the present was a universalizing practice. Identities were fabricated that no longer seemed to belong to a particular geographical space but which moved in multiple places and different calculated spaces as home, such as found in the new organization of work and liberal politics. In this context, it was possible for almost all of the first American social sciences to travel to Europe to understand the new sciences and to transport and translate them back into an American imaginary. It is also possible to understand discussions today about the global citizen in light of this historical universalizing of the cosmopolitan self and the centrality of discourses of the child, childhood, and the school in the historical making of the citizen who has a traveling home.

The invention of the calculable child is inscribed in the emergence of a worldwide educational system that Meyer, Boli, Thomas, and Ramirez (1997) have studied. In today's narratives is a subjectivity that is collaborative and community oriented, with a problem-solving disposition that seems to move individuals beyond the local and the national through an individuality that has no context, history, or nation. The systems of reason that circulated about family, childhood, development, and pedagogy are, today, naturalized as a global construction in the productive practices of the modern school. The discourses of curriculum through which the child becomes calculable and disciplined are themselves hybrids that circulated among multiple geographical settings in Europe as well as settling in the colonies that existed after the seventeenth century.

But one should not speak of globalization as a phenomenon that is outside and divided from local production and the national imaginaries in which the cosmopolitan self is produced (Popkewitz, 2000b). While there are universalizing characteristics of the cosmopolitan individuality that seem to cross nations, those universals are not universal but particular normalizations and divisions that move with anxieties and displacements that include unequal playing fields. The universalized norms of the cosmopolitan self that seemed inclusive of all individuals are not. The normalizations embody differentiations and divisions that are historically worked through in the relation of the global and the local, and with continual slippages. When considering the relation of the global and the local, we need to think about their relations and connections rather than their divisions. Further, there is a continual need for historicizing the relations of the global and universalized, and the construction of collective or imagined communities in order to understand how subjectivities are re-territorialized, at least in the current conjuncture, as a problematic of the registers of social administration and freedom.

Notes

[1] See Lasch (1977) for a historical discussion of this relation, although we diverge with Lasch's argument in multiple respects, especially his reductionism. However, this does not assume that the concept of childhood appears in these transformations (see, e.g., Ariès, 1965; Hunter, 1994), but only that it assumes a particular configuration in relation to problems of social administration. Some of these issues are discussed in Bloch and Popkewitz (2000).

[2] We use the concept of "register" to recognize that there were multiple and overlapping ideas, events, and occurrences that historically came together in the linking of social administration with the problem of freedom.

[3] It is important to note here that our construction of the problem is historical and related to multiple trajectories in which the outcomes are never predetermined and thus open to interventions rather than causality.

[4] We can think of the past and present as did Althusser's (1972) notion of "hailing" in relation to this argument about change. Our interest, however, is with a historicizing that is not concerned with causal or origin narratives but with the productive qualities of power and with a notion of history in which multiple trajectories overlap to form a single plane rather than a history of origins. Our raising a relation of our concern with governing and Althusser is to recognize that certain Marxist traditions in France and Germany (the Frankfurt school, for example) overlap with postmodern theories in the sense of turning to knowledge as a material practice. There are, however, important differences in that the latter concern with knowledge is with how classes are produced and the micropatterns in which power circulates as a productive practice (see Popkewitz, 1998a; Popkewitz & Fendler, 1999).

[5] It is a mistake, we believe, in not understanding the modern state as a welfare system of administrating the freedom of the individual, although the system has different trajectories; for example, in the United States (Fine, 1956) and northern European states. For state development, see Hindess (1996); Skowronek (1982); also Skocpol (1992) as it relates to early state pension schemes; Wittrock and Wagner (1996) on development of the state and social science.

[6] There are at least two different periodizations given to modernity: one in the seventeenth century with the production of ideas about reason and science as a bringing of progress through individual action, and a modernity associated with the nineteenth century industrialization, urbanization, and professionalization of knowledge. It is the later one that we deploy here. We use "modern," then, in this historical and analytic sense to focus on the reconfiguration of discourses and institutions that care for the child through a bringing of a new expertism and epistemologies of social administration that becomes evident in the nineteenth century. Our placing of modernity in the nineteenth century is to emphasize the processes of rationalization, science, liberalism, and industrialization that emerge as overlay in the constructions of identities.

[7] Our assumption is that all scientific discourses are governing ones in the sense discussed here, including our own (see Popkewitz, 1991, 1993 for further discussion). The problem of modern scholarship requires what Bourdieu, Chamboredon, and Passeron (1968/1991) call an epistemological vigilance (also see Bourdieu & Wacquant, 1992).

[8] In the court system, for example, children were put into juvenile courts up to the age of seventeen (thereby marking them as children), where previously a child over age seven was considered as criminally responsible in most states and, therefore, culpable as an adult.

[9] While Grubb and Lazerson (1981) suggest the principle of *parens patriae* resulted in state intervention into the family being rare, or only when absolutely necessary, the principle of possibility and actuality of intervention was reinforced.

[10] See Hindess (1996) and Bloch and Blessing (2000) for a discussion of the gendered nature of this position. There is a particular form that the organizational development of state governmental administration took in the United States that was different from most European welfare state developments (see, e.g., Orloff & Skocpol, 1984; Bledstein, 1976, for discussion of the new cultural representations of self among the middle classes; also Popkewitz, 1996).

[11] Religious systems of authority were also redefined, in part, through the merging of the state with religion, and also through changes in social cosmologies in which religion was constructed (see, e.g., Berger, 1969; Berger & Luckmann, 1967).

[12] This shift in focus and emphasis to social reform and state intervention is found in the American Social Science Association (ASSA) by the 1880s, the association from which many of the specific disciplines of U.S. social science emerged.

[13] First in loose connections of people concerned with rationalizing reform through social science and later in disciplinary departments in the university, women joined the settlement house movement that overlapped the worlds of social science and social reform, in large part targeting poor women and their children as the "others" to be helped. Women social scientists took the tools of social science to promote what was seen as the welfare of the whole society while enabling women to use these opportunities to inform their practical approach and validate their ethical solutions to social problems. *The Hull House Papers and Maps* (1885), for example, incorporated the latest technologies of lithography to illustrate the relations of racial and ethnic populations in tenement conditions of the district in which Hull House was located. The maps join an appreciation for empirical details through the use of social surveys with a moral vision of change that was present in the 1890s; see Sklar (1998).

[14] In Hall's 1893 *The Contents of Children's Minds*, he positioned the child within a set of norms that defined a rural-ness as a universal to order the growth and development that was to be nurtured in the child who was to become an adult.

[15] While it seems natural to talk of children as learners and child development as a way of memorializing school, we tend to forget that psychology was not an organized or necessarily privileged discourse to speak of the educated subject until the late nineteenth century (Fendler, 1999). Further, this privileging of the child as the focus of pedagogical content is still part of the reform efforts in education.

[16] The title of this section should be read in its ironic quality, as we are not concerned with who did what to whom (a theory of origins and structure) but with the relational quality of connections and amalgamations in which the registers of social administration were constructed.

[17] There was a prophetic quality to notions of the New World replacement of the Old World as it overlapped with biblical notions about the meaning of "new" and the manifest destiny of the Republic. Protestant notions of a millennial were brought into secular calls for change and order. The prophetic qualities are carried into today's political rhetoric about a "new world order" and the U.S. role in the spread of democracy and liberalism.

[18] Russell was a leader of the American Institute for Instruction, which later became one of the two major professional organizations of U.S. teachers, the American Education Association.

[19] There is an ironic quality to this logic as the U.S. political efficiency movement of the late nineteenth century and early twentieth century tried to remove local communities from decision making to promote good, efficient, and responsive government.

[20] There is continual debate about the relation of the social to the individual in pedagogical constructivism although these debates exist within a common sense.

[21] The issues of inclusion/exclusion are discussed in Bloch and Popkewitz (2000); Popkewitz (1998b, 2000a); and Popkewitz and Lindblad (2000).

[22] Rose suggests that the movement of governing in the present shifts the focus to surfaces rather than the soul, with a constant and never-ending modulation of flows and transactions in which the individual acts. Our reading of the literature in education

suggests that the soul is still the focus through concerns with, for example, the dispositions and sensitivities of the child and teacher in the reform of schools and welfare systems, but within the enclosures and internments described.

[23] See, for example, the National Association for the Education of Young Children's (NAEYC) document on *Developmentally Appropriate Practice* that states: "Developmentally appropriate practice is based on knowledge about how children develop and learn. As Katz states, 'In a developmental approach to curriculum design, . . . (decisions) about what should be learned and how it would best be learned depend on what we know of the learner's developmental status and our understanding of the relationships between early experience and subsequent development' (cited in Bredekamp & Copple, 1997, p.109). To guide their decisions about practice, all early childhood teachers need to understand the developmental changes that typically occur in the years from birth through 8 and beyond, variations in development that may occur, and how best to support children's learning and development during these years. Following is a list of empirically based principles of child development and learning that inform and guide decisions about developmentally appropriate practice . . ."(Bredekamp & Copple, 1997, p. 9).

[24] Recent reviews of child development publications in the United States, for example, suggest that well over 80 percent of the articles published in the 1990s on child development were still based on research studies of middle-class white and Western children (New, 1994).

[25] The issues of inclusion/exclusion are discussed in Bloch and Popkewitz (2000); Popkewitz (1998b, 2000a); and Popkewitz and Lindblad (2000).

[26] We am not arguing against certain notions as useful to serve as foundations for organizational or social purposes; rather, the purpose is to suggest that universals are historically formed and always to be treated with partial irony and thus problematically.

References

Althusser, L. (1972). Ideology and ideological state apparatuses. In B. R. Cosin (Ed.), *Education: Structure and society, selected reading* (pp. 242–80). Middlesex, England: Penguin Books.

Anderson, B. (1991). *Imagined communities: Reflections on the origin and spread of nationalism.* London: Verso.

Ariès, P. (1965). *Centuries of childhood: A social history of family life.* New York: Vintage Books.

Baker, B. (1998). Childhood-as-rescue in the emergence and spread of the U.S. public school. In T. S. Popkewitz & M. Brennan (Eds.), *Foucault's challenge: Discourse, knowledge, and power in education* (pp. 117–43). New York: Teachers College Press.

Balibar, E., & Wallerstein, I. (1991). *Race, nation, class: Ambiguous identities.* New York: Verso.

Berger, P. (1969). *The sacred canopy: Elements of a sociological theory of religion.* New York: Doubleday Anchor Book.

Berger, P., & Luckmann, T. (1967). *The social construction of reality: A treatise in the sociology of knowledge.* Garden City, NY: Anchor.

Bhabha, H. (1994). *The location of culture.* New York: Routledge.

Bhabha, H. (1995). Freedom's basis in the indeterminate. In J. Rajchman (Ed.), *The identity in question* (pp. 47–62). New York: Routledge.

Bledstein, B. (1976). *The culture of professionalism, the middle class and the development of higher education in America.* New York: Norton.

Bloch, M. (1987). Becoming scientific and professional: An historical perspective on the aims and effects of early education. In T. S. Popkewitz (Ed.), *The formation of school subjects: The struggle for creating an American institution* (pp. 25–62). New York: Falmer Press.

Bloch, M., & Blessing, B. (2000). Restructuring the state in eastern Europe: Women, child care, and early education. In T. S. Popkewitz (Ed.), *Educational knowledge: Changing relationships between the state, civil society, and the educational community* (pp. 59–82). New York: State University of New York Press.

Bloch, M., & Popkewitz, T. S. (2000). Constructing the parent, teacher, and child: Discourses of development. In L. D. Soto (Ed.), *The politics of early childhood education* (pp. 7–32). New York: Peter Lang.

Bloch, M., & Tabachnick, B. R. (1994). Improving parent involvement as school reform: Rhetoric or reality? In K. M. Borman & N. P. Greenman (Eds.), *Changing American education: Recapturing the past or inventing the future* (pp. 261–96). New York: State University of New York Press.

Bloor, D. (1997). What is a social construct? *Vest, 10* (1), 9–22.

Boltanski, L. (1993/1999). *Distant suffering, morality, media, and politics.* Trans. Gramam Burchell. New York: Cambridge Press.

Borman, K., & Colleagues. (Eds.) (1998). *Ethnic diversity in community and schools.* Norwood, NJ: Ablex.

Bourdieu, P. (1979/1984). *Distinction: A social critique of the judgment of taste.* Trans. R. Nice. Cambridge, MA: Harvard University Press.

Bourdieu, P., Chamboredon, J., & Passeron, J. (1968/1991). *The craft of sociology: Epistemological preliminaries.* Ed. Beate Krais and Trans. R. Nice. New York: Walter de Gruyter.

Bourdieu, P., & Passeron, J. (1970/1977). *Reproduction in education, society, and culture.* Trans. R. Nice. Beverly Hills, CA: Sage.

Bourdieu, P., & Wacquant, L. (1992). *An invitation to reflexive sociology.* Chicago: University of Chicago Press.

Boyer, R., & Drache, D. (1996). *States against markets: The limits of globalization.* New York: Routledge.

Braverman, H. (1974). *Labor and monopoly capital: The degradation of work in the twentieth century.* New York: Monthly Review Press.

Bredekamp, S., & Copple, S. (Eds.) (1997). *Developmentally appropriate practice in early childhood programs* (revised ed.). Washington, DC: National Association for the Education of Young Children.

Burke, A. (1923). *The conduct curriculum.* New York: Teachers College Press.

Charter, W. W. (1923). *Curricular construction.* New York: Macmillan.

Cherryholmes, C. (1988). *Power and criticism: Poststructural investigations in education.* New York: Teachers College Press.

de Swann, A. (1988). *In care of the state.* Cambridge, UK: Polity Press.

Dean, M. (1994). *Critical and effective histories: Foucault's methods and historical sociology.* New York: Routledge.

Delpit, L. (1995). *Other people's children.* New York: New Press.

Durkheim, E. (1938/1977). *The evolution of educational thought: Lectures on the formation and development of secondary education in France.* Trans. P. Collins. London: Routledge and Kegan Paul.

Edelman, M. (1977). *Political language: Words that succeed and policies that fail.* New York: Academic Press.

Epstein, J. (1995, May). School/family/community partnerships: Caring for the children we share. *Phi Delta Kappan,* 701–12.

Evans, P., Rueschemeyer, D., & Skocpol, T. (1985). *Bringing the state back in.* Cambridge, UK: Cambridge University Press.

Fendler, L. (1999). Making trouble: Predictability, agency, and critical intellectuals. In T. S. Popkewitz & L. Fendler (Eds.), *Critical theories in education* (pp. 169–90). New York: Routledge.

Fine, S. (1956). *Laissez faire and the general welfare state: A study of conflict in American thought.* Ann Arbor: University of Michigan Press.

Foucault, M. (1979). Governmentality. *Ideology and Consciousness, 6,* 5–22.

Franklin, B. (1986). *Building the American community: The school curriculum and the search for social control.* New York: Falmer Press.

Freedman, K. (1987). Art education as social production: Culture, society and politics in the formation of the curriculum. In T. S. Popkewitz (Ed.), *The formation of school subjects: The struggle for creating an American institution* (pp. 63–84). London: Falmer Press.

Furner, M. (1975). *Advocacy and objectivity: A crisis in the professionalization of American social science, 1865–1905.* Lexington: University of Kentucky Press.

Gee, J. (1996). *The new work order: Behind the language of the new capitalism.* Boulder, CO: Westview Press.

Gee, J. (in press). Progressivism, critique, and socially situated minds. In C. Edelsky & C. Dudley-Marley (Eds.), *Progressive education: History and critique.* Urbana, IL: National Council of Teachers of English.

Giroux, H. (1992). *Border crossings: Cultural workers and the politics of education.* New York: Routledge.

Greek, C. (1992). *The religious roots of American sociology.* New York: Garland.

Grubb, W. N., & Lazerson, M. (1982). *Broken promises: How Americans fail their children.* New York: Basic Books.

Hall, G. S. (1893). Aspects of child life and education: The contents of children's minds on entering school. *Princeton Review, 2,* 249–72.

Haskell, T. (1977). *The emergence of professional social science: The American social science association and the nineteenth-century crisis of authority.* Urbana: University of Illinois Press.

Haskell, T. (Ed.) (1984a). *The authority of experts: Studies in history and theory.* Bloomington: Indiana University Press.

Haskell, T. (1984b). Professionalism versus capitalism: R. H. Towney, Emile Durkheim, and C. S. Pierce on the disinterestness of professional communities. In T. Haskell (Ed.), *The authority of experts: Studies in history and theory* (pp. 180–225). Bloomington: Indiana University Press.

Hill, P. S. (1923). Introduction. In A. Burke, *The conduct curriculum.* New York: Teachers College Press.

Hindess, B. (1996). Liberalism, socialism, and democracy: Variations on a governmental theme. In A. Barry, T. Osborne, & N. Rose (Eds.), *Foucault and political reason: Liberalism, neo-liberalism, and rationalities of government* (pp. 65–80). Chicago: University of Chicago Press.

Hunter, I. (1994). *Rethinking the school: Subjectivity, bureaucracy, criticism*. New York: St. Martin's Press.

Kliebard, H. (1986). *Struggle for the American curriculum*. London: Routledge & Kegan Paul.

Kohli, W. (1995). *Critical conversations in philosophy of education*. New York: Routledge.

Ladson-Billings, G. (1994). *The dreamkeepers: Successful teachers of African American children*. San Francisco: Jossey-Bass.

Lasch, C. (1977). *Haven in a heartless world: The family besieged*. New York: Norton.

Latour, B. (1999). *Pandora's hole: Essays on the reality of science studies*. Cambridge, MA: Harvard University Press.

Locke, J. (1693). *Some thoughts concerning education*. London: Printed for A. and J. Churchill.

Mattingly, P. (1977). *The classless profession: American schoolmen in the nineteenth century*. New York: New York University Press.

McCaleb, S. P. (1994). *Building communities of learners*. New York: St. Martin's Press.

Meyer, J., Boli, J., Thomas, G., & Ramirez, F. (1997). World society and the nation-state. *American Journal of Sociology, 103* (1), 144–81.

Michel, S. (1999). *Children's interests / mother's rights: The shaping of America's child care policy*. New Haven, CT: Yale University Press.

Murphy, M. (1990). *Blackboard unions: The AFT & the NEA, 1900–1980*. Ithaca, NY: Cornell University Press.

Napoli, D. (1981). *Architects of adjustment: The history of the psychological profession in the United States*. Port Washington, NY: Kennikat Press.

New, R. S. (1994). Culture, child development, and developmentally appropriate practices: Teachers as collaborative researchers. In B. L. Mallory & R. S. New (Eds.), *Diversity and developmentally appropriate practices: Challenges for early childhood education* (pp. 65–83). New York: Teachers College Press.

Nieto, S. (1992). *Affirming diversity: The sociopolitical context of multicultural education*. New York: Longman.

O'Donnell, J. (1985). *The origins of behaviorism: American psychology, 1870–1920*. New York: New York University Press.

Olneck, M. (1989). Americanization and the education of immigrants, 1900–1925: An analysis of symbolic action. *American Journal of Education, 97,* 398–423.

Orloff, A., & Skocpol, T. (1984). Why not equal protection? Spending in Britain, 1900–1911, and the United States, 1880s-1920. *American Sociological Review, 49,* 726–50.

Paoletti, J. B., & Kregloh, C. L. (1989). The children's department. In C. Brush Kidwell & V. Steele (Eds.), *Men and women: Dressing the part* (pp. 22–41). Washington, DC: Smithsonian Institution Press.

Popkewitz, T. S. (1976). Reform as political discourse: A case study. *School Review, 84,* 43–69.

Popkewitz, T. S. (1981). Qualitative research: Some thoughts about the relation of methodology and history. In T. S. Popkewitz & B. Tabachnick (Eds.), *The study of schooling: Field methodology in educational research and evaluation* (pp. 155–80). New York: Praeger.

Popkewitz, T. S. (1987). *The formation of school subjects: The struggle for creating an American institution*. London: Falmer Press.

Popkewitz, T. S. (1991). *A political sociology of educational reform: Power / knowledge in teaching, teacher education, and research*. New York: Teachers College Press.

Popkewitz, T. S. (1992). Social science and social movements in the USA: State policy, the university, and schooling. In D. Broady (Ed.), *Education in the late twentieth century:*

Essays presented to Ulf P. Lundgren on the occasion of his fiftieth birthday (pp. 45–79). Stockholm, Sweden: Stockholm Institute of Education Press.

Popkewitz, T. S. (1993). *Changing patterns of power: Social regulation and teacher education reform.* Albany: State University of New York Press.

Popkewitz, T. S. (1996). Rethinking decentralization and the state/civil society distinction: The state as a problematic of governing. *Journal of Educational Policy, 11* (1), 27–51.

Popkewitz, T. S. (1998a).The culture of redemption and the administration of freedom in educational research. *Review of Educational Research, 68* (1), 1–34.

Popkewitz, T. S. (1998b). *Struggling for the soul: The politics of education and the construction of the teacher.* New York: Teachers College Press.

Popkewitz, T. S. (2000a). *Educational knowledge: Changing relationships between the state, civil society, and the educational community.* New York: State University of New York Press.

Popkewitz, T. S. (2000b). Reform as the social administration of the child: Globalization of knowledge and power. In N. Burbules & C. Torres (Eds.), *Globalization and educational policy* (pp.157–86). New York: Routledge.

Popkewitz, T. S., & Fendler, L. (Eds.) (1999). *Critical theories in education.* New York: Routledge.

Popkewitz, T. S., Franklin, B. M., & Pereyra, M. (Eds.) (2000). *Cultural history and critical studies of education: Critical essays on knowledge and schooling.* New York: Routledge.

Popkewitz, T. S., & Lindblad, S. (2000). Educational governance and social inclusion and exclusion: Some conceptual difficulties and problematics in policy and research. *Discourse, 21* (1), 5–54.

Popkewitz, T. S., & Simola, H. (1996). Professionalization, academic discourses, and changing patterns of power. In H. Simola & T. S. Popkewitz (Eds.), *Professionalization and education* (Research Report 169; Dept. of Teacher Education) (pp. 6–27). Helsinki, Finland: University of Helsinki.

Rice, J. M. (1893/1969). *The public school system of the United States.* New York: Arno Press and The New York Times.

Richardson, T. (1989). *The century of the child: The mental hygiene movement and social policy in the United States and Canada.* Albany: State University of New York Press.

Rose, N. (1989). *Governing the soul: The shaping of the private self.* New York: Routledge.

Rose, N. (1999). *Powers of freedom: Reframing political thought.* Cambridge, UK: Cambridge University Press.

Rose, N., & Miller, P. (1992). Political power beyond the state: Problematics of government. *British Journal of Sociology, 43* (2), 173–205.

Rueschemeyer, D., & Skocpol, T. (1996). *States, social knowledge, and the origins of modern social policies.* Lawrenceville, NJ: Princeton University Press.

Sears, R. R. (1975). Your ancients revisited: A history of child development. In E. M. Hetherington (Ed.), *Review of child development research*, vol. 5 (pp. 1–73).

Silva, E., & Slaughter, S. (1984). *Serving power: The making of the academic social science expert.* Westport, CT: Greenwood Press.

Silverberg, H. (Ed.) (1998). *Gender and American social science: The formative years.* Princeton, NJ: Princeton University Press.

Simola, H., & Popkewitz, T. S. (Eds.) (1996). *Professionalization and education* (Research Report 169; Dept. of Teacher Education). Helsinki, Finland: University of Helsinki.

Sklar, K. K. (1998). Hull-house maps and papers: Social science as women's work in the 1890s. In H. Silverberg (Ed.), *Gender and American social science: The formative years* (pp. 127–55). Princeton, NJ: Princeton University Press.

Skocpol, T. (1992). *Protecting soldiers and mothers: The political origins of social policy in the United States.* Cambridge, MA: Belknap Press.

Skowronek, S. (1982). *Building a new American state: The expansion of national administrative capacities, 1877–1920.* New York: Cambridge University Press.

Swadener, B. B., & Lubeck, S. (Eds.) (1995). *Children and families "at promise": Deconstructing the discourse of "at risk."* Albany: State University of New York Press.

Tabachnick, B. R., & Bloch, M. N. (1995). Learning in and out of school: Critical perspectives on the theory of cultural compatibility. In B. B. Swadener & S. Lubeck (Eds.), *Children and families "at promise": Deconstructing the discourse of "at risk"* (pp. 187–209). Albany: State University of New York Press.

Wagener, J. (1998). The "normal" body: Foucault and sex education. In T. S. Popkewitz & M. Brennan (Eds.), *Foucault's challenge: Discourse, knowledge, and power in education* (pp. 144–72). New York: Teachers College Press.

Wagner, P. (1994). *The sociology of modernity.* New York: Routledge.

Wald, P. (1995). *Constituting Americans: Cultural anxiety and narrative form.* Durham, NC: Duke University.

Walkerdine, V. (1988). *The mastery of reason: Cognitive development and the production of rationality.* London: Routledge.

Wiebe, R. H. (1995). *Self-rule: A cultural history of American democracy.* Chicago: University of Chicago Press.

Wittrock, B., & Wagner, P. (1996). Social science and the building of the early welfare state: Toward a comparison of statist and non-statist western societies. In D. Rueschemeyer & T. Skocpol (Eds.), *States, social science, and the origin of modern social policies* (pp. 90–114). Princeton, NJ: Princeton University Press.

Wittrock, B., Wagner, P., & Wollmann, H. (1991). Social science and the modern state: Policy knowledge and political institutions in western Europe and the United States. In P. Wagner, C. Weiss, B. Wittrock, & H. Wollmann (Eds.), *Social sciences and modern states: National experiences and theoretical crossroads* (pp. 28–85). Cambridge, UK: Cambridge University Press.

Woody, T. (1932). *New minds: New men? The emergence of the Soviet citizen.* New York: Macmillan.

6

Educating Flexible Souls

*The Construction of Subjectivity through
Developmentality and Interaction*

Lynn Fendler

The prime function incumbent upon the socius has always been to codify the
flows of desire, to inscribe them, to record them, to see to it that no flow exists
that is not properly dammed up, channeled, regulated.

Deleuze and Guattari, *Anti-Oedipus*

The term "flexible" has recently been used to describe desirable traits, not
only in education but also in business and politics. Analyses of developments
in these fields and others have shown that current social circumstances call
for "flexible" and "fluid" ways of being. These terms rightly pertain to a shift
away from the rigidly defined social roles characteristic of modernity, such as
the assembly-line positions in a Fordist factory or the efficiency models in a
Taylorist school. The conception of a fixed role or position has now shifted
to a more multifaceted and response-ready capacity, exemplified in a recent
television commercial in which the members of a chamber orchestra drop
their musical instruments to play basketball when a ball is thrown into their
midst. Flexibility is vaunted as the cutting-edge solution to the challenges of
productivity in a fast-moving global economy, and the goals and objectives of
education reinscribe the values of flexibility through curricular and pedagogical practices.

The shift from fixed role to situation response does indicate a new kind
of flexibility relative to modern organizational structures, and on that basis
many liberal and critical analyses of education suggest that this flexibility entails some essential sort of freedom, liberation, or release from regulation. The
argument of this chapter, in contrast, suggests that assumptions about freedom—as a metaphysical essence, a teleological imperative, or a rhetorical
deployment by critical theorists—should be problematized. I argue that in

education a particular form of subjective flexibility is constituted through the confluence of three disciplinary discourses—epistemological, curricular, and pedagogical—whose technologies construct the educated subject. First, I analyze the epistemological assumptions by referring to the discourse of "whole child" education. The literature that uses the language of the whole child constructs aspects other than cognition as the aspect of the subject that learns, knows, and is taught. In some educational literature, the whole child is called the "active learner," the "constructivist learner," or the "autonomous learner." The epistemological assumptions embedded in this discourse construct a particular target or substance to be educated. I characterize this construction of the educative substance as "responsive desire." In my analysis of responsive desire, I hope to critique the valorization of flexible response-ability and problematize the essentialization (Freudian or otherwise) of desire, which in educational literature is often called "internal motivation."[1]

The second disciplinary discourse is "developmentally appropriate curricula," a widely applied curriculum theory that correlates lesson plans with a sequence of capabilities.[2] The discourse of developmentally appropriate curricula interweaves three distinct discursive threads. It appeals to developmental psychology for its scientific base, it inscribes assumptions of progressive efficiency, and it assumes a behaviorist approach to establish educational objectives.[3] In this section, I argue that the interweaving of developmental psychology, efficiency, and behaviorism in educational curricula becomes a technology of normalization. I call this technology *developmentality* as a way of alluding to Foucault's governmentality, and focusing on the self-governing effects of developmental discourse in curriculum debates. Developmentality, like governmentality, describes a current pattern of power in which the self disciplines the self.

The pedagogical regimen that frequently accompanies developmentally appropriate curricula is interactive pedagogy, the third disciplinary technology investigated in this chapter. Interactive pedagogy is a recent pedagogical innovation; it was promoted as a solution to the problems associated with previous "teacher-centered" and "child-centered" pedagogies.[4] Interactive pedagogy stipulates that the teacher be responsive to the child in the process of teaching; for example, by engaging in dialogues or conversations instead of lectures. In this section I argue that interactive pedagogy is isomorphic with other aspects of governance in contemporary society. Specifically, I relate interactive pedagogy with Deleuze's (1992) characterization of "societies of control." I suggest that the social technologies inscribed by interactive pedagogy are different from those technologies of previous pedagogies, and so a different sort of educated subject is constructed. Overall, then, the educated subject is produced by the confluence of whole child education, developmentality, and interactive pedagogy.

I anticipate one line of objection by saying that when I analyze the discursive construction of the educated subject, I do not imply any sort of determinism. I am not talking about how institutional demands dominate people. Rather, I am talking about educational practices that may appear to be exercises of freedom but, on closer examination, turn out to be repetitions and reiterations of the status quo. I believe that any given moment of education is comprised of myriad and varied dynamics—more than can be accounted for in any theoretical sweep, regardless of how broad or inclusive. So I do not mean to suggest that the discursive confluence of the whole child, developmentality, and interactionism is in any sense totalizing or inevitable; my analysis is limited, narrow, and focused on one particular constellation of practices. I mean to suggest that at the historical moments when these particular discourses do converge—and this could happen in a classroom, in a policy, in a research design, or in a textbook—the convergence embodies consequences of power relations that may be unintended and unproblematized. The analysis of this chapter is an attempt to interrupt these unproblematized exercises of power. Therefore, in the conclusion I suggest that flexible is not necessarily free, developmentality is not necessarily appropriate, and interaction is not necessarily democratic, although in some instances, democracy and/or freedom may indeed be served.

When the educated subject is analyzed as a product of discursive technologies, the workings of power at the level of subject become susceptible to critique. The critique is an attempt to effect a more nuanced view of the relations among educational practices that embody assumptions about the whole child, developmentality, and interactionism. In that way, those of us who engage in educational practices may become more aware of the ways discourses have already shaped our thinking about what it means to teach and to learn.

Responsive Desire as the Substance to Be Educated

The thrust of whole child education is that the child's entire being—desire, attitudes, wishes—is caught up in the educative process. Educating the whole child means educating not only the cognitive, affective, and behavioral aspects but also the child's innermost desires. There must be no residue of reluctance to learning; success for whole child education means not only that the child learns but the child desires to learn and is happy to learn. No aspect of the child must be left uneducated; education touches the spirit, soul, motivation, wishes, desires, dispositions, and attitudes of the child to be educated.

The substance to be educated in this discourse is unlike the substance of other historical moments, which focused on, for example, aesthetic sensibility, religious spirit, and deductive cogito. Nineteenth-century educational reform was concerned primarily with intellect, moral behavior, and citizenship, so curricula and pedagogies were designed to cultivate the intellect, discipline behavior, and encourage social responsibility. Today, classroom management techniques generally maintain intellectual, behavioral, and civilizing disciplines, but more recent reforms have tended to assert that intellectual mastery and behavioral compliance are not enough. The current substance to be educated is constituted by fears, wishes, aspirations, attitudes, inclinations, and pleasures. Educational goals now require that students be "motivated" and have a "positive attitude." I argue that the recent education of desire—motivation, attitudes, fears, wishes, and dispositions—suggests a shift from previous targets of education and therefore a shift in the construction of the educated subject.

Changes in the meaning of the word "motivation" can illustrate this shift. Motivation has been a concept in educational psychology for decades, but its meaning has changed in accordance with other changes in educational discourse. Motivation was inscribed in early twentieth-century psychological discourses of behaviorism, in which motivation was defined, evaluated, and cultivated through reinforcement and punishment of physical acts. This construction rendered motivation understandable in terms of a mechanistic cause and effect. In later discourses of cognitivism, motivation was understood in one of two ways. A child's motivation could be understood in moralistic terms, referring to the essential tendency of a child to do good or to learn or to please. Otherwise, motivation could be conceived as being more instrumental; a child would act or think out of self-interest or rational choice when the consequences of various positions were explained.[5] More recently, however, motivation has been inscribed in discourses of temperament, attachment theory, and relationships. In these more recent constructions, motivation is explained in terms of feelings, love, fear, hope, pleasure, and aspiration. These aspects of the whole child (or sometimes "inner child") constitute new targets of educational technologies—new educated subjects—and construct the substance to be educated as the "soul."

Evidence of the ways the soul is being constructed in education can be found in various pedagogical techniques. For example, in "metacognitive monitoring," a student is not only required to solve a math (or writing, or science) problem but also to reflect on and attest to the motivational steps involved in that computation: "Why do you want to do that?" Some forms of reflective and autobiographical learning, such as writing journals, require allocutions of a student's attitudinal or affective state as a part of the learning process: "Describe a personal story in which you felt like the character in the book." Similarly, in teacher education, reflective and autobiographical research methodologies construct the educated soul in the process of becoming a teacher.[6] In "constructivist" approaches, a teacher or student participates actively in the construction of an identity that includes desire to participate— usually referred to as motivation—as an essential aspect. Resnick (1998) advocates "knowledge-based constructivism" in which the "core pedagogy" is understood to include "meta-cognitive learning" and "self-monitoring." Character education, which regulates affect and disposition, is replacing behavioral modification, which regulates actions, as a pedagogical technique. David Elkind (1996) has begun a new study: "We are presently gathering data on a new instrument called the Personal Fable Scale, which will assess young people's sense of specialty, their sense of invulnerability, and their propensity for risk taking" (p. 82).[7] Finally, complex batteries of standardized tests and assessment portfolios, no longer limited to assessing an informational knowledge base, have been developed to measure students' and teachers' attitudes, self-discipline, personality, disposition, type and levels of motivation, and willingness to adapt.

Jacques Donzelot analyzes an analogous phenomenon with regard to the creation of pleasure in a working identity:

> It is not a question here of creating joy through work (nor joy despite work), but of producing pleasure and work, and, so as better to realize this design, of producing the one in the other. (Donzelot, 1991, p. 280)

Both Foucault (1990) and Rose (1989) use the term "soul" to refer to aspects of humanity that were previously sacrosanct but that have recently been constructed as objects of psychological and regulatory apparatuses. The term soul deliberately alludes to what have been held as the innermost qualities of being human; Rose uses this term to emphasize the depth to which modern technologies of discipline have extended. Aspects of the soul[8] have become the focus of considerable research and attention, especially since the 1950s when "[n]on-intellectual behaviour was . . . rendered into thought, disciplined, normalized, and made legible, inscribable, calculable" (Rose, 1989, p. 147) through technologies of psychological observation, measurement, and intervention. Constructions of desire, fear, and pleasure have become teachable technologies of the self.

Educational programs that inscribe aspects of desire, fear, and pleasure as calculable objects of science are generally based on the assumption that such research represents progress in scientific understanding; aspects of the inner self that had been mysterious or vague can be brought to light and rationalized through scientific investigation. Another, less obvious, consequence of this scientific gaze is that it renders more aspects of human life susceptible to educational management. Previous constructions of the educated subject targeted the cogito, natural virtue, or potential citizenship as the substance to be educated. However, fears, desires, and hopes were not similarly rationalized as objects of scientific intervention in educational discourse.[9] Now, curricula are designed to engage a child's soul in order to facilitate its "normal" development.

The discourse of educational psychology has constructed desires, hopes, and fears as rationalizable attributes; significantly, however, as a condition of governance in a liberal democracy, the educated subject is self-disciplined. This means that the reinforcement or the motivation to "have a positive attitude" must be exercised by the self on the self. In order to be recognized— or recognize oneself—as educated, the subject understands and reflexively disciplines desires, feelings, loves, wishes, and fears. The construction of the whole child[10] is a relatively new configuration in educational discourse and inscribes a new target—or substance—for pedagogical technologies and self-discipline. Later in this chapter, I will suggest that the new substance to be educated has normalcy as its object of desire.

Developmentality as the Mode of Subjectification

The substance to be educated has recently undergone changes, and aspects of those changes have been effected in the mode of reasoning deployed to justify educational practices. Quite a bit has already been written about the deployment of psychological reasoning in disciplining and normalizing the self (see, e.g., Herman, 1995; O'Donnell, 1985; Popkewitz, 1991, esp. Chapter 6; Rose, 1989, esp. Chapter 12; Walkerdine,1984). For the purposes of this chapter I analyze only one aspect, namely, the deployment of a specific kind of reasoning that is inscribed in discourses of developmentally appropriate curricula. I focus on developmentally appropriate curricula not because they are the source or origin of power but because educational literature so frequently deploys the language of developmental appropriateness to justify curricula and practices. Developmentally appropriate curricula claim scientific validity because the curriculum design is purportedly based on the results of scientific study in developmental psychology.

Developmental psychology has become increasingly complicated and nuanced since its inception a century ago (Walkerdine, 1984).[11] Throughout its increasing complexity, many strands of developmental psychology have tended to retain their claims as empirical science through methodological commitment to observation, experimentation or field study, statistical analysis, and interpretation of findings. Methodologies in developmental psychology have also become more diverse, including nonverbal, dynamic-model, and context-specific approaches. Significantly, developmental psychology has expanded its scope of observable objects to include aspects of the inner child and the soul.

I understand developmental psychology as a discourse that constructs human growth and change in scientific terms.

Developmental psychology per se is a scientific discourse, but in this chapter, I focus on the ways developmental psychology is brought into educational discourse through curriculum design. Much educational literature takes for granted the legitimacy of relying on developmental psychology to justify a curricular design; however, in this chapter, I problematize the tacit acceptance of developmental psychology in education as a means of legitimating specific curricular or pedagogic reforms. In this way, I investigate how developmental psychology functions not as a descriptive science but rather as an instrument of authorization or validation. In effect, then, the findings of developmental psychology are not treated as objects of science to be questioned or tested; rather, they are deployed as rationalistic, a priori truths upon which a curriculum can be designed or evaluated according to its degree of appropriateness. Findings of developmental psychology are assumed; they function as Cartesian proof texts for the design and reform of curriculum. Insofar as curriculum design unquestioningly appropriates the findings of developmental psychology as truth, that curriculum makes a characteristically modern (and Deweyan) leap, namely that science, particularly psychology, is the appropriate foundation for curriculum design. When the findings of empirical science are used as the basis or justification for curriculum design, educational discourse conflates rationalism and science in its discursive practices.

Under what circumstances did this conflation become possible? Historically, the deployment of psychology in education occurred together with the deployment of efficient (or "scientific") management and behaviorism. This particular discursive configuration constructs a mode of subjectification I call developmentality in order to convey the workings of power through discourse:

> In the complex web they have traced out for us, the truths of science and the powers of experts act as relays that bring the values of authorities and the goals of business [schools] into contact with the dreams and actions of us all. These technologies for the government of the soul operate not through the crushing of subjectivity in the interests of control and profit, but by seeking to align political, social, and institutional goals with individual pleasures and desires, and with the happiness and fulfillment of the self. . . . They are precisely therapies of freedom. (Rose, 1989, p. 257)

The purpose of my analysis is to historicize the shifts in various modes of subjectification that have all been termed "reason" or "rationalism"; it does not essentialize the meaning of rationalism as if there were such a reified thing. In this section I analyze four aspects of developmentality that are embedded in current curricular discourses: developmentally appropriate objectives, the definition of normal, the mind-body dualism, and social constructionism. This critical analysis highlights the ways developmentality, in its language of justification, exercises power and normalization in the construction of a specific regime of truth.

Developmentally Appropriate Objectives

Today, it is virtually impossible for educators to imagine a syllabus[12] without the concept of "objectives." Since the 1960s, educational encyclopedia and handbook definitions of syllabus have included the assertion that "a syllabus begins with a statement of objectives." However, writing syllabi in terms of objectives is a relatively recent innovation. Educational objectives were formally inaugurated into curricular design with the publication of B. S. Bloom's *Taxonomy of Educational Objectives,* in which volume one (1956) specified cognitive objectives, volume two (1964) focused on affective objectives, and volume three (1966) was devoted to psychomotor objectives (see also Eraut, 1989). In the nineteenth century, syllabi were written in terms of questions and exercises that the students were supposed to know. Beginning in the 1870s, the syllabus began to include suggestions for readings. At the turn of the century, there was evidence of a notion of educational goals, but objectives were not stipulated formally or stated explicitly.

Before education was conceived in terms of outcomes, it was conceived in terms of procedures. Before the 1960s, for example, syllabi were organized according to procedural steps: "first write the new vocabulary on the board, then pronounce each word," and so on. The shifts in the organization of syllabi inscribe broader historical shifts from procedure-driven to goal-driven governance. For example, the procedure-driven pattern of organization is commensurate with Fordist assembly lines, which were explained as a series of ordered steps or procedures. In the case of procedure-based syllabi, the sequence of steps is stipulated, so the teacher is not free to improvise a method or approach; the steps on the assembly line are fixed. In procedure-driven governance, the outcome is unspecified and undetermined; the methodological steps are controlled, but the outcome is not explicitly stated. In contrast, when syllabi began to be written in terms of objectives, the converse was the case. Objective-driven syllabi leave the procedure unspecified but the eventual outcome is stated explicitly. Pedagogies are evaluated on the degree to which they attain the explicitly stated predetermined objectives. Objective-driven syllabi are commensurate with bottom-line management, target quotas, and outcome-based mechanisms in related fields. Goal steering in social and political sectors is often (vulgarly) called "pragmatism," in which the means are subordinated to—and determined by—the goals. In all of these technologies, the mechanism of governance is not procedure driven but objective driven.

The shift to objective-driven syllabi in educational discourse is historically related to behaviorism. The system of reasoning inscribed by behaviorism requires that the desired outcome—the response—be known and articulated in advance. In this system of reasoning, learning is redefined so that it comes to mean the fulfillment of predetermined objectives. Learned responses are really a form of demonstrated compliance. Learning shifted its meaning: Enlightenment learning was conceived as a discovery process that went from the unknown to the known; modern learning is more of an integrative process that goes from the known to the internalized. In this learning paradigm, teachers must have a clear idea of which behaviors to reinforce in order to be able to teach. Students are not expected to discover what was previously unknown; rather they are expected to internalize what is already known.[13]

In the 1990s, what is already known is a post-Fordist productive capacity for flexibility and a positive, willing attitude. The developmental goals, then, are different from the Taylorist/Fordist goals of fixed-role efficiency. Recent developmental goals of the curriculum reinscribe historically specific values of flexibility and desire to adapt. Curricular objectives serve as the mode of subjectification that construct a flexible and responsive educated subject. When this mode of subjectification is put together with the educative substance of desire and the power relations of governmentality, then the educated subject is one who freely disciplines the innermost aspects of the self to comply with the developmental objectives of society in order to be educated.

Normal

There has also been a crucial historical shift in the meaning of normality.[14] The term "normal" was first used in a medical discourse and then transferred to social sciences following the work of Comte (Hacking, 1990). From the beginning, pathological was defined in opposition to healthy. Before 1800, pathology was the central and specified term, and healthy was the general or default condition; anything that was not designated pathological was assumed to be healthy. The desirable condition, then, was not specified, not circumscribed, and the possibilities for ways of being healthy were theoretically unlimited. After 1800 however, in scientific and social scientific discourse, the term "normal" became the central and specified term in opposition to "pathological." Moreover, the specifications for the term were constituted in a measurable population, either in terms of an average or socially defined virtue. In this definition, anything that could not be specifically defined as normal/average was then regarded as pathological or not-normal. In this newer sense, then, the possibilities for being normal are theoretically limited and circumscribed as those characteristics that are average or common; in contrast, the possibilities for being not-normal are theoretically limitless. Even the shift in terminology—from pathological to not-normal—connotes the shift in specificity and determination.

Normalization operates through the discourse of developmentality when the generalizations that stipulate normal development are held to be defined and desirable, and all departures from that circumscribed stipulation are held to be not-normal or deviant. The generalization serves—more or less explicitly—as the norm, and the lives of individual children are evaluated with reference to that norm. The analytical generalization takes precedence over the broad range of variations by calling some statistically specified ways of being normal and assuming all other ways of being are not-normal.

Educational discourses that advocate developmentally appropriate curricula reinscribe the knowledge and assumptions that were constructed by historical power relations. For example, early twentieth-century developmental psychology specified patterns of development that varied depending on race, based on established nineteenth-century scientific assumptions about racially specific natures. Indications of developmental stage were measured, for example, by phrenology (see Gould, 1981). More recent renditions of developmental psychology specify development in terms of "critical metatheoretical reflection" (Teo, 1997) in which a child is expected to develop the reflexive capacity to monitor his/her own development.[15] Developmental psychology and the developmentally appropriate curricula that are based on it both inscribe historically specific understandings of the parameters of development.

In this way, developmentally appropriate curricula normalize the educated subject in discourse. These days, the reasoning inscribed in questions of developmental appropriateness assumes that "normal" pertains to a specific set of qualities that have been rationalized by statistical and scientific justifications. Conversely, any qualities other than those so specified are assumed to be not-normal.

Mind/Body

Seventeenth-century Cartesian rationalism drew a strict line between reason, which was of the mind, and feelings or sensations, which were of the body. Cartesian consciousness, which consisted of deduction and intuition,[16] was the substance to be educated. Consciousness was the natural repository of god-given reason, and education targeted the consciousness in order that the educated subject be able to distinguish the reasonable/godly/true from the unreasonable/ungodly/false. For Descartes, all appetites, feelings, emotions, sensations, and even imagination belonged to the domain of the body, which was subject not to reason but to its own mechanical and physiological laws and therefore not subject to education.

This contrasts sharply with recent discourses of developmentality in which affect and emotion are construed as aspects to be educated. The history of developmental psychology has been described as "the expansion of the initially narrow and biologically-oriented concept of development into a more comprehensive and liberal one" (Weinert, 1996, p. 1). The line that distinguishes mind from body has been redrawn. The use of the term "liberal" in this construction puts an emancipatory spin on the "expansion" of regulatory capacities that are possible in developmentality.

The "comprehensive" feature of developmental psychology refers to the expansion of approaches from psychoanalytic and cognitive to "socioemotional" development (Weinert, 1996, p. 6). Jerome Kagan (1994) describes the new developmentalist studies as having a focus on "temperament," which includes fear, timidity, and frustration. John H. Flavell's (1994) predictions for the future of developmental psychology point to studies of the inner world of the child: "When knowledge and abilities are subtracted from the totality of what could legitimately be called 'cognitive,' an important remainder is surely the person's subjective experience: *how self and world seem and feel* to that person, given that knowledge and those abilities" (Flavell, 1994, p. 582, emphasis added). Finally, the recent popularity of "attachment theory" (Ainsworth and Bowlby, 1991) inscribes the developmentalist focus on the psychology of love. In each case, the multiplication and discovery of new aspects of human being that can be described, measured, evaluated, and improved are celebrated as indications of scientific progress and advances in knowledge.

This developmentalist concern with the construction of desire contrasts strikingly with the focus of Cartesian rationalism, which was constructed as godly, and limited to conscious faculties of intuition and deductive reasoning. Throughout this century, developmentalist discourses have begun to focus on psychological aspects other than cognition and behavior. The more recent developmentalist construction of desire, in discursive connection with the normalizing effects of statistical reasoning, constructs a relatively new target of education, namely the subjective desire to be normal.

Social Construction

Another aspect of a current mode of subjectification is the relationship between the individual and the social that is inscribed in the discourse of developmentality. Developmentality has construed individual development increasingly in terms of the social. Resnick's (1998) and other constructivist learning theories—including some deployments of Vygotskian psychology—propose that all cognitive development ought to be understood in social terms because all knowledge is understood to be socially constructed. Even arithmetic calculation is understood to be a constructed process insofar as different people use different strategies to do arithmetic, and a variety of strategies can only be learned through contact with a variety of people in society. In intellectual fields outside the psychology of Piaget and Vygotsky, research characterizes— more or less critically—modern subjective development in terms of social development, including Durkheim's (1961) "moral education," Elias's (1978) "civilizing process," and Foucault's (1991) "governmentality."

Beginning after World War II, however, the constellations of relations began to suggest a reconfiguration in the meaning of the social. This reconfiguration consists of shifts away from fixed social roles, Fordist production techniques, procedure-driven regimes of regulation, and homogeneous categories of social identity. Deleuze (1992) goes so far as to term this "the death of the social."

The changes in the scope of psychological development are demonstrated in the sequential appropriations of the work of two major contributors to developmental psychology, first Jean Piaget and then Lev Vygotsky.[17] A Piagetian term that describes using knowledge to understand the world is "assimilation"; and his term that describes learning about the constraints of the world is "accommodation" (see, e.g., Weinert, 1996, p. 5). Moreover:

> The innate tendency to search continuously for a better balance between
> the two processes of assimilation and accommodation is the foundation
> of the fundamental mechanism of self-regulation, which directs and
> maintains cognitive development. (Weinert, 1996, p. 5)

This Piagetian epistemology constructs knowledge as a relation between the individual and the external world. Nevertheless, Piagetian theories in education still construct the psychological subject as an independent individual, and development as an "intrapsychic process that is largely independent of social interaction and social-cultural contexts" (Weinert, 1996, p. 5).

This Piagetian type of social independence is transmuted in the subsequent discourses of developmental psychology that refer to Vygotsky. Although Piaget and Vygotsky were contemporaries, Vygotsky's work has only recently (1980s and 1990s) gained popularity in the United States. So why is Vygotsky now more fashionable than Piaget? This relatively recent reception of Vygotsky (re)inscribes the discursive shift to a particular form of the social construction of development, namely one that is constituted through social interaction:

> In this [Vygotskian] perspective, higher psychological functions are nei-
> ther "implanted" in the child through social transmission nor developed
> independently of social-cultural contexts. Instead, social interaction and
> instruction in shared, goal-directed action contexts provide the tools for
> change that the child must then actively interiorize and transform. (Wei-
> nert, 1996, p. 6)

Psychological constructions of the individual-social relation ascribed to Vygotsky depart from those ascribed to Piaget insofar as Vygotskian knowledge
cannot be regarded as the "intrapsychic" phenomenon that Piagetian knowledge is. The construction of knowledge inscribed in a Vygotskian discourse is
one in which social interaction constitutes the basis for an individual's knowledge; this is what "socially constructed" means in this schema. Development,
then, becomes inscribed in an interactionist discourse in which interactions
(or in some approaches, "relationships") constitute the basis for knowledge in
general and specifically for knowledge of the self. This discursive relation is
another technology that constructs the self as a social entity.

    Another example of the construction of the self as a social entity is the
discourse of culturally appropriate curricula. In a troubling way, the discourse
of culturally appropriate curricula reinscribes the discursive patterns of developmentally appropriate curricula.[18] "Developmentally appropriate" and
"culturally appropriate" may appear to be disparate terms, but they play homologous roles in the exercise of power through curricular technologies. Both
expressions are constructed in terms of populational referents; both are understood as generalizations that apply to sociological categories—in the first
case of age and in the second case of culture. Both discourses function in a
recursive way to define and reconstitute the populational categories that they
allegedly describe. Developmentally appropriate and culturally appropriate
curricula are progressively motivated discourses that attempt to resist domination while they recognize and affirm alternative ways of being. At the same
time, both discourses construct normative standards and regulatory pedagogies that normalize particular educated subjects. For example, Gilligan (1982)
states, "the sequential ordering of identity and intimacy in the transition from
adolescence to adulthood better fits the development of men than it does the
development of women" (p. 163). This essentializes the meaning of "woman"
as one who values intimacy and caring. In multicultural education, Sleeter
(1993) documents that "cooperative learning" (as opposed to "whole class or
individual teaching strategies") is "culturally compatible" with minority
"learning styles." While the recommendations are intended to counteract the
injustices of racism, the discourse simultaneously essentializes minority students as different from white students and also as homogeneous in terms of
learning styles. The systems of reasoning that constitute the meanings of appropriate inscribe historically specific power relations and have the effect of
normalizing possibilities for educated subjectivity.

Regimen of Interactionism

In the previous section I analyzed the curricular discourses of developmentality that normalize what is considered to be developmentally appropriate.

Now, in this section, I focus on the pedagogical discourse that is shared by interactive pedagogy and interactive development, which, for convenience, I call interactionism. I regard interactionism as a pedagogical technology that constructs the meaning of educated and, simultaneously, as a technology of the self that constructs the self to be educated. Interactive pedagogy is a technology of the late twentieth century.[19]

Interactive pedagogy is posited as the pragmatic solution to the unsatisfactory alternatives of child-centered and teacher-centered pedagogies. Bredekamp (1993) writes that the literature "frequently oversimplify[ies] the teacher's role to a dichotomy between teacher-directed and child-initiated learning. The reality is far more complex and far more interesting" (p. 16). In interactive pedagogy, the teacher does not lecture (that would be teacher centered), and the child does not independently pursue his/her interests (that would be child centered). Rather, the teacher teaches by adapting the material to the children's momentary interests and imparts information at a pace that is set by the children's questions. This pedagogy requires the teacher to respond flexibly to the child's feelings, words, and actions.

Developmental psychology, itself, also posits a theory of interactive development. It is a theoretical construct to deal with the perennial nature/nurture problem, or in the language of developmental psychology, the "two equally unsatisfactory alternatives of socially-autonomous development and socially-determined development." In attachment theory, for example, "the attachment system was conceived as being neither innate nor entirely predetermined; instead, its course is determined by social interaction, that is, it grows through feedback in response to active behavior" (Weinert, 1996, pp. 6–7).

Because an interaction (both in interactive pedagogy and interactive development) is described as neither child directed nor teacher directed, it may appear that the interaction is autonomous or free form and not directed at all. However, I argue that interactionism is itself a disciplinary technology. This discourse of interactionism constitutes a technology of the self whose particular sort of flexibility is response-able and response-ready. Moreover, the identity of the response-able and response-ready subject is keyed to developmentally appropriate norms.

At the level of teacher-student or teacher-child interaction, interactionism constructs both a response-able/-ready child and a response-able/-ready teacher. On the one hand, the teacher's words and actions are responsive to the child's words and actions; on the other hand, the teacher's (inter)actions serve as a model of the preferred, normal, and developmentally appropriate outcome to the child. The interactive agenda is not specified in advance, in order to allow for flexible interaction in the classroom. However, interactive pedagogy is usually combined with developmentally appropriate curricula in classroom practices. The interaction may seem to be open-ended, but the objectives of the curriculum are specified in advance and justified by appeals to developmental psychology. So sometimes in educational practices, inter-actionism combines with developmentality in ways that embody unintended disciplinary effects.

The two-part construction of this notion of pedagogy is significant: de-velopmentally appropriate and interactive. It may seem that the discourse of interactionism and the discourse of developmentality are autonomous trends, but they are not. Interactionism and developmentality are flip sides of the same coin, in a way that is analogous to the relation between freedom and self-discipline in a modern liberal democracy.[20] This relation pertains to changes in historical social relations. Specifically, traditional (premodern) re-lations were characterized by a predominance of coercive force implemented by the sovereign on the subjects. Modern relations, on the other hand, do not rely on the forceful domination of a sovereign, but rely instead on a construc-tion of citizenship in which freedom is understood to mean that the individual takes responsibility for self-discipline: "Fundamentally modern is exactly 'the idea that we construct our own social identity' " (Wagner, 1994, p. 157, quot-ing Martin Hollis). Modern freedom is an effect of governmentality in which the self, acting responsively and reflexively, disciplines itself to become the socially constituted self. Analogously, interactive pedagogy is practiced in re-lation to the developmental norms that—implicitly or explicitly—drive the interactions. In the 1990s, interactionism is a historically specific approach that is isomorphic with a whole raft of interrelated discourses that can be characterized as fluid, dynamic, situation responsive, pragmatic, and virtual.

Interactive pedagogy and developmentality are analytically separable, but I regard them as historically inseparable in order to examine the effects of their simultaneous deployment. Interactive pedagogies provide a way to moni-tor development at frequent intervals, and developmentally appropriate out-comes provide standards for quantitative evaluation. More importantly, de-velopmentality and interactionism typically coexist in contemporary educational discourse, but the effects of their simultaneous deployment are rarely explored. The procedures used in interactive pedagogies may appear to be free because they are not specified in advance; but the success of a pedagogy is evaluated according to the degree to which the specified objective is achieved. The procedure may be flexible, but the outcome is ironically predetermined. Flexible interactive pedagogies are not necessarily instances of freedom or emancipation but rather effective and efficient technologies for attaining predetermined, socially stipulated objectives.

It is significant, then, that the developmental goals are specified and in-tegrated into the pedagogical discourse, more or less explicitly. And because the developmental goals are specified, there is no theoretical possibility for the subject to have any features or characteristics other than those specified as normal—as defined by their developmental appropriateness. The notion of flexibility, then, may pertain to the course of interaction. However, there can be no flexibility or variation in the outcome per se; the outcome of current pedagogies is paradoxically limited to a response-able and response-ready subject.

The construction of the response-ready subject is exercised through various discursive technologies that are recognizable in educational fields. For example,

> The roles of the teacher are discussed . . . again as part of an integrated conceptualization of the educational system. . . . Among the concepts encompassed in a discussion of the roles of the teacher are relationship, reciprocity, co-construction, research, collaboration, partnership, observation (in the active sense), and documentation. (Bredekamp, 1993, p. 16)

Interactive pedagogies construct flexible subjects in subtle and nuanced ways. The rhetoric of interactionism gives the impression that a teacher's response to a child is driven by the child's stimulus. In educational literature that refers to interactive pedagogy, there is seldom any acknowledgement that a response is governed by multiple discourses—scientific, political, aesthetic, pragmatic, and ethical—including the discourses of developmentality. Further, the shift from procedure-driven to objective-driven mechanisms of regulation gives the impression that governance has somehow been lifted or diminished. However, interactionism and developmentality are not necessarily instances of newfound emancipation and democratization. They are also instances of new technologies of governance, discipline, and normalization.

Again, I am not arguing that people are determined by these discourses. I do not draw any conclusions about the multiple and various ways people engage in educational practices (e.g., compliance, negotiation, rebellion, amusement, forbearance, and critique); that is not the focus of my investigation. Rather, I focus on the system of reasoning that tacitly permeates educational discourse practices when developmentality converges with interactionism. I investigate the productive effects of that system of reasoning on what it is possible to think of as educated.

Societies of Control

Deleuze has analyzed a very recent and emerging form of governance as "societies of control" in contrast to "societies of discipline":

> The administrations in charge never cease announcing supposedly necessary reforms: to reform schools, to reform industries, hospitals, the

armed forces, prisons. But everyone knows that these institutions are finished, whatever the length of their expiration periods. It's only a matter of administering their last rites and of keeping people employed until the installation of the new forces knocking at the door. These are the *societies of control*, which are in the process of replacing the disciplinary societies. (Deleuze, 1992, p. 4, emphasis in original)

The contrast between "disciplinary society" and "control society" inscribes many of the aspects that distinguish modernity from postmodernity. Governance in modern democracies could be characterized as governmentality, as in Foucault's work, and the society could be characterized as a society of discipline. However, Deleuze suggests that new or emerging patterns of power relations are sufficiently distinct from the relations of modernity, that a society of discipline no longer pertains to all aspects of society, and that the emerging power relations constitute societies of control. I understand Deleuze's control society as different from a disciplinary society in three respects that are elaborated throughout this section. To summarize briefly: first, both discipline and control societies are characterized by the self-monitoring gaze; however, in a control society the monitoring is more frequent and continuous than in a disciplinary society. Second, standards in a disciplinary society tend to be fairly centralized and long lasting; however, standards in a control society are more heterogeneous and quickly changing. Finally, a disciplinary society afforded the promise of closure or completion of a project; however, a control society offers no possibility of closure or completion.

The first salient aspect of the disciplinary society that is now different in the control society is in the nature and rhythm of its regulatory mechanisms. In a disciplinary society, the outcome or product may be evaluated only once, perhaps by a final exam or quality control unit at the end or completion of a session. At the end of the term or assembly line, students or factory products are inspected, tested, and evaluated. The members of a disciplinary society are self-disciplined and productive members of society.

According to Deleuze, monitoring in a control society is more frequent than in a disciplinary society. A control society is characterized by "continuous monitoring": "Indeed, just as the corporation replaces the factory, *perpetual training* tends to replace the school, and *continuous control* to replace the examination" (Deleuze, 1992, p. 5, first emphasis in original; second emphasis added). In schools, there is evidence of a shift from grading on the basis of a final exam to grading many more frequent tests throughout the semester. Smaller, weekly papers are replacing the one big research paper required in previous decades. The popularity of an increased frequency of monitoring was also evident in the U.S. presidential race in 2000. In his campaign, George W. Bush publicly and emphatically criticized Al Gore for proposing a national education program that required high-stakes examinations for students every three to four years, while Bush's program would require the exams every year. Interactionism as a pedagogical technique constitutes continuous monitoring; the discourse directs attention to each turn of dialogue—each interaction—in a way that is more frequent than previous lecture-based or discussion-based pedagogies. The shift in frequency of monitoring is evident in fields other than education, including the move in economics when a fixed gold standard was replaced by floating rates of exchange; in criminology, electronic tracking devices are locked onto prisoners rather than having prisoners locked up in a (fixed place) prison; and in business, marketing in the form of continuous multimedia advertising is replacing brand-name loyalty and market niches.

The second aspect is in the heterogeneity of standards in a control society. Standards in a disciplinary society could be regarded as relatively centralized or uniform. In contrast, a control society is one in which "standards and demands can come from anywhere at any time, in any form" (Ball, 1999). For example, a school curriculum is no longer accountable only to school board criteria of education. School curricula are now also answerable to local businesses, churches, parents' groups, social service providers, psychiatrists, and police forces. In order to manage a classroom, teachers must be familiar with a wide range of experts in order to make appropriate referrals for children to social services, parent representatives, community liaisons, and legal services. Education must be understood to serve a multicultural, multilingual, and culturally fragmented constituency. In some places, school curricula are influenced by the McDonalds or Taco Bell franchises that operate in the school lunchrooms (Kaplan, 1996).

According to Deleuze, the final contrast between the discipline society and the control society is in the possibility for completion. In a disciplinary society, one could graduate or be promoted to another rank. However, in a control society, completion is not an option:

> In the disciplinary societies, one was always starting again . . . , while in the societies of control one is never finished with anything—the corporation, the educational system, the armed services being metastable states coexisting in one and the same modulation, like a universal system of deformation. (Deleuze, 1992, p. 5)

The notion of "never finished" is also inscribed in recent developmentalist programs of whole-life and life span development, as well as in lifelong learning and continuing education programs in schooling. One never graduates; one never completes an education.

These features of the control society—never finished, heterogeneous standards, and continuous monitoring—are evident in pedagogies that purport to be developmentally appropriate. However, these features are also evident in other sorts of pedagogies that purport to be critical or alternative, and that appeal to justifications other than science or developmentality such as moral education and critical pedagogy.[21] Such pedagogical approaches typically include having students write several short papers during the semester rather than one long paper at the end of the course. In addition to a greater frequency of monitoring, the pedagogies include the notion of being never finished. "Never finished" contrasts with modern Taylorist-based pedagogies that construct learning in terms of discrete and finishable units. More recently, pedagogies construct learning as in process or incomplete or lifelong.

Aspects of a control society are inscribed in diverse pedagogical approaches, whether or not they use the explicit terminology of desire, developmentality, or interactionism. Sometimes the features of continuous monitoring and never finished are articulated with such terminology as "the postmodern condition," "on-line interaction," "site-based management," "decentralization," "pragmatic response modes," and "multiple and shifting subject positions." In any case, the mode of subjectification and the stipulated outcome of pedagogical technologies no longer inscribes the fixed role, coherent identity, unidirectional development that is characteristic of modernity and the disciplinary society.

Flexible Conclusions

The use of the term "flexible" to describe methods—management, pedagogy, diagnosis—and to describe the subjective outcome—educated subject, worker, facilitator—gives the impression that regulations have been lifted, or that more possibilities have been opened. I argue, instead, that flexible and interactive technologies are constituted in historical relation to developmentally defined outcomes. In this historical relation, the education of flexible souls does not necessarily constitute an instance of emancipation, release, or empowerment. Rather, the educated subject is produced as the effect of the confluence of current discursive practices.

In one aspect, the definition of "flexible" has come to mean response-ready and response-able; and the definition of "freedom" has come to mean the capacity and responsibility for self-discipline. Obviously, response-ready cannot be an autonomous state; there must be a "stimulus" to prompt the response. In current discourses, however, the stimuli are also flexible, meaning various and changing. There is no fixed or specified source or pattern of stimuli; if there were, the corresponding subject would not have to be response-ready, just obedient to some designated authority. Response-ready is a mutable and dynamic subject position, but it is a very specific subject position, one that is effected by current historical power relations and normalized in educational discourse.

The current discourse of developmentality is also constitutive of this historical moment. Its methods are changing in order to respond to changes in context and focus; the entities of development have expanded from cognition to affect, temperament, self-esteem, and love. These words have been used for decades in educational psychology, but the meanings are different now that they are inscribed in current discourse practices. There is now a developmental analysis of the stages of critical thinking.[22] The discursive construction of "normal" allows for the expert definition of desirable traits, and all nonspecified possibilities are not-normal by default. "Normal" has a meaning other than "average" or "common," though. "Normal" also has the meaning of correct, right, ideal, healthy, and moral. This double-barreled deployment of "normal" has allowed for some remarkable effects:

> The normal stands indifferently for what is typical, the unenthusiastic objective average, but it also stands for what has been, good health, and for what shall be, our chosen destiny. That is why the benign and sterile-sounding word "normal" has become one of the most powerful ideological tools of the twentieth century. (Hacking, 1990, p. 169)

This deployment of "normal" is characteristic of most of the twentieth century; however, the corresponding historical changes in substance, mode of justification, and practices render the recent meaning of "normal" as different from earlier meanings.

The historical correlate of developmentally specified outcomes is interactionism. Interactionism also inscribes the flavors of the moment: dynamic, fluid, and responsive. Interactive pedagogy provides for continuous monitoring—and modeling—for the construction of a response-ready and response-able subject. Interactionism and developmentality both imply continuous and never-ending responsive change. Donzelot (1991) writes that the new discourse invites the person "to become 'an agent of change in a world of change' " (p. 252). However, change cannot be regarded as free floating or power free. Rather, changes are effected by the discursive regimes that constitute what counts as change and what can be recognized as a response.

In a sense, this genealogical approach—in which essentialized assumptions are historicized and problematized—is a way of reconstructing the deployment of "normal" in discourse. In the discourse of developmentality since 1800, "normal" has been the central and specified term to the effect that there are infinite possibilities for being not-normal. As a critical move, the genealogical approach takes "normalized" as its central and specified term to the effect that there are infinite possibilities for being not-normalized. Other possibilities, then, become unbounded and undetermined. Unspecified and unnamed subjectivities are thereby inscribed in the space of the possible and the desirable.

Notes

Thanks especially to Thomas S. Popkewitz, Kenneth Hultqvist, Lisa Hennon, and Thomas Broman for critical comments on earlier versions of this chapter.

[1] By "desire" I do not mean to imply an essential or psychoanalytic drive. I do not assume that there is some innate desire, and that social circumstances can induce a repression or sublimation of that innate faculty. I do not refer to the rationalization of bodily pleasures. Rather, I assume that desire, in all its myriad historical forms, is always produced as an effect of discourse. Therefore, this analysis assumes that power and desire are always present in every discourse, and that historical changes in the relations of languages and practices create different forms of power and desire. I mean to problematize the meaning of desire by analyzing how its meaning is constructed in recent educational discourse.

[2] Early developmental psychology focused on cognitive capabilities, but the scope of features that are analyzable by developmental criteria has increased continuously. The incorporation of affective and dispositional features as being developmental is discussed in the "Responsive Desire as the Substance to Be Educated" section of this chapter.

[3] Efficiency is characteristic of "progressive" educational discourse around 1900 and exemplified by Frederick Taylor's *Principles of Scientific Management*, published in 1911. See Kliebard (1986) for a thorough discussion. Behaviorism also entered educational discourse in the early decades of this century, based on the writings of John B. Watson and Ivan Pavlov.

[4] Teacher-centered pedagogies were deemed too authoritarian to be appropriate for a democratic classroom, and child-centered pedagogies were not practical for classrooms of twenty or more children. In addition, they offered no mechanism for "covering the material" of the course.

[5] The debate between behaviorism and cognitivism is exemplified in the intellectual exchange between B. F. Skinner and Noam Chomsky in 1952.

[6] Some certification and licensing agencies administer assessments (e.g., Wisconsin's "Teacher Perceiver") that measure a person's attitudes, dispositions, and personal feelings about issues in order to determine whether a person is fit to be a teacher.

[7] Interestingly, Elkind identifies this approach as being "postmodern."

[8] Foucault (1988) and Rose (1989) use the term "soul" to indicate "the minutiae of the emotional economy, of ethics, and the management of personal conduct" (Rose, 1989, p. 221).

[9] Hopes and fears were certainly not absent from religious discourses that also shaped education. However, these "inner" features were not constructed in scientific terms until they were subsumed by psychology at the end of the nineteenth century.

[10] The discourses of Comenius and Froebel indicated an idea of whole child; however, earlier ideas of wholeness are not the same as those constructed in the late twentieth century. Recent discourses inscribe wholeness in terms of psychologically defined attributes that were not present in earlier versions of whole child education.

[11] For critical analyses of developmental psychology by developmental psychologists, see, e.g., Teo (1997) and Burman (1994).

[12] For this summary of historical and archival work on syllabus design, I am indebted to Inés Dussel, who kindly and generously shared her research findings with me over e-mail.

[13] Again, to emphasize, I do not mean that any discourse is totalizing or universal. So, I do not mean that new learning is impossible; obviously, it is not impossible. I only mean to say that insofar as the discourses of developmentality and objectives-based syllabi converge, learning is constructed in a way that contrasts with previous constructions of learning.

[14] See Hacking (1990) for a thorough discussion of this historical shift.

[15] I cannot resist quoting the following excerpt from Teo's (1997) article for its shocking irony: "From a liberation point of view, Foucault turned later to subjectivity, and discussed the subject's possibility to install his or her life as a piece of art. On this view, the subject has the possibility to develop an aesthetics of existence, and thus, it becomes possible to develop an individual lifestyle in the area of sexuality, body, and other forms of self-expression. Subjective life can be constructed as a piece of art; resistance can be turned aesthetically. *Could this not be a meaningful research topic for developmental psychology?*" (paragraph 37, on-line version; emphasis added).

[16] For Descartes, intuition is not a "mysterious non-rational faculty." Rather, intuition is a cognitive faculty: "[W]hat Descartes means by intuition is intellectual cognition of the simplest and most direct kind. For the educated seventeenth century reader, the primary connotation of the Latin verb *intueri* which Descartes uses here would have been the quite literal and ordinary meaning of to 'see,' 'gaze at,' or 'look upon' which the verb has in classical usage" (Cottingham, 1986, p. 25).

[17] See Popkewitz (1998) for a comparative discussion of the context and reception of Piaget and Vygotsky in the United States and Russia.

[18] I think of the relationship as troubling because the original formulations of developmentalism by G. Stanley Hall and Edward Thorndike occurred in connection with turn-of-the-century projects of eugenics.

[19] For comparative purposes, it may be useful to mention that the pedagogical regimen of Cartesianism was the catechism, for the Enlightenment it was rhetoric, and the modern practice was recitation (see Fendler, 1999).

[20] See, for example, Popkewitz (1998) for a discussion of "the administration of freedom" and the power relations that constitute liberal democracy.

[21] Ellsworth's (1996) notion of "situated response-ability" pertains to a teacher's accountability, and it has some partial relation to the changes in student-teacher interaction.

[22] See Elder and Paul (1996).

References

Ainsworth, M. D. S., & Bowlby, J. (1991). An ethological approach to personality development. *American Psychologist, 46,* 331–41.

Ball, S. (1999, February 24). Policy sociology: Critical and postmodern perspectives on educational policy. Havens Center Lecture, Madison, WI.

Bredekamp, S. (1993). Reflections on Reggio Emilia. In *Young Children* (a publication of the National Association for the Education of Young Children), 49 (1), 13–17.

Burman, E. (1994). *Deconstructing developmental psychology.* New York: Routledge.

Cottingham, J. (1986). *Descartes.* New York: Basil Blackwell.

Deleuze, G. (1992, Winter). Postscript on the societies of control. *October, 59,* 3–7.

Descartes, R. (1954). *Philosophical writings.* E. Anscombe & P. T. Geach (Trans. and Eds.). New York: Bobbs-Merrill.

Donzelot, J. (1991). Pleasure in work. In G. Burchell, C. Gordon. & P. Miller (Eds.), *The Foucault effect: Studies in governmentality* (pp. 251–80). Chicago: University of Chicago Press.

Durkheim, E. (1961). *Moral education: A study in the theory and application of the sociology of knowledge.* London: Collier Macmillan.

Elder, L., & Paul, R. (1996). Critical thinking: A stage theory of critical thinking: Part I. *Journal of Developmental Education, 20* (1), 34–35.

Elias, N. (1978). *The history of manners: The civilizing process.* (Vol. 1; E. Jephcott, Trans.) New York: Pantheon.

Elkind, D. (1996). *David Elkind: A history of developmental psychology in autobiography* (pp. 71–83). Eds. D. Thompson & J. D. Hogan. Boulder, CO: Westview Press.

Ellsworth, E. (1996). Situated response-ability to student papers. *Theory into Practice, 35* (2),138–43.

Eraut, M. R. (1989). Specifying and using objectives. In M. Eraut (Ed.), *The international encyclopedia of educational technology* (pp. 341–52). New York: Pergamon Press.

Fendler, L. (1999). *The educated subject: Discursive constructions of reason and knowledge in history.* Unpublished doctoral dissertation, University of Wisconsin-Madison.

Flavell, J. H. (1994). Cognitive development: Past, present and future. In R. D. Parke, P. A. Ornstein, J. J. Rieser, & C. Zahn-Waxler (Eds.), *A century of developmental psychology* (pp. 569–87). Washington, DC: American Psychological Association.

Foucault, M. (1988). *The care of the self.* (R. Hurley, Trans.) Vol. 3 of *The history of sexuality.* New York: Random House.

Foucault, M. (1990). *The use of pleasure.* (R. Hurley, Trans.) Vol. 2 of *The history of sexuality.* New York: Random House.

Foucault, M. (1991). Governmentality. In G. Burchell, C. Gordon, & P. Miller (Eds.), *The Foucault effect: Studies in governmentality* (pp. 87–104). Chicago: University of Chicago Press.

Gilligan, C. (1982). *In a different voice: Psychological theory and women's development.* Cambridge, MA: Harvard University Press.

Gould, S. J. (1981). *The mismeasure of man.* New York: W. W. Norton.

Hacking, I. (1990). *The taming of chance.* Cambridge, UK: Cambridge University Press.

Herman, E. (1995). *The romance of American psychology: Political culture in the age of experts.* Berkeley: University of California Press.

Kagan, J. (1994). Yesterday's premises, tomorrow's promises. In R. D. Parke, P. A. Ornstein, J. J. Rieser, & C. Zahn-Waxler (Eds.), *A century of developmental psychology* (pp. 551–68). Washington, DC: American Psychological Association.

Kaplan, G. R. (1996). Profits R us: Notes on the commercialization of America's schools. *Phi Delta Kappan, 7* (3), K1-K12.

Kliebard, H. (1986). *Struggle for the American curriculum.* London: Routledge & Kegan Paul.

O'Donnell, J. M. (1985). *The origins of behaviorism: American psychology, 1870–1920.* New York: New York University Press.

Popkewitz, T. S. (1991). *A political sociology of educational reform: Power/knowledge in teaching, teacher education, and research*. New York: Teachers College Press.

Popkewitz, T. S. (1998). Dewey, Vygotsky, and the social administration of the individual: Constructivist pedagogy as systems of ideas in historical spaces. *American Educational Research Journal, 35* (4), 535–70.

Resnick, L. (1998, November 19). Learning organizations for sustainable education reform. Keynote address, American Education Week, Madison, WI.

Rose, N. (1989). *Governing the soul: The shaping of the private self*. New York: Routledge.

Sleeter, C. E. (1993). How white teachers construct race. In C. McCarthy & W. Chrichlow (Eds.), *Race, identity and representation in education* (pp.157–71). New York: Routledge.

Teo, T. (1997, July/August). Developmental psychology and the relevance of a critical metatheoretical reflection. *Human Development, 40* (4), 195–210.

Wagner, P. (1994). *A sociology of modernity: Liberty and discipline*. New York: Routledge.

Walkerdine, V. (1984). Developmental psychology and the child-centered pedagogy: The insertion of Piaget into early education. In J. Henriques, W. Holloway, C. Urwin, C. Venn, & V. Walkerdine (Eds.), *Changing the subject: Psychology, social regulation, and subjectivity* (pp.154–210). New York: Methuen.

Weinert, S. (1996). A general framework of human development, learning, and instruction in educational perspective. In E. De Corte & F. E. Weinert (Eds.), *International encyclopedia of developmental and instructional psychology*. New York: Pergamon Press.

7

Bringing the Gods and the Angels Back?

A Modern Pedagogical Saga about Excess in Moderation

Kenneth Hultqvist

Introduction

In the normalized view, childhood is the natural space of the child. This space prescribes the limits and the possibilities of being a child as long as it is inscribed in the natural habitat of childhood. For all its advantages, this view of childhood fails to recognize that childhood is a technology that fabricates the child in the "mirror" of the imaginaries, theories, and ways of reasoning that delineates such a space for the child.

Historically, the school has been a major institution of childhood. To be in school or in preschool is a part of a journey, a becoming, that is by definition different from work. This is the historical meaning of childhood as education: to be free from work. Childhood in the twenty-first century is still about a becoming, but the way this becoming is construed is different from the past. Also, there are new patterns of transactions between the major institutions of childhood (e.g., the school, the preschool, and the family) and the practices that were not formerly included in the concept of childhood, for example, today's media industry. My limited purpose in this chapter is to present an overview of how the space of childhood is constructed in today's Swedish educational context. I will also make a few suggestions of how the new regulatory ideals of the child are constructed. "Space," in this context, is used to designate the imaginaries, knowledge, techniques, and institutions that construct the child as a subject and object of childhood.

Until the middle of the 1980's, the obligatory school in Sweden was a centralized and rule-steered system that was supervised by the former Skolöverstyrelsen (the Board of Education). It comprised all levels from the elementary school to the upper secondary school. In the early 1990s the school was formally decentralized and rule steering was replaced with goal-steering procedures.[1] Also, the system expanded and the preschool was formally integrated with the school in 1998. In this expanded and goal-governed system, the national goals and obligations became the task of the government and parliament while their enactment was transferred to the local school authorities, the teachers, the students, and their parents. This is the most obvious feature of today's changes. Perhaps less obvious, the new principles of governing also implied new ways of reasoning about the child. New links were forged between the child, his or her assumed personal aspirations and ambitions, and the national imaginaries embedded in schooling and that link schooling with the national projects of the economy, culture and welfare. These links and this child were not there in advance but had to be envisioned by educational thought and by the art of pedagogy.

From this vantage point, one of the most salient aspects of today's Swedish educational discourse on the child is the move from the child of psychology of the post-World War II period toward a broad conception of the child as the subject of humanistic discourse.[2] Curricula and programs for the school, educational research, and pedagogy somehow rely on visions about a humanistic subject; the undivided/whole subject of cognition, feeling, will, and aesthetics (see, e.g., Skola för bildning, 1992). In the prevalent constructivistic pedagogy, this humanistic subject actively both constructs and organizes his inner and outer worlds. This is a significant shift as it makes the child the locus of change.

In the early 1990s, the humanistic child was officially sanctioned in the governmental report "Skola för Bildning" (School for Bildung) (1992). The report drew on previous conceptions of a humanistic education, in German Bildung, that flourished in Sweden and continental Europe during the nineteenth and early twentieth centuries. In such an education, the growing child was personally engaged in an educational journey, a new becoming. Bildung, in this sense, "means to accomplish something that is not there in advance. Bildung is something that human beings do with themselves, an active endeavor in order to invent themselves, their abilities and judgements as a precondition of freedom. The concept of Bildung has its roots in the mystique of the Middle Ages: man carries the image of God inside him. She, the fallen Angel, is able to develop her abilities through the realization of this imago domine" (see Broady, 1992, p. 348).

This view of humanistic education was for an elite (see Hunter, 1988), but similar views, slightly transposed, entered both the popular school and the preschool during the nineteenth and twentieth centuries, for example, in the shape of Froebelian children's gardens (kindergartens).[3] The growth of the child was compared with the growth of a plant that would be cultivated in the rich soil of a humanistic garden. During the 1920s the garden images lost much of their persuasive power in the Swedish context and were eventually substituted by "the psychological laboratory" and the "psycho-biologically appropriate environment." Alva Myrdal's book *Stadsbarn* (*City-child*) (1935) is a good illustration of this shift. In her book, which was about the construction of a modern preschool, Myrdal disturbed the taken-for-granted boundaries between nature and technology. The bathing in fresh lakes and the enjoying of healthy sunlight at the countryside were substituted by indoor pools and electricity in a city environment.

This transformation of "nature" was part of an ongoing transformation of the Swedish national imaginaries of community, identity, and subjectivity.[4] Nature for the pioneers of school and preschool referred to an ideal way of living and, most succinctly, their ideas were about the natural bonds that were supposed to prevail between people in small communities, in the towns, or at the countryside. Significantly, the early preschool teachers tried to reconcile what they saw as traditional ways of life with the modernizing trends in society. In their vision of the children's garden they saw a means to save the (working-class) child's soul[5] from the disruptive influence of the streets and, generally, from the moral uncertainties of their times (see Hultqvist, 1990). During the 1930s and 1940s, industrialization moved ahead and efforts were made to mobilize the people for an industrial society. A series of government programs were developed to change the people's hearts and minds.[6] In the process, the garden image of community and the child was "industrialized" and technology, formally opposed to nature, became the natural means to realize the nation's resources, material as well as human. The pastoral image of nature continued to play an essential role, but new lines were drawn and the man-made nature now figured as an extension of the naturalness of the child. It was this new configuration of thought, the social engineering of the soul, that made possible the idea of a People's Home.

The People's Home was a pedagogical and rhetorical device that was invented and used in the early 1930s to mobilize support for the vision of an industrialized society (see Hultqvist, 1990).[7] It united the idea of a gemeinschaft of a traditional society (the pastoral visions of community held by the early pioneers of school and preschool) with ideas about a large-scale modern society (gesellschaft) that was based on the presence of large cities. It also merged religious discourse about a forthcoming golden age, when the heavens will reign on the earth[8] (see Popkewitz, 1996), with technological visions about a healthy, well-regulated, and efficient population (see Hultqvist, 1990). In the prevailing views of the time, the social-liberal discourse of the welfare state replaced the discourse of religion (see G. Myrdal, 1931). It was exactly this assumption of a break with the past that made the influence of religious discourse go unnoticed. and thus reinscribed the long-lasting Protestant heritage and the Lutheran theology of Christian liberty "where the service of others is the hallmark and goal of how Christian liberty is to be used" (Lull, 1989 p. 5).[9]

Finally, the scaffolding of these diverse and often contradictory discourses inscribed an educational path for the child that would set him or her on course toward citizenship in a cosmopolitan society (see Chapter 5 of this book). Alva Myrdal's efforts to construct man-made nature in the 1930s and 1940s, in the context of preschool, were part of this transformation.

The reappearance of the subject of Bildung, and more generally the reappearance of the humanistic subject, may look somewhat confusing as it seems to imply a return of more traditional ideas about the child. A few observers in the Swedish context also have made comments about "going back" (see Englund, 1998). However, this is not my way of reviewing current events. Using the notion of modern governance that was developed by Michel Foucault (Foucault, 1991), I will argue that the new conception of the child in the Swedish context is about changing governmentalities.

"Governmentality" implies an assumption that ruling in modern societies is based on a mentality toward the subject (see Foucault, 1991). It is not the child or the human being in a natural state that is the subject and object of governing but the child as it is constructed within the framework of historically produced political thought. Such thought derives from many sources (e.g., as in the case of the People's Home idea), but they intersect on a single plane to form a more or less coherent image of the child (see Popkewitz & Lindblad, 2000). Knowledge plays an essential role in this context, as it makes the child/subject manageable within the range of assumed qualities and dimensions of political thought. Another important feature is that government in today's context is enacted in a decentralized way. It thus does not emanate from a central point (e.g., the state) but rather assumes in this decentralized form the character of a network in which both political and nonpolitical players are involved—the media, the government, various market players, volunteer organizations, and so on.

Following this line of reasoning, I also argue that the new governmentalities link the child with the changing national imaginaries that are embodied in the governing principles of curricula, educational research, and pedagogy. My strategy will be to pursue these arguments in relation to the concept of Bildung. First, I relate the concept of Bildung to the conditions that made it possible to once again think about the child in terms of it. Second, I will try to delineate what I believe are distinctive marks of the new discourse of the child. Part of my strategy is to historicize current conceptions of the subject of Bildung. My tactics involve an effort to establish a perspective on the present, which will make it seem untimely in relation to our conception of it. Of course, I do not believe that it is possible to leave one's own age; rather it involves trying to gain a perspective on our present, from the inside of the present itself.

The chapter is organized in two parts. In the first part, I make an outline of the new subject of Bildung. This part ends with a preliminary description of the problematizations and the ways of reasoning from which it merged. In the second part, I contrast today's version of the subject of Bildung with a few examples of earlier versions; all of them have been influential in the Swedish educational context. I use two historical texts—an autobiographical text by Carl Linné (Linneus), the famous Swedish "botanist"[10] and one text by Friedrich Fröbel about the preschool or kindergarten. In the process I shall also make references to other historical figures like Maria Montessori.

The Knowledge Journey of the Active Self

In May 1995, I read an article in the biggest Swedish newspaper *Dagens Nyheter* in which the then director general of the National Agency for Education (in the following referred to as the director general) gave his views on the role of school in society. I use that article as a jumping-off point for my own thoughts, as it brings out the main features of the political government of the schools during the 1990s in an almost exemplary manner. The headline was "Pupils should be daring and become as free as Angels," and the article asserted that the school should "foster Angels, which dare to move freely between different areas to seek their own unique educational paths" (*Dagens Nyheter*, 1995). The quotation asserts two things. On one side there is the freedom of the individual, and on the other side the thought that each individual has a unique educational path that corresponds to his/her own nature. The state of freedom is central in this context, since it concerns an ongoing process through which the individual is both offered the possibility of discovering who he/she is and simultaneously making use of this insight in a practical way. Thus one discovers who and what one is after assiduous trials.

Detached from its actual context, the director general's statement is just a rehearsal of similar statements made long before, both inside and outside of Sweden. One such example was a statement made by Fridtjuv Berg, the influential leader of one of the major Swedish teacher's organizations at the turn of the twentieth century and also one of the architects of the modern Swedish school system. Berg did not speak about the free flights of the angels, but like the director general and our own contemporaries he spoke about the individual's Bildungs journey. It would be a mistake, however, to argue that it is about identical statements. The statements are similar with regard to their wordings, but they are inscribed in different reasoning complexes and they will also differ in their consequences when enacted as educational practices. I will return to this comparison in my final section.

In this section I will explore the difference between the past and the present in two ways. First, I will make an outline of the expectations and the ways of reasoning that construct the subject in today's government reports, curricula, educational research, and pedagogy. The section ends with a diagnosis of the conditions that made it seem reasonable to once again talk about the child's Bildungs journey in the context of Swedish education.

In short, my hypothesis is that the free subject in the present school development, the one spoken about in the previous quotation from *Dagens Nyheter*, does not have its reference point in the pupil's so-called natural leanings. Rather than being the author of him- or herself, then, the free child is the end product of a long chain of interventions that constitute the new technologies of governing. These technologies provide links between a variety of measures, ranging from a decentralized and goal-governed school system, new forms of curricula and evaluation, as well as new paradigms of knowledge and pedagogy, to all those minor technical inventions and tools that are used in today's Swedish schools to promote the free and autonomous child.

This is not the way, however, that the child's route to knowledge and self-knowledge is presented. The child is rather the free angel that I referred to in the opening part of this section; a creature who is assumed to be willing and capable of making the necessary decisions to realize the route toward self-realization. This way of reasoning covers vast ground; for example, the practices of educational research, pedagogy, book publishers, commercials, and the official reports of the government. The language of the latter documents is particularly revealing. Whereas the child of the post-World War II period was addressed in a bureaucratic and formal way, today's official report communicates directly with the child (and the adult) and addresses him or her in almost a personal manner and as a partner in the national objectives of schooling:

> Our mission has been to support the pedagogical development in the school, to identify the obstacles for this development and to suggest that government and parliament remove these obstacles . . . We shall not tell the personnel of schools what we believe that they should do, but we should engage in a dialogue with the schools of Sweden, their teachers, school leaders, children and parents." (see Skolkommitteir, 1997, p. 5)

Angels or not, the child that is assumed to be responding to this kind of interpellation is not the actual or authentic child. The responsivity of the child is not there in advance but is stimulated in different ways and along many routes. Today's curricula constructions are apt examples. In the national Läroplaner of the World War II period, the demands on the teacher and the child were partial: to obey the rules of the national document education and be loyal to the spirit of it. Today's curricula or Läroplaner move beyond this purely formal level and address the child and the teacher at the level of his and her subjectivity. Anything, even the personal desires and beliefs of the actors can be part of the national curriculum as it is interpreted and transcribed to suit the demands of a local school, a particular class, and an individual child. Furthermore, the use of specific techniques and tools, like diaries, individual planning, and self-evaluation procedures (often including parents), provide additional means that shape the free and self-conducting form of individuality that is at stake in current Swedish school reform. The teacher is supposed to be in charge, but as the child grows older he or she is progressively more involved in this "hermeneutics" that turns the national into the local and personal.

This shaping process is further stimulated by innovations of the methods of teaching and instruction. A decentralized model for guidance replaces ex cathedra teaching and the control practices earlier, in the form of a centrally placed teacher (in both the literal and other senses). Previous boundaries between school subjects are destabilized and reorganized in patterns of knowledge that are more flexible and more suited to the child's personal aspirations and competencies. In the new landscape of schooling, the task of the teacher is less to teach and more to link and regulate the child's border crossing and "free" knowledge seeking. Furthermore, this border-crossing activity is extended both in time and space; in time as the child's journey of education turns into a lifelong involvement (lifelong learning), in space as the content of the journey now is coextensive with the concept of society (the learning society). In the twenty-first century, almost anything can be part of the child's educational journey, even the journey itself (see Hultqvist & Petersson, 1998).[11] Finally, as I described in my introduction, the child that is mobilized is no longer the partial individual of the post-World War II period but the entire child with all his or her abilities, competencies, and aspirations:

> In the kind of society that is now about to take shape, education must be based on humanistic values, i.e. the standpoint that declares that human beings are able to develop morally, aesthetically and intellectually. All of the child's abilities for growth and creativity must be promoted. (Lärarförbundet [Teacher's Organization], 1998, p. 17)

In comparing the picture I have just drawn of the child with an earlier version, one is struck not only by the expanded borders but also, equally significantly, by the change that has taken place in the child's relationship to society or to the greater national community. Governing seems less concerned with the social conditions of learning and knowledge and more with the child's own constructive capacities. The duty of the child is to establish him- or herself in an active form and to realize his/her freedom and him- or herself in a knowledge "marketplace" of seemingly expanding opportunities. It is silently assumed that the child is both highly motivated as well as capable of accomplishing such an extended self-regulated journey of knowledge (see Chapter 6 of this book).

It must be pointed out that we are talking here of tendencies, and that the manufacturing of the new child is not free of conflicts and divergent views. The opposition is demonstrated in the discussions about independent schools and generally in the discussion about the so-called increased market orientation of public facilities. The direction is, however, quite clear, and there is an ongoing mobilization of people—preschool/school children, other children, and adults—moving this way (see Hultqvist & Petersson, 1998).

Bringing the Gods and the Angels Back

Now we come to the title of this chapter, "Bringing the Gods and the Angels Back." I chose it with the idea of saying a few words about the significance of knowledge in the forming of the new subject. It is not my intention to bring the angels back, but I find it significant that they are in fact brought back and used as models to envision subjectivity in the late modern Swedish society. The reappearance of the angels carries an irony, even a double irony when situated in today's context. It is an irony that angels carry on their duties in late modernity, but it's also an irony and probably an unintended critique of current reform to use the figure of angels to speak about freedom. Angels weren't ever free and to be free like an angel would at best mean to fly in accordance with the divine order. I will revert to this issue in the final part of my chapter. Let me, however, pursue this untimely line of thought for a moment.

According to the myths, gods not only need guardians such as the angels, they also need messengers to provide them with information and knowledge about the events that occur in the periphery of the divine territory. The myth of Hermes would be exemplary in this context. Hermes, who is a primary figure in hermeneutics, was the messenger of the gods, the one who was to inform us mortals of the latest news from the heavens as well as to report back to the gods his version of how things were going on earth. He was, in other words, a form of expertise. The myth gives quite a good picture of the situation in knowledge production even now, and it is regrettable that the insights contained in it have not gained it the success it deserves among Swedish school researchers and pedagogues. Few can, however, avoid seeing the breaking of trends in research in the last three decades, and an alert eye easily sees that knowledge speaks approximately the same language as that which governs the political agenda of schools, preschools, and other institutions and practices. New concepts and theories are being created on a broad front, and although they differ in theoretical ties, research methodology, and other aspects, they still have in common the fact that they articulate a view of the subject like that I sketched previously. The children in the literature of educational research have become a good deal more cunning than they were just a couple of decades ago. It is not only that they can do more than what was formerly believed; they are also seen as the creators of themselves and their own lives, and so on (see Dencik, 1995; Kristjansson, 1995; Dahlberg & Lenz-Taguchi, 1996).

If we replace the gods in the mythical description of Hermes with the concept of governmentality, we obtain a more modern terminology for the same thing. By "governmentality" I mean, as stated earlier, an attitude or mentality toward or a view of how people, both children and adults, should be governed. Like Hermes, present-day researchers have accepted the summons of the gods, and like Hermes, there are also attempts to produce or implant the new knowledge in a practical form. The knowledge thus becomes a part of the new strategies of governing and contributes in this way to molding and giving direction to the creation of the new subjects. Knowledge and power are therefore productive elements in shaping ourselves to the kind of subject referred to in the *Dagens Nyheter* quotation. The notion of a nature seeking itself and its own truth is a figure of thought, a way to think of ourselves and the world, and it doesn't necessarily imply that there is a nonhistorical foundation or substance to subjectivity.

Examples are not hard to find. Talk about the active individual—the individual who chooses him-/herself and his/her relationship to him-/herself, others, and the community—takes shape in a time when international competition increases, and when national borders are opened economically, culturally, and socially. As matters stand, the traditional form of the individual appears almost obsolete. Individuals are stimulated to be active, border-transgressing subjects (with some limitations, of course; I shall return to these). To once more refer to Greek mythology, today's individuals are encouraged to accept a time-adapted form of hubris—to fly as close to the sun as possible without burning themselves. In this process of transformation many historical and imaginary figures must move aside. One of these is Jante,[12] known in Scandinavia as Jantelagen, "the Jante law"—"You shouldn't believe that you're any better than anyone else". This was a product of the industrial society, a social invention that promoted fellowship and solidarity in a time of great social upheaval. Today, when the conditions for governing have changed, there is a reduction in the need for a Jantelag, as well as for other worn-out regulators of individuals' relationships with the social order. It is no longer incorrect (in principle) to diverge from the crowd, and it is possible to excel, even in preschool and school. In an interview study[13] on the development of schools in Sweden, which I did in different parts of the country in 1999, this characteristic is very apparent. In one of the schools where I interviewed, the principal had hung a Jante figure from a string in the entrance hall, as though to remind people of the authoritarian regime that had existed earlier in this school. It was also to serve as a jumping-off point from which to eventually get rid of the Jante, which, according to the principal, remained in all the school staff, pupils, and their parents. It was right to excel, said this principal, and those who excel can also be rewarded for it without having to pass out consolation prizes to the others who are not able to excel. In another set of interviews, representatives of one of the major teacher's unions, the so-called Lärarförbundet, expressed similar concerns. The representatives were worried about the tendency of teachers to see themselves as victims instead of active problem-solving subjects. In the strategies that have been developed by the Lärarförbundet, efforts are made to stimulate new ways of reasoning that would promote the active and self-assured teacher (and pupil), an example of which would be the effort to reinterpret the concept of "security." Security, according to the representatives, "should" no longer be given a collective meaning, but be individualized and attached to the individual teacher's competencies.

The mentalities that guide us at present stimulate us to an excess in moderation, and give to the individual who is permitted the right degree of pride, to fly just the right distance from the sun—and thereby the subtitle of this chapter. Examples are, as I have said, not hard to find. Göran Kropp bicycled from Sweden to the Himalayas and, without flinching, climbed the world's highest mountain.[14] People parachute from Kaknästornet, Stockholm's highest building, and bodybuilders push their bodies to their outermost limits. Even Friskis och Svettis, a fitness organization for amateurs, can be seen as a regime for creating the active and self-affirming individual. In earlier times this sort of activity was for bourgeois adventurers who went to the Arctic (André, the Swedish hot air balloonist) or explored dark continents (Hedin, the Swedish explorer). Now adventure comes within everyone's reach. The freedom to be "arrogant" has even become an obligation, and thus it is perhaps not so odd that preschools and schools go in the same direction.

A Series of Problematizations

The director general of Swedish Agency for School, to whom I referred earlier, probably wanted the students to be free like angels and he probably also thought that the subject of Bildung would realize such ends. However, the author of a statement, whether it is about Bildung or any other subject, is not in control of the discursive field where statements are made and used (see Walkerdine, 1995). The latter point will be pursued in some detail in the final part of my chapter.

I will end this section with a few suggestions about the discursive conditions that have given rise to the subject of Bildung and similar conceptions of it. As I hinted at in my introduction, the new subjects are not of a singular origin but are heterogeneous and appear in multiple places, both in the school system proper and outside of its borders. I also suggest that they are not confined to their place of "origin," but that they travel beyond their spaces and cross the borders of singular institutions and practices. They are linked in chains of communications and translations, and "they interpellate us through the radio-calls, through the weekly magazines columns, through the gentle advice of the health visitor, teacher or neighbor, and through the unceasing reflexive gaze of our own psychologically educated self-scrutiny" (Rose, 1990, p. 208). In today's context of educational policy, when learning, creativity, and other achievements of the pupils are supposed to transcend the limits of the school walls, the Bildungs subject easily connects with other images—for example, mountain climbers, parachuters, and other of today's adventurers.

Let me now turn to the conditions of thought from which the new figures of schooling derive. The new subject(s) emerged from a series of problematizations of the welfare practices that were established after World War II. Nationally and internationally, the Swedish "model" of government was seen as a third way, between liberalism and socialism (see Hultqvist, 1990; also see Larsson, 1984). The administrative and technical resources of the centralized state were among the most striking features, but equally significantly, the governing by the state relied on Enlightenment ideas and humanistic conceptions about the liberty and rights of individuals as well as on religious ideas and pastoral images about community and the child's nature (the director general's angels suggest that the pastoral images of the past are still active). During the 1970s and on, the welfare arrangements were criticized and the critique emerged as a series of problematizations.

One of the critique points focused on the assumed inability of the welfare arrangements to deal with issues of multiculturalism and pluralism; how can one, for example, deal with such issues within the framework of universal norms? Another point of critique concerned the paternalism inscribed in welfare discourse and practices, for example, the tendency toward taking charge of the lives of the citizens (Hirdman, 1989), and the institutionalized learning to helplessness that followed. This kind of critique, then, concerned itself with the problem of too much governing. Other forms of problematizations focused on unexamined assumptions of welfare practices. The welfare programs were constructed in the image of a People's Home (see my introduction) and according to the rhetoric of the days, the People's Home would not favor any citizens, whether low or high. Now, the critiques argued that the People's Home had not always been the good and decent home it was designed to be.

It was founded on a population politics that segregated parts of the population, for example, through the use of eugenics and programs for the sterilization of so-called subnormal populations (see Runcis, 1998). The 1970s and 1980s also saw a major critique of the positive state that emerged during the post-World War II years and the social sciences that underpinned this conception of the state. The social sciences were critiqued for their involvement in the state's apparatuses of control and management, which, according to the critics, led to the establishment of conditions of alienation that divorced individuals and collectives from their real selves. The latter critique was phrased in the emancipatory language of humanistic and neo-Marxist discourse.[15] This critique was part of a broader debate, the so-called positivism critique, that flourished in Sweden and the other Scandinavian countries in the 1970s and 1980s. It is interesting, and perhaps also ironic, that the former critics and the positivists now are mutually involved in the promotion of an "efficient" government; the humanistic current inscribes the interpretative and humanistic subject of the whole man, while positivism calculates the efficiency of the goal-directed subject. Finally, in the eyes of the critics, it was precisely the lack of efficiency that made rule governing a failure. In the early 1990s, this critique was instrumentalized in laws and programs for decentralized goal governing.

The new discursive subjects are embedded in these and similar forms of problematizations. New lines were drawn, old ones were linked in new ways, and eventually a portrait of the new subject emerged that became part of the new programs and techniques for governing the schools and other practices. I believe that this new subject is succinctly drawn by Larsson in his book *The Home We Inherited* (1994):

> The creation of the People's Home became a search of grandeur after the universal mechanisms of human action. The goal was to predict, decide and distribute resources in accordance with the need of the modern democratic citizen and this goal in turn, became a national principle of order for the growing bureaucracies. . . . However, we now realize that the rational conviction, translated into a project to subordinate human beings to a science based national project to build the modern society, has lost sight of the needs of human beings in its eagerness to guide and govern in accordance with standardized system solutions. . . . The human being cannot be reduced to an economic or social partial being. She is a cultural whole being with unique genetic characteristics, with her own reason and creativity . . . To grow as a citizen means, in accordance with this line of thought, to live under one's own risk, to be active and exercise one's responsibilities without endangering the freedom of others. (p. 254)

Larsson's description is not necessarily a valid description of a past that now lies behind us. More likely, it is about a way of reasoning that produces the past while envisioning the future (see Hacking, 1995). Inscribed in Larsson's statement is the mission to replace the citizen of the social with the cultural citizen, a whole being who is able to deal with the contingencies of life at his or her own risk. This is a very significant shift in Swedish discourse of the subject. Of course, today's search for wholeness is not new. All sorts of authorities, past and present, have tried to govern in the name of wholeness, whether it be in the name of religion, administration, science, or technology, but the newness of today's search for wholeness is the increasing focus on the individual. The idea has taken shape that wholeness can be governed in the name of free and responsible individuals. In such a scenario, society and the national community assume less importance. Community is something one chooses and not something to which one is under obligation, as was the case earlier (see Rose, 1996).

This adds up to a new way of governing subjectivity, where the World War II conception of the Swedish state gives way to a facilitating, enabling state of the sort that I have tried to describe. This is the state of partnership, the almost personal state that interpellates the child and the other subjects of government at the level of their subjectivity: the whole child (of humanistic discourse).[16]

The subject of Bildung is part of this new emergent pattern of the whole-part relationship. The outcome is still uncertain. Conflicts and battles are fought over subjectivity and the saving of souls, in and outside of schools; a reminder that religious discourse is still active and provides fuel for the combatants (see Popkewitz & Brennan, 1998).

I will end this chapter with two historical examples that I believe are interesting as comparisons with today's visualized educational paths. The one example is an autobiographical text by Carl von Linné (Linneus) and the other one is a text on the kindergarten by Friedrich Froebel. I prefer to call these figures heroes of the past to suggest that there are certain recurrent historical personas that are used to report on "the past" (see Deleuze & Guatteri, 1994). The way these historical personas reasoned about the cultivation (Bildung) of the child's nature became part of the Swedish educational imaginaries during the nineteenth and twentieth centuries, both in the context of school and preschool. My purpose here is not so much to show how these historical personas shape our present but to use the contrast created by my historical examples to explore differences between today's reasoning about the child's Bildungs path, which I suggested in the form of my earlier quotation from *Dagens Nyheter,* and that which preceded it.

Heroes of the Past

Linné, God's Monitor in the Botanical Class

In his autobiography *Carl Linné*, Carl von Linné (Linneus) describes his own educational path: he was born in 1707, grew up in Stenbrohult in Småland,[17] later made his great discoveries, became world renowned, and was raised to the nobility. There is a point in my interpretation of this text that it is thus Carl von Linné, world-renowned botanist, who writes about himself.

First I would like to report on how Linné saw his educational path—what kind of a story he tells about himself. The text begins with the author's description of the place where he was born and grew up. It is a vivid description of the landscape, the geographical position, and the beauty of the surroundings. Then Linné goes into family connections, who his paternal and maternal grandparents were, their professions, certain information on their circumstances, and in some cases descriptions of characteristics and temperaments.

After this background, he starts the real story about the young Linné's educational path and gives a fairly detailed description of his first years. His father, who was a pastor, plays an important role in this part of the story, and special attention is paid to the garden his father created at the parsonage: "It was the most beautiful garden in the whole county, filled with specially selected trees and the loveliest flowers. My father sought leisure in the garden when he was free from his pastoral duties" (p. 5).

His father's garden thus plays an important role during these years, and his father's knowledge of flowers and herbs made a deep impression on the young boy, who "regarded this with great pleasure, and was the theme song most often played in the boy's ingenuity." The garden that first aroused Linné's interest actually turned out to have certain educational and disciplinary effects, for the boy who showed such a great interest in everything that had to do with the garden showed a weakness. "In the manner of children he forgot the names, and (once) was sternly upbraided by his father, who said he would never give the boy any of the names of the herbs if he were only going to forget them. Thus the boy's entire mind was put to use to remember the names so that he would never lose this most pleasurable privilege" (p. 5).

This was the starting point of the tale. It was a garden that first aroused Linné's mind, and it was gardens that returned in one guise or another when Linné later began his studies at the university and eventually started on the path of botany and attained fame. I will not report on the details of Linné's writing of history, but wish to briefly give some basic points of his tale. Firstly, the reader is struck by how preordained Linné's educational path appeared to be; it was rather as though it was put on rails. It starts with the father's garden lighting a spark in the young Linné, and after that we see how he kept the spark alive with varying degrees of success. Linné turned back and forth between his real self and his unsuccessful self, and he tells honestly and even with a measure of self-irony how bad he was at certain tasks. According to some authorities Linné was completely incapable of further studies (which at that time meant studying for the priesthood), and they stated that it would be better to let the boy do something practical. Here his father intervened and managed to set the boy straight. He provided new allies, and soon Linné found expression for the impulses awakened in the father's garden but that had been stifled by so many of his contemporaries. "The boy had found a fervent spirit for a science which in that time and place lay hidden in barbarism, and no other sciences were practicable than those which fostered priests, to which even his parents, especially his mother, had doomed her son since infancy" (p. 7).

Even his parents were apparently obstacles in his way, perhaps mostly his mother. The obstacles were many, and his educational path is described as crooked, but there were still enough favorable contemporary conditions to allow Linné to find himself. The compulsory primary and secondary school was such a place, and "the young people in these schools can be likened to small trees in a nursery . . . when they have finally been transplanted, change their raw natures and become beautiful trees which bear delightful fruits" (p. 9).

What is so remarkable about this story? On the surface it appears to be identical with the educational path the director general talks about. Linné is the one who finds his proper place in life. In other words, there's nothing new under the sun. Now I wish, however, to introduce a difference that really is a difference in relation to our time's visualized educational path.

One key to my interpretation is the title of the text, *Carl Linné*. The subject of Linné's reflections is Carl's educational path, and the one who writes about it is Carl von Linné, the famed botanist. The construction of the story is thus done from the position of the botanist, and this is probably not just by chance. The presentation of Carl is reminiscent of the kind of presentation Carl von Linné makes in his scientific theses on plants. Linné classifies and organizes his life into compartments and subcompartments in the same way as he classifies and organizes plants. Each plant has its own characteristics and needs certain soil conditions in order to develop. I think we find a key to the story if we continue and ask questions about the knowledge-creating subject, that is, Carl von Linné. What kind of a figure was he and what kind of a view of knowledge did he express?

To answer that question we will leave Carl von Linné's text for a moment and turn to contemporary literature. Michel Foucault described in his epoch-making work *The Order of Things* (1970) the thinking and knowledge of the eighteenth century in similar terms. At that time, states Foucault, thinking revolved around the tableau and thus around a way of thinking that was based on classification and order. The order of things was given, and it was only a matter of the subject of knowledge recreating as carefully and accurately as possible in his/her thoughts that which existed outside them. Ultimately this order is a divine gift. Therefore it was God who gave Linné the duty to, like Hermes, convey the testimonies of the godly order to a (probably) ignorant mass of people, and thus get the "wild trees . . . to give delightful fruit" (p. 9).

Linné is thus God's monitor in the botanical class. As a monitor, Linné really has a sense of what belongs and what doesn't belong. He demonstrates his skill in determining the genders of plants, for instance, and moreover shows an ability to discover deviations among human flowers, perhaps especially female ones. For example he reports, in passing, of a woman who has been unfaithful to her husband—and doesn't follow up with any further information. He doesn't mention women and women's qualities in many places in the text, but when he does it isn't always in a favorable light.

The distinctions between the former and our present educational paths have been established, and not much imagination is required to see that Linné had other clients for his life work than is the case with today's subject. The educational paths of today's preschool children, schoolchildren, and others are decentralized and neither knowledge nor life are to be taken for granted. Between the godly order and ourselves a theory of knowledge has been established, an opportunity for reflections on knowledge and its conditions. Thus it will also be possible to orient oneself to the activities with which we create knowledge, ask questions about knowledge's constructive character, and finally ask questions about how we are created and create ourselves as actively knowledge-creating subjects. This opportunity was outside the reach of Linné; he did only what he was obliged to do—he reported on the divine order as it appeared in the botanical garden.

Linné's way of reasoning about the garden was influential both in the Swedish national context and abroad. In the nineteenth century, it entered the colonial discourse and was used to classify and order the visible features of the races and their assumed qualities, for example, in terms of distinctions made between wild nature and civilized nature/Bildung. Eventually, Linné's thought was popularized in geography books and maps that were used in schools. Through these and other channels his thought became part of the Swedish standardized beliefs about the "other" (see, Lester, 2000)—the non-Swedes and the non-Europeans; a tool, then, to imagine what it takes to become a Swedish and a European child.

Finally, I believe that the concept of governmentality is not completely adequate when it comes to characterizing Linné and his contemporaries. The liberal form of government as exercised in the name of self-guiding or self-regulating individuals was not fully established in Linné's time. Linné's ambition was to recreate the divine botanical order in his scientific work and since he himself, as God's obedient subject, belonged to this order, it was logical that in his autobiographical presentation he saw his own Bildungs journey as an act of God, as in the predetermined order of flowers (or trees).

Friedrich Froebel and Swedish Preschool

Friedrich Froebel is usually considered to be the father of the Swedish preschool, and there is something to be said for this (see Johansson, 1994, and Tallberg-Broman, 1991).[18] It was, in any case, Froebel's thoughts about kindergarten that became a source of inspiration for Ellen and Maria Moberg and several other more or less renowned advocates of a Swedish preschool education. In this way, the thought was established that children other than those of the upper social classes could have a Bildungs path.

On the surface, Froebel's kindergarten was strikingly similar to Linné's garden for the cultivation of human and nonhuman flowers and trees. Froebel writes thus:

> "You people who wander through gardens, meadows, and woods, why do you not open your ears to what Nature in its mute language can teach you. Look at the plants that you call weeds. When they grow up in bondage and restraint, they can hardly show any inner adherence to law. Regard them when they are allowed to develop freely—what adherence to law, what a pure inner life, harmonious in all its parts, they exhibit; how one shows a sun in miniature, another a gleaming star. Parents, so should your children be able to develop and bloom, if you wouldn't try to force them so early into unnatural molds and duties, making them weak and artificial. (Froebel, 1912, p. 6)

Like Linné, Froebel perceived children to be malleable plants, and we also see that Froebel emphasizes that each person should follow his own life path—that is, that there is a deterministic principle built into his order. I would, however, like to point out two aspects that I believe make Froebel different from Linné and the early eighteenth century. One is that in Froebel and especially in Froebel's followers, the early psychologists and educators, there was a much greater measure of distance and technical competence in the possibility of forming children's and young people's educational paths. Linné constructs his educational path afterward (he is, of course, writing for another purpose) while Froebel, on the other hand, thinks ahead of time what will be necessary to accomplish the proper educational path, what knowledge will be necessary, how the children can be influenced, and what relationships must be built up between the child and the adult. The other aspect, which is connected to the first point, is that Froebel's image of God is different from Linné's. Both subscribe to the "divine order theory," and both try in one way or another to recreate this, in autobiographical form or as a practically functioning educational operation. Froebel's God is, however, the good liberal God, a spirit that believes in and affirms the good sides of the child (and the adult), while Linné's God still has characteristics of Nemesis Divina, that is, the punishing God (see Ödman, 1995). I will try briefly to illustrate both of these theses, and I do it with a quotation. The adult must, says Froebel, "be positive, protective, corrective, and shielding, and not dictating, decisive, and interfering" (Froebel, 1912, p.7).

Today we would say that Froebel expresses here the progressive thought, that all pedagogical activity must be based on the child's interest and that the main principle must therefore be to support the child's will to provide him-/ herself with knowledge, rather than to delineate borders or to punish. This is also a technical principle, to the extent that it requires new "regulations" regarding the relationship between the child and the adult. The distance that should be established gives the adult new opportunities to set himself up in a reflective relationship to the child. By keeping a distance from the child and his/her activities, by taking a protective position, the adult gets increased opportunities to see different expressions of the child's nature as these appear in his/her daily activities—play and other occupations. Everything goes well for the most part, but sometimes the "order" in the garden is disturbed; weeds and less popular flowers rear their heads in the child's activity, and then it is important to find out what it is in the child's nature that causes this meandering. It is thus through this technical innovation that the adult gets the opportunity to get a glimpse into the inner child, to get under the child's skin and guide, as it were, from a distance. This reflexive apparatus is hardly present in Linné. It is a present-day invention, and its continued development is in the hands of modern psychology and pedagogy.

I would like to conclude this part of the chapter by citing some words of Maria Montessori. The quotations are interesting because they point out the strong historical connection between the development of more liberal principles for the governing of children (and adults, of course) and the pedagogical and scientific development of knowledge about children. These two sides are as closely connected as Siamese twins and cannot operate independently of each other:

> The fundamental principle of scientific pedagogy must be, indeed, the liberty of the pupil—such liberty as shall permit a development of individual spontaneous manifestation of the child's nature. If a new and scientific pedagogy is to arise from the study of the individual such a

study must occupy itself with the observation of free children. (Montessori, 1912, p. 69)

Montessori thus claims that children's freedom to do themselves justice is in fact the prerequisite for a scientific pedagogic development of knowledge. If the true child, the natural child, is not allowed to speak or express him-/herself, then there is indeed nothing of which to seek knowledge. Montessori and her colleagues in the areas of psychology and pedagogy need, in other words, the support that Froebel's technical innovation gives them. It is the liberal form of government, in Froebel's form or others', that renders possible a scientific development of knowledge about the child. It can even be claimed that it is in this process that the child's nature is created, first as a mental construction and subsequently as a reality. The nature of the child is, says Montessori,

> a nearly unexplored landscape. We thus know very little, but what we do know indicates that there is more to find out. How can we know, however, that there is such a thing as the nature of the child, when we are so ignorant of its existence? (Montessori, 1936, p. 124)

These lines are almost transparent. Nature appears in front of our very eyes because we assume its existence. I do not believe that it is this productivity of knowledge that Montessori discovered; other things in her work speak for the opposite. However—and here she is more modern than both Linné and Froebel—she points out that the gaze of knowledge is conditional; if we are going to see, we must know what we are looking for. Linné felt that seeing was generated out of acquaintance with the real "things." The world was more complicated for Montessori and her successors; it had become opaque, and the subject of knowledge after that had to create order with its own activity.

The Routes of the Angels Have Changed

The historical personas of Linné, Froebel, and Montessori significantly shaped the Swedish discourse on the child for the past two or three centuries. Their ways of reasoning are still present in the Swedish national context. Linné's procedures for the classification of plants would be akin to the classificatory procedures that are used in today's apparatuses to administrate the child's freedom. Likewise, Froebel's and Montessori's modernist efforts to produce knowledge about the deep and underlying core of the child's nature are part of contemporary educational thought.

I will now use my historical examples to delineate what I believe are distinctive marks of current mentalities of governing. Let me return to Fridtjuv Berg, the Swedish pioneer of the school during the latter part of the nineteenth century and early part of the twentieth century. Berg made frequent use of the idea of Bildung and for him this concept made available two distinct lines of thought. These two lines of thought merged in his visions about the tasks of the educational system in modern societies:

> The goal of society is justice, namely the right of each and all to free development of all the hood powers of his [sic] nature. The view that the state is a huge machinery, an immense mechanism of cogs and wheels that are being replaced continuously when worn out, is false. The state is rather an organism of autonomous cells, renewing themselves through the development of new cellular individuals from the constant supply of new living materials.
>
> The health of the state is conditioned on the principle that everything will be put in its right place. It is the same with society. The "tissues of society" must be renewed continuously through the incorporation of similar materials from a never ceasing stream of the rising generation. If the supply were to be diverted from its natural cause through artificial means, symptoms of disorder will appear in the society's body. To prevent this from happening each new member of the state must receive proper guidance to assure that he or she will find the way just to those "tissues" to which he (or she) naturally belongs. For the educational system to act on behalf of the welfare of society, it may not hinder the talents of anyone, independent of (their) social class, from finding (their) right place in Society. The educational system diverts from its mission, if it should in an arbitrary way intervene in the course of natural development. (Berg, 1921, p. 50)

In Berg's organic view, Bildung and education tied the population reasoning of the state with the reasoning of the child and this twofold goal would be realized through the self-regulating mechanisms of nature. Nature would set the child on his or her course toward the goal of self-realization and, unknowingly, this way he or she would also realize the ends of the society and the state.

This conception of the individual's Bildungs path is enacted at a distance from Linné's times, and although there are a few similarities Linné would not have recognized his own path in this version of self-development. For Linné, the distinctive marks of the self, as revealed in his classificatory system, referred to the divine order. Berg's thought, on the other hand, was informed by the nascent biological thought of his time (see Hultqvist & Petersson, 1998). The gap is even wider compared with the discourses that govern the conceptions of individuality in the twenty-first century. Although the wordings may look familiar, today's construction is different from that of Berg, Froebel, and the early psychologists of the twentieth century. To identify difference one has to look beyond the words and to the discursive structure of the statements. In fact, the director general's free angels are governed in neither the name of the divine order nor the name of the early twentieth-century conception of nature. Today's angels move in an orbit defined by the constructivist ethos of our actuality.

Nature has receded into the depths of history and is replaced with a different model of the subject and subjectivity. Or perhaps one should say that it is the previous versions of nature that have changed, that is, the ones that were developed by historical heroes such as Linneus, Froebel, Montessori, and Alva Myrdal. The natural journey of the self in today's governmentalities seems no longer to be about the discovery of the child's fixed nature or obligations toward a predefined conception of society. This journey, or becoming, seems more to be about being a motivated learner that is able to explore and deal with today's comparably more flexible landscape of learning and knowledge. The child has become an entrepreneur of him- or herself.[19]

This is a mentality that corresponds with the language and ethos of today's constructivistic conceptions of science and research. In a very interesting article, Nikolas Rose (see Rose, 2000) claims that with the emergence of modern technology of genetic steering, the governing of ourselves now has reached the domain of the human vital order. The new technical inventions—for example, in the areas of biomedicine and genetic engineering—have made our biology look less deterministic and more open to choice and manipulation. Should this be a reasonable argument, then a whole set of assumptions and distinctions—that is, nature and nurture or hereditary endowment and culture—need to be rethought. As the matter stands, it seems unlikely that Fridtjuv Berg's ideas about nonintervention in the work of nature will stand the test of this new advanced liberal epistemological mutation. Perhaps less important, the angels might finally emancipate themselves from the divine order.

Or will they? In the beginning of the twentieth century, the school child and the preschool child certainly were inscribed in the religious discourse. The project of schooling was about the saving of the child's soul in a world undergoing rapid change. Progressively, this moral objective was inscribed in a population reasoning that made the child a healthy and ambitious cosmopolitan citizen capable of contributing in an industrialized society (this renewed form of "population reasoning" was present in Fridtjuv Berg's thought). The home that was constructed for the child during the 1930s aimed at reconciling traditional ways of reasoning and living with the emergent trends of large-scale society. Still, the child's soul was to be saved. In today's Swedish imaginaries, the child has been given the task of inventing him-/herself and, not unexpectedly, past authorities and the forces of religion and morality seem to have receded into the past. Or have they? Perhaps not. There is still struggle going on about the child's soul, with the difference that now it is the child him-/herself who is supposed to be the main actor. However, this displacement hides the fact that the child's adventure is well regulated and governed and there is probably not much surprise to be found on the other side of the Bildungs journey. For one thing, the journey itself is goal governed. Where is the adventure, when the goals are there in advance (see Chapter 6 of this book)? As in the 1930s and 1940s, there is a whole technology set in order for him or her to achieve the status of citizenship. The difference is that today's child is not inscribed in the national imaginaries of the People's Home, to which I referred in my introduction, but more likely, for lack of better words, in the local/global home envisioned in today's Swedish national imaginaries. The People's Home has become individualized and attached to the individual's soul, a soul that is flexible enough to enable the child to feel at home in different contexts and circumstances, local/national or global. Should the child fail to invent him-/herself accordingly, there are always professional resources available to save his/her soul and to empower his/her nature.

The irony and paradoxes of today's making is in the use of many and seemingly contradictory discourses. On the one hand there is the discourse of the social engineering of the welfare state of the post-World War II years and on the other the humanism of the nineteenth century. There is also the new epistemology of today's biotechnology. The paradoxes, however, are the result of assumptions about the character of the sciences and their "worldly" effects. The historical self-understanding of humanism, for example, puts humanism on one side and power and technology on the other (this heritage is certainly inscribed in the intellectual currents of preschool education in Sweden and elsewhere). But humanism never was located on the outside of technology and the orders of power. And as is shown by current governing practices in Sweden, the logic of practice makes other connections than those that are available in the practice of logic (on this subject, see Popkewitz, 2000). There is even room for angels. This is the kind of logic that fabricates the child in the new millennium.

Conclusions

In the traditions of childhood thought, there is the presupposition that the child is there from the start and that he or she eventually will become a mature and well-reasoned adult. This narrative is not very convincing. In the beginning there were children, but to become a child these children must first be transformed to fit the patterns of thought and practice that are inscribed in childhood. In today's Swedish educational context this becoming of the child is thought of in terms of Bildung and similar conceptions. In this chapter, I have tried to make it plausible that current talk about Bildung can be comprehended in terms of governmentality or political rationality. My historical examples also serve the purpose of showing the historicity of all knowledge and government.

Today's subjects should be free, they should be autonomous, and they should be flexible. The latter characteristic is not entirely easy to combine with a more traditional idea about Bildung. In order to make it possible we will probably need to visualize the education-thirsty pupil/child as being equipped with several natures, to which he or she can revert when required by circumstances. At any rate, the work of education today makes other demands on the child, and it is these that are placed in the various current programs and activities for school development. They are used in the setting up of teamwork in schools, in the requirement for a holistic viewpoint (also see Chapter 6 of this book), in the new school role casting, or in the form of new curriculum constructions. None of this is, parenthetically, especially original; it can be found elsewhere, especially in the new management culture and in private industry (see Gee, Hull, & Lankshear, 1996).

In the early 1990s I wrote a thesis about the preschool child (see Hultqvist, 1990). I entitled it "The Preschool Child, a Construction for Individual Liberation and Solidarity." I was and still am quite satisfied with that title, since the thesis was concerned with a period in Swedish preschool development when there was vacillation between the social community and the individual's liberation and development. For reasons that I have indicated it is not, however, equally certain that this title can be applied to today's developments.

Finally, I want to say a few words about humanism and my own theoretical efforts. Humanism is, as I have indicated in this chapter, the keyword in almost any document of significance in today's Swedish educational context. Is it not a fact, then, that poststructuralist thought, to use a common label, expresses a determinism or even antihumanism? Where has the pure humanism gone, that which psychologists and others have tried to expose in their efforts to protect children's rights in society?

Nothing could be more wrong. Trying to describe the forms of power and governing that have been shaped in the name of one or another theoretical position is hardly being deterministic. To make that claim would be to overestimate the true effectiveness and meaning of the various programs and practices of governing. The historical registers of thought that we use to envision the past tell us rather that humans have shown a certain measure of disobedience in one respect or another, and this is probably true even when there are requirements that they should be free. "Freedom" is not an unambiguous concept, and in a democratic society peopled by differing wills and interests there should be diverging opinions of whether we should be as free as, for example, angels.

Every modern society has equipped itself with a subject policy that is based on an immanent pedagogy (see Ödman, 1995). The concept of immanent pedagogy emphasizes the situation of influence existing not only in rationalized programs for pedagogic guidance but also embedded in the situations of daily life—in the family, the schoolyard, during leisure time, at the workplace, and especially in advertising and the media. The specific matrix of immanent power relations that made childhood as education possible during the nineteenth and twentieth centuries has changed, but as I have tried to show in this chapter, past discourses and techniques of government reappear in new clothes in today's settings. Today's adventures and adventurers, in and outside schools, might be free, but it is not self-evident that current versions of freedom cover the full range of meanings that can be attached to "freedom."[20] Discussions of this subject-shaping "machine" occur seldom in pedagogical connections and in political debate and if a study of governmentalities can clarify some of the aspects of this concealed subject shaping, issues of freedom and power might enter the realm of public dialogue. Thus, what do we mean by freedom, and how, when, and where is it reasonable and right to allow oneself to be governed in the name of freedom? It seems to me that such issues are based on a democratic and humanistic disposition. They are, moreover, important issues. The increased emphasis on individuals' freedom is a historic step forward, but one cannot ignore the reverse side of current versions of freedom.

Notes

I want to thank Thomas S. Popkewitz for his valuable comments on various versions of this manuscript. I also want to thank members of the so-called Wednesday group at the Department of Curriculum and Instruction, University of Madison/Wisconsin, who read and made comments on the almost-finished version of my manuscript. Finally, I wish to thank Per-Johan Ödman for directing my attention to the autobiographical work of Carl Von Linné that I use in this chapter. I also want to thank Per-Johan for his critical comments on earlier drafts of the manuscript.

[1] There is a tendency today to make a sharp distinction between goal governing and governing by rules. However, the difference between the past and the present is not between goals and rules but in the ways goals are created and enacted. The Swedish school in the World War II period was as goal governed as today's system. In fact, it represented an extreme form of goal governing. The difference from today's system of governing, however, is that the goals never entered the local context as goals to be pursued by local school boards, politicians, teachers, and parents, but were translated into detailed prescriptions and regulations that the local actors were supposed to follow. The connection with Taylorism and the Fordist mode of production is very pronounced. Today's goal governing reintroduces the teacher, the child, and the parent as local actors and as semi-experts in the arts of hermeneutics to interpret and to enact the national curricula at the local level.

2 During the period after World War II, when the pedagogical science developed concepts and theories to explain and describe schools and education, this was done in light of the views at that time on how schools and other public facilities should be governed. The norm was universality, and the development of concepts in education followed this and "spoke" in terms of general laws of learning, that is, the way the individual in general learned. Today the norm has been decentralized, and efforts are made to rethink previous universal conceptions, witnessed by the concepts of multi-culturalism and pluralism. It is the latter development that conditions today's educational research and in the process reshapes it.

3 Historically, the preschool branch in Sweden saw its own function as differing from the school. Thus it has been customary since the beginnings of preschool in the early part of the twentieth century to make a differentiation between school's and preschool tradition's view of the child. Many battles have been fought over this difference and the fight continues even now. It received even more fuel when the development of schools at the end of the twentieth century tended to support the more liberal and holistic view of children as found in Fröbel's manifesto and in the writings of other renowned historical advocates with similar views, for example, Ellen Key (see Key, 1900). However, differences have been exaggerated (see Hultqvist, 1997; also see Dahlberg & Taguchi, 1994).

4 There is a huge international literature on the subject of nature, pastoralism, landscape, and national imaginaries. See, for example, Marx (1967), Mitchell (1994), and Jehlen (1986).

5 The children's garden was supposed to transform the wild nature of the children of the streets (streetwise intelligence) in the early twentieth century. Wild nature in the Froebelian garden was referred to as weeds.

6 The most significant contribution in this context is Alva and Gunnar Myrdal's *Kris i Befolkningsfrågan* (Crisis in the population question) (1934). In their book, the Myrdals created the theoretical framework to deal with the issues and problems of mobilizing the Swedes for the industrialized large-scale society. The population question was used to create links between heterogeneous elements such as sexual hygiene, education, family politics, housing, and the national economy. Thus, older mentalities would be superseded by new ones and the conditions of possibility would be set for the new and industrialized Swede to emerge. Part of this program was pursued in a series of governmental reports in the late 1930s and 1940s. See, for example, *Betänkande i Sexualfrågan* (1936) and *Betänkande angående Barnkrubbor och Sommarkolonier* (1938).

7 The idea of a People's Home originated in Germany in the nineteenth century. In the Swedish context it was used in conservative circles at the turn of the twentieth century and was reused in the late 1920s to promote the politics of the Social Democratic Party.

8 In the early part of the twentieth century, the religious discourse still provided the horizon for the school, preschool, and other public institutions. The rationalization of the political discourse during the 1920s was supposed to remove religion from the political agenda, but this never happened. While there was a change in language, basic elements of previous religious discourse became reinscribed in social science thought and the political agenda of the nascent welfare state. One particularly good example is Alva Myrdal's reinterpretation of Fröbel's preschool discourse (see Hultqvist, 1990).

9 The link between the religious discourse of Luther and the social liberalism of the Swedish welfare state also cast some doubts on the now popular but ahistorical use of "neoliberalism" to reason about current changes in economy and government.

[10] It would perhaps be more appropriate to say that Linneus was a man of science. The profession of the botanist belongs to the nineteenth century and thereafter.

[11] Efforts to reconceptualize school are evident in many corners of the Swedish educational system. In an interview study I did with centrally located representatives of the major Swedish teacher's organization, the so-called Lärarförbundet, there were clear signs of going beyond previous strategies that focused on the school. Today's strategies link the teacher, the child, and the parent with conceptions of community work.

[12] The law of Jante was described and documented in a novel from 1933, *En flykting korsar sitt spår* (A refugee crosses his track) by the Danish-Norwegian author Aksel Sandemose.

[13] Included in my project on the development of schools in Sweden, 1960–1995. The project is funded by the National Agency for Education.

[14] Göran Kropp is one of the many Swedes who have been following the tracks of the early bourgeoisie adventurers. At present he is skiing to the North Pole. The media reports almost every day from his new adventure and they seem to be especially concerned with the dangers that Kropp encounters on his route to the pole, for example, being attacked by polar bears and other wild animals.

[15] Herbert Marcuse and Eric Fromm were among the influential voices of this period of time. See, for example, Marcuse (1991) and Fromm (1941).

[16] Interestingly, in today's reasoning about the state, the previous positive state coincides with a humanistic and hermeneutic conception of the state. On the one hand, the actors are interpellated as humanistic subjects to interpret the national curricula, but the evaluation of their performances, on the other hand, relies on behaviorist approaches and statistics.

[17] Småland is a county in the southern part of Sweden.

[18] In earlier contexts I have claimed that preschool's connection with Fröbel in research literature has perhaps been emphasized a little too strongly, and that changes in methods of governance, knowledge development, and so on mean that there is perhaps very little left of Fröbel in today's thinking about preschool. See Hultqvist (1998).

[19] See *I Entreprenörskapets tecken- en studie av skola i förnyelse,* Närings och Handelsdepartementet, 1997:3.

[20] The adventure of Göran Kropp is a good example of such well-governed adventurers. Before Kropp climbed Mount Everest, a group of servicemen went ahead of him, just to secure a safe route to the top of the mountain. The event was also broadcast on radio and television.

References

Berg, F. (1921). *Folkskolan som bottenskola.* Pedagogiska skrifter, Stockholm: Lärarförbundet.

Broady, D. (1992). Bildningstraditioner och läroplaner, in Skola för bildning. Betänkande av läroplanskommittén. Stockholm: SOU (Government reports on social issues), 94.

Dagens Nyheter (1995, May 17). Eleverna ska våga och bli fria som änglar, Insidan.

Dahlberg, G., & Lenz-Taguchi, H. (1994): Förskola och skola—om två skilda traditioner och om visionen om en mötesplats, I Grunden för ett livslångt lärande. En barnmogen skola. Stockholm: SOU, 45.

Dahlberg, G., & Lenz-Taguchi, H. (1996). Visionen om ett Möte mellan förskola ochskola. *Pedagogiska Magasinet, 1*, 20–24.

Deleuze, G., & Guatteri, F. (1994). *What is philosophy?* London: Verso.

Dencik, L. (1995). Modern childhood in the Nordic countries: Dual socialization and its implications. In L. Chrisholm, P. Buchner, H-H. Kruger, & M. Du Bois-Reymond (Eds.), *Growing up in Europe* (pp. 105–19). Berlin/New York: de Gruyter.

Englund, T. (1998). En vindkautring har skett still de svagares nackdel. *Pedagogiska magasinet, I*, 44–49. Stockholm: Lärarförbundet.

Fergusson, R. A. (1997). *The American enlightenment 1750–1820.* Cambridge, MA: Harvard University Press.

Foucault, M. (1970). *The order of things: An archaeology of the human sciences.* New York: Vintage Books.

Foucault, M. (1991). Governmentality. In G. Burchell, C. Gordon, & P. Miller (Eds), *The Foucault effect: Studies in governmentality.* London: Harvester Wheatsheaf.

Froebel, F. (1912). *Om uppfostran dess mål och medel i allmänhet.* Svensk översättning ingående i Froebelarkivet, Stadsarkivet i Norrköping.

Fromm, E. (1941). *Escape from freedom.* New York: Farrar & Rinehart.

Gee, J. P, Hull, G., & Lankshear, C. (1996). *The new work order: Behind the language of the new capitalism.* Sydney: Westview Press.

Hacking, I. (1995). *Rewriting the soul: Multiple personality and the sciences of memory.* Princeton, NJ: Princeton University Press.

Hindess, B. (1993). Liberalism, socialism and democracy: Variations on a governmental theme. In A. Barry, T. Osborne, & N. Rose (Eds.), *Liberalism, Neo-liberalism and governmentality.* London: Routledge.

Hirdman, Y. (1989). *Att lägga livet tillrätta. Studier i svensk folkhemspolitik.* Stockholm: Carlsson.

Hultqvist, K. (1990). *Förskolebarnet, en konstruktion för gemenskapen och den individuella frigörelsen.* Stehag/Stockholm: Symposion förlag.

Hultqvist, K. (1997). Changing rationales for governing the child: A historical perspective on the construction of the child in two institutional contexts—the school and the pre-school. *Childhood*, no. 2. London: Sage Publications.

Hultqvist, K. (1998). På spaning efter det nya barnet. *Pedagogiska Magasinet, 7*, 6–11.

Hultqvist, K. (1998). A history of the present of the Swedish welfare child. In T. S. Popkewitz & Brennan, A. *Foucault's challenge to the knowledge, curriculum and political projects of schooling* (pp. 91–116). New York: Teachers College Press.

Hultqvist, K., & Petersson, K. (1998). Iscensättningen av samhället som skola. Konstruktionen av nya nordiska människotyper mot slutet av det tjugonde århundradet. I samfundet som skole. Konstruktionen af nye nordiske mennesketyper i slutningen af det tyvdende århunderede. In Jens Bjerg (Ed.), *Grundbok i Pedagogik* (pp. 517–49). Stockholm: Liber.

Hunter, I. (1988). *Culture and government: The emergence of literary education.* London: MacMillan Press.

Jehlen, M. (1986). *American incarnation: The individual, the nation and the continent.* London: Harvard University Press.

Johansson, J-E. (1994). *Svensk förskolepedagogik under 1900-talet.* Lund: Studentlitteratur.

Key, E. (1900). *Barnets århundrade.* Stockholm: Albert Bonniers förlag.

Kristjansson, B. (1995). Vardandets barndom –(Be)varandets barnforskning. In L. Dahlgren & K. Hultqvist (Eds.), *Seendet och Seendets Villkor. En bok om barns och ungas välfärd* (pp. 29–61). Stockholm: HLS förlag.

Larsson, J. (1994). *Hemmet vid ärvde. Om folkhemmet, identiteten och den gemensamma framtiden.* Stockholm: Arena.

Lester, L. A. (2000). *"De andra" i pedagogiska texter. Afrikaner i svenska pedagogiska texter (1968–1965).* Stockholm: Stockholm Institute of Education.

Linné, Carl von (1823). *Egenhändiga anteckningar af Carl Linneus om sig sjelf.* Utgiven av Adam Afzelius, Uppsala.

Lull, T. F (Ed.) (1989). *Martin Luther's basic theological writing.* Minneapolis: Fortress Press.

Lärarförbundet (1998). *Forma framtidens lärande, ett utbildningspolitiskt diskussionsmaterial* (Shaping the learning of the future; policy document).

Marcuse, H. (1991). *One-dimensional man: Studies in the ideology of advanced industrial society.* Boston: Beacon Press.

Marx, L. (1967). *The machine in the garden.* New York: Oxford University Press.

Mitchell, W .I. T (Ed.) (1994). *Landscape and power.* Chicago: University of Chicago Press.

Montessori, M. (1912). *The Montessori method.* London: Heineman

Montessori, M. (1936). *The secrets of childhood.* Bombay: Orient Longmans.

Myrdal, A. (1935). *Stadsbarn: en bok om deras fostran i storbarnkammare.* Stockholm: Kooperativa förbundet.

Myrdal, G. (1931). Socialpolitikens dilemma, I och II. *Spektrum, 3,* 13–31.

Myrdal, G., & Myrdal, A. (1934). *Kris i befolkningsfrågan.* Nora: Nya Doxa.

Närings-och Handelsdepartementet (1997). *I entreprenörskapets tecken—en studie av skola i förnyelse.* En utredning på uppdrag av Närings-och Handelsdepartementet, 3.

Osborne, T., & Rose, N. (1997). In the name of society, or three theses on the history of social thought. In *History of the Human Sciences,* vol. 10, no 3, pp. 87–104.

Ödman, P-J. (1995). *Kontrasternas spel del II.* Stockholm: Nordstedts förlag AB.

Popkewitz, T. S. (1996). Rethinking decentralization and the state/civil society distinction: The state as a problematic of governing. *Journal of Educational Policy, 11* (27), 27–51.

Popkewitz, T. S (2000). *Educational knowledge: Changing relationships between the state, civil society and the educational community.* New York: State University of New York Press.

Popkewitz, T. S., & Brennan, A (1998). *Foucault's challenge to the knowledge, curriculum and political projects of schooling.* New York: Teachers College Press.

Popkewitz, T. S., & Lindblad, S., (in press). Educational statistics as a system of reason: Relations of governing education and social inclusion and exclusion.

Popkewitz, T. S., & Pitman, A. (1986). *The idea of progress in educational research: The social function of the intellectual.* New York: Falmer Press.

Rose, N. (1990). *Governing the soul: The shaping of the private self.* London: Routledge.

Rose, N. (1996). The death of the social: Refiguring the territory of government. *Economy and Society, 25,* 327–66.

Rose, N. (2000, February 8). The politics of life itself: Biosociality, genetics and the government of the human vital order. Paper presented at an open lecture at the Stockholm Institute of Education.

Runcis, M. (1998). *Steriliseringar i folkhemmet.* Stockholm: Ordfront.

Skola för bildning (1992). *Huvudbetänkande av Läroplanskommitten.* Stockholm.

Skolkommittén (1997). *Skolfrågor. Om skola i en ny tid.* Slutbetänkande av Skolkommittén, SOU:121. Stockholm: Nordstedts.

Tallberg-Broman, I. (1991). *När arbetet var lönen. En kvinnohistorisk studie av barnträdgårdsledarinnorna som folkupplysare*. Stockholm: Almqvist och Wiksell International.

Walkerdine, V. (1995). Utvecklingspsykologi och den barncentrerade pedagogiken: införandet av Piaget i tidig undervisning. In Hultqvist K. and Petersson, K., (eds), *Foucault, namnet på en modern vetenskaplig och filosofisk problematik*. Stockholm: HLS förlag.

8

Childhood, School, and Family
Continuity and Displacement in Recent Research

Mirian Jorge Warde

Opening Scene

A municipal cemetery was opened, in São Paulo, in the beginning of the '90s, with the perspective of having its urbanized portion occupied by the first decades of the next millennium. The cemetery overlooks a hillside; looking at this slope, the official statistics had planned the use of the land: there would still remain a few decades, considering the slower dying pace of the elderly.

Before the '90s were over, the urbanized part of the cemetery had already been virtually taken. The municipal statistics reaffirm the rhythm of elderly deaths, but they also indicate what had not been forecast: the serial dying of children and adolescents born in the '80s and '90s. They are children killed by adults in slaughters in poor neighborhoods because of fights for drug dealing territories; they are children killed by adults in holdups; they are children killed by other children fighting for drugs or robbery spots; and they are children killed by drug abuse. These weekly corpses also include those who die in the periodic escapes/breakouts from Febem—the Underage Welfare State Foundation.

Febem was founded in the '70s, during the military dictatorship. It receives offenders and abandoned children. The state action toward extremely poor children and adolescents is today virtually reduced to maintaining institutions like Febem, managed and financed by state governments. Its role is just to keep children and teenagers under custody, no matter whether they are "abandoned" kids or "offenders."

One of Febem's units, in the outskirts of São Paulo, from where over 1,000 interns have escaped, lives in a permanent state of conflict. Monitors, on behalf of discipline, make torture and insult to human dignity a daily routine. The 1,400 underage kids kept in custody in this unit are awakened at six o'clock every day, generally with the noise of punches on the wall. Because of overcrowded conditions, two or more have to share the same mattress. Asking to go to the toilet during the night is grounds for reprimand. J. C. S., who ran away last week, says this was the reason for one of the four severe beatings he got from the jailers during the three months he was in the institution. He says: "I had to stay with my head leaning over the wall, supporting the weight of my body onto the wall, for about an hour, then I was hit with the handle of a broom." O. P. R. says he was punished due to an even more trifling reason: he asked the monitor where he was born. One of his mates laughed at the curious question and he ended up being beaten.

The list of tortures implemented at Febem is comprehensive and creative. One of the most frequent torments is called "gecko." The boy is forced to open his arms and put his whole body in contact with the wall, supported by his tiptoes only. If he is unable to stay like this for a time longer than he can stand, he is hit with elbow strokes in the back. Beatings are done with wood and iron sticks wrapped with towels so they will not leave blemishes. During the day, in certain periods, the kids are allowed to play soccer, dominoes, or checkers. Usually, however, they are forced to sit on the floor and they cannot talk to each other. Monitors say they can control the movements of interns this way, avoiding the formation of gangs and escape plans.[1]

Children and adolescents under custody in public institutions have the field and the nature of their future expectancies narrowed. Their language is dominated by negative terms: they don't want to be beaten anymore; they don't want to be in custody anymore; they don't want to go to school. Affirmative phrases are rare; confronted with choices, they accept to work, but not without reserves.

They do not have a family they can turn to. Some know where their mothers are; few know where the father is, but there is no turning point. As a matter of fact, all of them are where they are now because of a lack of family. Regarding the original condition in which they started, these interned children and adolescents have a lot to say.

About the mother:

She worked night and day and had no one to take care of us, because we are six (children), and my mum worked night and day. Then she took us to Febem. . . .

She would go to work, she had nobody taking care of the house, she went to the judge and sent us here.

About the father:

He's been in Bahia, for a long time. All letters that have been sent to my dad are returned; all phone calls that are made, wrong number.

About the family:

I have a grandma whose name is Dilma, but she died. My mom died when I was a little girl. My grandma died when I was already a teenager. . . .

I also had a little brother who died. His name was Pedro. When my mom gave birth to him, he was the first of all, but he was only born first, then he only stayed good for two months, he got sick, and then he died. . . .

Then when my mother died, she was wearing a nice dress, all blue, light blue and dark blue. Then I stayed there and missed my mom a lot. . . .

After that, we grew up and we came to school [Febem] . Because my mom died and my dad could not keep us, because my dad had to work. . . .

My mom wanted to kill my sister and my dad, she wanted to kill everyone. I don't know why, she used to drink! She got drunk! She talked a lot of bullshit. . . .

I don't know my father. My mother left home and my dad went away on a trip.[2]

In these statements, the children charge the environment and the family with the cause of their abandonment and misdemeanor. They also do not have faith in themselves because they already incorporate and embody the stigma.[3] In their talks, disbelief in themselves is patent when they mention poverty and the lack of a family. Being poor and with no family seems to be the prior condition to risk; their paths, for them, represent the confirmation of what had already been inscribed in their origin.

Introduction

An increasing number of studies are dedicated to children and childhood in Brazil (see, among others, Del Piore, 1999; Freitas, 1997; Marcílio, 1998; RBH, 1999; Rizzini, 1993a, 1993b; Santos, 1996). Recent assessments (see Rizzini, 1997) of social research allow one to see continuities and displacements between the prescriptions, valuations, and concepts they operate with and devices that normalize childhood, put in action since the mid-nineteenth century.

In this chapter, I discuss recent research based on three perspectives, in order to capture in them the homologies and displacements: the family as the place where the family itself is instituted; the school as a place of preservation and development of childhood; and the state as the guardian of the uncared-for child.

The types of research I examine restore, on one hand, the association between "full childhood" and "structured family"; on the other hand, they introduce limitations in their conception of childhood while associating it with school. My argument is twofold: I try to show that recent research is constrained between a Catholic culture of a wide and remote tradition and the urgencies of economic adjustment into the world order. In addition, I intend to demonstrate that the relations between childhood, family, and school present themselves as private relations from which the state is absent.

Family and Childhood

There is really little current research that denies or relativizes the role of family in the constitution of childhood. Zaluar (1985) warns about the increasing process of disappearance of the instituted nuclear family (in the large Brazilian metropolises such as São Paulo and Rio de Janeiro). But, in the spots where criminality abounds, Zaluar has not confirmed the current assumption of "family disorganization," as most of the families are complete; in addition, one can notice the increasing process of redimensioning the cultural pattern in force where clearly separated father and mother roles were distinguished, because "what one can see, as a general standard, is a decrease in the importance of the male figure in favor of the expansion of the female role. Far from being a characteristic of the Brazilian urban proletariat only, the so-called matrifocal family is, no doubt, a reality in the social organization of the poor workers" (Zaluar, 1985, p.98; see also Zaluar, 1992, and Adorno, 1991).

In the current sociological research, however, abandonment and delinquency are directly and repeatedly associated with "family de-structuring" and parental thoughtlessness. Thus, in the very family roots lie the social inviability of these children and their condemnation to a nonchildhood, the result of low levels of income, morals, and intelligence.

Rooted in the assumption that the so-called child marginality is a product of the de-structured nuclear family, children are photographed throughout the cities; they are found under custody in a situation of embarrassment; they are calculated in the crop fields and in the coal mines, in slave and semislave labor. The sociological research has become the depository of philanthropic essays at the end of the nineteenth century and the beginning of the twentieth century, produced by jurists and health scholars, in their role of making the cartography of child penury and refeeding the charity of the governmental and nongovernmental sector. This recent sociology shares the same discourse field produced by government agencies and domestic and international charity agents, and they are the permanent interlocutors of newspaper denounce-ments (see Martins, 1991).

This discursive field, in which this recent sociology takes part, affirms the epistemological inviability of providing marginalized children with singularity and individuality. These children are the very mirror of the metropolis; they are the violence of the city; they are Febem; they are the gangs, the hordes. This sociological cartography epistemologically justifies the lack of inroads on the individual and the subjectiveness: socially excluded children are nonindi-viduals and nonsubjects. At the same time, by ascribing the de-structured family as the cause of the impracticable childhood for the marginalized child, this sociology replaces the family's primary social role, its status of celula mater.

This trend decants the modern family's (postcolonial) constitutive dis-course, which emerged in the nineteenth century and was present in the first decades of this century. Once the family were/had become instituted within scientific, rational standards, there would remain no salvation for the individ-ual outside of this institution: there would only remain the condemnation of the streets or seclusion by the state. Where the family and the state failed, there would be the damnation of the norm.[4]

It was necessary to create the family "intimacy" in order to affirm that the construction of childhood could only take place within the home, under the intimate zeal of the family's adult members, against the street's harmful-ness. It was necessary to institute the street as the external side of the family world in order to affirm in it the inviability, the risk, and the denial of childhood.

"Showing the world as a lair of ruin or, deliberately, stressing the risks of assault to decency and other forms of moral violence was an effective way of withdrawing the family from the street's promiscuity and turning it in to the home" (Costa, 1979, p. 136). While creating the evil of the world, consensus was established to say that only within the family is there protection. "The obscene world, morally destructive was invented to create, within the family, terror to what is exterior and tenderness by means of intimate conviviality" (p.136). The family's protecting intimacy was set up simultaneously with the creation of the world's evil.

But the doctors, jurists, and hygienists of the nineteenth century had no doubt that the constitution of the rational family, subject to scientific inter-vention, could flourish only in the social environments adverse to deviations and degradations. If poverty was a natural hindrance to the coming of har-monic family, the state should be in charge of directly intervening on behalf of parents and children in jeopardy. In Brazil in the second half of the nine-teenth century, black, mulatto, and dun-colored people were the racial foci requiring direct state action, as they lacked the natural condition on which science could act to erect physical and moral health; the physical degradation of black, mulatto, and dun-colored people was naturally followed by moral degradation.[5] In the beginning of this century in Brazil, the state's direct intervention was requested regarding immigrants, whose "racial inferiority" was taken as a reason for their "moral degradation." Worse than the black people—who at least had shown to be pacific, even though degenerated— the immigrants were socially rowdy and politically threatening.

Some physicians and pedagogues of the nineteenth century had attempted to petition the care of children by means of the state, with the fear that the mixed-breed Brazilian family would be unable to get rid of its colonial past. But the prompt results obtained with the subordination to the hygiene claims and parental affection (with a great contribution from the Catholic Church[6]), drove such attempts backward. Soon, the normalized, whitened,[7] bourgeois-styled, European-like family became the ideal place to cultivate the normalized, whitened, orderly childhood.

Acquiring habits would be the family's primary task, starting at the youngest age. No other institution could do it. Taken from the cradle and molded with tenderness, the child would foreshadow the adult person contained in his/her "evil inclinations" and resist harmful external agents. Consisting of a practice of "good habits," the child would become an adult with no suffering and without being aware of how or why.

Doctor José Lino Coutinho said in 1849:

> this is how the plants are cultivated and also that's how men are educated, when still young and flexible, they get—without being aware of it—all the impressions and doctrines, but, when tough and big, sooner or later, they never straighten. The well-defined man is an animal of habits. (in Costa, 1979, pp. 173–74)

Thus, the "de-structured family," which is found in the research and denounced in the diagnostics, is the family constructed in the second half of the nineteenth century by means of a systematic intervention of medical, hygienic, psychological, pedagogical, and legal normalization. Disciplined, the modern family yielded the well-educated, refrained, and repressed individual. It produced his/her intimacy and capacity to share the public order. The de-structured family of today is also the product of its permanent dependence on external normalization, the constant disciplinary intervention. As it is no longer able to function without being dictated the rule of correct conduct— as man and woman are to live together, get married, love each other; as parents are to love and take care of their children; as children are to love and hate their parents; as adults are to relate to the children; as children are to relate to adults; as adults and children are to relate to the elderly . . . the family has de-structured itself because it was strict in complying with the rules of health, balance, civility, and good manners imposed on it (see Costa, 1979,

p. 15). The family is blamed for its own de-structuring and for producing the "violated childhood."[8]

Childhood and School

In Brazil, social research has been involved, since the end of the '80s, in the systematic campaign that Boom and Narodowski (1996) called "worldwide education." These are studies of strong doctrinal contents that put into action two argumentative sets to defend schooled education as a path for the national development: on one hand, indicators from the so-called developed countries are evidence of the direct relation between the development indices and the schooling rates; on the other hand, they bring forth arguments based on the new productive technology that is demanding not only the dissemination of schooling but also the rise/change of the cognitive standards.

Boom and Narodowski examined two movements occurring in Latin America (they can certainly be applied to Brazil as well) in which school education was used as an anchor to national projects. In the first one, dated from the nineteenth century, the constitution of nationwide teaching systems was defended as a prerequisite for the constitution of the nation and the political education of the citizen; school was defended as a primary place where the national unity was created, by sharing common values and the same language. Today, the discourse of "spreading education worldwide" engages the school in the project of economic development so that "(school) education begins to be a basic necessity of first order, by increasing people's demand, as well as investments of resources and international loans" (see Boom & Narodowski, 1996, pp. 7–16).

Although the authors are correct about the social perspective of the discourses that feed the belief in the transforming power of education, implemented in the mid-nineteenth century and resumed in the 1980s, they do not sufficiently stress what these discourses convey in their essence, aimed as they are at creating not only consensus about the collective changing power of schooled education but also the subjective incidence of such discourses. In them and by them, the school takes the place of a true institutor of individuals and their subjectivity. Between the mid-nineteenth century and the beginning of this century, one used to talk about the "new man"; current research now mentions a "new subjectivity."

As a complementary issue, and a central one as well, current research reiterates school/family as a complementary pair and a support to the societal project and condition for the construction of the "new subjectivities." Nor could they state it differently; without its complement—the family—school would stop working immediately. Even if the alliance device has changed direction, the alliance still remains. This is so true that the parties—with heavy losses caused by the delegitimation they have suffered (especially from the '60s on)—admit that when one party stops working, the functioning of the other party is affected.

Many of these studies (and the bibliography they use) refer to the discourse that defends a "new subjectivity" as having characteristics of the constructivist self: flexible, problem solving, active, enterprising (see, among others, Popkewitz, 1998a and 1998b, and Corazza, 1998). As an offset, the new nationwide curriculum parameters[9] and the nationwide teaching exams,[10] as well as the requirements imposed by the new technological centers, indicate an operation to reduce the possibilities to be reached by the new subjectivity: if the new man—potentially contained in the child—was the result of intercrossing moral choices, citizenship, and rational and cognitive capacities, then the new subjectivity is strictly delimited by specific cognitive skills, from which, one expects, their moral choices and forms of societal insertion are derived.

This reducing force has been strongly produced by the decline of the modern pedagogy—in the forms projected by Comenius—and its incorporation to psychology. Comenius had thought of the child as a plant:

> with the ax and the saw and the scythe of their law, cut at their feet and after pruning the half-died and dry trees of our heart, there [He] planted new shoots chosen in paradise; and in order to make them come to life and grow, He irrigated them with his own blood and never did He stop watering with several gifts of his Holy Spirit, which are like brooks of living water: and He also sent his workers, spiritual gardeners, to take good and faithful care of God's new plantation. (Comênio, 1985, p. 58)

He calls children "heaven's little plants," "paradise's little plants," "God's little plants," comparing them to "new little trees," which are to be treated with great care so that they will grow "pretty and strong" and it will be possible to "renew the orchard," as their minds are "simple and have not been occupied and spoiled with vain prejudices and mundane customs," and for this reason, they are "more inclined to love God" (Corazza, 1998, p. 12).

Comenius (mid-seventeenth century) thrust modern pedagogy on the belief of education as regenerating by means of the art of teaching everything to everybody in a total manner. In his missionary-pedagogical preaching everyone was included and everybody could receive the full word.

In his last pedagogical work—*Pampaedia*—Comenius includes everyone, even those who were still outside the Didactica Magna. Everybody fit in, including the barbarians, he said:

> one must also wish that even the extremely barbarian nations may be enlightened and drawn out of the darkness of the barbarism and thus,

because they are part of Mankind, resembling their whole, as, actually, the whole is not complete if some of its parts are missing. (Comênio, 1971, p. 47)

To teach everyone everything:

one desires that every man is straightly formed and entirely educated, not only in one thing or in a few things or in many things, but in everything that improves the human nature: to know the truth and not be seduced by the evil; to do what is to be done and to refrain from what is to be avoided; to talk wisely about everything, with everyone, when it is necessary, and never see oneself forced to be silent; in short, to act, under all circumstances, toward things, toward men and toward God, in a non-frivolous manner; but prudently and thus, never be apart from the purpose of their happiness. (Comênio, 1971, p. 38)

And, in order to teach in a total manner:

not for ostentation and external splendor but for the truth. That is, to make every man as much as possible similar to the image of God (in compliance with which we were created), that is, truly rational and wise, truly active and quick, truly thorough and honest, truly pious and holy, and thus, truly happy and blissful, in this world and for eternity. (Comênio, 1971, p. 38)

Comenius's belief in the naive and passive spiritual inclination of the "little plants" to grow and germinate is not shaken until the end of the nineteenth century. But "the vain prejudices and mundane customs" walked more rapidly than the dissemination of the "full word," and some branches of the "tree of life and knowledge" were contaminated. The view on the child, at the end of the nineteenth century, started the process of ambivalence: children are not all alike. There are children in danger and there are dangerous children.

It is also the image of the plant that the director of public instruction in São Paulo, Oscar Thompson, takes in 1914 at the opening of the Experimental Pedagogy Laboratory, in the Pedagogical Anthropology and Psychology Office of the Secondary Normal School of São Paulo, to sustain pedagogy in psychology (see Carvalho, 1997, and Tavares, 1995). Basing his comments on the image of a tree split in two halves—one is leafy, the other is withering with wilted fruits—he said:

The tree of scientific pedagogy that is erected from the base of several disciplines, extends and gives life to two major branches: abnormal and corrective pedagogy and normal pedagogy which, as we have seen, provided practical education with a new direction, reformed it, showing the scientific reason of each principle in the different educational means.

Regarding the pedagogy for abnormal individuals, it is evident that new educational criteria are in progress at the light of which our guidance in this arduous and delicate field will be safer and more rational. Through them, the teacher will learn to confront and distinguish the normal cases from abnormal cases in order to take care of everyone according to their precise worth. (Thompson, 1914, p. 15)

But if the normal individuals are different from the abnormal ones— through the "safe and rational" act of discriminating and classifying (and all may still be the target of the teacher's action, although "everyone according to their precise worth" and more precarious results)—from them all the fallen or "degenerates" are distinguished:

It is important not to confuse the cases of simple anomaly with those of severe and deep degeneration. The first ones may be, within a certain limit, compatible with the nature and purpose of school, they may attend the schools for the normal individuals, they may be corrected and changed by means of special methods, which the teacher must know if he/she does not want to commit what one could call crimes of lese-profession. On the contrary, the degenerates are absolutely excluded from the school for the normal children no matter the form of their degenerative character. I think it is suitable to indicate this distinction, not because certain anomalies, more than others, are of interest to pedagogy, but because this study is also considered one of the forms of activity, a manifestation of normal or abnormal life. It is a subject matter of interest and, similarly to so many others, it shows how scientific pedagogy provides the teacher with new means and new aids, as well as it can indicate to his/her mission a new route, that is, to attempt a cure and the education of children who are not absolutely degenerated, but partly defective or late in the development of some activity, poor children almost always looked at as an obstacle to the free and regular functioning of school life and, therefore, they are abandoned to their own fate. The education of the morally or intellectually defective child is less likely to achieve the results achieved by the normal and sane child. That is why the attempt of improving even if just a little the condition of this unfortunate being is an act of the most beautiful human nobility and truly worthy of the educator's holy mission. (Thompson, 1914, p. 16)

If science gives the teacher a hand in teaching him how to discriminate "the tares from the wheat," only Christian charity can justify the effort to educate those who will yield little fruit: the educator's mission is "holy." One must start with nature—because they are abnormal children by nature—and replace such nature with what it cannot do by itself:

> If educating a normal child follows nature, educating an abnormal child is something completely different, that consists of replacing the nature present in the child, repairing the faults it causes to the child and satisfying the necessities that such replacement requires. The study of this subject matter and the corrective means takes an increasing importance and it would be enough to highlight the humanitarian purpose of scientific pedagogy. Without a scientific pedagogy we would not be able to study the child in his/her special character, we would be able to distinguish the student with a slow intelligence from the cretin, the imbecile from the idiot. If not long ago this child was lost for society and exiled to the madhouse to expiate the parent's faults, we see him/her now, thanks to a better study, in the hands of special orthophenic institutes, where the child is educated and corrected to take his/her place in social life. (Thompson, 1914, pp. 17)

The school is then no place for the "degenerates"—those morally decayed due to their own nature.

Thompson was one of the persons mainly responsible for disseminating the principles of the modern and scientific pedagogy in Brazil in the beginning of the twentieth century. In constant contact with the United States and Europe, Thompson, in his position as director of public instruction, undertook efforts to disclose the "latest findings in Child Psychology" and promote the practices of psychic measuring of children. His speech opens the leaflet in which elementary teachers and students of the normal school are presented studies on child psyche (child reasoning, child graphism, the child's kinetic memory, intellectual types, association of ideas) and institutes the adoption of the school biographic card, an instrument to record data measured on a yearly basis and future classifications of students at the elementary schools.

From Comenius to Thompson (from the seventeenth to the nineteenth century/beginning of the twentieth century) the belief in the dual power of school education is disseminated: on one hand, under the form of a nationwide system, school education becomes one of the most central political devices for the education of the citizen and constitution of the nation; on the other hand, it had the role of controlling and molding the individuals for a healthy psychological and moral life. Thus, school education becomes the anchor both of the production of the amalgam of societal life and condition of the modern individual. Between Comenius and Thompson, the exclusion of the "barbarian" was inscribed as one of the possibilities of modernity.

Schooling strategy is twofold. It takes place on one hand in the economic project as a "way out" for a horizon of social survival. On the other hand, the replacement of the schooling discourse reappears as an individual alternative, with a double meaning: it can save the individual from the objective point of view as well as from the subjective point of view. On both hands, children deprived from prior social conditions—to be clear, family conditions—are excluded from this possibility. Thus, the child-individual, the infantile-subjectivity this discourse is aimed at, is the one whose social conditions make its emergence possible. School reappears such as in the nineteenth century and beginning of the twentieth century as a complement—for the purpose of the public environment—of the family.

Recent psychological research covers that portion of childhood for which remains the assumption of existence of the individual, and that is the child at school; but due to conceptual and methodological artifices, this child is turned into a universal being and concretizes all forms of childhood. Child and childhood appear in this research under the form of the actual student or the potential student. Thus, by disjoining the normal from the pathological, child psychology or infantile psychology in recent research has reduced, and in the extreme has eliminated, the incursions into the moral, affective, attitudinal field to focus on the processes of cognitive development. Taking this route, it establishes a common discourse with the school diagnostics and reforms sponsored by the state. Both for the psychological research and for the state, the target is the children at school age, cut from the component of psychic life that is interesting to them, that is, the normalized cognitive processes. These may be measured and examined.

Narodowski says:

> it is prudent to stress that this discourse differentiation between the discourse development promoted about childhood in general (psychology-psychoanalysis-pediatrics) and childhood specifically at school conditions (educational psychology-pedagogy) assumes, beyond the multiple and complex relations found between the two fields, a differentiation on the level of the object under study: while the former ones study the child, the latter claim a childhood integrated into school institutions that specialize in producing adults: the school. The object of the latter is the child regarded as a student only. (Narodowski, 1994, p. 26)

The argument being made here is in favor of Narodowski's position as related to the process of construction of these disciplinary fields. However, recent research conducted in Brazil indicates the subsumption of the pedagogical discourse in the psychological discourse and vice versa.

The process of reducing the psychological object to the childhood under school conditions, which implies identifying the child with the student, represents the subsumption of pedagogy by psychology, and both had, at the very first moments of their discourse institution, a great deal of convergence and separation. Child and student corresponded existentially, but on an epistemological basis they were different objects. In the framework of recent psychological (and pedagogical) investigation, child and student are identified existentially and epistemologically; being a student became sine qua non for making childhood real.[11]

With such a view, recent research reiterates governmental guidelines intended to cognitively encourage the child, and they operate with the aim of producing evidence that the social and technological changes underway ask for a cognitively skilled child; the cognitive-technological child. "A more adult and more rational child, especially adult and rational too early, a child from and for the technical civilization" (Trisciuzzi & Cambi, 1989, p.140).

This reduction of childhood to phases of cognitive development and its mirroring in the process of technological development may be thought of as the outcome of the same movement of hyper-naturalization of the child and the economical/social processes.[12] Acting as the bearing of this hyper-naturalization of the child, one can find evolutionist assumptions that support the psychology of development, that is, "the development has become the metaphor that directs the theorization about children" (Skolnick, 1975). Archard (1993) mentions three basic assumptions: teleology, necessity, and endogeny.

Development assumes there is a purpose, a telos to be reached, which is the adult status. It is in this phase that all biological characteristics are defined and the organism achieves its plenitude. Thus, the progress of the child development is measured against the proximity to the adult phase, which is used as a term of comparison. The adult capacities serve as a parameter, that is, "the apex of the developmental sequence is an adult age which mirrors a general standard for the culture or the species" (Archard, 1993, p. 34).

But development has intrinsic laws: development is a necessity of development itself. Each stage to be gone through is the prerequisite of the progress necessary for the next stage. The need for development thus assumes the cultural invariability—all beings, regardless of the cultural context where they are found, must go through the same stages. Also, development is self-impelled. It draws driving forces from the very structures and functions contained in the child's nature (see Santos, 1996).

State, Church, and Social Intervention

The constitution of the modern school and family in Brazil took place in a temporal continuum; the postcolonial family was already consolidated, from the mid-nineteenth century, when the discourse orders around school were laid out and their instituting practices were started off in the beginning of the twentieth century. Thus, when school started to take its present form, the family was already socially rooted and lent itself to the discourse of extra-familial dangers. This is so true that by the end of the nineteenth century and beginning of the twentieth century, there came the speeches that denounce the street child, outside the family, and to this child is imputed the condition of "morally dangerous" (Thompson writes about the third kind of child—the degenerated child—in 1914; up to that moment, two other kinds—the normal and abnormal child—were mentioned in the scientific milieu, and the concept of the "naive" child, unaware of the original sin, prevailed).

In Brazil, the defining power of the family over school form and culture—form and culture of exclusion—has to be thought of, in the long run, in reference to two combined elements: a) the Brazilian republican state, which conserved strong links inherited from the Portuguese state, that is, high administrative and bureaucratic concentration, with low political and moral legitimacy[13] and b) the capillary penetration of the Catholic Church on different levels of social life, supported by the effective strategies of aggiornamento, put in action since the beginning of this century.

The postcolonial Brazilian state born in the nineteenth century was configured by a high administrative/bureaucratic concentration, fed by a strongly excluding process of social recruitment, and became decisive over time by effective mechanisms of socialization and training of bureaucratic-administrative staff. This configuration allowed maintenance of a very organized, cohesive, and powerful state apparatus (see Carvalho, 1996), but strongly referred to the property-owning social classes, at the same time strongly opposed to the other social groupings.

The multiple modernizing discourses, put into circulation from the mid-nineteenth century on, provided arguments for breaking with the imperial state with the aim of instituting the republic, but they did not change the configuration of the state. The particularities of the Brazilian state are supported by the porous relations between these two forms of arrangement—the state and the family. The process of transgressing the family milieu to give rise to the state was conducted by the intermediation of public servants strongly instituted by means of patrimonial education and practices.[14]

The fact is that, even if very modern and universalistic in its administrative-bureaucratic practices, the Brazilian republican state configured an antisocial and peculiar standard in dealing with the citizenship issues. It is within this long-term perspective that one can observe the inclusion on the state level of social welfare practices, but not the configuration of a welfare state.[15]

If the impotence of the state to compose the republican imagery from transcendent (supraparticular) political and moral values was caused by the prevalence of patrimonialist standards, this impotence was counteracted by the potency of the Catholic Church to more easily operate with discourse and nondiscourse devices of moral and political shaping. The Catholic Church

undertook a massive effort, by the beginning of the twentieth century, to update its discourse and practice in order to halt the process that unfastened the
state from the family; the most effective operation occurred in the very familial
ambience. The Catholic action over the families took place through a modernizing intervention of its practices and by means of the intermediary access
to scientific knowledge.

Two central and complementary strategies led the displacements of the
Catholic Church from the primitive Tridentine theology to papal ordinances
set forth after the *Rerum Novarum* encyclical: on one hand, it made the scientific
branches of knowledge compatible (and their discourse and nondiscourse
forms of circulation) with the practices of moral and religious education[16]; on
the other hand, it created and controlled agencies for the education of medium
and upper cadres, which spread through the state apparatuses (bureaucratic
and representation apparatuses) and the elementary and high schools and in
the university scientific institutes.[17]

An Attempt at Conclusion

Childhood entered the level of state intervention by means of two excluding
paths; on one hand, by incorporating children into the elementary school
system. This is the only field of systematic action of the state; for this path the
'90s have been producing the discourse of possibilities of reinserting Brazil
into the worldwide economic development. On the other hand, the state maintains secluding institutions for abandoned children and offenders who are
"underage"; for most of these underage individuals, school is virtually out of
their possibilities.

During the '70s, when the present seclusion institutions were created for
the abandoned and the offenders, the state project included the complementary aspect of these institutions with the public schools and, whenever possible,
training for a profession. This state project, tried out in the '70s and '80s, was
a total disaster in the '90s. School and seclusion institutions no longer have
any channel of social communication.

The result makes patent the fissure in the social imagery associated with
childhood: part of the children are included in future social possibilities, another part of them are definitely excluded. Moreover, against this part society
must protect itself because it compromises the possibilities of the imagined
future. While presenting recent statistics on the children's situation in Brazil,
an assistant to the government declared that 40 percent of Brazilian children
between birth and fourteen years of age live under abject conditions, that is,
the monthly family income does not exceed half of the minimum wage; they
are the product of structural unemployment, of social changes, of family dis-

aggregation. The state can do nothing for them, at least not in the short run. Among these children, a small amount can be "saved" if they are lucky enough to be adopted, another small amount may be included in some nongovernmental aid program. But the great majority will not stand a chance of witnessing and much less taking part in better times.

A fundamental point to be incorporated in the analysis of the place delimited by the state, both through scientific and religious intervention, both inscribed in the construction of modernity, concerns the heavy resources these segments have applied on the family. Thus, thinking the state as depositary of expectations of child intervention implies considering that the state is not an exclusive or even privileged land of action, but instead and preferably the family is; through the family, the construction and consolidation of the state occurs. It should not remain unnoticed that since the second half of the nineteenth century—when the discourses of systematic intervention on childhood started to be disseminated—the family was turned into the target and main consumer of such discourses.

Return to the First Scene

After two more bloody escapes and the death of a few interns, the government of the State of São Paulo decided to close down some units of Febem in the capital and transfer them to other locations in the countryside. Inhabitants from these cities have already turned to courts of law, organized demonstrations, and formed political alliances no one could have ever thought of, in protest against the government's decision. One leader of such movements soon declared: "instead of taking the peace of mind away from our families, it should be better to kill those monsters."

Construction of new units has been stopped by order of a Court of Justice.

Notes

This chapter received excellent suggestions from my program colleague, Maria das Mercês Ferreira Sampaio, who was once again my ingenious reader, and from my translator, Luiz Ramires.

[1] Based on a news story.
[2] Speech of children secluded at Febem, recorded in research by Kosminsky (1991).
[3] In meaning E. Goffman has given to "stigma" (1975).
[4] This expression—"damnation of the norm"—is a play on words (damn and nation) taken from a brilliant study by Roberto Machado et al., published in 1978

under the title *Danação da norma: medicina social e constituição da psiquiatria no Brasil* (Damnation of the norm: Social medicine and constitution of psychiatry in Brazil). This study, rooted in Foucault's work, was the basis for a great number of studies starting in the '70s dedicated to the history of medicine, hygiene, pedagogy, and other disciplines as well as the family and childhood. A highlight in this line is Costa (1979), Herschmann (1996), and Antunes (1999). The same period must also include a series of studies on the same topics in France, where the highlights are Murard & Zylberman (1978), Joseph et al. (1977), and Fourquet & Murard (1973).

[5] The boy and the girl, children of black slaves, used to live within the colonial house and this remained so until the mid-nineteenth century; the boy was the toy of the "little lord"; the girl was the deposit of learning for the pleasure of the boys of the manor house. Thus they could enjoy the space of the lord's family, a custom that lasted until censures and disciplinary rules began. Up to that moment, the white boy and the black boy did not carry a differentiated image. They had the same practices. The patriarchal and colonial certainty that their social roots and destinies were so definitely intertwined meant that for centuries neither laymen nor religious men took charge of distinguishing blacks from whites. The sixteenth-century papal bill that blessed black slavery and relegated slaved blacks to animal condition did not reach the child; as such, it shared the same "natural" condition of the child; neither one nor the other had yet been conceptualized. With no concept, the white and black child took part in the universe of naturalness. That was how many patriarch families disseminated the habit of including the black boys in the practices of baptism. When the chaplain headed for the manor house to baptize the lord's boys, the black boys (children of the household slaves) were also included. Something different occurred with the indigenous child in the beginning of colonization; the Jesuits converted the Indian boy into a specific chapter of the sermons and practices of catechization. In the nineteenth century, Indians had already been wiped out or interned into the woods.

[6] One should not think, however, that the goals of scientization of the social practices were conducted in detriment of religious-biased discourses and practices. If it is true that the Catholic Church has to yield to the technical/scientific interventions, it is also true that the defeats suffered by the religious field in the last decades of the nineteenth century were followed by a rearrangement of that field so that it could also be updated, incorporate science precepts, and, within bounds, include itself in the process of construction of modernity. Thus among the modernity projects in Brazil that took shape from the last decades of the nineteenth century on, one has to include those associated with the scientists and also with different sectors of the Catholic Church. To be sure, this strategy was part of the process of "Romanization" of the Catholic Church in the Western world and of the significant expansion of its social and state intervening power.

[7] Racism is a phenomenon deeply connected with scientific discourse. The black person was seen as a holder of evil, and statements that the black person was a threat to order and a hindrance to progress were found in the scientific academies and schools of medicine and in the scientific journals, from where the information was disseminated. Interfering with the family was meant to attack the presence of the black slave circulating among whites. The medical/hygienic discourse did not take a position against slavery but encouraged disgust toward black people. It normalized their expulsion from within the house and barred their contact with children. Due to racial arguments, blacks did not enter the level of medical benefits. There was no direct intervention toward black people—their racial degeneration made scientific charity

useless. Their presence in the house was a challenge to hygiene; from animals useful to the assets and property, they became animals harmful to health. Because of the academic theses submitted to the Medicine College of Rio de Janeiro in the second half of the nineteenth century, black people were included in the harms to health caused by "miasmas, insects, bad atmosphere and bad habits . . . among the female slaves, who are not only stupid, rude and have vicious morals, but also their body is usually the seat of a great deal of diseases, such as syphilis and scrofulous diathesis, limphatism" (Murilo Mendes Vianna, 1869, in Costa, 1979, p. 122). "Therefore, Black slavery and the great number of slaves are the causes which appear in the first place in the prostitution of Rio de Janeiro" (Herculano A. Lassance Cunha, 1845, in Costa, 1979, p. 265). "Black people who are stupid and rustic by nature and education, unaware of the feelings of decency and chastity, and having an erotic and consequently very lustful disposition, are thus sent into the core of our families as actual automatons of our will, our *fac totum*, mainly the female ones" (José A. A. Macedo Júnior, 1869, in Costa, 1979, p. 122).

[8] Not only by the production of the "violated childhood"—the one that feeds police reports, official statistics, and newspaper pages—but also the "expropriated child"—the child produced by consumption and technology, because he/she was abandoned by the adults in his/her own home and turned to television, to electronic games, and to the computer. Recent sociological research reveals an increasing concern not only with what they call the "violated child" but also with the so-called "expropriated child," in the meanings indicated above. This is research particularly sensitive to arguments like the ones contended by authors such as Postman (1984) and Trisciuzzi & Cambi (1989), who impute to "familial disorder" the cause for the increasing risk of end of childhood and increasing need to appraise the school as a way out. About this, see Narodowski (1998).

[9] National Curriculum Parameters are the guidelines for the curriculum reorganization in the elementary and high schools set forth by the federal government in the '90s. They are based on constructivist pyschopedagogy rooted in Piaget.

[10] The national teaching exams, implemented on the different levels of schooling in the '90s, represent a privileged tool for the federal government to control the cognitive results obtained in the state, municipal, and private schools. They will be used for the purpose of allocating financial resources as well as for the control of the international financial agents over the loans made in the '80s and '90s.

[11] "Schooled childhood led to a childhood minutely made pedagogical, in their hearts and minds, by the educational disciplines so that their entire behavior is then encoded by concepts of normality, by means of normalization methods more and more accurate and judicious. The 'conquer of child by science' was followed by a pedagogy which 'populates the path of human life with signaling posters,' but it also deals with the infantile life that is deviant, deficient and pathological with pharmacological, chemotherapy, orthopedic, psycho-therapeutic resources" (Corazza, 1998, p. 141).

[12] About the hyper-naturalization of the technological processes, see Marcuse (1999)

[13] About the organizational standard of the modern Portuguese state and its roots in the Brazilian state, see Faoro (1976) and Carvalho (1996).

[14] About the Portuguese patrimonial root of the Brazilian state, see Holanda (1995).

[15] This patrimonial root is patented in the state's low moral and political capacity to produce adherence to the lay and positivist republican symbols, which were sub-

jugated in the people's imagery by the religious symbols. About the struggle between the lay and positivist symbolism, defended by the elite in control of the process of constitution of the republic, by the end of the nineteenth century, and the religious symbolism resulting in the success of the latter over the former, see Carvalho (1987, 1990).

[16] In Brazil, medical intervention on the family, in the long run, did not mean the loss of moral intervention by the Catholic Church. Penetration of the latter into the university scientific institutions was part of the strategy of aggiornamento conducted by the Catholic Church in Brazil. On the other hand, the outstanding presence of the Catholic religious education over the male intelligentsia is remarkable from the second half of the nineteenth century until the 1980s. An outstanding example of this scientific/religious merger is found in the insistence of medical theses in the second half of the nineteenth century on the necessity to operate a strict control at the schools over male masturbation (not one single thesis was found dealing with female masturbation), as it was considered the major cause of physical and moral decadence of children and young men. Masturbation—as the church shepherds used to preach— "causes phthisis, madness, epilepsy, hypochondria, chronic phlegm of body organs and eventually death" (Antenor Augusto Ribeiro Guimarães, 1858, in Machado et al., 1978, p. 122).

[17] The Catholic Church, based on Vatican ordinances, among which *Rerum Novarum* is only the opening one, put in action different strategies for different countries and continents. Thus the strategic operations successful in Brazil were not the same ones found in the European Catholic countries and were not even the same applied in other countries of Latin America. Even so, the very strategic differentiation was part of the Vatican's central strategy: *aggiornare* (update) the intervention on the social level by adopting the diversity of practices and discourses.

References

Adorno, S. (1991). A experiência precoce da punição. In J. de S. Martins, (Ed.), *O massacre dos inocentes: a criança sem infância no Brasil* (pp. 181–216). São Paulo: Hucitec.

Antunes, J. L. F. (1999). *Medicina, leis e moral: pensamento médico e contemporâneo no Brasil (1870–1930)*. São Paulo: Ed. Unesp.

Archard, D. (1993). *Children: Rights and childhood.* New York: Routledge.

Boom, A. M., & Narodowski, M. (Eds.). (1996). *Escuela, Historia y Poder.* Buenos Aires: Novedades Educativas.

Carvalho, J. M. de (1987). *Os bestializados: o Rio de Janeiro e a República que não foi.* São Paulo: Companhia das Letras.

Carvalho, J. M. de (1990). *A formação das almas: o imaginário da República no Brasil.* São Paulo: Companhia das Letras.

Carvalho, J. M. de (1996). *I—A construção da ordem.* Rio de Janeiro: Ed. UFRJ/Relume Dumará.

Carvalho, M. M. C. de (1997). Quando a história da educação é a história da disciplina e da higienização das pessoas. In M. C. de Freitas (Ed.), *História social da infância no Brasil.* São Paulo: Cortez; Bragança Paulista: USF.

Comênio, J. A. (1971). *Pampaedia.* Coimbra: Faculdade de Letras da Universidade de Coimbra.

Comênio, J. A. (1985). *Didactica Magna: tratado da arte universal de ensinar tudo a todos.* Lisboa: Fundação Calouste Gulbankian.

Corazza, S. M. (1998). *História da infantilidade: a-vida-a-morte e mais-valia de uma infância sem fim.* Porto Alegre: UFRGS (tese de doutoramento).

Costa, J. F. (1979). *Ordem médica e norma familiar.* Rio de Janeiro: Graal.

Del Piore, M. (1999). *História das crianças no Brasil.* São Paulo: Contexto.

Donzelot, J. (1977). *La police des familles.* Paris: Minuit.

Faoro, R. (1976). *Os donos do poder.* Porto Alegre: Globo (2 vols.).

Fourquet, F., & Murard, L. (1973). *Les équipements du pouvoir.* Fontenay-sous-Bois: Recherches.

Freitas, M. C. de (Ed.) (1997). *História social da infância no Brasil.* São Paulo: Cortez; Bragança Paulista: USF.

Goffman, E. (1975). *Estigma: notas sobre a manipulação da identidades deteriorada.* Rio de Janeiro: Zahar.

Herschmann, M. (1996). Entre a insalubridade e a ignorância. A construção do campo médico e do ideário moderno no Brasil. In M. Herschmann, S. Kropf, & C. Nunes, *Missionários do Progresso: médicos, engenheiros e educadores no Rio de Janeiro— 1870–1937* (pp. 11–67). Rio de Janeiro: Diadorim.

Holanda, S. B. de (1995). *Raízes do Brasil.* São Paulo: Copanhia das Letras.

Joseph, I., et al. (1977). *Disciplines a domicile: l'édification de la famille.* Fontenay-sous-Bois: Recherches.

Kosminsky, E. V. (1991). Internatos—os filhos do Estado padrasto. In J. de S. Martins (Ed.), *O massacre dos inocentes: a criança sem infância no Brasil* (pp. 155–80). São Paulo: Hucitec.

Machado, R., et al. (1978). *Danação da norma: medicina social e constituição da psiquiatria no Brasil.* Rio de Janeiro: Graal.

Marcílio, M. L. (1998). *História social da criança abandonada.* São Paulo: Hucitec.

Marcuse, H. (1999). *Tecnologia, guerra e fascismo.* São Paulo: Ed. Unesp.

Martins, J. de S. (Ed.) (1991). *O massacre dos inocentes: a criança sem infância no Brasil.* São Paulo: Hucitec.

Murard, L., & Zylberman, P. (1978). *L'haleine de faubourgs: ville, habitat et santé au XIXe. Siècle.* Fontenay-sous-Bois: Recherche.

Narodowski, M. (1994). *Infancia y poder: la conformación de la Pedagogía Moderna.* Buenos Aires: Aique.

Narodowski, M. (1998). Adeus à infância (e à escola que a educava). In L. da Silva (Ed.), *A escola cidadã no contexto da globalização.* Rio de Janeiro: Vozes.

Popkewitz, T. S. (1998a). A administração da liberdade: a cultura redentora das ciências educacionais. In M. J. Warde, *Novas políticas educacionais: críticas e perspetivas* (pp. 147–72). São Paulo: PUC/SP.

Popkewitz, T. S. (1998b). Reforma educacional e construtivismo. In T. T. da Silva, *Liberdades reguladas: a pedagogia construtivista e outras formas de governo do eu* (pp. 95–142). Rio de Janeiro: Vozes.

Postman, N. (1984). *The disappearance of childhood.* New York: Laurel.

Revista Brasileira de História (RBH) (1999). Vol. 19, no. 37. Dossiê: Infância e Adolescente. São Paulo: Anpuh.

Rizzini, I. (Ed.) (1993a). *A criança no Brasil hoje: desafio para o terceiro milênio.* Rio de Janeiro: Ed. Universitária Santa Úrsula.

Rizzini, I. (1993b). *Assistência à Infância no Brasil: uma análise de sua construção*. Rio de Janeiro: Universitária Santa Úrsula.

Rizzini, I. (1997). *O século perdido: raízes históricas das políticas públicas para a infância no Brasil*. Rio de Janeiro: Ed. Universitária Santa Úrsula/Petrobrás/Ministério da Cultura.

Santos, B. R. (1996). *A emergência da concepção moderna de infância e adolescência: mapeamento, documentação e reflexão sobre as principais teorias*. São Paulo: PUC/SP (dissertação de mestrado).

Skolnick, A. (1975, Summer). The limits of childhood: Conceptions of child development and social context. In *Law and Contemporary Problems, 39* (3), 25–40.

Tavares, F. A. R. (1995). *A ordem e a medida: Escola e Psicologia em São Paulo (1890 a 1930)*. São Paulo: Universidade de São Paulo (dissertação de mestrado).

Thompson, O. (1914). O futuro da pedagogia é scientífico. In Escola Normal Secundária. *O Laboratório de Pedagogia experimental*. São Paulo: Typografia Siqueira, Nagel & Comp.

Trisciuzzi, L., & Cambi, F. (1989). *L'infanzia nella società moderna*. Roma: Riuniti.

Veiga, C. G., & Faria, L. M. de (1999). *Infância no sótão*. Belo Horizonte: Autêntica.

Warde, M. J. (1997). Para uma história disciplinar: psicologia, criança e pedagogia. In M. C. de Freitas (Ed.), *História social da infância no Brasil*. São Paulo: Cortez; Bragança Paulista: USF.

Zaluar, A. (1985). *A máquina e a revolta: as organizações populares e o significado da pobreza*. São Paulo: Brasiliense.

Zaluar, A. (Ed.) (1992). *Violência e educação*. São Paulo: Cortez.

9

Childhood and the Politics of Memory in Argentina

Inés Dussel

For almost a century, childhood has been considered a universal and stable category that encompasses a chronological period of our life. Since the irruption of progressive pedagogies, schools and other public institutions have been organized upon a notion of the "nature of the child." As other contributors to this book have argued, these claims to universality have had the effect of producing particular scripts for children, enabling certain practices and authorizing specific discourses about who is to be considered a "child" while disabling and repressing other discourses and practices (Baker, 1998; Hultqvist, 1998; Popkewitz, 1998; Walkerdine, 1990, 1997). Childhood has functioned as a regulatory ideal that prescribes a "self-regulating individual and a notion of freedom as freedom from overt control" (Walkerdine, 1990, p. 19). Yet this freedom is regulated, administered through minute devices that one learns from one's own early experiences and continues doing so throughout the whole life. In the oxymoron of an administered freedom, one can trace the paradoxes faced by modern pedagogy (Donald, 1992).

In this chapter, I intend to put these critical arguments in a different context, that of the struggles around memory/forgetting in Argentina. After discussing the historical construction of childhood in the context of an educational system that marginalized child-centered pedagogies, I will focus on the recent rearticulation of "childhood" within the discourses of human rights. The emergence, in the past four years, of an organization that nucleates the children of the disappeared people, called H. I. J. O. S. (literally "children" or "sons/daughters" in Spanish, acronym for Hijos por la Identidad y la Justicia contra el Olvido y el Silencio, Children for Identity and Justice and against Forgetting and Silence), has renewed the struggle against impunity. It has also implied a generational relay in the field of human rights from the Mothers of Plaza de Mayo to the children, an event full of semantic and political consequences. While they are not children any longer, their ages now being around eighteen to thirty years old, the H. I. J. O. S. speak of their "robbed childhood" and of their rights to know their identities, thus producing a radical rearticulation of the concept of childhood within a new constellation of meanings.

I will claim that this shift in the concept of childhood and its occupation by other strategies compel us to "eventualize" the notion of discursive concepts—that is, to produce a more radical theoretical movement toward discontinuity and singularity than what we have done so far with the critique of childhood as a "regulatory ideal." Using Foucault's theoretical approach combined with a Derridean sensibility for issues of justice and responsibility,[1] I will deal with the historical construction of childhood in Argentina, characterized by the marginalization of child-centered pedagogies, and the current production of new memories of children that reclaim the language of identity and voice. Drawing also on Ernesto Laclau's political theory of articulation, I will argue that childhood has to be understood as an empty signifier whose temporary signifieds are a matter of political, historical competition. This competition will not be considered in terms of a dialectical movement of action and resistance (as in critical pedagogy) but as a contingent trajectory of discourses, a trajectory that continues to be written today.

Introduction: The Names and Memories of Childhood

> The name: What does one call thus? What does one understand under the name of the name? And what occurs when one gives a name? What does one give then? One does not offer a thing, one delivers nothing, and still something comes to be which comes down to giving that which one does not have. (Derrida, 1995, p. xiv)

Derrida's comments on the power of the name provide a point of entry to the issue of childhood and of how discourses and "names" shape us and yet leave room for indeterminacy. As I read this paragraph, I would say that being called a name is to be offered something, a space or locus in a social grid, a filiation or affiliation; but those who give a name are giving something that they do not have, or do not totally have, and one can relate this not-totally-having with the limits of freedom and the desire to be sovereign subjects and have command over other people's selves. What's in a child's name, then? What's in the name of "childhood," and what's done on its name? How do discourses produce and also constrain (exclude other possibilities of being) our selves?

"On the Name," on the other hand, is the title of a short essay by the Argentinean poet Juan Gelman about the children of the disappeared. According to Gelman, children are rarely inscribed in national histories, which are monopolized by adult-centered narratives. However, there is enough courage and protagonism in children's lives so as to include them in Argentina's narrations of the nation. Gelman tells the stories of three children who were taken away by the military in the same operations in which their parents were kidnapped or killed in the 1970s. The first child, Paula, was kidnapped by a police officer when her parents were disappeared and was illegally adopted by the officer's family. She was twenty-three months old and knew that her name was Paula. Those who took her away tried to rename her as "Luisa" but she refused and insisted on being called Paula instead. Her keeping her name was of great help for her grandmother to locate her. The second child, Anatole, a four-year-old boy, was taken to a Uruguayan clandestine concentration camp with his parents and his eighteen-month-old sister Victoria. He learned to say the names of all the inmates at the detention center. Some months later, his parents were killed and the two children were taken to Chile, where they were left at an orphanage.[2] A couple tried to adopt him and not his sister, but he refused and convinced them to adopt the two of them together. Again, his keeping his name, staying with his sister, and recalling the names of the people he had seen at the concentration camp were useful for locating him and knowing the fate of dozens of persons. Gelman wonders at the power of the name and the power of memory, and claims that Paula, Anatole, and Victoria's obstinate memories should be incorporated into the narration of the nation.[3]

These stories are true, and it is not by chance that Juan Gelman tells them. His own daughter-in-law disappeared (she was kidnapped by the military) when she was seven months pregnant and had her child while at the same Uruguayan camp where Anatole and Victoria were kept. Through other reports he learned that the baby was born healthy but the mother was never seen alive again. Twenty-three years later, just weeks before I wrote this article and after long and exhausting struggles to know what happened to the baby, Gelman finally found his granddaughter, who lives in Uruguay.[4]

The children of the disappeared continue to be an open wound in Latin America. Recent reports on El Salvador also show that among the casualties of the civil war there are hundreds of missing children who in most cases were seized away by the military and given up for adoption (Rosenberg, 1999). In Argentina, the struggle of the Grandmothers of Plaza de Mayo has been central not only in locating the missing children but also in keeping several military chiefs in jail. Despite the general amnesty declared in 1990 to all those militaries condemned for human rights violations, the *comandantes* are being incarcerated again on a legal argument: The crime against the children continues to be perpetrated until they are found and their identities are restored, and thus it is not a crime of the past but of the present.

In all these cases, the discourses of human rights and of the rights of children to their real identities have been invoked to fight with considerable success for locating and identifying the missing children and for punishing the perpetrators. These discourses have been traditionally grounded on a liberal, modern conception of the self as a freewill agent who is the "source and center of meaning of the world" and whose ethical values have become the universal standard on which to measure all human experiences (Douzinas, 1999, p. 101[5]). At first sight, then, the project of putting together these discourses of human rights and poststructural thinking seems very capricious, if not self-contradictory. More so, if we take into account, for example, Michel Foucault's "confession" that his "general project has been, in essence, to reverse the mode of analysis followed by the entire discourse of right, . . . to invert it." Thomas Keenan elaborates on this statement, saying that Foucault wanted to show "not which rights (whether divine, individual, or human) are legitimate, justified and authorized, but rather, how force relations have been enabled and naturalized in the name of 'right' " (Keenan, 1997, p. 162; quote by Foucault on the same page). In relation to the children, the appeal to innocence and free will, and also a naturalized conceptualization of identity, might be read as the consolidation of the dominant power régime. It seems as if rights were so deeply rooted in the methods of subjugation and epistemes of modernity that it is hard to believe that Foucault, as well as many other poststructuralist thinkers, would propose to reinscribe them in a different way.

However, I will claim in this chapter that these contemporary struggles can show how the discourse of rights is producing paradoxical, even subversive, effects and can be reoccupied strategically by an "inventive politics" (using Nikolas Rose's term; Rose, 1999, p. 490) that de-fatalizes our present and calls for new power relations, ethics, and subjectivities. This shift in the articulation of childhood compels us to "eventualize" the notion of discursive concepts—that is, to produce a more radical theoretical movement toward discontinuity and singularity than what we have done so far with the critique of childhood as a "regulatory ideal."

I will use two different theoretical frameworks for this project of "de-stabilizing" our certainties about childhood. The first one is related to Foucault and will focus on his notion of history and particularly on what I translate as "strategic occupation" of a given "dispositif" or device. In "Nietzsche, Genealogy, History," Foucault asserted that "[t]he great game of history is who is going to seize the rules, who will take the place of those who use them, who will disguise [herself/himself] so as to pervert them, invert their meaning, and use them against those who had initially imposed them; who, through entering into the complex apparatus, will make it function in a way that those who are dominant will in fact be dominated by their own rules" (Foucault, 1984, p. 86, translation modified).[6] The notion that laws and apparatuses/devices can be reoccupied by other strategies is a relevant methodological tool for analyzing how these discourses of children's rights to memory have more complex political effects than those that can be assumed by a decontextualized reading.

It is also important to remark, following Keenan, that in his "History of Sexuality" Foucault spoke about which direction should be taken by our struggles, and he pointed to the need of a new kind of right, antidisciplinary and liberated from the principle of sovereignty (Keenan, 1997, p. 165). Keenan sees in this rewriting of the term "right" the possibility that it can be recuperated in democratic struggles; in other words, Foucault did not close the possibility that rights could be inscribed or articulated in a different kind of politics. At this point, I would like to make it clear that I am not interested in "rescuing" Foucault or other poststructural thinkers for the "good causes." Rather, my project is to intervene in contemporary theoretical debates about the limits of a politics based on poststructural tenets, showing that poststructuralism can provide important gains both for theoretical and political innovations, and can help us read contemporary events in a different, more creative way inspired by the hope of justice.

The second theoretical framework I will use is Ernesto Laclau's political theory of articulation (Laclau, 1996; Buenfil Burgos, 1996), acknowledging that there are contradictions and incompatibilities between them but stressing their points in common.[7] In this reading, childhood functions as a "floating signifier" whose temporary signifieds are a matter of political, historical competition. I will quote here Costas Douzinas's argument about rights as floating signifiers:

> As a signifier, [the "man" of the rights of man] is a discursive element that is not automatically or necessarily linked to any particular signified or meaning; on the contrary, the signifier "man" is empty of all meaning and can be attached, therefore, to a large number of signifieds. As a result, it cannot be fully and finally pinned down to any particular signified, because it transcends and overdetermines them all. But the "man" of human rights is not just an empty signifier; the signifier is full of symbolism, it carries a surplus of meaning, value and dignity endowed by the early modern revolutions and augmented by every new struggle for the recognition and protection of human rights. This semantic excess turns it into a floating signifier and explains its importance for human-rights campaigns. (Douzinas, 1999, p. 104).

I will argue that, if we think of childhood as a regulatory ideal that has a historical, contingent trajectory and that carries its own "semantic excess," then we have to acknowledge that this trajectory continues to be written today. Thus, it is important to look at what other contents are now being articulated by the notion of childhood, in what ways, through which discourses, and with what effects.

This reference to struggle and competition does not intend to bring back the traditional tale of "power" and "resistance" that has been heard of too many times already. Rather, I intend to point to the process by which "alternative values and their constituencies have labored to mark themselves in discourse" (Morse, quoted in Morris, 1993, p. 465). Childhood as a regulatory ideal may imply different things across time (Hultqvist, 1998), and this ideal may be plural, incoherent, made of layers of sedimented discourses, and may be mobilized in different ways by different strategies. As Rose remarks, "resistance . . . needs no theory of agency" if one states that human beings "live their lives in a constant movement across different practices that subjectify them in different ways" (Rose, 1996, p. 35). It is to this movement inscribed within the articulation of childhood that I would like to point in this chapter, through analyzing the construction of discourses of childhood and its links to the politics of memory in Argentina.

With this heuristic device, I will argue in this chapter in favor of expanding our critiques of the discourses of childhood in two directions. The first moves from the level of the political rationalities of the discourses of human rights and children's rights to the level of political events,[8] not easily reducible to the level of political rationalities. The second is related to the geopolitical shift from a theory formulated and grounded in societies where modernization has achieved particular goals to a part of the globe in which modernization has had different effects.[9] Particularly, I will claim that the school system in Argentina was not organized upon a progressive pedagogy; on the contrary, the progressive pedagogy remained a marginalized discourse, and liberal individualism never achieved the status of commonsensical knowledge as I believe it has in the United States and some European countries. This "discursive constellation," then, provided a different horizon in which discourses of children's freedom and autonomy were inscribed and will be dealt with in the next two sections. In the final section, I will show how this constellation also frames the way in which childhood is being mobilized today in human rights discourses.

The Politics of Memory and the Construction of Childhood at the Turn of the Twentieth Century

Argentina shares with France and the United States a history of mass immigration that shaped in significant ways the construction of the nation. Initially colonized by the Spaniards, the southern part of the continent was a marginal settlement that produced no remarkable wealth compared to the gold and silver that came from Peru and Mexico, and achieved its independence in 1810. After several decades of political unrest and civilian wars, a national state was organized during the second half of the nineteenth century. Local elites of the provincial states had to subject themselves to the power of a centralized oligarchy, and provincial identities, which up to that point had been the primary collective identities, had to be abandoned (Chiaramonte, 1989). At the same time, a genocide was committed against the nomad tribes of native peoples in a military campaign that was significantly called "The Conquest of the Desert," as if EuroAmericans were advancing in a vacant land, in a similar way to what happened in North America since the first settlers (Shapiro, 1997, pp. 28–30).

Immigrants were called upon to unmake the effects of the "barbarians" and to bring into the country the culture and civilization that it lacked. The diagnostic frame, structured in colonial language,[10] was established by a seminal book written by Domingo Faustino Sarmiento (1811–1888), president of the republic and a prominent educational leader in the second half of the nineteenth century. In *Civilization or Barbarism* (1845/1950), Sarmiento sought to understand the "origin of the Argentine tragedy," as he called the civilian wars that followed the independence from Spain. He found a cultural explanation: "barbarism" was the obstacle for unifying the nation. It could be healed through a series of actions that ranged from extermination ("The Pampas have to be watered with the gauchos' blood," he claimed unapologetically) to immigration and education. The immigration that he had in mind was the northern European, Protestant family, which he pictured as hard working and austere.

Part of Sarmiento's dreams were fulfilled, but some others turned into his most feared nightmare. From 1860 to 1930, six million people came to the country, most of them southern Europeans and Middle Eastern immigrants, accounting for 75 percent of the total population growth in Argentina. They were overwhelmingly illiterate, Catholic, and poor. The great majority settled down in Buenos Aires, the capital city, where almost 80 percent of the population were immigrants or children of immigrants by 1914 (Sarlo, 1993).[11]

By the turn of the century, concerns about the impact of this massive immigration on the viability of national unity became more common and were expressed through legislation, newspapers, and the arts. Even Sarmiento, so ardently in favor of immigration, became a quasi-chauvinistic nationalist and devoted his last years to struggle against the Italian community, which he perceived as the new obstacle for the country's development. Besides, some events—such as the semiofficial declaration of the King Vittorio Emmanuele of Italy that Argentina should become an Italian colony, and the protagonism of immigrants in the organization of labor unions and leftist parties—contributed to shape a climate of ideas that supported active nationalization campaigns and that broke away from the cosmopolitanism that characterized the earlier appeals to immigration.

In this nationalizing climate, education was to play a key role, as will be shown in the next section. But there were also several other ways in which "nationalization" was to be achieved: a national judicial system, a compulsory military service for all young men, and the production of a national memory that entailed a particular "structure of memory and forgetting" (Shapiro, 1997). Soon after, everything turned out to be part of the crusade for the nation. The urban historian Adrián Gorelik states this clearly with the following example:

> The patriotic liturgy invades different realms, and in this movement several institutions and discursive supports are added. [For example,] As an homage to the centenary of our country, the oil "Bou" gives to Argentine children a copy of a plate belonging to General José de San Martín [a hero in the war against the Spaniards], as exhibited in the Historical Museum, adhering to the motto with which the English reproduced the dinner service of Admiral Nelson: "to eat in the plate of a hero is to be inflamed with the fire of the highest patriotism." (*Caras y Caretas*, Buenos Aires, January 21, 1911, quoted in Gorelik, 1998, p. 217)[12]

One of the privileged realms in which this campaign was enforced was on the construction of monuments and buildings ("the most significant markers" according to the European image of "culture"; cf. Shapiro, 1997, p. 23). Statues epitomized which events and characters were to be included in the national pantheon of heroes and which ones would be excluded and were specially powerful due to their spread distribution across the city. One of the leading intellectuals of the nationalistic movement in the first decades of the century said that: "History is not only taught in class lessons: the historical sense, without which lessons are sterile, is formed in the spectacle of daily life, in the traditional names of places, in the sites that are associated to heroic memories, in the remains and pieces preserved at museums, and even in the commemorative monuments, whose influence on the imagination I have called the pedagogy of statues" (Ricardo Rojas, quoted in Gorelik, 1998, p. 206).[13] For example, in the capital city, Buenos Aires, during the first decade of the twentieth century, there were fervorous debates around the statue erected in honor of the Italian leader Garibaldi in 1907, and an older one to pay homage to Mazzini in a central square near the city's port, erected in 1878 (Gorelik, 1998, pp. 206–8). Both were the object of severe scrutiny and complaints due to their association with Italy. While decades before the statues symbolized cosmopolitan values (liberalism, republicanism) that were thought to be central to the newly constituted Argentine republic, by the turn of the century the nationalism that became prevalent was too exclusivist and chauvinist to tolerate the integration of foreign heroes in the national pantheon. However, Gorelik notes that paradoxically the sculptors and aesthetic patterns used to produce the nationalistic statues were also of European origins, show-ing that the quest for an "authentic" national style was much more sinuous than it was intended.

These debates were also expressed in the urban plans for the moderni-zation of cities. Buenos Aires was perceived by part of the elite as an enemy, a cosmopolitan monster. Its central avenue, Avenida de Mayo (in honor of the month of the Revolution), was seen as a mask ball that represented the new civic barbarism, the new rich immigrants. The historian Ricardo Rojas up-dated Sarmiento's opposition between civilization and barbarism in terms of urban decay and degeneration: "[Barbarism's] theatre is the city, and no longer the country; the barbarians do not ride horses but tramways" (in Go-relik, 1998, p. 214). The monuments and statues had to stand in opposition to the city, producing a new sense of the past as a collection of patriotic icons (Gorelik, 1998, p. 216). This conviction led Rojas to build his Buenos Aires house imitating the facade of the building in which independence from Spain was declared in the northern province of Tucumán. This house, already de-molished, was for him the symbol of the "true," authentic nation, against the urban Babel that mixed all styles and confused all symbols. He declared in his will that his house should be transformed into a museum after his death. One can see here how the "invention of tradition" of which Eric Hobsbawm and Terence Ranger have talked is at work: the creation of a historical house in the 1920s was to be transformed into a landmark of Argentina's memory of the early nineteenth century.

The national imaginary that was constituted through these interventions was thus based on a particular account of the past, that posed as its Other first the native peoples and the gauchos, and later on the new immigrants. In the next section, I will deal with its impact on the construction of a national educational system and on how childhood was conceived and regulated.

The Modern Educational System and the Construction of Childhood

As it has been said, the organization of the educational system was a key factor in the integration of a disparate population into a nation. The "literate citi-zenship" (Sábato, 1992) educated by the schools would be the pillar of the republican order and the national union imagined by the founding fathers, most of them subscribers to a loose liberalism (Schwarz, 1977). Sarmiento, about whom I talked in the past section, said that "An illiterate people will always vote for the local leaders or 'caudillos'." Sarmiento thought that the construction of the nation would be achieved only if new, "civilized" subjects were produced through education. His generous educational plan, which in-cluded the education of women and poor children, was based however on the prior extermination of all those who fell into the description of "barbarians." It seemed as if modern education that would guide the nation into a more democratic and productive organization was only possible at the expense of repressing or exterminating parts of the population, deemed uneducable (Puiggrós, 1990). These assumptions were at the basis of Argentine pedagogical optimism and supported the feeling that in order to achieve a structural transformation, there had to be a schooling process of the masses, for which there was a strong distrust. This suspicion can be seen in Sarmiento's own efforts to organize local boards of education following the U.S. example, efforts that were frustrated when the social participation did not have the results he intended but instead produced the occupation of civic spaces by political cliques. Sarmiento ended up supporting their suppression or marginalization (Caruso & Dussel, 1996).

From 1870 on, several laws were passed that established free, secular education for all. Public instruction was conceived of as the best guarantee that the sovereign people would exercise their duties in the right way. As in France, secularism became an important feature in the common culture created by schools. It was thought that everyone should be socialized on the same grounds, irrespective of their national and social origins or religion, and these grounds were seen as "neutral," "universal" terrain that would embrace all peoples.

Thus conceived, the public school turned into a formidable machine of assimilation of the immigrant and provincial population. The extension of elementary schooling and the introduction of a centralized teacher training system were the means through which these heterogeneous masses became integrated into Argentine society (Tedesco, 1986). Illiteracy rates soon achieved the levels of western European countries, and a large reading public emerged that consumed textbooks, magazines, and books.[14] It is interesting to note that the popular literature had many points of contact with "high culture," and it was usual to find the writings of Borges or of European philosophers in the magazines that were bought massively by these new literates (Romero & Gutierrez, 1992). In the collective myths that forged the national imaginary, Argentina was presented as a melting pot in which everyone would be welcomed and move up in society and in culture. It was also presented as a leading country in Latin America, the most European-like and "Europeizing."

Schooling as a Patriotic Crusade

The last section has shown that, no matter how inclusive national identities proclaimed themselves to be, they brought along other exclusions. The Argentinean common national self required avoiding particularistic identities and liberal individualistic philosophies (a source of "anarchy" for most of the organizers of the school system). In order to become national subjects, immigrants had to abandon their languages, mores, heroes, and costumes. The school system participated actively in this campaign (which was called the "Patriotic Crusade" in 1908–1912), policing the boundaries of "proper Spanish," "proper memories," and "proper rules." One school officer, Juan P. Ramos, wrote in a seminal report on the state of schools in 1910:

> We have not known how to make schools contribute to affirm the principle of nationality. . . . We lack the aptitude to be a melting pot. . . . Collective persuasion, produced by imitation, is unavoidable during the childhood years. . . . We lacked the principle of a national school textbook, even of a national history itself from which we only knew the chronicle and fragmented episodes. [From now on,] We have to establish a patriotic cult in schools, a cult for our Patriotic symbols and heroes, we have to retain the facts, the dates, and the names in our national history. (Ramos, quoted in Quatrocchi de Woisson, 1995, p. 41)[15]

Patriotic rituals and "liturgy", as Gorelik calls it, became part of the daily life of schools. The honoring of the flag, the marching ceremonies of patriotic celebrations, and mural pictures and inscriptions proliferated across the country. This shift can be observed in the transformation of school rituals. While in the last decades of the nineteenth century there was a day that commemorated "The Tree," celebrating nature and its positivistic laws, in the first decades of the twentieth century it disappeared and gave way to a continuous schedule of patriotic feasts commemorating independence, revolution, the founding fathers, and the "discovery of America." Also, it should be noted that Andrés Rodríguez, the writer of one of the best-selling textbooks of all times (*The Kid*, 1895, reprinted as late as the 1940s), started writing a series of books that were called *The Patriot*, *The Family*, and *The Soldier*. The space of the "child" had to be filled with particular semantic associations, attached to this militaristic nationalism.

This nationalistic crusade was supported by a medicalized pedagogy, through which children were "normalized" and subjected to strict disciplinarian rules and rituals (Puiggrós, 1990). Teaching practices were supposed to follow scientific methods that could be replicated across the country. There was a whole set of rules and devices to classify the school population into different categories, either related to their ethnic origins or their intelligence coefficients.

To illustrate this point, which shows how nationalism can be at the same time an inclusive and an exclusive identity, combining acculturation with claims to equality and social progress, I will refer to the narrative of a teacher.

Daughter to illiterate immigrants, she attended the normal school and became the headmistress of a school in a low-income area in the city of Buenos Aires in the early 1920s. In her first day as principal, she lined up her little pupils and separated several of her male students. Leaving them standing in the school playground, she called the barber and had him shave the heads of the kids. She still remembers that the playground was covered with a soft carpet of thin hair. According to some other data, more than 10 percent of her students were immigrants themselves, and many more sons of recent immigrants. One can imagine that most of them might have had difficulties in speaking Spanish, and a large portion of them might have been Jewish. She justifies her action saying that, if left with their hair, these kids would have brought lice to the whole school, and that the first thing she wanted to do was to give a practical lesson (Sarlo, 1997, p. 187). While the narrative may shock for its brutality, it should be made clear that for this teacher it seemed perfectly right to perform this task in the name of health and literacy. "Children's rights" (whatever one fills this up with) did not have a place in this system, except as "the right to be educated"—which could be easily transformed into an obligation. This naturality provides some insights about the kind of intervention that the public school system performed on the educational subjects in Argentina.

Another example of this imaginary, which shows the extent to which "individual's rights" or the nature of the child were not central issues in the constitution of the modern school system and of the prevalent school culture in Argentina, is the introduction of white aprons (*guardapolvos*, literally: dusters) as school uniforms in the early twentieth century. To avoid social differentiation by appearance, the educational authorities decreed that children should attend schools wearing an identical white cloth or smock over their clothes. This uniform, which resembles the one worn by medical doctors or nurses, also had some prophylactic aims, such as to prevent germs and bacteria from spreading throughout schools. Soon after, the teachers were obliged to wear them as well. Here, there are visible links between uniformity, particular notions of equity, and a medicalized pedagogical discourse. The notion of a liberal individual who can express "freely" through "choosing" his or her way of dressing, as it happened in the U.S. educational history, was excluded from the beginning.[16] It is interesting to note that "inclusion" in the social order was not made on the name of individuals exercising their rights but on the name of a state that assumed to know what was best for the individuals. My point here is not to advocate for a liberal affirmation of rights, but rather to emphasize that the "technologies of the self" (Foucault, 1988) put in practice in Argentinean schools were different than the ones employed to form a "self-governed citizen." I will deal with these differences in more detail in the next section.

The Marginalization of Child-Centered Pedagogies
and the Absence of a Discourse of Rights

It goes without saying that the notions of childhood that were authorized by such a pedagogical organization did not leave room for a child-centered pedagogy. Some reservations about child-centeredness should be expressed here. While I do not intend to support a romanticized notion of progressivism, I want to point to the different ways in which childhood and political cultures have been constituted in different countries. I agree with Valerie Walkerdine's argument that progressive pedagogy, despite its claims to liberate the individual, is really an administration of freedom. It implies a naturalization and internalization of rules in the name of the child. " 'The Child' is created as a sign, to be read and calibrated within the pedagogic discourses regulating the classroom. The child is defined and mapped in its relations of similarity and difference with other signs: activity, experience, play rather than passivity, recitation, work, and so forth. Through the regulation of this pedagogy children become subjected in the classroom" (Walkerdine, 1990, p. 25).

However, there is a difference in establishing rules in the name of the child or against him/her. Paraphrasing Rose, I would say that the technologies of the self that were effected through the prevalent pedagogy in Argentina were based on a calculable individual, an individual whose performance was to be judged and measured against a norm, but that this individual was not seen as calculating him/herself, as a self-regulatory being that had to enact these calculations on his/her own (Rose, 1999, p. 133). One can take, for example, the history of physical education in Argentina and compare it to Britain or the United States. While in these two countries sport practices played a pivotal role in the training of the body (see for example Kirk, 1992), in Argentina the practice of sports was explicitly prohibited in 1908 because they were thought to promote too much competitiveness and no solidarity. The privileged content for physical education became the drills and marching. One can speculate that the body that was imagined by Argentinean educators was one that had to respond to commands but that was not required to calculate its autonomous contribution to a collective endeavor.

Childhood (as part of a "political rationality" [Hultqvist, 1998], namely, the way in which the world of politics becomes a practice) was defined as immaturity, incapacity, instinctivity that needs to be governed and protected, both from others and from itself. It is remarkable that this definition encompassed both the schooled children and the unschooled ones. Along with the educational laws that established a compulsory secular education for children from six to twelve years of age (1882/1886), there emerged child labor laws and laws of childhood protection that implied the confinement in orphanages and minority institutions of the children of the poor and the deviant. For example, one of the first comprehensive pieces of legislation in relation to childhood, the Law of Childhood Trusteeship *(Patronato)* (Nr 10903, October 21, 1919), established that the state would be in charge of the children abandoned or neglected by their parents, including "moral and intellectual neglect." The other category of children to be "rescued" (Baker, 1998) by the state was the juvenile delinquent (Carli, 1991). Deviancy, delinquency, abandonment: those were the futures of children who did not attend schooling.

Remarkably, these associations between childhood and delinquency also invaded the school terrain and are nowhere clearer than in the writings of educational psychologists of that time. Two historians of psychology claim that "From the academic discourse, medicalized and biologized, the notion of the child gets severed from the figure of the innocent, angel, free of sins. In the context of a Haeckelian biogenetic law, according to which the development of the individual recapitulates the stages of development of the species, the fact that the child has outbursts of violence from his primitive and less developed personality in his adaptation to the environment acquires the category of evidence. It constituted an analogy between the child-like stage of humanity and the child-like stages of the future adult" (Ríos & Talak, 1999, p. 142).

The child, then, could not be abandoned to his or her instinctive tendencies; instead he/she has to be molded through education, an education that was conceived as the outline of natural, evolutionary laws that defined normality. The educational psychology that emerged out of this framework was not, then, one that valued "child development" but one that tried to steer it into a very defined pattern. This is clear in the writings and actions of Víctor Mercante (1870–1934), the creator of "Paidology," a branch of psychology specializing in the study of children. Unlike some of his North American colleagues, Mercante put the child under suspicion: "Philogenetically considered, criminal tendencies are natural to children such as they were natural in primitive men. . . . The child is not born as a good, all-loving being; on the contrary, the delinquent germination is much more active and varied than in the adult" (quoted in Ríos & Talak, 1999, p. 144).

Mercante gave a primordial role to memory. He suggested that one of the most important tasks of schools was to contribute to "anamnesis" or historical filiation. Given the fact that children bring along bad as well as good tendencies and drives, the school's problem was to cultivate the good ones and to get rid of the bad ones. In order to do so, the school had to know the child's background: the family profile, their criminal history, their ethnic origins, their school records. That is why he said that "Psychology has two defined fields of application: the school and the prison, culture and crime" (Mercante, 1927, p. 47). The anamnesis was to be achieved through visits to the children's homes and through a detailed recording of their school histories. Mercante conceived of these records as "biographical files" that may or may not be useful in the future but that should be compiled in case any other state agency needed them to establish a case. Knowledge and power were totally intertwined in his conceptualization of children's memories.

Educational psychology, led by Mercante and his followers, was pivotal in structuring an adult-centered pedagogy. Thus, the progressive pedagogies that were prevalent in other countries, and which were read and followed by many teachers, found scarce or little echo on the organization of schools and on the prevalent school culture. Some efforts to introduce the "child self-government," reportedly based on North American and northern European experiences, were soon marginalized in the school system and their promoters expelled (Carli, 1993). By the time the New School pedagogy turned into an official discourse, in the 1930s, it included an alliance with a conservative Catholicism and a growing fascist trend in society. One of its leaders was Juan Bautista Terán (1880–1938), who was the president of the National Education Board from 1930 to 1932. Terán led a movement to "spiritualize the school" (Terán, 1932). He criticized both positivism and pragmatism, which he accused of reducing the child to a "beam of instincts and tendencies." "School should not only be a gym to awake and give full shape to child spontaneousness," as Dewey and Montessori sought (Terán, 1932, p. 4). The aim of education, in Terán's view, should be to build a moral being with freedom and responsibility and project it to a transcendental level. He defended spiritualism as an educational philosophy, as it implied a return to intelligence in opposition to the cult of life advocated for by pragmatism. In his argument, activism was to be subordinated to discipline, order and respect to the rules, and these were the educational principles to be followed. This version of the New School was the prevalent one during several decades in Argentina and it occupied the discursive space of the school reform and of childhood protection, until the irruption of psychoanalysis in the 1950s and 1960s. This latter movement favored the reintroduction of child-centered pedagogies, although they were confined to private secular schools and microexperiences that generally did not extend to the public system.[17]

In Argentina, the 1970s were marked both by a political upheaval and radicalization and by the subsequent most fierce repression known to date by the military forces. Besides the guerrilla movement, one of the privileged targets of the repression was "youth": rock music, miniskirts, long hair, piercing all became metonomic representations of an alterity that was threatening and was dissolving "the national self" (Dussel, Finocchio, & Gojman, 1997). Children were considered at risk of becoming such "youth," and needed to be protected. Some of the guidelines of the military government in the educational area, as forbidding group activities, peer conversation, and "sharing attitudes" (all "germs of future communists"), would be laughable, had they not had such tragic consequences. Child-centered pedagogies were considered "subversive." Interestingly, the educational policies of the government relied on a conservative Piagetianism, in a reading that stressed its biologism and defended school abstentionism.[18] The "nature of the child," then, was articulated by an authoritarian pedagogy.

From the reinstitution of democratically elected governments, the educational field has undergone several attempts at reform and undoubtedly has changed profoundly. The current educational reforms in Argentina, which combine efficientism, World Bank orientations, and populist philantropism in varied ways, have represented an abrupt interruption of the traditional school culture. The notion of a uniform system has been replaced by compensatory programs that focus on "target populations," classifying the school children as "normal" or "needy" (those needing special assistance). The enactment of overt differentiation through lunch snacks and special aids to poor children has transformed the landscape of schools, breaking the tradition of uniformation. In many cases, classrooms and even schools have been closed due to the lack of funding. Competition among schools for the scarce resources has been implemented as a rule. However, if one looks at the curricular prescriptions and the new regulations, there are few mentions of children's rights or a child-centered pedagogy. The emphasis is being put on flexible organizations, management techniques, and new curricular contents such as computing and foreign languages. Remarkably, the space of childhood is still predominantly defined as the "object/target" of education.

Childhood and the Obsession with Memory in Contemporary Argentina

Let me now move out of the educational arena and discuss some broader cultural politics in which the notion of childhood is being redefined and restaged in different ways. I will refer to the politics of memory/forgetting that has been central to Argentine politics since the last dictatorship, and to the role played by the notion of childhood. I will claim that there is a "rewriting" of the notion of children's rights in the current articulation of human rights struggles in Argentina, which has to be read in line with the marginalization of child-centered pedagogies and the politics of memory/forgetting that structured the national imaginary at the turn of the twentieth century.

According to Andreas Huyssen, we live in a time obsessed with memory. This obsession is evident in the increased numbers of museums, historical exhibitions, antiques, and nostalgic fashions, which speak of the role that the past has come to play in legitimating certain ways of experiencing the present. Moreover, for Huyssen, it spectacularly denounces the crisis of that "structure of temporality that marked the age of modernity with its celebration of the new as utopian, as radically and irreducibly other" (Huyssen, 1995, p. 6).

There are, however, other places in the world in which this obsession with memory becomes more urgent and dramatic, where, to put it crudely, the obsession is populated with corpses left by past struggles, corpses that are still warm. This warmth does not necessarily mean that the events recalled are immediate, but that they have a particular presentness, an astonishing capacity to pervade the life of a society, as Henry Rousso puts it for the memories of the Vichy Regime in the French case (Rousso, 1991). This is the case of Argentina. Remarkable for the proximity of trauma in time and for the presentness of "corpses still warm" (a metaphor particularly adequate for this country, where the absence of corpses has led to a prolonged mourning of the disappeared people), the Argentine obsession with memory is being played out dramatically in the last years. As in many other societies emerging from a period of violence and trauma, the command to remember is very strong in Argentina (Jelin & Kaufman, 1998). The saying that "to remember avoids repeating" is probably linked to the spread of some basic tenets of psychoanalysis in the political culture, which stress the link between repression and repetition, making it difficult at times to critically interrogate current constructions of memory (Jelin & Kaufman, 1998, p. 3).

I will briefly refer to two facts that I believe are crucial for understanding how these politics of memory/forgetting have been constructed along these years. From 1983 (the end of the military dictatorship) to 1998, the sites of memory have gradually shifted from the state-centered research commissions, trials, and amnesties at the beginning of this period, to the multiplicity of testimonies and sites of memory, as it became evident when the twentieth anniversary of the military coup in Argentina aroused many commemorations. That is, it became more microphysical, if I may use the term, more visible in the daily life, and less important in the political arena. The second fact is that, while the Mothers of Plaza de Mayo were the center of human rights struggles in the 1980s—and continue to be important— lately the H. I. J. O. S. (sons and daughters of the disappeared) have become pivotal in the articulation of new memories and alliances. This generational relay may be speaking of the end of a certain "state of emergency," as John Beverley calls it, and the birth of a new orchestration of time on the ruins of the old desire of testimony (Beverley, 1996).

In the past four or five years, childhood has been mobilized within these politics of memory/forgetting. One of these mobilizations has been the movement to derogate the Law of Childhood Trusteeship *(Patronato)* already described, which is still the norm that regulates what the state does with abandoned and delinquent children and which gives enormous power to the police. According to its advocates, the space of childhood appears as the last trench of authoritarianism, from where it needs to be eradicated. Through a press campaign and the organization of symposia and publications, a coalition of human right activists, politicians, judicial agents, teacher union leaders, and academics is trying to develop a new consensus around the notion of children's rights and freedom and denouncing the structures of repression and corruption that are still present. In this context, Rosario, the second largest city in the country, has started a pilot project called "the city of children," which proposes to adapt the city's architecture and activities for the youngest people and to abolish juvenile institutions and asylums as spaces of confinement for the youth. The "rights of the children" becomes a new signifier around which new coalitions are built that disentangle or question the prior association between childhood and delinquency or deviancy.

However, quite more radical in its rearticulation of the notion of childhood has been the emergence of H. I. J. O. S. Organized in 1994, it groups the children of the disappeared and of victims of the repression both in Argentina and abroad. The coming out of new memories of their childhood is shaking the grounds of the dominant narratives on the recent past that have proclaimed the national reconciliation between perpetrators and victims. After years of silence and shame, these teenagers and young adults are starting to talk about their stories and are staging in new ways the claims and debts left by their parents. After years of demonization and repression of their parents' memories, their response is not to perpetuate the silence but to get together and speak out. They feel unified by their parents' struggles to transform the world into a more just, better place.

Their first journal was called "The Gaze." Finding new ways of representation seems to be a common quest for them. "This is the only place where I don't need to use words to be understood," says twenty-nine-year-old Verónica. "The gaze is what first brought us together. I went to the first meeting and I felt that I already knew everybody, all faces looked familiar, but in fact it was the first time we were all together," says another activist (Dillon, 1998). They dismiss institutionalized, traditional ways of organization, and inherited discourses and rhetorics seem insufficient to help them deal with their wounds. The power structure of their organization is horizontal and does not include any representation or delegative posts; they meet weekly and decide their next steps through voting.

The H. I. J. O. S. have organized successful demonstrations and artistic gatherings in front of the homes of the perpetrators, putting traffic signals that say "Beware, a genocidist lives nearby," or writing graffiti with their parents' name on the walls of these houses. The *escraches* or outings of the perpetrators have been assimilated to a commemorative ritual that combines the figures of the tribunal, the demonstration, and the popular upheaval, in a way that actualizes the past and produces social knowledge about the present (Vezzeti,

1998). They renewed the participation of young people in human rights demonstrations in 1997 and 1998, after years of decaying numbers.

While they are not children any longer (their ages being around eighteen to thirty years old), the H. I. J. O. S. speak of their "robbed childhood" and of the rights of children to know their identities. Childhood, then, clearly appears as a discursive space and not a biological reality. It is interesting to note that they called themselves *"hijos con puntitos"* (punctuated children); the expression shows to what extent their identities are defined by punctuation, by cuts, by interruptions. Also, their support groups increasingly include young people who are not sons or daughters of disappeared people but of exiled or former activists (Meyer, 1998).

One of the interesting results of the irruption of the H. I. J. O. S. has been to disentangle the notion of childhood from the schooled context. It is remarkable that, since the spread of mass schooling, the identity of the child as a student has become more stable and pervasive than any other. Even those who valued childhood as a subject of rights, like the socialists and anarchists, suggested that children should be interned in educational institutions. It was very difficult to imagine a different identity for children than that of a student in a nationally organized educational system (Ríos & Talak, 1999, pp. 158–60). Yet childhood appears, in the actions of H. I. J. O. S., as defined outside schooling, as a product of political actions and cultural creativity.

Somehow, however, the notion of an innocent and pure childhood has helped in the process of getting recognition and support, and here the notion of childhood as a floating signifier is useful in reminding us of the semantic associations that are carried over by names. One feature in the Argentine legislation toward human rights violations is significant in this respect. While most crimes have been amnestied by the democratic governments, the cases of children who were kidnapped by the military and were given up for adoption to other militaries or their relatives have been excluded from the pardon and continue to be fought for in the judicial terrain. On that basis, after having been freed for several years thanks to a presidential amnesty in 1990, the former chief of the Junta Jorge Videla was put in jail again in 1998, in an unforeseen twist of events in a case regarding the illegitimate appropriation of children during the dictatorship. The photograph of a senile and defeated Videla behind bars circulated as a refreshing image among those who shared the hopes of the human rights movement. What seems remarkable is that this is done in the name of children. Childhood appears as a subject position that is unquestionably innocent and vulnerable, and the crimes against it are to be considered worse than any other crimes. Given its current articulation with the action of H. I. J. O. S., however, this innocence is not an apolitical terrain. Brought along other discourses on human rights and for justice, and most of all, in the context of a political mobilization that denies any kind of "innocence" of children but that on the contrary pictures them as active, angry citizens, the semantic associations that are constructed are very different from the "natural," innocent child of the eighteenth century.

These struggles have been powerful in establishing an opposing ethics, based on the notion of truth against power, which one analyst equals to Foucault's description of "parrhesia" (Font, in press). Parrhesia is "a verbal activity in which a speaker expresses his personal relationship to truth, and risks his life because he recognizes truth-telling as a duty to improve or help other people (as well as himself)" (quoted in Font, 1999, p. 30; also in Bernauer, 1999, p. xv). The parrhesist holds to this truth against the sovereign or the governing majority, and in doing that he or she reinvents the game of truth. The opposition of the H. I. J. O. S. to the established rules of truth and power and their radical activism can be read as a parrhesian attitude that is founding a new ethics.

The psychoanalyst Hugo Vezzeti has presented a critical view of this movement, in terms of the politics of memory that it is producing. First, the prevalence of direct activism and the dismissal of parliamentary and judicial ways of achieving justice seem to be dangerous, according to Vezzeti, in a country in which the usual way of dealing with conflicts was to disregard institutionalized ways and resort to violence or military coups d'état. More importantly, in my view, is his consideration of the burdens of the name of "children" in political action, its association to family memories, and the threat to repeat the past instead of reclaiming it. Children are supposed to occupy their parents' place, and in Vezzeti's opinion, given that this place and the role of political violence have not been sufficiently questioned by the new generation, the invocation of the name of children as their primary identity marker may not contribute to further reevaluations (Vezzeti, 1998). He warns us about the complex relationships between a mythologized vision of the past (in terms of the romanticization of the disappeared or their demonization) and family representations and (af)filiations, and is less optimistic about the contribution of H. I. J. O. S. to an "inventive politics."

While I do not agree with Vezzeti's somewhat acritical view of institutional politics and his fear of any kind of political action that runs through other channels than the juridical or party lines, I think that his warning about the burdens of a name can be put together with Derrida's remarks in order to interrogate ourselves about the uses and reoccupations of the name of childhood. Vezzeti seems to be more preoccupied with what is given when one receives a name: a particular mandate or legacy, a family affiliation, a relationship to authority. But he seems to disregard the space of indeterminacy given along with a name, that which cannot be given, that which cannot be passed on. Particularly, I find the H. I. J. O. S. definition of themselves as "punctuated children" very compelling, as a useful resort to remind themselves and everybody else that the space they reclaim for themselves is not a safe, innocent childhood but that of a cut-across, politically charged period of their life that dramatically intersects with Argentina's recent history and creatively recombines past and present.

Concluding Remarks

Is it possible that the antonym of "forgetting" is not "remembering," but "justice"?
Yerushalmi, 1989, p. 117

There is a beautiful short essay written by Foucault on the eve of the Iranian revolution. He plays with the question of whether it is useless to revolt. The question, he says, must be left open, acknowledging that there are revolts by people being oppressed, by delinquents who challenge absurd punishments, by the mentally ill who can no longer accept confinement. Their voices may not sound better than the rest or may not express any ultimate truth. But we have to remember that "it is due to such voices that the time of men does not have the form of an evolution, but precisely that of a history" (Foucault, 1999, p. 134). It is the task of the intellectual to watch out for the singular that arises against the universal, that breaks it and agitates it, and ultimately limits it.

I stated in the introduction that my project was to destabilize our critiques of childhood as a regulatory ideal and to place it in a different geopolitical context, in which the discourses of children's rights have been traditionally marginalized and are now being mobilized creatively by the human rights movement. How to accommodate this movement, this irruption of singularity, with our conceptualizations about the naturalization of childhood and participation in the regulation of bodies and "souls"? Certainly, our critical stance can denounce that there are ontological claims in these new memories of childhood, claims that speak of robbed identities (as if they had been pure and uncontaminated had history been otherwise), claims that are hard to accept if one wants to engage in a different politics than "progressivism" or liberalism.

However, Judith Butler makes a strong case for the use of ontological categories, as long as we acknowledge their history and try to recirculate and resignify them so as to produce ontology itself as a contested field. This is similar to Rose's remarks on identity: "to declare 'I am that name': woman, homosexual, proletarian, African American—or even man, white, civilized, responsible, masculine—is no outward representation of an inward and spiritual state but a response to that history of identification and its ambiguous gifts and legacies" (Rose, 1996, p. 39).

From my point of view, both Butler's and Rose's stances seem to do justice to the problem of theorizing the social from an antifoundationalist point of view and engaging in rethinking politics poststructurally. Butler goes on to say that "there is no other way to counter those kinds of (transcendental) grammars except through inhabiting them in ways that produce a terrible dissonance in them, that 'say' precisely what the grammar itself was supposed to foreclose" (Butler, 1998, p. 279). Would it be the case of the H. I. J. O. S. who speak in the name of a childhood that was not allowed to be? Would the notion of "punctuated children" be one of these dissonances that cry out for justice and the remaking of the past and the present? Would it be the case of those expelled from a "normal childhood" and confined to asylums and jails?

These questions don't have definite answers, and the fact that it is a movement-in-the-making whose effects are too incipient to assess makes it harder for me to write these final paragraphs. If I have put together both sections of this chapter, it is because I believe that the construction of childhood through the modern educational system was part of a political rationality that is not unrelated to the political violence and genocide that took place in Argentina two decades ago. Also, I find that the marginalization of child-centered pedagogies and of children's rights discourses needs to be taken into account when considering their contemporary reemergence. As I said before, we need to look at what other contents are today being articulated by the notion of childhood, in what ways, and with what effects. If childhood is a floating signifier that can be articulated by diverse strategies, then I suggest that we have a lot to learn from putting our claims in different political contexts and seeing where they can take us, and also where they can not, and what productive dialogues we can establish in these cases.

Finally, I have produced this essay from a particular point of view. Formed under the tradition of "academic activism" that is so prevalent in Latin America (Taylor, 1997), many times I find myself posing questions related to a "so what" that can be heard as an anti-intellectual stance. My activism, however, has a different ground, which I like to define as a sense of responsibility, in a Derridean sense, about what the effects of our writings are (Spivak, 1994). Probably that is related to the thin wall (almost inexistent) that separates the academic and political fields in Argentina, due to constitutive traditions and the poverty of resources and positions that academics have. These different traditions, when put to work together, may collide, or may be used as a permanent reminder of their limits. I want to think that they help me remind this "lesson" taught by Foucault, however uncomfortable he might have been with this term: "Never consent to be completely comfortable with your own certainties. Never let them sleep, but never believe either that a new fact will be enough to reverse them. Never imagine that one can change them like arbitrary axioms. Remember that, in order to give them an indispensable mobility, one must see far, but also close-up and right around oneself. One must clearly feel that everything perceived is only evident when surrounded by a familiar and poorly known horizon, that each certitude is only sure because of the support offered by unexplored ground" (Foucault, 1997, p. 144). The unexplored ground—shifting our frames of thought about childhood and interrogating them from unfamiliar places—seems to be a good way to start that journey.

Notes

[1]To attempt to define Derrida's notion of justice is a very ambitious task that exceeds this chapter. "Justice" seems to refer to the openness of the hopes of human beings for a better future, always unattainable; something like an ethical reminder that there will always be injustices to fight against and wounds to heal. I will present some quotes that can help the reader get a sense of where I'm pointing to. I begin with Derrida's: "[The more radical program of deconstruction is] not, doubtless, to change things in the rather naive sense of calculated, deliberate and strategically controlled intervention, but in the sense of maximum intensification of a transformation in progress, in the name of neither a simple symptom nor a simple cause (other categories are required here)." (Derrida, 1992, p. 9).

"Justice" then has to be thought through/within other categories that exceed the legal discourse and even the philosophical one. Mariana Valverde, in a compelling essay on Derrida, justice, and responsibility, states that: "Addressing justice is for Derrida . . . a matter of praxis. The question of justice that Derrida asks is not 'what is justice?' but rather: 'how can we, in our particular time and place, work in the direction of justice?' " (Valverde, 1999, p. 302). Justice is defined as an aspiration, a desire, a hope, a force, always concerned with singularity. It is "a movement towards the particularity of the Other. The desire for justice is thus destined never to be fulfilled." Law obliges us to calculate, and justice remains as the incalculable, as that which reminds us of the unjust character of our calculations. Yet there is a need to calculate how to dispense or make justice: "if one neglects the everyday political and legal struggles going on at the level of law and rights in favour of a philosophical quest for pure ethics, one may find oneself in a dubious if not downright unjust political position—as happened most memorably to Heidegger" (Valverde, 1999, p. 302).

My final quote lays on David Campbell's seminal work on the Bosnian conflict. He summarizes "justice" in this way: "Justice is the relationship to the other; it is justice when we are open to the surprise of the other, acknowledge the other's summons, or are willing to be unsettled by our encounters with others. The relationship to the other is the context of the political, it is the site of an irreducible responsibility, and yet it is in the relationship to the other that responsibility is often suppressed or effaced by violence" (Campbell, 1998, p. ix).

[2]This case was important in establishing in international and national courts that there was an articulated plan forged by the armed forces of Argentina, Chile, and Uruguay, called "Operación Cóndor," to combine their efforts in repressing political insurgency.

[3]On the narration of the nation, I draw on Bhabha (1990).

[4]DNA tests are still pending to provide definite evidence that the young woman is his granddaughter.

[5]Douzinas criticizes this view of human rights but convincingly argues that human rights can be rearticulated within a poststructural framework if we recognize their links to the logic of indeterminacy and the principle of negativity (Douzinas, 1999). His argument has inspired part of my reflections in this chapter.

[6]In this quote, while there seems to be a dualistic rhetoric in its assumptions of winners and losers, there is also an extremely mobile picture of history and of social conflict that keeps Foucault at a distance from a dialectical history. Also, it makes it clear that he never subscribed to an overwhelming, absolute notion of power that is always victorious and never changes, as some critics have accused him of doing.

[7]Buenfil Burgos analyzes the differences between these two thinkers. Particularly, Foucault's notion of discourse is clearly different than Laclau's, who incorporates such psychoanalytic approaches as Zizek's and is decidedly post-Marxist (Buenfil Burgos, 1996). But both work against essentialist and transparent conceptualizations of the social and of discourse as a "reflection" of reality and make room for contingency and indeterminacy.

[8]The notion of "event" is taken as opposed to the *longue durée* of Braudel. I draw here on Foucault's consideration of events as discontinuous unities that cannot be reduced to generalizations (in Foucault, 1972).

[9]In the 1960s and 1970s, there was a lengthy debate about whether Latin America (but the same can be said about Africa or Asia) had been part of modernity or was underdeveloped and still needed to go through the processes associated with modernity (industrialization, institutionalization, secularization). I refer to Walter Mignolo's works (1995, 2000), for his account of Latin America's incorporation to and production of modernity, and for his urge to look at global histories from a local standpoint.

[10]Much could be said about the structuring of the "criollo" (creole) discourse in the nineteenth century and its links to colonial discourse. Mary Louise Pratt refers to this production in the "contact zone" in her brilliant book *Imperial Eyes* (1992). The Argentinean historian of literature Adolfo Prieto has also shown how the language and categories of European travel writers shaped the emergence of a "national literature" during the nineteenth century (Prieto, 1996). The creole elite saw itself as part of the same civilizing, imperialistic expansion, and the awareness of being subjects themselves to imperial powers emerged late in the nineteenth century, if not later.

[11]Even in 1936, foreigners accounted for 36.1 percent of the total population of the big cities of the Littoral provinces (Sarlo, 1993, p. 12).

[12]"La liturgia patriótica invade distintas esferas, y en este movimiento se suman diversas instituciones y soportes discursivos. El Aceite 'Bou' . . . regala a los 'niños argentinos' en homenaje al centenario de la Patria una copia del plato del general San Martín expuesto en el Museo Histórico, haciendo suya la consigna con que los ingleses reproducían, a su vez, la vajilla del almirante Nelson: "comer en el plato de un héroe es inflamarse en la llama del más acendrado patriotismo." [Véase revista *Caras y Caretas*, Buenos Aires, 21 de enero de 1911].

[13]"La historia no se enseña solamente en la lección de las aulas: el sentido histórico, sin el cual es estéril aquélla, se forma en el espectáculo de la vida diaria, en la nomenclatura tradicional de los lugares, en los sitios que se asocian a recuerdos heroicos, en los restos de los museos y hasta en los monumentos conmemorativos, cuya influencia sobre la imaginación he denominado la pedagogía de las estatuas" (Ricardo Rojas, La Restauracion Nacionalista, 1909).

[14]As early as 1930, 95 percent of the population of Buenos Aires was literate and 30 percent attended high schools (Sarlo, 1993; Tedesco, 1986).

[15]"Nosotros no hemos sabido hacer servir a la escuela para afirmar el principio de la nacionalidad. . . . Nos faltó la aptitud para ser crisol de razas. . . . La sugestión colectiva, producida por la imitación, es ineludible en la infancia. Nosotros no supimos aprovechar como los yanquis ese principio. . . . Faltaba el libro de texto nacional, faltaba la historia nacional misma de la cual sólo se conocía la crónica y episodios fragmentarios. Debemos instaurar en la escuela el culto patriótico, el culto a los símbolos y los héroes de la Patria, debemos hacer retener los hechos, las fechas y los nombres de nuestra historia nacional."

[16] This point is dealt with more extensively in my dissertation in progress, "School uniforms and the regulation of appearances from a comparative perspective: The cases of the U.S., Argentina, and France" (University of Wisconsin-Madison, 2000).

[17]This is a very tight synthesis of a complex process with many contradictions and subtleties. I refer to Puiggrós (1990) and Carli (1991, 1993, 1997) for a more detailed account of it.

[18]One of the regulations for language teaching was the split of the teaching of the alphabet in three years, each year consisting of thirteen, ten, and five letters, respectively. Severe punishment was granted to teachers who did not follow this rule and intended instead a "meaningful approach" (Caruso & Fairstein, 1997).

References

Amuchastegui, M. (1995). Los rituales patrióticos en la escuela pública. In A. Puiggrós (Ed.), *Discursos pedagógicos e imaginario social en el peronismo (1945–1955)* (pp.13–41). Buenos Aires: Galerna.

Baker, B. (1998). "Childhood" in the emergence and spread of U.S. public schools. In T. S. Popkewitz & M. Brennan (Eds.), *Foucault's challenge: Discourse, knowledge, and power in education* (pp. 117–43). New York: Teachers College Press.

Bernauer, J., SJ (1999). Cry of spirit. In J. R. Carrette (Ed.), *Religion and culture: Michel Foucault* (pp. xi–xvii). New York: Routledge.

Beverley, J. (1996). The real thing. In G. Gugelberg (Ed.), *The real thing: Testimonial discourse and Latin America* (pp. 266–86). Durham, NC: Duke University Press.

Bhabha, H. (Ed.) (1990). *Nation and narration.* New York: Routledge.

Bourdieu, P. (1994). *Distinction: A social critique of the judgment of taste.* Cambridge, MA: Harvard University Press.

Buenfil Burgos, R. (1996). Foucault y la analítica del discurso. Paper submitted to the conference "Aniversario del nacimiento de Michel Foucault." ENEP-Iztacala, Mexico.

Butler, J. (1997). *Excitable speech: A politics of the performative.* New York: Routledge.

Butler, J. (1998, Winter). How bodies come to matter: An interview with J. Butler by I.Costera Meijer and Baukje Prins. *Signs. Journal of Women in Culture and Society, 23* (2), 275–86.

Campbell, D. (1998). *National deconstruction: Violence, identity, and justice in Bosnia.* Minneapolis: University of Minnesota Press.

Carli, S. (1991). Infancia y sociedad: la mediación de las asociaciones, centros y sociedades populares de educación. In A. Puiggrós (Ed.), *Sociedad civil y Estado en los orígenes del sistema educativo argentino (1885–1916)* (pp. 13–45). Buenos Aires: Galerna Ed.

Carli, S. (1993). El campo de la niñez. Entre el discurso de la minoridad y la escuela nueva. In A. Puiggrós (Ed.), *Escuela, Democracia y Orden (1916–1943)* (pp. 99–160). Buenos Aires: Galerna.

Carli, S. (1997). Infancia, psicoanálisis y crisis de generaciones. In A. Puiggrós (Ed.), *Dictaduras y utopías en la historia reciente de la educación argentina* (pp. 221–88). Buenos Aires: Galerna.

Caruso, M., & Dussel, I. (1997). *De Sarmiento a los Simpsons. Conceptos para pensar la escuela contemporánea.* Buenos Aires: Ed. Kapelusz.

Caruso, M., & Fairstein, G. (1996). A las puertas del cielo. Hipótesis sobre la recepción de la psicogénesis en la Argentina. In A. Puiggrós (Ed.), *Dictaduras y utopías en la historia reciente de la educación argentina* (pp. 157–220). Buenos Aires: Galerna.

Caruth, C. (Ed.) (1995). *Trauma: Explorations in memory.* Baltimore: Johns Hopkins University Press.

Chiaramonte, J. C. (1989). Formas de identidad en el Río de la Plata (1810–1850). *Boletín del Instituto de Historia Argentina, 1* (2), 13–30.

Dean, M. (1994). *Critical and effective histories: Foucault's methods and historical sociology.* London: Routledge.

Derrida, J. (1992). Force of law: The "Mystical Foundation of Authority." In D. Cornell, M. Rosenfeld, & D. G. Olson (Eds.), *Deconstruction and the possibility of justice* (pp. 3–67). New York: Routledge.

Derrida, J. (1995). *On the name.* Stanford, CA: Stanford University Press.

Dillon, M. (1988, July 24). "Hijos de la Ausencia." *Página/12,* Buenos Aires.

Donald, J. (1992). *Sentimental education: Schooling, popular culture and everyday life.* London: Verso.

Douzinas, C. (1999). Human rights at the end of history. *Angelaki: Journal of theoretical humanities, 4* (1), 99–114.

Dussel, I., Finocchio, S., & Gojman, S. (1997). *Haciendo Memoria en el País de Nunca Más.* Buenos Aires: Eudeba.

Duschatzky, S. (1998). *El valor simbólico de la escuela para jóvenes de sectores populares.* Buenos Aires, Fundación Banco Patricios, M.A. thesis.

Font, E.A. (in press). Confrontando los crímenes del Estado. Poder, resistencia y luchas alrededor de la verdad: Las Madres de Plaza de Mayo. *Criminología Crítica y Control Social,* Vol. 2, Rosario.

Foucault, M. (1972). *The archeology of knowledge & the discourse on language.* Trans. by A. M. Sheridan Smith. New York: Pantheon Books.

Foucault, M. (1984). Nietzsche, genealogy, history. Trans. by D. Bouchard and S. Simon. In P. Rabinow (Ed.), *The Foucault reader* (pp. 76–100). New York: Pantheon Books.

Foucault, M. (1988). "Technologies of the self." In L. Martin, H. Gutman, & P. Hutton (Eds.), *Technologies of the self: A seminar with Michel Foucault* (pp. 16–49). Amherst, MA: University of Massachusetts Press.

Foucault, M. (1997). For an ethics of discomfort. Trans. by Lysa Hochroth. In S. Lotringer (Ed.), *The politics of truth* (pp. 135–45). New York: Semiotext(e).

Foucault, M. (1999). Is it useless to revolt? Trans. by J. Bernauer SJ. In J. R. Carrette (Ed.), *Religion and culture: Michel Foucault* (pp. 131–34). New York: Routledge.

Gelman, J. (1998, May 12). Del Nombre. *Página/12,* Buenos Aires, p. 32.

Gelman, J., & La Madrid, M. (1997). *Ni el flaco perdón de Dios. Hijos de Desaparecidos.* Buenos Aires: Planeta.

Gorelik, A. (1998). *La grilla y el parque. Espacio urbano y cultura urbana en Buenos Aires, 1887–1936.* Buenos Aires: Ed. Universidad Nacional de Quilmes.

Hacking, I. (1996). Memory sciences, memory politics. In P. Antze & M. Lamber (Eds.), *Tense past: Cultural essays in trauma and memory* (pp. 67–87). New York: Routledge.

Hultqvist, K. (1998). A history of the present on children's welfare in Sweden: From Froebel to present-day decentralization projects. In T. S. Popkewitz & M. Brennan (Eds.), *Foucault's challenge: Discourse, knowledge, and power in education* (pp. 91–116). New York: Teachers' College Press.

Hunter, I. (1994). *Rethinking the school: Subjectivity, bureaucracy, criticism.* New York: St. Martin's Press.

Huyssen, A. (1995). *Twilight memories: Marking time in a culture of amnesia.* New York: Routledge.

Jelin, L., & Kaufman, S. (1998, April 3–5). Layers of memories: Twenty years after in Argentina. Paper submitted to the conference "Legacies of authoritarianism: Cultural production, collective trauma, and global justice." University of Wisconsin-Madison.

Keenan, T. (1997). *Fables of responsibility: Aberrations and predicaments in ethics and politics.* Stanford, CA: Stanford University Press.

Kirk, D. (1992). *Defining physical education: The social construction of a school subject in postwar Britain.* London: Falmer Press.

Laclau, E. (1996). *Emancipation(s).* London: Verso.

Lurie, A. (1981). *The language of clothes.* New York: Random House.

Mercante, V. (1927). *La paidología.* Buenos Aires: Manuel Gleyzer.

Meyer, A. (1998, July 19). Carla, Gustavo, Fernanda y Muriel, Hijos. *Página/12,* Buenos Aires.

Mignolo, W. (1995). *The darker side of the Renaissance: Literacy, territoriality, & colonization.* Ann Arbor: University of Michigan Press.

Mignolo, W. (2000). *Local histories/global designs: Coloniality, subaltern knowledges, and border thinking.* Princeton, NJ: Princeton University Press.

Morris, M. (1992). On the beach. In L. Grossberg, C. Nelson, & P. Treichler (Eds.), *Cultural studies* (pp. 450–73). New York: Routledge.

Popkewitz, T. S. (1991). *A political sociology of educational reform.* New York: Teachers' College Press.

Popkewitz, T. S. (1998). *Struggling for the soul.* New York: Teachers College Press.

Popkewitz, T. S., & Brennan, M. (Eds.) (1998). *Foucault's challenge: Discourse, knowledge, and power in education.* New York: Teachers College Press.

Pratt, M. L (1992). *Imperial eyes: Travel writing and transculturation.* New York: Routledge.

Prieto, A. (1996). *Los viajeros ingleses y la emergencia de la literatura argentina, 1820–1850.* Buenos Aires: Sudamericana.

Puiggrós, A. (1990). *Sujetos, disciplina y curriculum en los orígenes del sistema educativo argentino (1885–1916).* Buenos Aires: Galerna.

Quatrocchi de Woisson, D. (1995). *Los males de la memoria. Historia y política en la Argentina.* Buenos Aires: Emecé.

Ríos, J. C., & Talak, A. M. (1999). La niñez en los espacios urbanos (1890–1920). In F. Devoto & M. Madero (Eds.), *Historia de la Vida privada en la Argentina. La Argentina plural: 1870–1930* (pp. 139–61). Buenos Aires: Taurus.

Romero, L. A., & Gutiérrez, L. (1992). Ciudadanía política y ciudadanía social: los sectores populares en Buenos Aires (1912–1955). *Indice* No. 5, 12–25.

Rose, N. (1989). *Governing the soul: The shaping of the private self.* London: Routledge.

Rose, N. (1996). *Inventing our selves: Psychology, power, and personhood*. New York: Cambridge University Press.

Rose, N. (1997). Identity, genealogy, history. In S. Hall & P. du Gay (Eds.), *Questions of cultural identity* (pp. 128–50). London: Sage.

Rose, N. (1999, August). Inventiveness in politics. *Economy and Society, 28* (3), 467–93.

Rosenberg, T. (1999, February 7). What did you do in the war, Mama? *New York Times Magazine*, pp. 52–59.

Rousso, H. (1991). *The Vichy syndrome: History and memory in France since 1944*. Cambridge, MA: Harvard University Press.

Sábato, H. (1992, August). Citizenship, political participation and the formation of the public sphere in Buenos Aires, 1850s-1880s. *Past and Present* No. 136.

Sarlo, B. (1993). *Borges: A writer on the edge*. London: Verso.

Sarlo, B. (1997). Cabezas rapadas y cintas argentinas.*Prismas. Revista de Historia Intelectual, 1* (1), 187–91.

Sarmiento, D. F. (1845/1950). Facundo: Civilización y Barbarie. In *Obras Completas*, vol. XII. Buenos Aires: Luz del día.

Schwarz, R. (1977). *Ao vencedor as batatas*. Sao Paulo: Duas Cidades.

Shapiro, M. (1997). Winning the west, unwelcoming the immigrant: Alternative stories of "America." In *Tales of the state: Narrative in contemporary U.S. politics and public policy* (pp. 17–26). Lanham, MD: Rowman & Littlefield.

Spivak, G. C. (1994). Responsibility. *boundary, 2* (21), 3, 19–64.

Taylor, D. (1997). *Disappearing acts: Spectacles of gender and nationalism in Argentina's "Dirty War."* Durham, NC: Duke University Press.

Tedesco, J. C. (1986). *Educación y sociedad en la Argentina (1880–1945)*. Buenos Aires: Hachette.

Terán, J. B. (1932). *Espiritualizar nuestra escuela. La instrucción primaria argentina en 1931*. Buenos Aires: Librería del Colegio.

Valverde, M. (1999, May). The personal is the political: Justice and gender in deconstruction. *Economy and Society, 28* (2), 300–311.

Vezzeti, H. (1998). Activismos de la memoria: el "escrache." *Punto de Vista* No. 65, pp. 1–7.

Walkerdine, V. (1990). *Schoolgirl fictions*. London: Verso.

Walkerdine, V. (1997). *Daddy's girl: Young girls and popular culture*. London: Macmillan; Cambridge, MA: Harvard University Press.

Yerushalmi, Y. H. (1989). *Zakhor: Jewish history and Jewish memory*. Seattle: University of Washington Press.

10

Constructions of the Child in the Mexican Legislative Discourse

Rosa Nidia Buenfil-Burgos

Concepts of childhood in Mexico in the educational field have been mostly studied from the perspectives of learning and teaching, the social conditionings of their achievement, and, only recently, from cultural, gender, and human rights perspectives.[1]

It has been generally assumed in Mexican educational research that children are the subjects of education par excellence. My interest here is to address how the child is constructed in recent legislative discourse stressing political relationships conditioning these productions. Legislation will be my historical "discursive surface"[2]; however, I will not address the question of rights but rather the conceptual textile whereby childhood is constructed. This question involves the inquiry about how this has come to be what it is today.

The legislative discourse cannot be analyzed without consideration to the educational discourse of the Mexican Revolution in its different shifts and emphases in history: its emergence (1917), radicalization (1934), its "rectification" (1946), and the educational "modernization" of 1988–1994. This is so because for almost a century the discourse of the Mexican Revolution has operated as a "nodal point"[3] weaving other national official narratives.

To address the question of the current construction of the child, this study relies upon logics and intellectual tools gathered around discourse political analysis—that is, the political analysis of legislative discourse—asking questions such as: How did the concept of the child in 1993 law become what it is today? What conditions allowed the production of this configuration of meaning rather than another? What was excluded and included in setting these boundaries? What other choices were forcluded in this decision? The analysis and interpretation I intend here rely on an articulation of contributions mainly by Laclau, Derrida, Foucault, and Wittgenstein.

Let me briefly sketch two theoretical issues now. On the one hand are the main conceptual tools equipping my reading: Discourse theory and political analysis (Laclau & Mouffe, 1985; Laclau, 1990, 1996) whereby I stress an approach to the political dimension of social practices (the latter considered as linguistic and nonlinguistic configurations of meaning, i.e., discourse). From this matrix I articulate three corpuses:

- A genealogical approach (Nietzsche, 1907; Foucault, 1977) in the search for discontinuities in the historical narratives, the contaminated, multiple, and contingent emergence of discursive configurations such as the Mexican legislation
- A deconstructive reading (Derrida, 1978, 1982) understood as a strategy for the desedimentation and reactivation of texts (text as textile, texture, weaving) in the search for reiteration, dissemination, and decentering of meanings
- A pragmatist position (Wittgenstein, 1963) understood as a postfoundationalist approach to meaning as use in a language game and in the search for family resemblance rather than literality, essences, or denotative meaning

Within this articulation elaborated elsewhere (Buenfil, 1990) a variety of concepts and categories (discursive surface, floating signifier, nodal point, antagonism, inter alia) are inscribed in my approach with a particular theoretical meaning. The reader will find some elucidation concerning their meaning in the endnotes.

On the other hand, I must pinpoint that the idea of "conditioning" here should not be understood as determination from the "context" to the "text" not only for conceptual reasons but also on analytical grounds. Conceptually, I do not subscribe to the idea that there can be "necessary and sufficient conditions" that are evoked by determination. Some conditions needed for an effect are likely to be detected, but "sufficient" conditions are evasive and can only be approached—hardly established—a posteriori.[4] Rather I sustain that causality is always in deficit and paradoxically in surplus, in insufficiency and also in excess. In addition there is never a neat and clear-cut frontier between the "context" and the "text" (Derrida, 1982). In analytical terms, I object to determination since in following its logic many processes would not be accountable. For instance, as we will see later in this chapter, in the law of 1942 when the dismantling process of socialist education had already started, the signifier socialist was still articulating the legislation.

This approach involves a reading against the grain of an idea of progression and linearity, which is a specific type of historization of education within the Mexican legislative discourse. I will draw from Article III—dealing with education—in the Mexican Constitution, and the Ley General de Educación, mainly in the recent reform (1993). I will search in its predecessors (i.e., the national unity law [1946], the socialist reform [1934], the Mexican Revolution [1917], and even the liberal reform [1857], if convenient). This will be done firstly by tracing the meanings associated to the child in legislative pieces; secondly, looking for the nodal points articulating these meanings in each case (e.g., education, rights, values, and administration). Then I will study shifts, continuities, and breaks among them, stressing the ambiguous moves of discursivity. And finally, from the marks found within the discursive fabric, the intellectual and political conditions will be traced. The political focus and the methodological procedure are organized to set the conditions for interpreting power relations involved in the construction of the child.

The struggle over the construction of childhood in Mexico has been embedded in the struggle over the moral and intellectual leadership on education in Mexican history. It has involved two main discursive articulations: the mystical/religious monopolized by and personified in the Roman Catholic Church, namely its top hierarchy (from the colony), and the liberal view embodied in the government (from 1857). In this chapter, I will focus only on the construction of the child within the educational discourse in its legislative modality where the systems of signification articulated around the Catholic imaginary and those structured by the Mexican liberal mentality antagonize but, paradoxically, also overlap. Liberalism was later articulated with the Mexican Revolution and its system of meanings, in what I have called the *revolutionary mystique*. The Mexican revolutionary mystique (MRM) was constructed through the fusion of different perceptions of the process and provided content to the struggle and a reason for sacrifice. It was an operation whereby the already heterogeneous perceptions of ideals, strategies, needs, battles, values, and so on elaborated by the masses (peasants, industrial workers, schoolteachers, inter alia) were going to be sometimes fused, sometimes only amalgamated with the also heterogeneous perception of the process elaborated by the intellectual leaders of the revolution (liberals, socialists, anarchists, etc.) and some other social agents.[5] In affirming that the MRM has operated in a way comparable to that of the religious discourse, I am stressing the attitudes, behavior, commitment, and so forth from the revolutionary groups, which in some cases were as passionate as those of the defenders of religion.[6] This was an incipient, precarious, heterogeneous, and overdetermined discourse proposing a social order to replace the previous one.[7]

The intellectual horizon where systems of signification articulate the meaning of education and the child in Mexico has involved the religious discourse rooted from the colony onward and formally excluded from the MRM and the official scheme wanting to preserve that exclusion. The Mexican revolutionary mystique emerged from a social popular movement but was later appropriated by the official sector; so far it has articulated politics and orientations of the Mexican political system. The process of appropriation and diffusion of the imaginary system operated as a translation of the historical process into a legend and the transformation of its conceptions and values into a myth. Paradoxically, one of its modalities is precisely the legislative discourse. [8] Many examples can be drawn to illustrate the unfixity of this legislative discourse, but for the purposes of this study, only the child has been chosen.

This chapter will be organized in three parts: first, the Enlightenment inscription in the discursive surface of education and the child; second, education and the child in the Mexican legislation; and third, political dimensions of the child constructions.

The Enlightenment Inscription in the Discursive Surface of Education and the Child

Education, understood as the organization of teaching strategies, learning means, administration, and certification within the school,[9] has been strengthened by Western thought from the seventh century onward and has played a key role ever since. In Mexico, during the second half of the nineteenth century and onward, with the separation of church and state, positivism rooted in the liberal official system of meanings.

Early Educational Thought

Let us move to the resignification of education within the Enlightenment system of meaning, where the crucial role of the teaching of reasoning was precisely assigned to school. Already in the seventeenth century Locke would claim that good education consisted of reconciling reason and nature in such a way that it would not "break the children's spirit." Reacting strongly against bodily punishment, Locke stated:

> Such a sort of slavish discipline makes a slavish temper. The child submits, and dissembles obedience, whilst the fear of the rod hangs over him; but when that is removed, and by being out of sight, he can promise himself impunity, he gives the greater scope to his natural inclination. (Locke [1693] in Kramnick, 1995, p. 225)

Another feature of good education stressed by Locke was the learning of a second language. Here the concept of childhood can be inferred as basically the natural, biological creature with intellectual faculties that should be nourished in order to form a balanced being.

In Rousseau's *Emile*, childhood is constructed as "a special stage of life with its own methods of thinking, seeing, and feeling." He stresses the civic dimension of education. Reasoning is seen as the result of a good education (not as its condition). Rousseau emphasizes that reason should not be imposed prematurely since children have their own timing to learn and develop different moments of perception and reasoning. Early education, he claims, "should be purely negative. It consists not in teaching virtue or truth, but in protecting the heart from vice and the mind from error" (Rousseau [1762] in Kramnick, 1995, p. 230). This negative approach means to free the child from prejudices and preconceptions, to open "the eyes of his understanding and reason" so that his mind would present no obstacle to the full effect of teaching. Thus "from a purely negative beginning, you would achieve an educational prodigy" (Rousseau [1762] in Kramnick, 1995, p. 230). He is also very much against punishment.

> Who knows how many children perish the victims of a father's or tutor's extravagant wisdom? Happy to escape their cruelty, the only advantage children derive from the ills they have been made to suffer is to die without regretting life, of which they have only tasted the sorrows. (Rousseau [1762] in Kramnick, 1995, p. 231)

In stressing the civic dimension of education Rousseau claimed the need of laws for infancy since men ought to begin learning civic values from the first moment of life.

> As at the instant of birth we partake of the rights of citizenship, that instant ought to be the beginning of the exercise of our duty. If there are laws for the age of maturity, there ought to be laws for infancy, teaching obedience to others; as the reason of each man is not left to be the sole arbiter of his duties, government ought the less indiscriminately to abandon to the intelligence and prejudices of fathers the education of their children, as that education is still of greater importance to the State than to fathers. . . . Families dissolve but the State remains. (Rousseau [1758] in Kramnick, 1995, p. 134)

Priestly (1765) acknowledges that while it has been in the hands of the clergy, rhetoric, logic, and school divinity were taught. He claims for a more liberal view of education "humbly proposing some new articles of academic instruction" such as those connected with active life: civil history and civil policy (Priestly in Kramnick, 1995). By the latter he meant theory of laws, government, manufactures, commerce, naval force, which in turn would change the meaning of the courses of reading, thinking, and conversation.

As stated previously, on the one hand school came to be the means for progress, thus becoming a central piece for the Enlightenment ideal of plenitude and the exclusive site for educational practices. On the other hand, a new concept of child emerged. Pedagogy, strongly embedded in medical discourses, stressed the biological features of age, stages of development, and teaching and learning strategies to educate the children's reason.

Liberalism and Positivism in Mexico

In Mexico Enlightenment, liberalism, and positivism were strongly embedded. After the Independence War (1810) but especially from 1833 onward, positivists were invited by the liberal forces to participate in the design of educational policies in the Dirección General de Instrucción Pública.[10] Within this system of meaning science, reason, progress, and education appear woven into a single ideal. Mass education (instead of elite education) is seen as the most necessary means for the "right use and exercise of reason" and as a means for a popular, representative, and republican government (Mora [1837] in 1949, p. 68)

The child and the youth within this configuration of meanings were constructed in relation with intellectual and biological faculties. They were said to deserve an education that excludes corporal punishment and emotional humiliation. Criticizing confessional schools, Mora wrote:

Education in colleges[11] is rather monastic than civilian; too much devoutness proper to mystical life rather than to that of the Christian; too much confinement, too much piety, too much stillness and silence, essentially incompatible with the active faculties of youth that should be developed. Too much corporal barbarian and humiliating punishment. (Mora [1837] in 1949, p. 80, my translation)

The strong complaint also included a lack of civic instruction (justice, honor, history) and hygiene, thus leading to the destruction of the *positive man* roots (Mora [1837] in 1949, p. 81). The criticism of syllabi, methods, routines, and orientation of the then current schools shows what they considered opposite to the good, positive education.

Another key representative of positivism in Mexico, Justo Sierra, can portray the way in which Enlightenment and positivism were inscribed in the intellectual and moral surface of the nineteenth century and beginnings of the twentieth before the Mexican Revolution. In his work one can understand the peculiar incorporation of Enlightenment and positivism in the grandiloquent manner of a traditionally Roman Catholic culture. Thus, in being strongly scientific he constantly evoked faith, in being uncompromisingly atheistic he permanently invoked the sacred.

Positivists are the greatest idealists of knowledge. They incarnate the intellectual consciousness of our century. Their will to truth at all costs, their faith in the absolute and unconditioned value of truth and science are not, however, but an infinitely refined, subtle and sublime form of the ascetic and Christian spirit. Our faith in science is always grounded upon a metaphysical belief, our faith in science; we, the thinkers of today, the atheistic, the anti-metaphysicians, [also share the millenarian Christian belief] teaching that God is the truth and the truth is Divine. (Sierra [1908] in 1947, p. 237, my translation)

Quoting Leon Gambetta, Sierra deploys his concept of positive teaching:

Due to the perseverance in the effort to acquire knowledge, the faculties were nurtured and developed, the training of the will and character were structured; due to the practice of method the notion and the necessity of order was acquired; and due to the scientific initiation love to truth [was acquired]. (Sierra [1908] in 1947, p. 240, my translation)

Or in a different piece he put his idea of positive teaching stressing the arrangement of sciences:

The truth is that in the plan of positive teaching, the scientific series constitutes a fundamental philosophy. The sky that starts in Mathematics and concludes in Psychology, in Moral, in Logic, in Sociology, is a philosophical teaching, an explanation of the Universe. (Sierra [1910] in 1947, p. 258, my translation)

Quoting Comte, the young child is depicted as a pyramid, where the top is the abstract capacity of logic, the middle of sciences and method, and below lies the body. The child has the capacity of abstraction and is depicted in the following idea:

[T]he teacher has managed to create the moral and physical habits orienting our instincts towards the good, [in] the child who is going to make out of his instincts the constant auxiliaries to reason when breaking through the decisive stage of youth and will acquire mental habits that will conduct him to truth. (Sierra [1910] in 1947, p. 248, my translation)

By the beginning of the twentieth century in Mexico, this intellectual horizon, and especially the educational field, was the arena of antagonism[12] between the two main forces interested in leadership: the Catholic hierarchy and the liberal government in turn.

Education and Enlightenment

The Mexican Revolution brought about the revivalism of an Enlightenment view of education articulated to a hybrid intellectual, moral, and political utopia: the Mexican revolutionary mystique.

Within this discursive configuration "education" was constructed as equivalent to instruction, a means for national greatness, the formation of the citizen, Enlightenment, a condition for the preservation of the revolutionary conquests, a passage to progress, love of freedom, a subject of very special political concern, and so on. The replacement of the prerevolutionary order by the proposal of a new one is also clear. Religious education and—to be precise—schooling in the hands of the clergy, "which divides the Mexican people, produces great fear and fanaticism," would be replaced by secular education, laicism, and true, rational, positive, and scientific knowledge.

Education as a component of the MRM condensed values that preserve the links between people and government into a manifold element of identification: firstly, a necessity formulated by the popular sectors and the promise to resolve it, formulated by the government; secondly, since it operated as a popular desire and the possibility of its being fulfilled by the government of the revolution; thirdly, it condensed an ideal shared by the people and the new ruling bloc, that is, an imaginary element of identification, an unachievable fantasy preserving their links. Finally, it synthesized a constitutive part of the mystical organizing principle of the revolutionary discourse.

It also condensed part of the meaning of other components of the MRM, since the definition and fulfillment of these other values partially depended on the delimitation and achievement of the educational target. Education was thus construed as a popular demand, a requirement for the configuration of the national identity, a means to improve agrarian and industrial productivity, and so forth.

The meaning of the educational component displaced itself (i.e., it circulated) throughout the other components of the imaginary system of the Mexican Revolution (thus the emphasis and reiteration of agrarian education, education for democracy and the progress of the nation, education for the Indian and the people, etc).

The educational component of the MRM emerged in the imaginary construction of the revolution, as an idealization of the Enlightenment powers; it was thought of as a principle that goes beyond history, as an intrinsic and transcendental value. Education as a mystical object was instituted in the symbolic order through its legitimization by the legislative discourse, rhetorical intervention of all kinds, financial discourse, social institutions and apparatuses. However the *Real* (in the Lacanian sense) imprinted its traces in it since struggles prevented this ideal identity from being fulfilled. This radical impossibility of plenitude or full realization was evident when antagonisms prevented the symbolic system from being fully constituted, in the case of the educational component of the MRM, when, for instance, the Catholic priests of the 1930s prevented the constitutional precept from being fulfilled (see note 16).

Education as a mystical component was materialized and has had effects at the level of reality, that is, in Mexican social relations and institutions, in the daily social practices of the people. In the early years of the revolutionary process and the postrevolutionary governments, only the first ingredients were condensed and tentatively established. Their consolidation can be thought of as a result of the different political processes that sometimes challenged and sometimes fixed these values. The necessary sedimentation that would set these values, initially appearing as "floating signifiers,"[13] in a mystique, can be understood through knowledge of the subsequent historical processes wherein some symbols and their meaning disappeared or were shifted and resignified while some others remained.

In this context was the necessity of replacing what had been associated with the old regime. Positivism was emphatically criticized, in my view, more for political reasons than for intellectual purposes. This was so because the Porfirista regime was very much identified with positivism. (As an example, let me mention that the cabinet was self-named the "Scientist Cabinet".) However, the explicit criticism to positivism and its replacement by "spiritualism," as the minister of education called it, in my view, was permeated by deep positivist values in the peculiar Mexican embeddedness of liberalism, positivism, and Enlightenment as an intellectual horizon.

José Vasconcelos, minister of education from 1921 to 1924, allegedly critical of positivism, used to display metaphors such as "the educational crusade," "education as the enemy of ignorance which is the worst enemy of the revolution," "the country craves for education," "in the whole country today there exists a yearning for enlightenment," and the "Nation shapes the people's educational will." Education was constructed as the means to a further end— progress, national redemption, justice—but also as the result of an action: "the conquest of the Mexican revolution." Education was signified as a means to national unification in terms of language, revolutionary ideology, cultural forms, and political structures, especially in a country as Mexico with so many ethnic groups and languages disseminated across the territory.

The inscription of Enlightenment in the Mexican revolutionary mystique can be thus observed in different moments, dimensions, practices, values, and discursive modalities. Enlightenment with its positivist mark under the guise of "spiritualism" became a strong orientation in the Mexican revolutionary schooling system (from primary to higher education); however, this does not mean that the Catholic imaginary disappeared. On the contrary, it has been struggling to recuperate its presence in the educational field, namely in two fronts: the legislative space regulating the school system and other social loci, for example, the family, temples, parents' groupings, civilian movements, and so on (Buenfil & Ruiz, 1997). The latter is today a key political arena for the Roman Catholic activities and quite an interesting subject to research (Ruiz,

1997–1999). However, the subject of this chapter is instead the legislative surface, where interesting debates have taken place.

Education and the Child in the Mexican Legislation

The legislative structure in Mexico is one of the three formal instances of the political system, together with the executive and the judiciary powers. Given that the country is formally ruled by a constitutional order, the system formed by the constitution, department laws (agrarian, educational, labor, tributary, and so on), and other more specific regulations makes up the legislative discourse, which plays an important role in the definition of the national orientation.

This section will approach the way in which both education and the child are constructed in two key pieces of legislation: the Mexican Constitution (Article III, dealing with education) and the General Law of Education.[14] As has already been stated, three legislative reforms will be studied here.

To put in context these legislative shifts, let me sum up a few historical facts in a sort of periodization: From 1921 to 1923 processes of institutionalization of revolutionary values, emblems, conquests, symbols, and so on—that is, the MRM—took place in deeds such as the reopening of the ministry of education, artistic productions about the Mexican Revolution, and literature and mural painting (by painters such as Rivera, Siqueiros, and Orozco). The peasant guerrilla was degraded and Villa was assassinated in Chihuahua (July 20, 1923).

From 1924 to 1932 under President Calles's de jure or de facto ruling the sedimentation of revolutionary forces, ideals, and symbols took place. A political system emerged and the political party so far organically linked to it was founded: the Partido Nacional Revolucionario, ancestor of the Partido Revolucionario Institucional, in power ever since. An energetic anticlerical battle took place, resulting in the Cristero War (Meyer, 1973).

From 1934 to 1940 with L. Cardenas's six-year presidency a "socialist" orientation was imprinted in the Mexican revolutionary mystique (Buenfil, 1994), and later in the forties, its "rectification" took place with Avila Camacho's administration, dismantling the socialist signs, especially in the educational field. Partido Nacional Revolucionario became Partido de la Revolución Mexicana, gathering the mass support (Buenfil, 1990).

In 1945 the Partido Revolucionario Institucional as we know it today came to be the party in power, heavily relying on the mass support previously achieved and strongly embedded in the government. From the forties onward a steady stability has been seen and only minor changes took place concerning the political system. Legislation on education did not change substantially until 1993, together with the policy of "Educational modernization" (1988–1994).

With these shifts in the political orientation of education and, in general, of the Mexican revolutionary mystique as a whole, the following reforms correspond to educational policies:

- *Socialist education* (1934–1940), where the socialist tendency within the hybrid revolutionary mystique was put forward, not only concerning education but also in other social fields, for example, labor, peasant and popular conditions, agricultural and industrial development, and the very character of democracy, the political system, and arts and cultural production (Buenfil, 1994).[15]

- *Education for national unity, for love, for international peace and solidarity* (1940–1946), where the "rectification" of the previous socialist tone was formally dismantled and instead the liberal tendency within the revolutionary mystique was stressed mainly in economic terms. In political terms, the mass-supported party inherited from the previous administration became the unconditioned platform for the presidentialist regime. Education and other intellectual and moral dimensions were articulated around pre-revolutionary values formerly excluded from the revolutionary mystique (i.e., a de facto reinscription of religious motives and a Porfirista morality).[16]

- *Educational modernization* (1988–1994), where the so-called "neoliberal" principles are inscribed in the national development plan. In political terms the rigidity of the political system, paradoxically, fissures in such a way that a slow but steady process of political reform starts. Relations between the Catholic Church and the government get closer and the revolutionary mystique, eroded, resignified, and for some in agony, reinscribes de jure the religious mark in the official discursive surface.[17]

Education and the Child in Article III

The Third Article of the Mexican Constitution is devoted to regulating education on a national scale and is the supreme law. Basically it establishes rights and responsibilities of the citizens, society, community, municipalities, states, and the federal state. It defines the civilian, political, and cultural criteria and delimits who can and who cannot conduct schools.[18] After more than fifty years of permanence Article III was reformed. The meaning of this reform gives evidence, inter alia, of the permanent struggle fought by the Catholic hierarchy in order to be formally acknowledged as a legitimate educator. Let us see some fragments[19] of the three versions of this law to illustrate the changes. By 1993 this article states:

> All individuals have the right to receive education. The State, Federation, states and municipalities will impart pre-school, primary and secondary education. Primary and secondary education is compulsory.
>
> Education imparted by the State will tend to harmoniously develop all the faculties of the human being and promote in him love to the Motherland and consciousness of international solidarity, in independence and justice.
>
> 1. Being the freedom of belief guaranteed by Article 24, the said education will be laic and therefore it will be completely aloof to any religious doctrine.
> 2. The criterion orientating this education will be grounded in the results of scientific progress, will combat ignorance and its effects: serfdom, fanaticism and prejudices. (*Diario Oficial*, 05/III/1993, p. 2)

The previous text starts with a consideration of the subject of education as one of rights, thus marking a difference with the article of 1946, which started with what, in 1993, became the second paragraph (i.e., "Education imparted by . . ."). Apart from this, the 1993 law shows no difference with that issued in 1946. The main change consisted of the previous regulatory laic education both in private and public schools (present in 1946 law and eliminated in 1993 law).

Another crucial difference appears when one reads the article of 1934 stating:

> Education imparted by the State will be socialist and in addition to excluding all religious doctrine, it will combat fanaticism and prejudices, in order to which school will organize its teaching and activities in such a way that allows to create in the youth a rational and exact concept of the universe and social life.
>
> Only the State—Federation, States and Municipalities—will impart primary, secondary and normal [20] education. Authorization to private agencies[21] willing to impart education in whichever of the three mentioned degrees can be conceded, according to the following norms . . .
>
> I. Activities and teaching in schools must fit without exception, to the first paragraph . . . [those in charge will be professionally qualified . . .] In virtue of which religious corporations, ministers of the cults and societies devoted exclusively or basically to educational activities, and the religious associations directly or indirectly linked with the propaganda of a religious creed, *will not intervene at all* in primary, secondary or normal schools.

... the educational function and the economic contributions corresponding to this public service, trying to unify and coordinate education in the whole Republic. (*Diario Oficial,* 13/XII/1934, p. 2, emphasis added)

In 1857 the law stated that education should be "free"(meaning free of doctrine), and in 1917 the law again stated that education would be free but it also specified that it would be laic (secular). As we saw previously, the liberal reform was taking place in many other spheres of national life. The political conditions under which these legislative reforms took place cannot be overlooked since they have imprinted their marks on the legislative surface, ergo, they are necessary to interpret and account for the shifts of the legislative meanings. However, as Derrida (1982) argues, this does not mean that the "context" determines the text.

Many studies have compared these laws (Ceniceros, 1954; Cisneros, 1970; Flores, 1996), stressing continuities and discontinuities among the texts. Considering the focus of this chapter, only some points will be emphasized in comparing the full versions[22] of the article.

1. Socialist education ruling in 1934 was eliminated in 1946.
2. Education as a public service articulating the article in 1934 was blurred in 1993.
3. Laic education—that is, secular and nonreligious education—had been the norm for both public and private schools in the laws of 1934 and 1946, but in 1993 a subtle modification made laic education not compulsory in private schools.
4. Religious education had been legally prohibited in official and private schools in the law of 1934 and in 1946, but a dramatic change occurred when it was officially legitimized in 1993.
5. The restriction for religious ministers to manage primary, secondary, and normal schools stated in the law of 1934 and preserved in 1946 was eliminated in 1993.

In brief, education was resignified in the Mexican Constitution and in other discursive modalities of the revolutionary system of meaning (speech, arts, budgets, and so on). These changes of meaning were an outcome of at least two angles of domestic political conflict: on the one hand, the struggle between church and government, and on the other, among the diverse factions within the party in government.

As it was elaborated previously, the Mexican revolutionary mystique was a hybrid but strongly unified system of representations. It involved liberal ideals and socialist utopias, both anarchist notions and democratic forms, both rationalist (anticlerical) positions and religious emblems (though not explicitly incorporated). Its political strength was due to its association with the popular root of the revolutionary process and later to the ways in which the party in government manipulated it.

However, this mystique has had different accents associated with the political inclinations in turn (e.g., liberal, anticlerical, socialist, conservative, anti-U.S., pro-U.S., and assorted combinations). I want to stress that Enlightenment values are inscribed in this hybrid and mobile discursive surface achieving a particular sense.

Let us move now to the discursive construction of the child. Reading the different versions of Article III (i.e., 1993, 1946, and 1934) in search of the constructions of childhood, it is quite surprising to realize that very scarce mention is made of infants, children, and subjects to education. However, the child construction can be analyzed in its context of enunciation in two dimensions: on the one hand, putting forward its movements stressing the relations of contiguity it establishes with other signs in a syntagmatic stream. On the other, it can also be analyzed putting forward the synonyms with which it is evoked. In other words, concentrating on how the meaning of the child is present in the use of other signifiers such as "pupil," "infant," "minor," "boys and girls," "sons and daughters," "tutored," "individuals," and the Spanish words *educandos* (those to be educated) and *párvulos* (children in kindergarten).

In 1993 there are only three explicit mentions of those for whom education was destined:

1. The first time the signifier is "human being" and it is constructed indirectly as he/she whose faculties have to be harmoniously developed. So we can see the child evoked as a developing biological entity, in a process of becoming in which the law wishes to intervene regulating how and where this development should go.
2. The second mention is to the *educando* (those to be educated) as a recipient of the educational action (that will contribute to better human coexistence . . . strengthening personal dignity and family integrity).
3. The third time it is referred to as "sons and daughters or those under their tutelage" since it is addressing parents and tutors, informing them about their obligations. Here children are implicitly evoked indirectly as the object of adult responsibility

In the Article of 1946 the first two references are identical as in (1) "human being" and (2) *educando* and no more. In the socialist Constitution of 1934 there is only one mention of the "youth" upon which state schools will "create a rational and exact concept of the universe and social life."

What we have here then is the permanence of a construction based on a sort of biological frame where the child is seen as an ensemble of capacities in the process of unfolding upon which the law is attempting to establish regulations as to how and where to direct them. This is enveloped in a legislative form. The basic difference among the three versions is that the law of 1934 refers to the child as "youth" without further elaboration of their developing capacities but rather in sight of their cognitive and civilian qualification. These are contained in the norm: "creating" a *rational and exact concept of the universe and social life* in the citizen. Here one finds the mark of an Enlightenment ideal embedded in the "socialist" law.

A second similarity is found in the signifier *educando* present in both the laws of 1993 and 1946, evoking the child as a supporter of the activity subject of Article III: education. As the paragraph did not change in these two laws, one can see the emphasis in some values: toward "better human coexistence . . . strengthening personal dignity and family integrity" as a permanent feature. This emphasis can be related, in the law of 1946, when the paragraph first appears, with the stress on "human and spiritual" values that was launched against the "materialist and antihumanist" values allegedly promoted by the socialist law. In the law of 1993, this paragraph simply was not revised.

The innovation of Article III in 1993 shows how the child is constructed in association with family relations in a legal perspective (sons and daughters); they are explicitly construed as a subject of rights but in an indirect way: as the object of parents' obligations. The appearance of this construction can be related with the dissemination of the discourse of human rights, especially the emergence of children's rights in international agencies in the Western world. It can also be related to the incorporation of new international educational policies tending to inscribe the parents' participation in public service. This incorporation shows the ambiguous status of, on the one hand, the politically progressive move to invite civilians to participate in public affairs, and on the other, the increasing tendency of the "thinning state" to abandon the responsibility upon public services.

Education and the Child in the General Law of Education

The General Law of Education was decreed on July 9, 1993, and has as its immediate predecessors the Ley Federal de Educación (1973) and others issued in 1975, 1963, and 1945. Here the Ley Orgánica de la Educación Pública (1942) and the Ley Orgánica Reglamentaria de los Artículos 3°, 27, Fracción III, issued in 1935, will be compared with the law of 1993.

These laws are much more extended and detailed than the constitutional article. They include several chapters, articles, and paragraphs dealing with issues such as the social role of education; its status as a public service; the faculty of the federal state to design, provide, and control it; and the role of private educational institutions.

Allow me now to go into some detail and display the amazing dissemination of the child construction in these laws, in order to set the historical discursive grounds upon which my analysis relies.

The Ley General de Educación (1993)

The Ley General de Educación was issued as the legislation for the Educational Modernization reform[23] (officially 1988–1994). It is comprised of eight chapters:

1. General dispositions
2. Educational federalism (divided in four sections: (1) The distribution of the educational social function; (2) Educational services; (3) Financing for education; and (4) Evaluation of the national educational system)
3. About equity in education
4. About the educational process (with three sections: (1) Education types and modalities; (2) Syllabi and programs; and (3) School calendar)
5. Education imparted by private entities
6. Official studies validity and knowledge certification
7. Social participation in education (with three sections: (1) About parents; (2) About the social participation councils; and (3) About the media)
8. Infractions, sanctions, and the administrative resource (with two sections: (1) About infractions and sanctions; and (2) About the administrative resource)

The transitory articles deal with the derogation of previous laws, dates of beginning, and other legal issues. Taking this law as an analytical unit, one can see that the child is construed in a chain of equivalence with *educando*, pupil, minor, individual, sons and daughters, and infants. Their meanings are associated as follows.

Educando In Chapter 1 it is constructed as follows:

- A pedagogical subject whose active participation should be guaranteed by the educational process
- A civic subject whose social responsibility should be stimulated—a wider reference is given to education as a means of cultural transmission and the individual and social development toward solidarity
- A subject and object of pedagogy and economics since they are bearers of an education enabling them to develop a productive activity
- A part of the national educational system

In Chapter 2 it is referred to as a beneficiary from a national system of equivalencies among syllabi.

In Chapter 3 it is construed as a beneficiary from scholarships and funds.

In Chapter 4 it is constructed in eight ways:

1. As a bearer of a special condition and in need of adequate attention (in relation with physical or mental impairment)
2. As an object exposed to verification
3. As a cognitive subject (in reference to knowledge: history, geography, etc.)
4. As a subject enabled to dialogue with parents and authorities
5. As an indirect object upon which the administrative authorities have the duty to inform parents
6. As beneficiaries from a school calendar
7. As an indirect object whose benefit will provide extra salary to teachers
8. As an indirect object receiver of the teacher's responsibility in working hours

Pupils In Chapter 2 they are construed in relation with evaluation of the national educational system, in the following ways:

- As an indirect object that together with teachers and school authorities will benefit from decentralization
- As objects that together with parents, teachers, and the society are entitled to be informed of the results of evaluation

In Chapter 3 they are referred to as the bearers of a learning process and benefit that should be supported by assorted educational institutions in the context of equity.

In Chapter 7 they are construed—together with teachers, school authorities, and employees—as the receiver of functions delegated to school councils, such as moral incentives and awards and social awards.

Minors "Minors with physical impairment" (Chapter 4) are construed as objects of *educación especial* (special education for the handicapped) considering either their integration into regular schools or satisfaction of their particular needs, toward an autonomous and productive social coexistence.

"Minors as *educandos*" (Chapter 4) are referred to as objects of protection in relation to physical, psychic, and social integrity; respect to their dignity; and in search of a type of discipline according to their age.

Individuals In Chapter 1 they are referred to as follows:

- As subjects of the right to receive education and object recipient of education, in a context of equal rights to access the national system of schooling

- As those who are going to develop through education
- As those whose integral development will enable them to exercise their human capacities
- As a philosophical object (human and biological) in terms of the "integral development of individual to fully exercise their human faculties"
- As an ethical, medical, and hygienic object and subject, referred to in terms of responsibility (parenthood, family planning, and health)

With reference to family relations:

- "Sons, daughters, minors and tutored (under tutelage)" (Chapter 1) as subjects of rights, objects of parents' and tutors' obligations to go to primary and secondary school, in the context of the national juridical frame
- "Sons and daughters or minor tutored" (Chapter 7) referred to as subjects of rights (to be registered and attend basic education[24]) and as objects of parents' obligations
- "Sons and daughters and tutored" (Chapter 7) constructed as subjects of pedagogical rights and as objects of obligations of parents and school authorities
- "Sons, daughters, minors and tutored" (Chapter 7) as subjects of the right to be supported in their educational process and object of parents' obligations

With reference to age:

- "Infant" (Chapter 3) appears only as the qualifier of types of educational institution (center for child development, center for social integration, boarding schools, school hostel, infant hostel); it is indirectly referred to as the object of the duties and obligations of school authorities
- "Younger than four years old" (Chapter 4) refer to biological, cognitive, sensitive, and social entities, as the pedagogical object of kindergartens in the context of the demarcation of educational types and modalities.

The Ley Orgánica de la Educación Pública (1942)

The Ley Orgánica de la Educación Pública was issued as part of the reform called *education for national unity, for love, for international peace and solidarity* (officially from 1940 to 1946; see Buenfil, 1990) that dismantled the previous "socialist reform" during the Second World War. This law consists of twenty chapters and five transitory articles. The twenty chapters are as follows:

1. General dispositions
2. State faculties and duties in educational matters
3. National educational system and types of education

4. General grounds for education imparted by the state (federation, states, municipalities, district and federal territories)
5. About curricula validity and revalidation
6. About public education imparted by private entities
7. Preschool education (kindergarten)
8. Primary education
9. "Constitutional Article 123" schools
10. Secondary education
11. Normal school or teacher preparation
12. Vocational education
13. Higher, technical, or professional education
14. Scientific research
15. Extra school education
16. Schools or other types of special education
17. Obligations and rights of tutors or minors' representatives
18. National unification of education
19. Coordination of educational services among federation, states, and municipalities
20. Sanctions

In this law the construction of children, pupils, minors, *educandos*, párvulos, infants, sons and daughters, and other constructions appear in the following cases.

Children The signifier "children" is constructed in the following terms:

- "Children younger than six years old," appearing as a pedagogical object of a type of education in the school classification in the context of the national educational system and its cycles (in this case, kindergarten).
- "All children of the country between six and fourteen years old," (Chapter 8) referred to as object of a regulation ("will attend primary school") in the context of juridical and administrative classification.
- "Representative of children" (Chapter 8), appearing as an object of legal representation and pedagogical assistance by adults (parents, tutors, etc.).
- "Children in schooling age," (Chapter 8) construed as objects of land-owners' and patrons' obligation to open schools (as long as there are more than twenty children), in the context of private sectors' obligations.
- "Niños infractores" (transgressive children) (Chapter 11), referred to as the user of a type of special teacher training, in the context of school classification and administration.
- "Children" (Chapter 11), referred to as pedagogical qualifiers of a school cycle in an age classification.
- "Mentally retarded, physically or mentally abnormal children" (Chapters

16 and 17), constructed as a pedagogical object with special requirements in a context of regulations to normalize them. They are also indirectly referred to as bearers of an exceptional status to be released of the compulsory character when adequate schools do not exist for their requirements, in the context of parents' obligations.

Pupils This signifier (Chapter 2) is constructed as follows:

- A pedagogical object in the context of military instruction and in the context of private schools
- An object of training for productive work in the context of an education useful to society

"Deprived pupils" (Chapter 2) are referred to as civilian and political objects of the ministry obligation in the context of scholarships that should be granted

In Chapter 3 they are referred to as follows:

- As the users of a curricula orientation to train them for productive work in case they desert school before finishing
- As the bearers of the educational value of productive work that has to be considered by curricula and syllabi
- As those "evidently poor pupils" who will get the benefit from scholarships that the state will assign in public education budgets

In Chapter 10 they are construed as the following:

- Subjects with the faculty to organize themselves in societies
- Qualifiers of the type of societies that by no means will intervene in school governing

In Chapter 11 they are construed as the following:

- Those who will benefit from a complementary course
- Those who will receive from school the adequate premises and equipment
- The bearers of a future action about which education will be oriented
- (Marked as female pupils) the receivers of an instruction especially for dealing with children of a certain age

In Chapter 12 they are construed as those towards which curricula, syllabi, and methods will be oriented.

In Chapter 13 they are referred to as the bearers of a future action for which higher knowledge should be imparted (in relation to higher education).

In Chapter 16 "pupils" are construed as the following:

- Receivers of aesthetic education
- Bearers of phases of development to be considered by the types of primary education

In Chapter 17 they are construed as indirect objects of faculties assigned to adults (tutors or children's representatives).

In Chapter 18 they are construed as items enumerated together with textbooks and calendars. The signifier operates as a marker for the noun "promotion."

Minors "Minors younger than fifteen years old" (Chapter 8) appearing as bearers of compulsory primary school in the context of civic obligations.

"Minors in social danger or transgressors of criminal laws" (Chapter 8) construed as indirect objects of the state policies that will not punish but adapt them to the social environment.

"Minors" (Chapter 17) are referred to as the following:

- Indirect objects of parents' and tutors' obligations to cooperate with schools and not to oppose school teachings at home,
- Objects of the parents' and tutors' faculties in surveying schools and denouncing abuse and ill treatment to children.
- An indirect object of adult tutelage whose representation is conceded to parents' societies.

Educandos *Educandos* (Chapter 4) are construed in six ways:

- As the recipients of a socialist education and a pedagogical object of physical, intellectual, moral, aesthetic, civic, military, economic, social, and productive training, for collective benefit
- As objects of an educational service oriented to civic values (solidarity, preeminence of the collective over the individual, against inequality)
- As the subject whose personal features should be respected,
- As objects of school discipline that is not allowed at all to administer corporal punishment (biological dimensions as well as human dignity are considered here)
- As the user of a free, public, state-guaranteed service, and
- as the receiver of a benefit (books and kits for school).

In Chapter 8 they appear as an indirect object whose "integral development" is the target of primary education ("integral" meaning physical, intellectual, moral, aesthetic, civic, military, economic, social, and productive training, for collective benefit).

In Chapter 12 they are referred to as pedagogical objects of vocational education and training for productive activities.

In Chapter 17 the signifier appears as the indirect object of the faculties conceded to parents' societies (that should survey and denounce abuse or mistreatment in schools and should also propose improvements).

Párvulos In Chapter 7 this signifier is constructed in seven ways:

1. The bearer of an age to be considered such (younger than six years old)
2. The pedagogical object whose age sets conditions for physical, mental, moral, and aesthetic development to be considered by teaching
3. The bearer of an age (younger than three) imposing pedagogical considerations (breeding, health, physical development, sentimental and mental maturing)
4. Pedagogical object with reference to educational activities: playing games, singing, dancing, rhythmical exercise, arts and crafts, etc.
5. Pedagogical object with reference to intellectual teaching against superstition, cruelty, hatred, selfishness, and other antisocial attitudes
6. Object of adult representation whose duty is to collaborate with the school
7. Object of a state obligation to provide assistance, succor, and adequate custody

Párvulos (Chapter 11) is referred to as an indirect pedagogical object target of teaching training.

Infants "Infants younger than six years old" (Chapter 11) are constructed as pedagogical objects in reference to the gender of their teachers (exclusively women).

"Infant population" (Chapter 7) is referred to as a user of a service that the state will try to guarantee, in the context of kindergarten features.

With reference to family relations:

- "Sons and daughters, and represented (children) younger than fifteen" (Chapter 8) appear as an indirect object of parents' obligations
- "Sons and daughters, tutored and represented (children)" (Chapter 17) refer to direct objects of parents' and tutors' obligations (both to send their children to school and to military instruction).

Other constructions:

- "Economically destitute or morally abandoned childhood" (Chapter 7), as the object of a state obligation to provide assistance, shelter, and adequate support
- "Population in school age" (Chapter 4), construed as the bearer of a ben-

efit: a service that should be expanded as an obligation of the federation, states, municipalities, and so on in the context of public educational funds

- "Boys and girls" (Chapter 8), constructed as the subject and object of a civic right in terms of gender, that is, equal educational rights
- "*Escolares*" (roughly meaning school-age children) (Chapter 4), construed as a pedagogical object bearer of a certain age and mental development
- "Individual" (Chapter 5), constructed as the object of a state faculty (studies revalidation)

The Ley Orgánica de Educación (1935)

This law was issued during the *socialist education* reform (officially operating from 1934 to 1940; see Buenfil, 1990, 1994). The law contains nineteen chapters:

1. General dispositions
2. Obligations and attributions of the state
3. About the aims of education
4. About private educational institutions
5. Schools "Article 123" (landowners' and patrons' obligation)
6. Compulsory and free (of charge) education
7. Revalidation of curricula
8. General regulations for the schooling system
9. Preschool education (kindergarten)
10. Primary school
11. Secondary school
12. Vocational and bachelor (preuniversity)
13. Normal school (teacher education)
14. Technical school and professional
15. Extra-school education
16. Scientific research
17. Schools for "special qualification" (technical qualification for labor, arts, retarded children, and others)
18. Functions of the federation, the states, and municipalities
19. Sanctions and transitory articles

This law also involves the regulation of Article III concerning private schools, with four chapters.

Mentions of the child, pupil, infant, student, and minor that were found in these thirty pages of legislation show the following cases.

Children "A number of children exceeding twenty" (Chapter 5) appears as a specification to the obligation of landowners and patrons to found a school.

"Their children younger than fifteen years old" (Chapter 6) appears as the parent obligation (fitting the compulsory mandate of education).

"Children who are not sons/daughters of their employees" (Chapter 6) indicates an obligation for landowners and patrons to receive pupils in their schools.

"Children younger than six years old," "infant houses," *"jardines de niños"* (kindergartens) (Chapter 9) appears as the specific target of a schooling cycle.

"Jardines de niños" (kindergartens) (Chapter 9) appears as the following:

- The qualifier of a schooling cycle that should be organically linked with primary school
- The qualifier of a school cycle for which women are getting trained (Chapter 13)
- (Regulation of Article III) the qualifier of a school cycle in which private associations are entitled to teach

"Children" (Chapter 10) appear as the bearer of a service whose vocational aptitudes should be explored and promoted.

"Primary school for children" (Chapter 10) appears as a precision about compulsory military instruction.

"Children and teenagers" and *"educandos"* (Chapter 17) are associated with the correspondence between regular school and that for the retarded.

"Children"(regulation of Article III) are associated with the moral and physical quality of the neighborhood to be considered when opening a school.

"Deprived children" (regulation of Article III) appear as bearers of assistance and social benefits from the private school.

Pupils "Scholarships for pupils and . . ." (Chapter 6) are associated with the obligation of the state to provide financing.

In Chapter 8, it indicates a recipient of a flexible curriculum foreseeing abandonment.

In Chapter 10 it is associated with the following:

- The user of a service whose biological faculties must be considered
- The spirit of initiative (energy to start an action), self-confidence, responsibility, and veracity to be developed by education

In Chapter 11 the signifier is related to the right to organize societies to cooperate with the school governing.

"Pupils" (regulation of Article III) are linked with two senses:

- Indicating the differences between boarding students, regular students, and others, and the number that should be attended by private schools

- Referred to students of private "normal" schools as the bearers of an obligation toward the community

"Pupils of private schools" (regulation of Article III) are associated with the obligation to fit the age of official schools in each cycle.

Párvulos *"Párvulos"* (infants in kindergarten) (Chapter 9) appears as bearers of biological and mental development.

"Párvulos" appear as bearers of biological and mental development whose main activities should be related with playing.

"Párvulos between four and six years old" (Chapter 13) appear as the qualifier of a schooling cycle and are associated with the curriculum particularities.

Educandos In Chapter 8 the signifier is associated with the following:

- The psychological features of the subject of education
- The exclusion of corporal punishment

"Men and women" and the *"educando"* (Chapter 8) are associated with the convenience of coeducation or both genders together regardless of their age.

In Chapter 10 it is constructed in three ways:

1. In association with biological and physical conditions that would be improved by the educational action
2. In terms of the socio-economic features of the environment to be considered
3. As those who should be acquainted with scientific knowledge of the world and society

In Chapter 14 it is referred to as the target of education linked with their future social role.

Other constructions:

- "Childhood" (Chapter 15) appears as the bearer of social activities that should be properly conducted.
- "Infancy" (Chapter 8) is associated with the knowledge of the features to be considered in syllabi.
- "The Mexicans younger than fifteen years old" (Chapter 2) appear as objects of a state obligation.

We have thus arrived at the end of this detailed and rich description of the specific features enhanced in the legislation about education and the construction of the child within it. The dissemination of signifiers has been largely shown and the need of some family resemblance appears as a means to provide some organization to this abundant proliferation of child constructions.

Dimensions and Tendencies of Child Construction

At this point I will attempt to weave some of the argumental threads displayed in the preceding sections. I will stress that the evident marks of the struggle between the liberal state and the Catholic Church and the traces of both Enlightenment and Catholicism, all put together and later resignified in the different versions of the Mexican revolutionary mystique, can easily be found in the six laws under consideration. Both the government and the church have shared that education has a key position as social action contributing to the very existence of all social organization, otherwise they would not have struggled for its leadership so intensely. Not only was there evidence of education's key position within both meaning constellations but also there were clear indications of the Enlightenment inscription in the official discursive surface from the nineteenth century onward, also present in the Mexican revolutionary mystique and still relevant in current legislation.

The persistent objection to corporal punishment, the supreme position assigned to scientific knowledge, and the search for a *rational and exact concept of the universe and social life* to fight against fanaticism and superstition present in Enlightenment are later recycled in the Mexican revolutionary mystique and its educational legislation. The same can be said about the frequent mentions of biological and intellectual faculties of children and their fragile physical and spiritual status susceptible to being injured by abuse (Locke, Rousseau or Priestly), later found in Mexican liberals, positivists in the nineteenth century, and also in the revolutionary mystique in the twentieth century when the grounds were established for the school system as we know it today.

Considering the variety of constructions of the child extracted from the three pieces of legislation, it is possible to propose some *family resemblance* (Wittgenstein, 1963) among the laws but also some differences and some opposed tendencies. From these extended, though not exhaustive, pieces of legislation some general features can be recognized. The child is construed in these legislative pieces as subjects of rights, in principle. However, the construction of the child is much more frequent as an object and as a bearer. In a general view, one can see this area of dispersion where children appear as the following:

- Subjects of rights (when they are construed as having the possibility to demand the fulfillment of the law, which is actually not that frequent).
- Objects or receivers (when they are construed in a passive way, as the entity to which an action is destined); they appear as objects of the following:
  — Legal representation
  — Pedagogical norms
  — Federation, state, and municipality obligations

- — Parent, tutor, and authority duties and obligations
- — Teaching and pedagogical attention
- — Paramedical services
- — Moral, civic, cognitive, and administrative consideration
- — Classification, prescription, regulation, and inspection
- Indirect objects (when they are construed in a passive way and subordinated to another object, i.e., the entity to which an action is destined)—for instance, special school regulations address parents of children with impairment; a norm is directed to schools ruled by municipalities in relation with kindergartens; or the child appears as the object whose features would be considered in syllabi of teachers' education.
- Bearers of a certain condition or feature; basically, bearers of biological or mental capacities, intellectual traits, or social and cultural conditions, bearers of a certain age making them able to attend certain types of schools.
- Qualifiers (when the signifier child or children appears only in an adjectival form, e.g., kindergarten).

The child is constructed in relation with a great variety of topics that can be articulated around four nodal points:

- Legal: concerning rights, duties, obligations, exemptions, representation, and protection
- Administrative: concerning the following classifications:
  - — Children, users, schooling cycles, schools, types of schools, etc.
  - — Administrative measures and normativity for schools, municipalities, states, federation, authorities, teachers, parents
  - — Roles and functions of those in charge—teachers, authorities, parents, tutors, and societies
- Pedagogical: when dealing with prescriptions related to scientific knowledge in curricula, syllabi, textbooks, teaching methods, and learning assumptions
- Axiological: concerning civic, political, national, moral, educational, and cognitive values and orientations

Let us consider now some movements of the signifiers throughout these law reforms. Of course changes in vocabulary due to linguistic transformation, academic trends, and political orientations are unforeseeable. This is why I presented some historical information. However, the idea to stress here is both critical of determinism from "context to text" and of advancing complete self-enclosedness of the text; it rather involves a type of *conditioning* that never manages to fully control the text, and the text can never manage to get rid of these conditions (see the introduction to this chapter). With this in mind let

us see some specific traits of the process from the postrevolutionary laws of
1934 and 1945 to the 1993 legislation.

- The radical exclusion of some signifiers found in the previous laws can
  be observed in the most recent law. This is the case of "children" precisely,
  which in a gradual way diminishes already in the law of 1942 and dis-
  appears in that of 1993.
- The increasing presence of other signifiers such as "individual," which
  had been excluded in 1934, appear timidly once in 1942, and have become clearly legitimate in 1993.
- Two signifiers evidently referring to the activity regulated by these laws,
  "pupils" and "educando," show an opposite tendency: while the former
  gradually decreases, the latter gradually increases.
- Signifiers such as "párvulos" become frequent in 1942 but then disappear
  by 1993.
- The references to gender are few and constant, those to age tend to decrease, and family relations (sons and daughters, tutored) increase in the
  most recent law.

Final Considerations: Political Dimensions of the Child Construction in Legislation

In this chapter the constructions of the child within Mexican legislative discourse were studied, locating its position in the constellation of educational
meanings. The characterization of the discursive horizon within which education is articulated has shown two forces antagonizing throughout history for
the intellectual, moral, and political leadership of the field (i.e., the Catholic
hierarchy and the government). It must be emphasized that even within the
Mexican revolutionary mystique, the traces of the former antagonism did not
disappear. This antagonism between Catholic and Enlightenment views of
education took different shapes and was present either within the MRM itself
(as a mobile and heterogeneous condensation) or between the MRM and the
opposition to this official discourse.

Among the great variety of discursive modalities susceptible of analysis
(curricula, syllabi, methods, budgets, national programs, etc.) legislation was
chosen here to study the constructions of the child in the struggle for their
management.

In order to understand how these child constructions have become what
they are today, the marks of *intertextuality*, the presence of other discourses in
the very system of meanings under scrutiny, led us to trace back their intellectual, political, and religious sources. Enlightenment and Catholicism have

been the strongest Western influences in Mexico concerning education and child construction from the seventeenth century onward and their traces may be found not only in the early years of the twentieth century (articulated with rationalism, anarchism, liberalism, and so on, in the incipient MRM) but also in contemporary legislation. Thus, another ingredient came to render this landscape more complex and more intellectually challenging—the overdetermined, heterogeneous, and hybrid character of the official constellation of meanings; that is, the Mexican revolutionary mystique ruling the imaginary parameters of the symbolic order that are incarnated in the legislation. This discursive constellation has been articulating key civic, moral, political, and intellectual values cherished by the government, legitimized by the law, and allegedly protected by the judiciary power.

However, this presence has remained, but not unaltered, throughout history. In this chapter, some salient moments of its trajectory have been mentioned as the legislation conditions of signification, therefore as conditions for education and child construction. Education from the Constitution of 1917 onward has been considered one of the five highest national priorities.

As we saw earlier there is rich material to analyze an enormous variety of child constructions in the context of Article III in its three versions, and in the context of the General Law (Organic Law in 1935 and 1942). The profusion of constructions appearing in both Article III and the law enabled us to analyze that the child is construed in principle as subject of rights (e.g., "All individuals have the right to receive education" [1993]). However, this was the poorest and least developed elaboration of the child. On the contrary, the richest conceptualizations were those in which the child appears as the following:

- An object of others' rights (teachers' rights, parents' rights, authorities' rights, etc.), duties, and obligations
- An object to be classified (in terms of age, the need of special care, an amount to justify the creation of schools, etc.), administered, taught certain topics, assessed, surveyed, protected, and shaped

The four nodal points articulating child construction in the laws, as I interpreted from the abundant material presented here, were the legal, the administrative, the pedagogical, and the axiological.

Depending on the issue developed in each chapter of the law the child would be more associated with its features as an age bearer or a supporter of family relations. Sometimes the child was depicted as a school regular (pupil, *educando*, and *párvulo*) and other times it was linked with the general status of a Mexican citizen, inhabitant, or individual. However, these variations did not occur completely subordinated to the issue approached by each chapter of the law. Information about historical conditions has enabled us to understand their movements vis-à-vis other discursive processes.

It is not surprising then to find that the child was articulated with the idea of a user of a public service more frequently in the socialist law (1934) than it is in 1993. It makes sense to find "individual" as a synonym of child in the latter and as a synonym of selfishness and antisocial attitudes in the former.

The increasing presence of "individual" as a legitimate signifier can also be related with a globalizing process. By globalization I do not mean a process of homogenization, universalization, and imperialization of cultural, intellectual, economic, or political values, (Braudel, 1991; Wallerstein, 1989) brought about by neoliberals (Chomsky & Dietrich, 1995). I rather take globalization as the encounter, the clash but also the interconnectedness and contact between different and also unequally empowered values, thus producing hybrid formations. In short, I share the view that in this globalized planet we have conflicting tendencies, fragmentation and integration, centralization and decentralization (see Giddens, 1990, p. 175; Kawame & Gates, 1997, p. xi; Perlmutter 1991, p. 911; or Robertson, 1990, p. 22). These conflicting tendencies can be perceived for instance in the political and intellectual trends circulating throughout the American continent (liberalism, constitutionalism, socialism, neoliberalism, and neoconservatism—to give them a name—Enlightenment, positivism, among others) and beyond it, in Europe. Accordingly, the association of the child with a bearer of a social right during the thirties can be easily traced to socialist ideals coming from the then USSR, Italy, the Spanish refugees of the Civil War, inter alia. However, the specific forms this ideal acquired in each case would differ depending on its combination with the specific cultural and political conditions in time and space. We thus have repetition with alteration (*iteration* in Derrida, 1982).

Considering the political dimensions of the child construction in Mexican legislation I must stress two points: (a) that the moments here analyzed coincide with educational reforms, and (b) that the operations' inclusion/ exclusion and rearticulation involve a hegemonic exercise (i.e., a political practice).

Education Reforms

As Popkewitz (1998) argues, reforms can be understood as an invention of the nineteenth century for the administration of social life. They bring into play a new economy of power "procedures which allow power effects to circulate in a manner at once continuous, uninterrupted, adapted and individualized throughout the entire social body" (Rabinow [1986] in Ball, 1994, p. 1). However, while accepting that reforms are carriers of power relations, my reading deals with a particular discursive modality: legislation.

Legislative reforms administer social life, bring about economies of power, bear power, and are the outcome of power relations but, in addition, they are considered the legitimate certification of authenticity of these economies of power. In formally constitutional regimes, legislation is constructed as the warranty of a supreme authority since it is supposed to represent a symbolic mandate achieved by popular consensus and thoroughly considered and debated before its approval. The mystical foundations of authority (Derrida, 1991), of course, are barely discussed.

Legislative History

The *iteration* of an Enlightenment ideal child shows the point I made in the introduction, that is, history against the grain of an idea of progression. The history of this legislation shows *iteration* in the Derridean twofold sense: as repetition and as alteration. The Enlightenment view is repeated and in each iteration it is altered since it is articulated around other different nodal points (e.g., both as inheritors of the MRM, "socialist education" in the thirties, and "education for national unity, for love, for international peace and solidarity" in the forties. The succession of inclusions/exclusions previously presented shows no linear progression to a "superior stage"; there is no reproductive repetition and there is no radically "new beginning" either.

- The child constructed in the legislation trajectory portrays, firstly, the hybridization of an Enlightenment ideal child with a "socialist" and welfare state ideal child (in the legislation of the thirties).
- Secondly, the fusion of an Enlightenment ideal child and a welfare liberal ideal child (in the 1940s legislation).
- And recently, an Enlightenment ideal child hybridized with a postwelfare "neoliberal" ideal child (in 1993 laws). During this course and much before, the legislation and the very concept of "child" within a wider horizon have both been objects of an intense struggle between (laic) government and (religious) opposition.

This hegemonic rearticulation of the signifier "child" shows how the discursive operation consisting of the rearticulation of the signifier child, its resignification and reoccupation, can be traced back from the contemporary individual member of a family, to an object or receiver of welfare benefits (in the forties), to a youth who would benefit from public education as a social good (in the thirties), and back to the nineteenth century when the child was conceived as the combination of instincts and reason. In other words, it shows the political practices enabling us to understand how the child has come to be what it is today in the Mexican laws.

Notes

I want to thank Silvia Fuentes, my research assistant, for her invaluable help with this chapter.

[1] Let me mention some approaches to the conceptual construction of childhood in contemporary studies. One can trace back from Montessori (1936) or Dewey (1944) pedagogical approaches that have continued to our days. The international agencies have also contributed to this enterprise; see UNICEF (1966, 1994) or UNESCO (1980). Cognitive studies (Piaget, 1929, 1980) and others related to the teaching strategies also deal with an idea of the child, for example, Winnicott (1980), Sauvy (1980), and Vergnaud (1991). Medical-educational and counseling views are present in the works by Cruickshand (1971), Knoble (1972), McAllister (1993) among others. Anthropological perspectives can be found in the work by Heuyer & Joulia (1978), and in Mexico, Bonfil (1997), Ovando & Morales (1990), and Orozco (1982). From a legal perspective the work by Tamés (1994) is an interesting contribution. Jiménez (1992) in Mexico and Carli (2000) in Argentina have studied the child from a historical viewpoint. An economic outlook is given by CREA-CEESTEM (1982). These and other pieces contribute to form notions of the child from multiple disciplinary standpoints.

[2] Discursive surface indicates the flow or stream of significations available in a specific moment conditioning the possible meanings to be conferred on a specific signifier, for example, the child in this chapter. These significations are incarnated in a variety of linguistic and nonlinguistic signifiers. However, due to the linguistic character of the discourse I will analyze here (i.e., the legislative) I will deal with linguistic signifiers only.

[3] Nodal point is a signifier occupying an articulatory position of a discursive field. It temporarily sutures the configuration of meanings and its centrality is an effect of power relations understood as hegemonic practices (i.e., antagonism and articulation—see Laclau & Mouffe, 1985, esp. Chapter 3).

[4] I also object to the idea of fixed causality even if it were multiple; instead I subscribe to the notion of overdetermination understood as condensation of multiple conditions and their displacement or circulation (Laclau & Mouffe, 1985). This amounts to a critique of fixity, self-enclosedness, and full causality.

[5] Democracy, secularism, the nation, land redistribution, popular will, education, people's identity, and the worker's identity were among the most noticeable concepts cherished by the revolutionary system of meanings. These components of the MRM were condensed in symbols and images that may be contradictory since they are hybrid and heterogeneous. They displaced themselves from one symbol and/or image to another, evoking a revolutionary principle or value, thus conferring a sense to the sacrifice, heroic acts, and hopeless expectations. Villa, Zapata, the rural schoolteacher, the peasant, the worker (with his invariable overalls), industrial action, land redistribution, and so on as values appeared repeatedly in different discursive modalities (speech, murals, music, budgets, programs, and, of course, curricula and syllabi). On

the other hand, the symbolization of the enemy was condensed in the image of the clergy, the landowner and his bodyguards, the capitalist with his selfish and relentless image, the *Porfirista* dictatorship, and U.S. imperialism, all of them constructed as forms of oppression against which the revolution struggled.

6 As it was argued previously, the MRM was constituted as an ensemble organizing and articulating what was dispersed and chaotic. The forms through which it has operated and impregnated social life permit the analogy with the mystical discourse. Paraphrasing Castoriadis (1983), I claim that the MRM is neither the Constitution of 1917, nor the *ejido;* it is neither land expropriation and redistribution nor the Cultural Mission that reaches the furthest corner of the country; nor Zapata's legendary image; nor the motto "Freedom and Justice." The MRM is rather their condition of possibility, thus instituting these signs as symbols of the Mexican revolution. It is what encourages the population to organize themselves and struggle against oppression; it is what articulates the different groups around an incipient national project; it is what distinguishes the antagonistic poles and gives cohesiveness to the people as a revolutionary agent.

7• It was incipient and precarious because in this initial moment, precise political orientation had not been yet decided. In the case of the MRM, it combined fragments of new political theories with elements of the old liberalism incorporated into Mexican political life in the nineteenth century, elements of the Catholic beliefs, and bits and pieces of popular wisdom, along with old symbols and new codes.

• It was heterogeneous not only because it combined elements of the past and the future but also due to the political diversity of the revolutionary groups:

— Anarchism, liberalism, and socialism, within the labor movement
— Socialism, liberalism, and rationalism, within the intellectual and professional dissidents
— An inexhaustible list of social demands and petitions (not necessarily attached to any specific political discourse) held together by the prevailing peasant common sense

• It was an overdetermined discourse because it condensed a multiplicity of equivalent elements in a relatively reduced set of components that were substitutable among themselves vis-à-vis the enemy and because it displaced some of the meanings grounding the equivalence (e.g., oppression, domination, freedom, justice, etc.) from one component to the other.

8 Probably the best example of how this fusion was represented (i.e., how a discursive object was produced through this complex process) can be studied in the Mexican Constitution promulgated in 1917 in Querétaro when Carranza had been elected constitutional president. The ambiguity present in the constitutional text, the unfixity of its meaning, is one of the features shared by the majority of the constituent elements of the revolutionary mystique. Both the exaltation of the peasant's rights and the legislation for advanced conditions for the workers, the most radical guarantees for the nation's right over the Mexican natural resources, can be found in the juridical text, coexisting along with the defense of some of the *hacendado's* privileges, private property, and so on. All these elements (and more) fused in one heterogeneous and chaotic unity were spread among different sectors of the population by different means, and particularly by the informal ones. An interesting example of the way in which the

images of the peasant leaders, the account of heroic battles, the dearest ideals and the most popular symbols of the revolution were being constructed by the masses, can be analyzed in the proliferation of Mexican *corridos* (at least some twenty different *corridos* were composed about Zapata). These popular songs developed during the armed movement contributed to spread the information and to preserve the memory of the events since they were familiar and accessible to the people. Elsewhere (Buenfil, 1990) I have analyzed six of its multiple components: democracy, the nation, land redistribution, popular will, people's identity, the worker's identity, and education (which will be discussed in "Education and Enlightenment").

[9] Education understood as school overlooks the rich and complex process happening beyond the school premises. A variety of agencies have been in action before, during, and after the reductionist concept in use today. My view is that regardless of our conceptualization of these agencies and their actions as education, they educate, they shape social subjects, they propose images of identification and succeed because sometimes they do this more effectively than schools.

[10] This refers to 1883 when the Ministry of Public Instruction closed the university and colleges due to their scholastic, monastic, and confessional orientation.

[11] Meaning private and almost always confessional schools of different degrees.

[12] Antagonism indicates a political relation of reciprocal denial of identities and involves the creation of a political frontier between two conflicting agencies. Antagonism and articulation are the two operations involved in a hegemonic practice (Laclau & Mouffe, 1985).

[13] Floating signifiers are discursive units available in a specific time and space whose meaning is unstable, polysemyc, and susceptible to be temporarily fixed around a nodal point as an outcome of an articulatory process (Laclau, 1996).

[14] Ley General de Educación in 1993, Ley Orgánica de la Educación Pública in 1942, and Ley Orgánica de Educación Reglamentaria in 1934. Before this the other important laws dealing with education in the country are found in Article III of the Constitution of 1917 (as an outcome of the Mexican Revolution), reforming that issued in 1857 by the first liberal government. It can be traced back to 1824–1835 and Article 5 of the constitution, which established as an "exclusive faculty of the General Congress, the promotion of enlightenment." It is also possible to track it back to the Título XI De la Instrucción Pública of the Spanish Constitution of Cadiz in 1812.

[15] Just to give an example of the counterconstruction of the child in those days, let me quote some fragments of the Mexican Catholic speakers. When the amendments of the Third Article were announced, the apostolic delegate Leopoldo Ruiz y Flores, writing a pastoral from exile in the United States, called the reform a war against religion. He warned that there were rights

> ... *above any Constitution, rights which the ... [State] should respect and uphold, such as religious rights, the right to educate one's children, the right to life, the right of private property and all other natural rights. Any law impairing those rights is unjust and null and void ...*
>
> ... *it was illicit for any Catholic person to establish or support any schools or to send their children to those already existing [under the reformed law].* .... (Beteta, 1935, p. 190)

Another example is given by the motto repeated to semirural people from loudspeakers in a car:

Parents Alarm! Rush to the schools and take out your children. General Calles has given orders that they all be branded on their foreheads with the letters PNR. If you don't want your offspring to become property of the devil and of the PNR, take your children out of school before it is too late. (Townsend, 1952, p. 78)

[16] Here is an example of the Catholic construction of those times:

Our State claims to defend freedom and to fight for human dignity, and this freedom is denied to family parents for educating their children, and this dignity is injured in the person of the child . . .
   There is only one civilisation: the Christian.
   There is only one justice: the Christian.
   There is only one peace: the Christian. (J. Guisa y Azevedo [May 1, 1939], in García Cantú, 1965, p. 949).

[17] At this point, the rearticulation of Catholic hierarchy and government produces a unified discourse where children are the bearers of an inalienable parent's right: the right to educate their children according to their own beliefs, which in this context means to teach religion in schools again.

[18] Education will be free, compulsory, and laic; defined and controlled by the state; will teach scientific knowledge; will lead the students to international solidarity in peace; and so on.

[19] The reader will have to deal with my free translation of old legislative writing. I cannot reproduce the entire text but I will try to quote the most crucial fragments.

[20] "Normal" education means teacher education.

[21] In the then current context, "private interests" alluded to the Catholic hierarchy and orders traditionally devoted to educational activities: Jesuits, Lasalleans, Franciscans, inter alia.

[22] Due to space considerations I cannot fully quote the articles.

[23] I analyze this policy in the context of globalization in Buenfil (1999).

[24] Basic education is the cycle comprising kindergarten (noncompulsory yet) and primary and secondary school (compulsory).

References

Ball, S. (1994). *Education reform.* Buckingham, UK: Open University Press.
Beteta, R. (1935). *Economic and social program of Mexico* (1–211). Mexico City, Mexico: Ministry of Economics.
Bonfil, G. (1997, April–May). Los diversos rostros. *Tierra Adentro,* no. 85. Mexico: CENCA/SEP, pp. 4–12.
Braudel, F. (1991). *Escritos sobre la historia.* Mexico: Fondo de Cultua Económica.
Buenfil, R. N. (1990) Politics, hegemony and persuasion: Education and the Mexican revolutionary discourse during World War II. Ph.D. thesis. Essex: University of Essex.
Buenfil, R. N. (1994) *Cardenismo: Argumentación y Antagonismo en Educación.* Mexico: DIE-Cinvestav-CONACYT.
Buenfil, R. N. (1997). *Revolución mexicana, mística y educación.* Mexico: Torres Asociados.
Buenfil, R. N. (2000). Globalization and educational policies in México, 1988–1994: A meeting of the universal and the particular. In N. Stromquist & K. Monkman

(Eds.), *Globalization forces in education* (pp. 275–97). Boulder, CO: Rowman & Littlefield.

Buenfil, R. N. (2000, February). Globalization, education and discourse political analysis: Ambiguity and accountability in research. *Qualitative Studies in Education, 13* (1), 1–24.

Buenfil, R. N., & Ruiz, M. (1997). *Antagonismo y articulación en el discurso educativo: Iglesia y gobierno (1930–40 y 1970–93).* Mexico: Torres Asociados.

Carli, S. (2000).*Niñez, pedagogía y política. Transformaciones en los discursos acerca de la infancia en la historia de la educación argentina.* Ph.D. thesis. Buenos Aires: Facultad de Filosofía y Letras, Universidad de Buenos Aires.

Castoriadis, C. (1983). *The imaginary institution of society.* London: Blackwell-Polity Press.

Ceniceros, A. (1954). *Nuestra Constitución Política y la Educación Mexicana.* Mexico: Instituto Politécnico Nacional.

Chomsky, N., & Dietrich, H. (1995). *La sociedad global.* Mexico: Joaquín Mortiz.

Cisneros, G. (1970). *El Artículo Tercero Constitucional. Análisis histórico, jurídico y pedagógico.* Mexico: Trillas.

CREA-CEESTEM (1982). *La participación económica infantil, adolescente, No. 2.* Mexico: Consejo Nacional de Recursos para la Atención de la Juventud/Centro de Estudios Económicos y Sociales del Tercer Mundo, A. C.

Cruickshand, W. (1971). *El niño con daño cerebral; en la escuela, en el hogar y en la comunidad.* Mexico: Trillas.

Derrida, J. (1978). *Writing and difference.* Trans. Alan Bass. Chicago: University of Chicago Press.

Derrida, J. (1982). *Margins of philosophy.* London: Harvester Press.

Derrida, J. (1991). Force of law: The mystical foundation of authority. Distinguished Annual Lecture at Essex University.

Dewey, J. (1944). *El niño y el programa escolar, mi credo pedagógico.* Buenos Aires: Editorial Losada.

Fendler, L. (1998). What is it impossible to think? A genealogy of the educated subject. In T. S. Popkewitz & M. Brennan (Eds.), *Foucault's challenge: Discourse, knowledge, and power in education* (pp. 39–63). New York: Teachers College Press.

Flores, N. (1996). La reforma salinista al Artículo Tercero constitucional ante 132 años de laicismo juarista. B.A. dissertation. Mexico: UNAM.

Foucault, M. (1977). *Language counter-memory, practice.* Oxford: Basil Blackwell.

Foucault, M.(1979). Governmentality. *Ideology and Consciousness, 6,* 5–22.

Furet, F. (1995). *El pasado de una ilusión.* Mexico: Fondo de Cultura Económica.

García Cantú, C. (1965). El Pensamiento de la Reacción Mexicana, Historia Documental 1810–1962, México Empresas Editoriales.

Giddens, A. (1990). *The consequences of modernity.* Cambridge: Polity Press.

Hall, S. (1996). Who needs identity? In S. Hall & P. Du Gay (Eds.), *Questions of identity* (pp.1–17). London: Sage.

Heuyer, G., & Joulia, P. (Eds.) (1978). *Paideia* (Bublioteca práctica de pedagogía, psicología y psicopatología de la infancia). Barcelona: Planeta.

Jiménez, M. A. (1992). *Los cuerpos y las cosas de la enseñanza.* Tesis de maestría. Mexico: Departamento de Investigaciones Educativas—Centro de Investigaciones y Estudios Avanzados.

Kawame, A. A., & Gates, H. L. (1997). *The dictionary of global culture.* New York: Alfred A. Knopf.

Knight, A. (1986). *The Mexican revolution.* Cambridge: Cambridge University Press.

Knoble, M. (1972). *Infancia y familia: orientaciones sobre salud mental.* Buenos Aires: Grancia.

Kramnick, I. (Ed.) (1995). *The portable Enlightenment reader.* New York: Penguin Books.

Lacan, J. (1956). Fetishism: The symbolic, the imaginary and the real (with W. Granoff). In M. Balint (Ed.), *Perversions, psychodynamics and therapy.* New York: Random House.

Laclau, E. (1990). *New reflections on the revolutions of our time.* London: Verso.

Laclau, E. (1996). *Emancipation(s).* London: Verso.

Laclau, E., & Mouffe, C. (1985). *Hegemony and socialist strategy: Towards a radical democracy.* London: Verso.

Laplanche, J., & Pontalis, J. B. (1985). *The language of psychoanalysis.* London: Hogarth Press.

McAllister, S. (1993). *La participación de los padres y su relación con los logros de los niños: lo que sabemos hasta ahora.* Santiago, Chile: CIDE.

Meyer, J. (1973). *La Cristiada.* Mexico: Siglo XXI.

Montessori, M. (1936). *The secrets of childhood.* Bombay: Orient Longman.

Mora, J. M. (1949). *El clero, la educación y la libertad.* Mexico: Empresas Editoriales.

Nietzsche, F. W. (1907). In *Genealogy of morals.* Trans. W. A Haussmann. New York: Macmillan.

Orozco, L. (1982). Los niños monolingües zapotecas ante la educación primaria (No. 38). Mexico: SEP/INI/CIESAS.

Ovando, L., & Morales, A. E. (1990). *Niños y niñas, palabras de Chiapas (Antología, cuentos y leyendas).* Mexico: Programa Editorial SNTE.

Perlmutter, H. V. (1991). On the rocky road to the first global civilization. *Human Relations, 44* (9), 897–1010.

Piaget, J. (1929). *The child's conception of the world.* London: K. Paul, Trench, Trubner & Co., Ltd.; New York: Harcourt, Brace and Company.

Piaget, J. (1980). *Six psychological studies.* Brighton: Harvester Press.

Piaget, J., & Inhelder, B. (1956). *The child's conception of space.* London: Routledge & Kegan Paul.

Popkewitz, T. S. (1997). Research and the study of educational reform: Social practice as an effect of power. Paper presented at the IV National Congress of Educational Research, Merida-Mexico, COMIE.

Popkewitz, T. S. (1998). *Struggling for the soul.* New York: Teachers College Press.

Robertson, R. (1990). Mapping the global condition. In M. Featherstone (Ed.), *Global culture.* London: Sage.

Ruiz, M. (1997–1999). *Política y alternancia en la educación de adultos.* Ph.D. research. Mexico: Departamento de Investigaciones Educativas Cinvestav (research working documents, field research, interviews, newspapers).

Sauvy, J. (1980). *El niño ante el espacio.* Madrid: Pablo del Río Editor.

SEP (1997). *Menores con discapacidad y necesidades especiales* (Antología, Biblioteca para la actualización de los maestros). Mexico: SEP.

Sierra, J. (1947). *Antología.* Campeche, Mexico: Gobierno del Estado.

Tamés, B. (Ed.) (1994). *El menor en el contexto del derecho familiar y los derechos humanos.* Mexico: Comisión Nacional de Derechos Humanos.

Townsend, W. C. (1952). *Lazaro Cardenas, Mexican democrat.* Ann Arbor, MI:.

UNESCO (1980). *Estudios y documentos de educación (El niño y su familia).* París: UNESCO.

UNICEF (1966). *Children and youth in national development in Latin America.* Report of conference. New York: UNICEF.

UNICEF (1994). *The best interests of the child: Culture and human rights.* Alston, P. (Ed.). Oxford: Clarendon Press.

Vergnaud, G. (1991). *El niño, las matemáticas y la realidad: problemas de la enseñanza de las matemáticas en la escuela primaria.* Mexico: Trillas.

Wallerstein, I. (1989). *El capitalismo tardío.* Mexico: Siglo XXI.

Winnicott, D. W. (1980). *El niño y el mundo externo.* Buenos Aires: Ediciones Hormé (distribución Paidós, Biblioteca: Psicología Infantil, Vol. XIV).

Wittgenstein, L. (1963). *The philosophical investigations.* Oxford: Basil Blackwell.

Official Documents

Diario Oficial (13/XII/1934), Mexico, Gobierno Constitucional de los Estados Unidos Mexicanos.

Diario Oficial (30/XII/1946), Mexico, Gobierno Constitucional de los Estados Unidos Mexicanos.

Diario Oficial (05/III/1993), Mexico, Poder Ejecutivo. Secretaría de Gobernación.

Documentos Completos del Vaticano II (1991). *Doctrina Social de la Iglesia. De León XIII a Juan Pablo II,* Ediciones Paulinas; S.A. De C.V., Mexico.

Poder Ejecutivo Federal (1941). Ley Orgánica de educación reglamentaria de los artículos 3°, 27, fracciones constitucionales. In *La educación pública en México desde el 1°. De diciembre de 1934 hasta el 30 de noviembre de 1940* (pp. 519–50). Mexico.

Secretaría de Educación Pública (1942). Ley Orgánica de la Educación Pública (publicada en el Diario Oficial 23/I/1942). In *Prontuario de la Educación Nacional* (pp. 26–46). México: SEP.

Secretaría de Educación Pública (1993). *Diario Oficial de la Federación. Ley General de Educación* 13/VII/1993 (pp. 42–56). México.

11

When Poststructuralism
Meets Gender

Julie McLeod

The excitement lies in the promise that young girls and boys might be able to
see and understand how they can resist gender as a limiting feature of their
identity. . . . The construction of gender begins from the cradle. . . . The logical
starting point must be the foundation stones.

Alloway, 1995, pp. 104–5

This chapter is motivated by a desire to understand the historicity and effects
of the poststructural moment and specifically to understand that moment in
relation to research in education, a field characterized by an engagement in
theory and practice as well as by policy making and implementation. I am
concerned, in particular, with exploring the influence of certain poststructuralist ideas on the direction and goals of feminist and progressive education
reforms in Australian schools, and the impact of these reforms on the governing of children's subjectivity. The "nature" and constitution of children's gendered subjectivity have been a central concern of feminist reforms in education, and in recent times this problematic has been commonly understood
through the lens of poststructuralism and the formulation of identity as "constructed." In the following discussion, I develop two main lines of inquiry. I
explore the coming together of a range of poststructuralist and feminist ideas
and pedagogical practices that promised to rescue the child from conventional
and constricting forms of gender identity, enabling them to embrace more
fluid and "gender-free" subjectivities. And, arising from this, I propose that
certain forms of poststructuralism have themselves become implicated in processes of governmentality, in inciting self-reflexive modes of subjectivity, and
in cultivating new norms of gender conduct. I begin by tracing some of the
intellectual and political lineages of these inquiries.

For over a decade, poststructuralist ideas, and particularly those bearing the marks of "Foucault," have permeated research in education—and the social sciences more generally—producing a diverse and influential body of work (Ball, 1990; Cherryholmes, 1988; Dean, 1994; Gore, 1993; Hunter, 1994; Luke & Gore, 1992; McNay, 1992; Meredyth & Tyler, 1993; Middleton, 1998; Peters, 1996; Popkewitz, 1998b; Popkewitz & Brennan, 1998). At conferences and seminars and in books and journals, we find ample evidence of the popularity of this approach, and of its relatively secure place in academic discourse (Schrag, 1999). At the same time, and even paradoxically, poststructuralism is often embraced as if it were still an oppositional, even marginal, intellectual orientation. I want to ask in this chapter how else—other than as oppositional or marginal—we might begin to understand the place of poststructuralism in education. In posing this question, I neither wish to denigrate poststructuralism, dismissing its insights as chimerical, nor to position it as savior, responsible for redeeming the project of educational research. Rather I want to extend the logic of certain Foucauldian insights and ask what effects poststructuralism itself is having in the field of education—what are its regimes of truth? What power/knowledge relations does it produce? What are its normative effects?

These questions have their own history. They also emerge from my engagement with feminist research and gender reform in Australian education. Since the early 1990s this body of work has been strongly and self-consciously influenced by poststructuralist ideas. Indeed, poststructuralism has become orthodox in this domain, both common sense and commonplace. Its mark has been imprinted in policy statements, in programs for teachers' professional development, in reports commissioned by government agencies, and in academic research. I am particularly interested in exploring the entry of poststructuralist discourse into the formal policy-making process. In Australia, this process needs to be understood in relation to the engagement of feminist projects—including gender reform in education—with state bureaucracies, of working with and through the state to achieve both institutional change and the transformation of personal attitudes (Yates, 1993a, 1993b; Franzway, Court, & Connell, 1989). As many commentators have noted, this is not because of a naive faith in the intrinsic fairness of the state but the result instead of a deliberate project for feminists to work strategically through existing arrangements—it has been a much-debated and, at times, fraught political practice (Eisenstein, 1991; Pringle & Watson, 1992; Yeatman, 1990).[1] In this most explicit way, we can see that feminism is not simply an oppositional politics working outside the "mainstream" or independently of state bureaucracies. Rather, feminism has become an integral part of the political and bureaucratic domains that govern us (see also Tapper, 1993). This is not simply due to the political successes of certain feminists within the bureaucracy—femocrats—

it is also a result of the manner in which feminism has operated through policy and bureaucratic mechanisms.

Further, the field of gender equity reform in education has been characterized by a relatively porous relation between the (feminist) academy and the policy arena (Yates, 1993a, 1993b, 1997). While feminist researchers and academics have developed critiques of policies and programs, they have also participated in the formal and informal processes of policy formulation through, for example, authorship of commissioned reports, secondments to work on specific projects, and involvement in teachers' professional development, all of which have promoted the vigorous circulation and crossover of ideas between the two spheres. It is inappropriate to conceive of this as a process of "infiltration" of feminist ideas, as those ideas were fundamentally important (not incidental, or post hoc) to the formation of the field of reform in the first place. Importantly, the relation between the two domains has been reciprocal, ongoing, and subject to change. In arguing this, I am wanting to refuse the misleading opposition between feminism and governmental and bureaucratic relations whereby the latter pollutes or corrupts the former, and the former is innocent of power and regulation.

There are two interrelated arguments arising from this. The first is that feminism can be analyzed as, in the Foucauldian sense, a governmental process, intimately connected to the management of conduct and to the regulation of individual desires and subject positions. In this analysis, "government" does not only denote the public administration of the state, which is the sense commonly conveyed by the term. Rather, as O'Malley, Weir, & Spearing argue, "One of the most formative general principles underlying governmentality writings has been the rejection of the identification of government with the state, understood as a centralised locus of rule, and the identification of programmes and practices of rule in micro-settings, including those 'within' the 'subject' " (1997, p. 510). In this way power "is decomposed into political rationalities, governmental programmes, technologies and techniques of government" (p. 510). For Foucault, "to govern . . . is to structure the possible field of action of others" (Foucault, 1983, p. 221). Such government, such conducting of conduct, is not the simple result of coercive or repressive practices being imposed on hapless individuals. Rather, this form of government produces and relies upon self-disciplining individuals who, through a variety of "technologies of the self," internalize governmental imperatives, making them their own. These technologies, or "arts of existence," are characteristic of modern forms of power and processes of subjectification, producing self-managing subjects, responsible for governing their own conduct (Foucault, 1988, pp. 16–49).[2] As Nikolas Rose writes, modern government enables "the citizen subject . . . not to be dominated in the interests of power, but to be educated and solicited into a kind of alliance between personal objectives and ambitions and institutionally or socially-prized goals and activities" (Rose, 1990, p. 10). I am arguing that feminist pedagogies and educational practices are governmental practices that promote particular "technologies of the self" and incite the regulation of "nonsexist," "feminist" subjectivities. My focus is thus on how feminism in education and in other social practices can be theorized as both a regulatory and emancipatory politics, and, in the case of education, my focus is on the manner in which feminist goals have been intimately connected to the "state" *and* to governmentality.

The second argument is that in the 1990s feminism and gender reforms in education have been shaped by certain poststructuralist ideas about identity and discourses, particularly claims that identity is constructed and nonessential and that discourses are productive. If we accept the former argument that feminism is engaged in governmental processes then we need to consider what impact these poststructuralist feminist ideas are having in terms of "governmentality." The question thus arises, What happens when poststructuralist ideas become part of governmentality? In summary then, in this chapter I am developing a Foucauldian analysis of the impact of poststructuralism on feminist and gender reform in Australian education, and this phenomenon is explored in relation to the production of truths about, and the government of, children's gendered subjectivity.

Let me make several matters clear from the outset. First, in describing poststructuralism as popular, I am not suggesting that it is utterly hegemonic, eclipsing all other diverse forms of contemporary educational research. But I am suggesting that in certain patches of that field, poststructuralism is ascendant and consequently has powerful effects on knowledge production and educational policy. Nor am I suggesting that such ideas have not met with debate, resistance, and challenge or that deploying poststructuralist precepts has become mandatory (e.g., Anyon, 1994). Second, my purpose is not to enter into an extended discussion about what is or is not truly "poststructuralist." Instead, I am trying to convey something of the distinctive intellectual character of Australian feminist educational research in the 1990s. My interest then is in exploring the kind of knowledges, insights, and practices made possible by poststructuralist analyses—what, in other words, does poststructuralism make possible to say? (see Fendler, 1998).[3]Third, I am conscious that the umbrella term "poststructuralism" is not always helpful, as its breadth can occlude differences in modes and traditions of analysis and give the misleading impression that all poststructuralists speak with the same (multiply accented) voice. Within educational research alone, a large number of ideas and modes of analysis fall under the rubric "poststructuralism." It denotes a range of work including the self-consciously transgressive and ludic kind, intent on subverting meaning (Lather, 1991), posthumanist accounts of the subject and critiques of master narratives (Lyotard, 1984), and histories of truth and the human sciences (Foucault, 1984a). In Australian educational research, however, Foucauldian ideas (however invented and represented) have had a powerful effect in shaping what constitutes poststructuralism in that domain.

Finally, it is also true that poststructuralism is not intellectually reducible to "Foucauldianism." Nor indeed, is there a single "Foucault"; and it is useful to consider the different ways in which Foucault or other "indigenous foreigners" (Popkewitz, in press) are embraced and (re)invented in different national settings (Butler, 1995, pp. 36–37). In one sense, part of the present chapter is, implicitly, a story about the particular Australian invention of Foucault—a story that stands against a globalized view of Foucault, whose presence is felt in unchanging and undifferentiated ways. Instead, the reception of Foucault is itself dynamic and inventive, a process linked to prior national intellectual and political cultures, and inadequately understood as the static imposition of foreign ideas on any new territory. Popkewitz (in press) deploys the concept of the indigenous foreigner "to direct attention to a particular type of hero and heroic discourse that brings global discourses of change into a relation with the construction of national imaginaries." Foreign authors give the imprimatur of success and progress to national reform efforts, their names and ideas circulating as if indigenous, signifying an apparently "seamless movement between the global and local." In this way, "the indigenous foreigner" becomes a "narrative without specific historical references and practices": "empty of history [it] appears an abstract, serial continuity rather than a series of specific historical contingencies in which the discourses of education are produced" (Popkewitz, in press).

This analysis is suggestive in relation to understanding the reception of Foucault (and other heroes) in Australian educational research. In terms of the focus of the present chapter, it alerts us to the question of why "Foucault" was taken up, adapted, pursued, and invented in particular ways in Australia. To answer this fully, we would need to consider the interplay of national political and intellectual traditions and identities that produced, reiterated, and recirculated a particular reading and identity of Foucault.[4] This formulation emphasizes both the invention (versus the straightforward reception) of ideas and the imbrication of the local in the global (hybridity) and not simply the colonizing of the local by the global. It is not possible in this chapter to address the myriad issues that flow from this analysis. I am noting, nevertheless, some questions that could be fruitfully explored in relation to educational discourses, indigenous foreigners, and national identities in Australia—I return to some of these issues later. In the following section, I briefly characterize some of the concerns of recent Australian educational discourses on gender equity.

Educational Reform and Gender Identity

Feminist research on education in Australia is a well-established and productive field of inquiry and is characterized by a high degree of self-conscious reflection on itself and on the project of gender reform. There have been numerous studies of the shifts in policy direction, most often examining the aims and effects of key policy statements. The policy documents usually discussed include the 1975 Commonwealth Schools Commission's report *Girls, School and Society,* followed by the Commonwealth's *Girls and Tomorrow* in 1984, the *National Policy for the Education of Girls* (1987), the *National Action Plan for the Education of Girls 1993–97* (Australian Education Council, 1993), and the recent national statement *Gender Equity: A Framework for Australian Schools* (Ministerial Council on Education, Employment, Training and Youth Affairs, 1997). Research on these policies includes analyses of the changing ways in which the question of the education of girls has been framed, changing conceptions of gender difference, shifts in the ways in which policy interventions are justified and implemented, and justifications or rationalizations of why one focus was pursued and not another.

In Australia, the administration of education has been relatively centralized, with the states responsible for the governance and funding (via the Commonwealth) of schools, but increasingly the management of schools (budgets, employment of staff, curriculum priorities, and so on) is being devolved to the individual school level. Since the 1970s, the Commonwealth government has played a strong role in relation to gender and education in terms of providing funding for special national projects and for establishing policies to which the states have been obliged to adhere. States, school regions, and individual schools can also have their own policies and programs. There are, then, several levels and forms of policy and while each has been important in relation to gender equity, policies and frameworks at the Commonwealth and national levels have been particularly influential (Henry & Taylor, 1999; Kenway, 1997).

The Commonwealth government itself has funded a number of major studies to analyze its changing policy concerns and current trends in gender equity reform, including a study of the changing terminology in Gender Equity Projects (Gilbert, 1996; Gilbert & Gilbert, 1994). In this regard, research on gender reform and educational policy in Australia cannot be defined as simply research directed toward policy or to changing practice. Rather, it is also constituted by a substantial body of research and reflection on itself.

Since the 1970s, the nature and formation of children's gender identity have been central issues for Australian research and policy on gender and education. While in the 1970s the problem of subjectivity was most often articulated (and resolved) through the language of the sex role and socialization (see later), in the 1990s the dilemma has been interpreted through the language of poststructuralism and the proposition that gender identity is a "construction," a social category that is "made" and open to change. The *National Action Plan for the Education of Girls,* the national *Gender Equity; A Framework for Australian Schools,* and numerous commissioned reports (Collins, Batten, Ainley, & Getty, 1996; Kenway & Willis, 1993, 1995) identify schools as places where this process of identity construction takes place, and advise schools, teachers, and educational systems to promote pedagogical practices that enable pupils and teachers to examine the process and effects of that construction. At school, these processes include the overt and hidden curriculum, forms of assessment, teachers' expectations, the attitudes of fellow pupils and so on (Alloway, 1995; Blair, Holland, & Sheldon, 1995; Collins et al., 1996; Connell, 1997; Davies, 1989;). The concept of "gender as a construction" stands in clear contrast to a view of gender identity as the expression of natural and unchangeable dispositions, capacities, and behaviors. One of the purposes of examining the construction of gender is to deconstruct the prevailing normative ideals of masculinity and femininity. This strategy, it is commonly believed, will help young people and children to see the many possible ways in which they can be male and female, and thereby help to break down narrow, rigid, and constricting gender stereotypes. Policies based on this view of gender identity emphasize the responsibilities of schools to work toward promoting broader and less conventional ideals of femininity and masculinity that, it is optimistically expected, will enhance options and life chances for both girls and boys.

Much research has also been conducted investigating how gender identity is constructed though schooling practices and the discourses of popular culture, often exploring how normative gender codes are practised, negotiated, or transformed. During the 1990s, the attention to gender identity expanded from a predominant focus on femininity (Gilbert & Taylor, 1989) to encompass practices of masculinity (Gilbert & Gilbert, 1998; Lingard & Douglas, 1999; Martino, 1999). In the educational policy arena and in popular and media discussion, there has been heated debate over the question of What about the boys?, and this too has often been framed in terms of the content and form of masculine identity (McLean, 1997; Lingard & Douglas, 1999). The "boys debate" condenses a number of anxieties about gender and education, including concerns that girls are now "outperforming" boys, that boys' needs have been neglected, and that feminism has unfairly advantaged girls at the expense of boys (e.g., Epstein, Elwood, Hey, & Maw, 1998). There is also an underlying concern about the reported difficulties many young men have with their emotional lives; from being prone to aggressive and abusive behaviors, to having poor skills in fostering affective relations, to having alarmingly high rates of suicide, and to not being as "naturally" good as girls at certain subjects such as English/languages and literacy (Gilbert & Gilbert, 1998). Again, a common policy and research response to this range of concerns has been to urge schools to examine the construction of masculinity, to encourage boys to consider other ways of being "male," and to challenge rigid gender stereotypes (or subject positions)

Represented as a way of rewriting the "gender script," examining the construction of gender becomes for both boys and girls a form of intense self-examination, a strategy for scrutinizing habitual conduct and for encouraging an improved understanding of oneself. What are the effects of and the antecedents to this way of governing children's gender identity? Much of the recent research on gender and identity has made clear its debt to poststructuralism, and mostly poststructuralism has been embraced enthusiastically, promising important new policy directions as well as answers to enduring questions about truth, subjectivity, and epistemology. In trying to understand the impact of poststructuralism on education, I am concerned with the accumulated effect of a range of ideas as well as the appeal and effects of specific "truths" associated with poststructuralist educational research in Australia—viz. "identity is constructed"; "discourses are constitutive"; "truth is partial"; and "meaning is multiple" (see also Anyon, 1994). These phrases distill a large and complex history of meaning, some of which is lost in their regular rehearsal.

In the following sections, I address the popularity and truth claims of the "construction of gender" in three main ways. One overall purpose is to identify some of the conditions that have made such a focus possible. First, I outline a history of the present formulation of gender identity through charting the immediately preceding accounts of gender difference as articulated in educational research and policy and professional advice literature. I suggest that the current poststructuralist-inspired view of children's subjectivity represents a kind of neoconstructivism and expresses both a break from as well as some continuities with earlier attempts to define and regulate gender difference and identities.[5] In other words, the shifting discourses about children's gendered subjectivity register both ongoing anxieties about the responsibilities of schools to govern that identity and disruptions to the ways in which that identity is imagined and intended to be managed. Second, I sketch one possible account of the emerging relationship between educational discourses and poststructuralist ideas in Australia and their intersection, in turn, with feminist concerns about gender and identity. Third, I examine the imbrication of poststructuralist discourse in recent gender equity policies and feminist pedagogies and outline some of the ways in which it is now possible to understand poststructuralism as itself part of governmentality. I conclude by raising some questions about what happens to educational and feminist reform once we have made the "poststructural turn."

The Truth about Children's Gender Identity

For the past twenty-five years in Australian education, the meaning and consequences of young people's gender identity has been an object of considerable research and policy activity (McLeod, 1996, 1998b, 1998c; Yates, 1998). Examining the various ways in which the dilemma of subjectivity has been formulated helps us to understand both shifts in feminist and social theory and the shifting authority of different accounts of identity. One purpose here is to challenge the notion (sometimes implicit, at others explicit) that poststructuralist discourses offer us the ultimate and inevitable truth about gender identity, one to which we have "progressed" in a movement away from less sophisticated and mistaken accounts. In tracing some of the previous ways in which gender identity has been imagined in educational research, I hope to underline both the specificity and the historical contingency of current understandings. The discussion developed in this chapter insists that poststructural accounts of identity are historically based (not quintessential or transcendent) truth claims. And, in the tradition of Foucauldian analysis, we must therefore examine their promise and their regulatory effects, as well as the way in which they too are particular effects of power.

What I offer in the following discussion, then, is not simply another narrative of policy shifts in gender equity from, for example, the 1970s focus on equal opportunities for girls to the "what about boys?" debate of the 1990s. Rather, I focus on the way in which questions about gender identity have been formulated in the 1970s and 1980s, in order to contrast and understand the claims and purchase of poststructuralist accounts in the 1990s. Further, I argue that while poststructuralism has provided an influential and productive way of conceptualizing gender identity, the broader "problem" of children's gender identity in Australian education both precedes and enables the turn to poststructuralism.

During the 1970s, sex-role and social learning theory provided the analytic and strategic focus for equal opportunity programs whose purpose was to expose the negative effects on pupils of stereotypical sex-role attitudes and behaviors. An understanding of identity (that of both children and adults) as formed by "sex-role socialization" underpinned much second-wave feminist discussion. As Kate Millet argued, "sexual politics obtains consent through the 'socialization' of both sexes to basic patriarchal politics with regard to temperament, role and status" (Millet, 1972, p. 26). For Millet, and for many other feminists writing in the late 1960s and early 1970s, women's sex role was narrow and confining in comparison to the diverse and rich roles available to men. Women were entrapped by their biology: if women were to overcome their subordination, they needed to transcend their biology. "The limited role allotted to women," Millet argued, "tends to arrest her at the level of biological experience." (p. 26). For second-wave feminists, the "sex role" was a foundational analytic category and was absolutely pivotal to their liberatory project: liberation from oppressive sex roles, from patriarchal expectations, and from the destiny of anatomy. The "sex role" enabled feminists (and others) to conceptualize the possibility of new ways of being, disconnected from biological imperatives and ingrained cultural habits. Women and girls were to be free to make themselves anew, to embrace hitherto repressed or denied characteristics and aspirations. The appeal of the sex-role concept was twofold: it provided a critique of patriarchy, and it made clear and possible the ways in which one could challenge and resist patriarchy and build a new form of politics. In the 1970s, the "personal was political" in many ways. Role theory, and its implicit promise that individuals could be resocialized, was integral to a feminist politics of personal and social transformation.

In education, teachers and pupils, through the scrutiny of their own sex roles, were urged to abandon traditional and sexist ways and aspire to androgyny, a state of being intended to transcend the poverty and limits of conventional and rigid gender difference. The influential 1975 Commonwealth Schools Commission report *Girls, School and Society* argued that "Until recently there has been little questioning of sex roles and so people have tended to adopt their sex roles without attempting at any stage to analyse the stereotype so formed in a rational way" (p. 16). Through values clarification exercises and role-plays, checklists, and quizzes, pupils were encouraged to scrutinize their conventional (and inappropriate) values and opinions and, once their folly was so rationally exposed, to jettison old-fashioned beliefs and adopt the new rationality of "nonsexism." In this way, children were incited to remake themselves into new nontraditional beings, freed from the constraints of sexual specificity. The purpose of equal opportunity and nonsexist education here (as with other forms of self-consciously defined radical and progressive education) was to expose and critique existing values and to create a learning environment that would emancipate and enlighten children and teachers. Feminist educators sought to regulate and re-form pupils' gendered subjectivity identities and saw this as a key element of gender reform projects in education. In this model of reform, children (and teachers) were discursively positioned as self-monitoring and self-reflexive and as desiring the transformation of subjectivity promised by the rational scrutiny of habit and inclination.[6]

In the 1970s, gender identity (the "sex role") was understood as unitary and as an artifact of culture or of socialization. In the 1980s, however, gender identity was more likely to be represented through discourses of difference. Difference had two sets of meaning here. In feminist debate, "difference" denoted differences among and between women as well as the intrinsic difference (embodied, affective, ontological, epistemological) of women from men (Alcoff, 1988). In education, during the 1980s, the view of gender identity as composed of a constellation of intrinsic capacities and dispositions became very influential. This understanding fostered many gender equity and curriculum programs that celebrated intrinsic gender difference and, following a combination of influences, including the work of Carol Gilligan (1977), embraced a belief in women's and girls' distinctive "ways of knowing" (Belenky, McVicker, Goldberger, & Tarule, 1986). Accompanied by commonsense assertions about women's and girls' special capacity for collaboration, conversation, and cooperation, the attention to difference generated much curriculum and professional development based on presumed gender differences in learning styles (Fowler, 1983; Suggett, 1987). In Australia and elsewhere this approach to reform was described as promoting "girl-friendly" schooling or "gender-inclusive" curriculum (Office of Schools Administration, 1990) . The role of schools was to create learning environments that would facilitate the unfolding of these inherent and immutable capacities: gender difference was valorized and girls' learning styles were held to be superior to boys' and as representing a preferred mode of learning for all students. The purpose of feminist education was thus to transform teaching and learning so that they became girl friendly and more sympathetically matched to the inherent qualities of girls. In this respect, femininity (and inversely and negatively, masculinity) was a kind of projection, one that essentialized and fixed gender identity, and children and teachers were incited to conform to its normative demands.

At the same time, the focus on difference brought a more complex understanding about gender and the differences, not only between girls and boys, but also within the genders. The 1987 *National Policy for the Education of Girls* declared that "Girls are not a homogenous category." In feminist theory and politics more broadly, the attention to differences within the category "women" registered a critique of the hegemony of essentialism and of gender universalism. On the one hand, the turn to "difference" in education promoted the circulation of relatively conventional ideas about masculinity and femininity and of gender difference (even if inflected positively). On the other hand, it encouraged a more nuanced account of the heterogeneity of gender identity. In both readings, important feminist debates were being exercised and having a definite effect on policies and programs.

The sex-role and the intrinsic difference views of identity represent distinct discourses about children's subjectivity. Yet both indicate that governing gender has been a pivotal task of educational reform, necessary to secure feminist and progressive agendas and to rescue children from inappropriate and repressive learning environments and modes of self-expression. In this way, the re-formation and regulation of gender identity is crucially linked to the discourse of "education as redemption" (Baker, 1998; Popkewitz, 1998a). Again, this redemptive discourse has a longer history, but what is of interest here is the different ways that rescue from a false subjectivity was articulated.

The view of gender identity as intrinsic difference was destabilized in the 1990s by a relentless focus on gender not as natural but as a "construction." (We can observe some resonances here with the earlier socialization models, despite strenuous attempts on the part of poststructuralists to distance themselves from the 1970s—see later.) Such a discursive shift was made possible by the political and theoretical attention to "differences among women" (McLeod, 1998a; Roman & Eyre, 1997) and by the increasing interest among many feminist researchers in poststructuralist ideas and especially ideas about the relation between subjectivity and discourse.

In the 1990s, poststructuralism offered a new and enticing way of conceptualizing and managing subjectivity and of working toward educational and gender reform. In the following section, I outline some of the poststructural ideas that came together and, intersecting with existing concerns about subjectivity, made possible the current truths about children's gendered identity.

Poststructuralist Discourse and Australian Education

In this section I survey, in a schematic fashion, some of the influential ideas that currently constitute poststructural discourse in Australian education.[7] It is not possible in this chapter to explore the complex intellectual and political genealogy of these ideas.[8] There is, nevertheless, a history to be written about the emergence, reception, and invention of such "foreign ideas" in Australia and about why some indigenous foreigners have a more lasting reverberation than others. There is also the question of at what point the metropole/peripherary binary breaks down and, as suggested by the notion of hybridity, we interpret the circulation of ideas not only in terms of origins and the indigenous foreigners who bear them, but in terms of their reinvention and recirculation in and across the local and global.

The influence of poststructuralism on educational research began to be strongly felt in Australia from the 1980s onward. Key ideas drawn from this body of thought have included the notions of subjectivity as "decentered," nonessential, and constituted; discourse as constitutive rather than reflective of meaning; and discourses as regulatory and productive of subject positions. Attention to subjectivity, discourses, and regulation has shaped a great variety of educational research and informed many feminist studies of gender and schooling (Davies, 1989b, 1993; Gilbert and Taylor, 1989; Kenway, 1993; McLeod, 1993). In this respect, the British collection *Changing the Subject* (Henriques, Hollway, Urwin, Venn, & Walkerdine, 1984) was very influential (at least in Australia) in providing a theoretical language for rethinking subjectivity and its relation to the social and for addressing the productive effects of discourses. The work of Valerie Walkerdine (1984, 1990, 1992), in particular, on the constitution of femininity and masculinity in relation to pedagogical practices and popular culture has had a very strong impact on research and policy on gender and schooling.

In the 1990s, there has also been a strong interest in examining the regimes of truth that govern schooling and educational practices. From such work we have learned, for example, that "nothing is innocent," "everything is dangerous," and that even emancipatory projects have their own disciplining truths and forms of regulation (Gore, 1993; Luke & Gore, 1992; McLeod, 1998c). Other genealogical work in education has developed research characterized as "history of the present," which seeks to unsettle the familiarity of the present and analyze the contingency of the emergence of now commonplace and dominant ideas and practices (Dussel, 1999; Foucault, 1984a; Hunter, 1994; Johnson, 1993; Meredyth & Tyler, 1993; Popkewitz, 1998b; Tyler, 1993). Often in conjunction with "histories of the present," poststructuralist research in education in the 1990s has explored the Foucauldian concepts of governmentality and technologies of the self (Donald, 1992; Hunter, 1994; Popkewitz, 1998b; Popkewitz & Brennan, 1998). Hunter, for example, recasts the administration of education as governmental process and addresses the intersections between schooling and pedagogical techniques that foster self-reflection and self-formation (Hunter, 1991, 1993, 1994).[9]

In much Australian feminist research in education, however, considerably more attention has been given to the insights that subjectivity is produced and discourses are constitutive. As I illustrate later, this constructionist perspective has become the hallmark of feminist poststructuralist discourses on gender equity reform and has had a significant influence on the direction of educational policy and reform. It is also equally true that neither poststructuralist discourse nor Foucault can be so neatly reduced to or contained within such a constructionist or neo-constructivist formula. However, assessing whether Foucault's work permits or contradicts or complicates such a perspective is not my primary concern in this discussion. Rather, what I am attempting to convey here are some of the intellectual conditions that made possible the prevailing truths about children's gender identity, and to sketch out some of the poststructuralist ideas that have been instrumental in shaping the current common sense about gender difference and the regulation of children's subjectivity.

Reforming Children's Gender Identity as the Object of Policy

I observed earlier that in Australia there has been a relatively porous relation between the (feminist) academy and the policy arena. This is especially ap-

272 Governing the Child in the New Millennium

parent in the gender equity field in the 1990s, where this relation has enabled the entry of poststructuralist ideas into policy discourses.[10]

In this section, I begin by identifying the influence of poststructuralist discourses on policies and government reports, noting some parallel trends in academic research, and discussing some of the ways in which the attention to the "construction of gender" has been regarded. I conclude the section by arguing that we need to address the normative dimensions of the "poststructural effect," particularly of the truth claim that "gender is constructed," and suggest that we might now be in a position to theorize poststructuralist ideas and practices as part of governmentality.

In the 1990s, numerous gender equity projects and reports commissioned by the Commonwealth Department of Education, Employment and Training explicitly drew on poststructuralism to explain gender relations and gender identity and the role of schooling practices and discourses in constituting subjectivities; many of these reports were written by feminist academics (Department of Education, Employment and Training [DEET], 1992; Gilbert & Gilbert, 1994; Kenway & Willis, 1993). Poststructural insights were also thought to provide the rationale and basis for effective strategies to deconstruct existing inequalities. In feminist academic research, the process of the construction and deconstruction of gender binaries was being explored, and there was a strong crossover between the policy and academic domains of ideas and authors (Davies, 1989a, 1989b, 1993; Gilbert, 1996; Kenway & Willis, 1993, 1995).[11] Kenway and Willis, in a government-commissioned report, "Enhancing Girls' Post-School Options," argue that "[a]n individual's identity . . . is the on-going result of the discourses that have shaped her/his story and which shape her/his world and the moment; it is constituted and reconstituted daily" (1993, p. 3). They advocate a poststructuralist perspective because it has:

> highlighted the complicated and ambiguous way in which meaning about gender is made in schools, and the highly subjective ways in which students "read" and indeed rewrite such meanings and take up their gender identities. (1993, p. 4)

Moreover, poststructuralism is said to offer "an understanding of girls which is able to accommodate the complex qualities of girlhood" (1993, p. 92). This consequently helps us see that "girls' identities are shifting and fragmented, multiple and contradictory, displaced and positioned as they are across the various discourses which historically and currently constitute their lives in and out of school" (1993, p. 11). Such arguments about the constitutive effects of discourse contradicted the view of intrinsic differences and underlined subjectivity as not given, but as an ongoing process, formed by discourses, not essences. In the 1990s, this became the widely accepted common sense about children's gender identity.

A Commonwealth-commissioned Project of National Significance, *Femininity and Reality: Factors that Affect Girls' Learning* located its work in the midst of "postmodern tensions" (DEET, 1992, p. 32) and explicitly drew on the work of Patti Lather and Valerie Walkerdine to explore the process of the construction of femininity. Addressed to teachers, this booklet of essays was a kind of primer on the connections between feminist theorizing and educational practice. Several of the authors explore the intersection of humanist and post-humanist accounts of subjectivity. They identify a tension at the heart of their work on femininity and reality that represents:

> one [position] which evolves from a humanist perspective which believes that identity develops within individuals through conscious reflection, experience and social interaction with the world outside oneself. The other evolves from what is called an anti-humanist or post-modern position and assumes that reality and the self are discursively constituted. (Leah & O'Brien in DEET, 1992, p. 32)

The working out of these tensions and ideas in such a publication indicates that feminist and poststructuralist debates were being grappled with in relation to the day-to-day practices of teaching. It also offers us a glimpse of how these debates were beginning to produce their own truth claims about gender and identity.

In the early 1990s, several studies were commissioned by the Commonwealth Gender Equity in Curriculum Reform Project to investigate how the national curriculum statements could become more gender inclusive. Many of these studies drew on "deconstruction" to explore gender relations and the production of meaning. For example, the supplementary guidelines for the subject "English" pose the following questions:

> What reality does this text produce?
> Whose reality?
> What are the gaps and silences and contradictions?
> Whose interests are served?
> What are the assumptions about gender/race/class?
> How can it be challenged, criticised, transformed, resisted?
> (Kinnane [1993] quoted in Kenway & Willis, 1995, p. 92)

Again, we can see here a deliberate harnessing of debates in contemporary social theory to questions about what and how to teach. Issues concerning "difference," textual strategies, and the idea of meaning as produced and contextual rather than immanent became central to the curriculum project of the subject "English." I am not suggesting that this movement between theory and practice is undesirable or mistaken. Rather, I am attempting to indicate some of the ways in which certain theoretical concerns were taken up and "put to work" in educational policy and professional discourses. In a related vein, other work published as part of the Gender Equity in Curriculum Reform Project examined "gender and disadvantage" and represented disadvantage as "a process of production of discursive positions and material circumstances" (Gilbert & Gilbert, 1994, p. 15). Developing a poststructuralist analysis, the authors conclude that "it is the interplay of these discourses [of masculinity and femininity, of class and geographical location, ethnicity . . .] and how they contradict and accentuate each other that explains how disadvantage is constructed, interpreted and experienced in particular sites" (Gilbert & Gilbert, 1994, p. 20).

A focus on discourses, difference, and identity construction is also evident in policy statements on gender equity. The Australian Education Council's *National Action Plan for the Education of Girls* (1993) and the Ministerial Council on Education, Employment, Training and Youth Affairs' *Gender Equity: A Framework for Australian Schools* (1997) nominated the examination of the construction of gender as a priority strategy. *Gender Equity: A Framework* specifies that: "The concept of gender construction will be acknowledged, examined and understood at all levels of schooling" (p. 12). The *National Action Plan for the Education of Girls* notes that the "prevailing belief about masculinity and femininity" can contribute to "girls and boys developing very limited concepts of their capabilities" (pp. 7–8). Several reports undertaken as part of the implementation of the 1993 *Action Plan* investigated the day-to-day operation and effects of "gender" in schools. The Commonwealth-funded report *Gender and School Education* was designed to investigate 'the construction of gender through the school environment' (Collins et al., 1996, p. 162). Following the criteria established in the *National Action Plan* and drawing on findings from the report *Listening to Girls* (Milligan & Thomson, 1992), *Gender and School Education* addressed two main questions: How do young people experience gender at school? What are schools doing, in a planned way, about the construction of gender? The report found there is "considerable evidence that attention to gender issues by systems, schools and individual teachers does make a difference to the gender experiences of students in schools" (p. xiv).

Across a range of government and professional reports, teachers were being encouraged to understand children's gender identity in a new light. They were exhorted to implement pedagogical practices that enabled the "examination of gender" and to foster within young people the desire to self-critique and remake their identities. In this way, we can analyze such pedagogies as themselves normative and as particular technologies of the self, practices for acting on and refashioning the self. What might this mean for children? We can see that the interrogation of gender itself is now regarded as a key element in the experience of childhood. And, further, the practice of actively and overtly forming subjectivity is now an explicit component of and rationale for curriculum and pedagogy. This is not, of course, to suggest that prior to this, gender identity was incidental to childhood. Rather, it is to suggest that the examination and reconstruction of gender is linked to a cultural and economic demand for flexible, self-scrutinizing individuals who are able to remake and endlessly adapt themselves. This is evident in calls for multi-skilled workers in the information age and by the project of "lifelong learning"—the capacity to reskill, retrain, and move flexibly between jobs. At the same time, individuals are required to be "ethically literate," to establish their own "value system" in a culture in which identities and communities are in flux—from the feminist questioning of gender, to processes of globalization and migration. Cultivating a reflexive and self-critical disposition is part of such transformations.

In relation to teaching, strategies broadly described as "critical pedagogy" or "critical literacy" have been widely promoted in Australian education. Pedagogies drawing on critical literacy have become particularly popular in relation to the education of boys and to working against the opposition of masculinity to literacy and language (the feminized knowledges). Alloway and Gilbert (1997) suggest that due to the operation of cultural binaries, literacy instruction is devalued for boys and young men and is perceived by them to undermine their masculinity. They argue that the practice of critical literacy—which uncovers the links between language and social practice—can be instrumental in enabling boys to understand the discourses that inscribe and construct them as masculine. In the context of the current concern about boys and poor literacy performance, Gilbert argues that it is unlikely that educators will make any difference "unless a close and careful examination of the social and embodied practices of masculinities, and of the social construction and value of school forms of literacy and literacy testing, become part of classroom learning" (Gilbert, 1997, p. 22). She continues: "Boys deserve access to knowledges about their social construction as gendered subjects, about the curricular processes they are inserted into, and about the ways in which they might position themselves differently in a range of social contexts" (p. 22; see also Davies, 1997).

In academic research, studies of the discursive construction of identity continued to proliferate. A popular focus for this work has been early childhood (Alloway, 1995; Davies, 1989b, 1993; Kamler, Maclean, Reid, & Simpson, 1994). This phase is represented as a kind of crucible of formative experiences, offering the potential to either cement or unsettle gender binarisms. The imperative is urgent and unequivocal. Children must learn to deconstruct their gender identity! In this way, the incitement to self-reflexivity becomes intrinsic to childhood development and to the soliciting of children to new norms of gender flexibility. As Alloway argues, "young children themselves need access to alternative discourses about gender before fundamental changes in gender relations can be achieved. Children need to be able to see and to talk about how they learn to 'do' their gender, to question socially-endorsed ways of being female or male that limit their possibilities" (Alloway, 1995, p. 103). Teachers must, Alloway suggests, "work together with young children to contest the discourses, the social practices, and the ways in which they begin to desire restrictive gender identities" (Alloway, 1995, p. 103). Deeply critical of developmentalism (Davies, 1989b) as a model for understanding the journey of childhood, poststructuralist accounts nevertheless govern childhood subjectivity through making gender reflexivity part of the necessary protocol of growing up. Gender identity is not imposed by social forces beyond one's control. Nor is gender the result of an intrinsic disposition or essence. No! Gender identity is an individual project.

The exhortation to examine the construction of gender has not passed unremarked. I shall first note some of the main ways in which it has been discussed. I shall then indicate some further issues to be explored in relation to the "poststructural effect" in educational research and policy. There has been much discussion among feminists about how attending to gender has enabled a focus on masculinity, and some concern that this signals a move away from attending to the specific needs of girls (Collins, Kenway, & McLeod, 2000; Gilbert, 1996, pp. 14–16; Lingard & Douglas, 1999). These concerns are also linked to the emergence of the "what about the boys?" debate and to a policy shift to investigate the specific factors impinging on boys' educational experiences and performance (Collins et al., 2000). (The attention to masculinity also registers a disruption to the alignment of gender as femininity that, in many respects, is an important discursive break.) It is also acknowledged that the strong focus on identity (either masculine or feminine) in gender equity policies has shifted attention away from analysis of the broader material and social conditions in which gender relations are formed and enacted. Borrowing from Nancy Fraser's formulation (1997), this has been analyzed as symptomatic of the ascendancy of the "politics of recognition" and the marginalization of the "politics of distribution" (Collins et al., 2000). There has also been some discussion of the limits of compelling young people to change their gender identities, and an appreciation that such a project risks being naively rationalist, oblivious to the emotional investments young people have in their (unreconstructed) identities (Gilbert, 1996; Kenway & Willis, 1997; McLeod, 1996).

The "construction of gender" has been reified as a stage in the periodization of gender reform. As the latest phase, it is often represented as the culmination of progress to more sophisticated understandings. Previous conceptions of gender identity and of gender reforms are thus cast aside as erroneous, simplistic, and naive. For example, the concept of identity as a construction is positioned in contrast to an essentialist view of femininity and to the "view of girls held within the liberal framework of highly rational, self-determining individuals with an essential and relatively stable self" (Kenway & Willis, 1993, pp. 3–4). Role theory, and strategies based on this understanding, are identified as especially flawed. In her study of preschool children and gender, Davies describes sex-role theory as "commonsense but inaccurate" because "of a profound confusion about what a person really is" (Davies, 1989b, p. 5). Role theories are, she argues, another illustration of the "individualistic humanist theories of the person that are so much part of the modern social world" (p. 6)

Sex-role socialization, while once a popular account, has, for legitimate reasons, now fallen from favor, and many critiques have been written explaining its limitations (Connell, 1983; Edwards, 1983). However, in some of the current educational research and policies recommending that we examine the ways in which we become feminine or masculine, the differences between this usually poststructuralist-inspired focus and the earlier accounts of role socialization are not always evident. There are, of course, significant differences in their theoretical traditions and approaches to the social and to subjectivity. Poststructuralism, for instance, offers a critique of role theory and repudiates its dependence on an implicit pregiven subject who "anchors" and selects the multiple roles that one—the essential self—adopts (Henriques et al., 1984). Role theory is more explicitly functionalist than poststructuralism and is unable to account properly for difference, contradiction, and instability. Nevertheless, there are arguably homologies between the two accounts of identity, especially insofar as they are evidenced in policy and professional discourses. In the recommendations and conclusions of contemporary researchers, I find it often hard to see how the latest, self-consciously sophisticated approach differs in effect from the earlier and often discredited approach. In terms of feminist educational strategies, what is the actual difference between arguing that identities are multiple and constructed and arguing that identity is socialized and comprised of many different roles? Both approaches view gender as profoundly social, as an object of rational examination, as a role or a category that can be remade and that, with proper feminist intervention, can be freed from patriarchal definitions and ways of being.[12]

In this sense we can see the "construction of gender" (and poststructuralism in education) as constituting a discourse of redemption (Popkewitz, 1998a) and as also normative and regulatory. Let me explain. As part of poststructuralism more broadly, it is represented as reinvigorating educational research on gender, rescuing it from innocent, old-fashioned "theories." As an exemplary "emancipatory discourse," the imperative to "examine the construction of gender" promises to free children from the confines of gender binaries and lead them to embrace an enriched, self-aware, and more authentic gender identity. Numerous commentators have examined the emergence of child-centered, constructivist pedagogies (Hultqvist, 1998; Hunter, 1994; Popkewitz, 1998a; Walkerdine, 1984) and the production of an individual who is "active, self-motivated, participatory and problem-solving" (Popkewitz, 1998a, p. 12). In some respects, the discourses of "gender construction" represent a continuation of these pedagogies. Gender reforms promote individual flexibility and responsibility, promising to empower girls and boys through the transcendence of traditional forms of identity. This represents both a particular way of understanding identity and the reworking of a more familiar set of progressivist dreams about the expectations of schooling—the blossoming of the fully rounded, self-aware, self-directed child, leading to the formation of responsible, socially critical citizens. In the current manifestation of this promise, however, the flexible, self-critical identity answers feminism's demand for nonsexist, nontraditional persons and matches the economic requirements for a multiskilled, adaptable workforce, well disposed to regarding the self as a project to be remade in the face of changing demands.

Yet, such a redemptive discourse must also (by the very logic of Foucauldianism) have its own "will to truth" and forms of regulation. In my view, there has been much work documenting the virtues of poststructuralism, but insufficient work that seeks to be reflexive about the truth claims of poststructuralism and its various (nonredemptive and dangerous) effects.[13] What then are the norms for the child governed by poststructuralist technologies? This is not simply a rhetorical question, with an answer known in advance—it is being posed in a speculative and exploratory manner. I have already suggested that one of the effects of the constructionist discourse is the incitement of the self-monitoring individual responsible for maintaining identity flexibility and regulating her-/himself in line with changing gender and feminist reform imperatives. The responsibility of students and teachers is to engage in educational processes that encourage the endless scrutiny of motive and inclination and refuse the possibility of a fixed and stable identity. Identity must be made time and again. This form of subjectivity demands self-reflexivity. The formation of self as a reflexive and self-conscious project is a key feature of modernity. Beck, for example, writes that in contemporary social life, "reflexive modernisation dissolves traditional parameters of industrial society: class culture and consciousness, gender and family roles. . . . These detraditionalisations happen in a *social surge of individualisation*" (Beck, 1992, p. 87). Beck argues that:

> The proportion of life opportunities which are fundamentally closed to decision-making is decreasing and the proportion of the biography which is open and must be constructed personally is increasing. Individualisa-

tion of life situations and processes thus means that biographies become *self-reflexive*; socially-prescribed biography is transformed into biography that is self-produced and continues to be produced. (p.135)

Examining the "construction of gender" is an emblematic project of modernity in which gender identities are (idealized as?) in flux, no longer fixed. Many poststructuralist and Foucauldian scholars have analyzed the process of modernity and the emergence of political rationalities that demand self-reflexive, autonomous, and flexible individuals (e.g, Rose, 1990). I am suggesting that as well as offering a compelling analysis and critique of modernity and its subjects, elements of poststructural discourse have themselves become, through pedagogies and educational reforms, both implicated in and symptomatic of the project of individualization and reflexivity.

In this section, I have been discussing some of the ways in which poststructuralist ideas have become a central part of educational discourse in Australia. I have addressed children's gendered subjectivity as the object of policy and reform discourses and indicated some of the ways in which their childhood gender identity is governed through pedagogies inspired by Foucauldian and poststructuralist ideas.

Conclusions and Questions

Throughout this chapter, I have analyzed certain poststructuralist discourses in education as intensely concerned with protocols for conducting oneself as a gendered subject and particularly with governing gender identity in childhood. I have suggested that poststructuralist discourse itself is implicated in governmentality—in the setting up of ways and norms to manage the conduct of conduct. In education, this has generated pedagogical practices that, as particular "technologies of the self," oblige individual children and teachers to monitor and regulate their gendered identity, to view subjectivity as a project and not as a given, fixed essence.

In arguing that poststructuralist ideas inform programs and policies on gender equity in Australia I have been focusing on the "mentalities of rule" dimension to governmentality (O'Malley et al., 1997). Another account could be told of the messy and contested nature of its implementation and reception (McLeod, 1998b, 1998c; Kenway & Willis, 1997). There is yet another story to be told about the complex process of policy formulation (whose voices are heeded?) within government bureaucracies and in the context of competitively and "externally" tendered research projects directed toward policy and program reform (Collins et al. 1999; Henry & Taylor, 1999).

In this chapter, however, I have been concerned with raising a different set of questions about the trajectory of certain kinds of poststructuralist and Foucauldian analyses. First, I have addressed the historical issue of the turn to poststructuralism in education and the social sciences more generally. My purpose here has been to consider the antecedents to this focus in the field of gender equity and to consider the appeal and policy effects of certain key propositions about subjectivity and discourses. I noted in particular the kind of neo-constructivist "Foucault" invented in Australian educational discourses as well as the emancipatory and redemptive promises of poststructuralism. Second, I have suggested that, at least in the field of gender equity, poststructuralist ideas can be understood as normative and as part of governmentality, both in terms of programs and "mentalities of rule" and in terms of the incitements and imperatives to practice certain forms of subjectification. Third, I have noted some homologies between the self-reflexive biographies produced by and required of late modernity and the kind of self-scrutinizing, reconstructing subjectivities invoked by poststructuralism in education and its call for each of us—child and adult—to endlessly examine the construction of gender.

One of the contexts for these analyses has been the Foucauldian proposition that all social practice is regulatory, and that even our most cherished emancipatory narratives have their own dangers and disciplinary effects. In terms of the analysis I have been developing about poststructuralism in education, I have emphasized the regulatory effects of certain truths and technologies. This has been in order to provide an alternative account to the predominantly celebratory ones that position poststructuralism ahistorically, as emancipatory, and, in some senses, as offering the final truth about subjectivity. I have also wanted to extend the reflexivity encouraged by poststructuralist and Foucauldian analyses and interpret poststructuralism as itself a particular regime of truth. However, I do not want to conclude only with the argument that these truths have had normative effects in education. I also want to retain a sense of education as a field of research, policy, *and* practice, and to consider which kind of discursive interventions are preferable to others. If all public policy is understood as governmental, implicated in managing populations and inciting modes of subjectivity, then we need to consider on what ethical basis we distinguish between desirable and undesirable governmental practices. Can one engage productively with governmentality and work with the possibilities enabled by "progressive" and feminist governmental programs? Is the only response to the "all is regulation/dangerous" argument simply resignation or ever more skeptical and sophisticated critique? Is a policy agenda based on the "construction of gender" preferable (and why or why not) to one based on the presumption of children's intrinsic gender difference and fixed identities? At the same time as the construction of gender produces its own dangers, it also positively and critically opens up possibilities for new, enriching subject positions. Certain forms of masculinity and femininity have been impoverished and confining and have obviously had serious educational and social consequences for girls and boys. Challenging the cultural authority of such gender norms, and instituting alternative (feminist) possibilities/norms, has been core activity for feminist reform in education and elsewhere. This underlines the tension arising from simultaneously deconstructing and reconstructing political and identity norms.

In raising these questions I am aware that attempting to establish normative ethical and political codes can, as Judith Butler suggests, foreclose the possibilities of what counts as "ethical" or "political" and reduce complex matters to a single pregiven version of "real" politics.[14] Butler writes that:

> To set the "norms" of political life in advance is to prefigure the kinds of practices which will qualify as the political and it is to seek to negotiate politics outside of a history which is always to a certain extent opaque to us at the moment of action. (Butler, 1995, p. 129)

Nevertheless, Butler continues: "To set norms, to affirm aspirations, to articulate the possibilities of a more full democratic and participatory political life is, nevertheless, a necessity" (p. 129). Butler's challenge to work across and with this paradox—of knowing the dangers of setting norms but still needing to—destabilizes conventional notions of foundationalist politics. Even though the answer to "what is ethical?" might not be determined in advance, the necessity to pose the question persists. In this sense, we do of course need to keep asking questions about the practices and effects of governmentality, but at the same time, we also need to ask more questions about the kind of educational policies and practices made possible by poststructuralism.

Notes

I wish to thank David Goodman, Lyn Yates, Kenneth Hultqvist, and Gunilla Dahlberg for their helpful, critical comments on drafts of this chapter. For their questions and interest in the work, I thank participants in the seminar "The Child in a Changing World," Copenhagen, August 1998, and the audience and members of the symposium "The Foucault Effect in Education" at the Australian Association for Research in Education annual conference, Melbourne, December 1999.

[1] There is a strong research tradition in Australia focused on the role and effect of feminists working in the bureaucracy—femocrats—and of assessing the consequences of feminist engagements with the state. Many feminist scholars, such as Eisenstein (1991), Watson (1990), Yeatman (1990), and Franzway, Court, & Connell (1989), have elaborated some of the dilemmas of the femocracy and of feminism

working with/for/against the state. This diverse body of work explores feminism as a powerful and productive politics, able to mediate reforms through state agencies, such as departments of education; in this way Australian feminism has had a significant institutional presence and definite effects.

2 This process, Foucault reminds us, takes place always in relation to technologies of domination and regulation. "Perhaps I've insisted too much on the technology of domination and power," reflected Foucault in a late article. "I am more and more interested," he continued, "in the interaction between oneself and others and in the technologies of individual domination, the history of how an individual acts upon himself, in the technology of the self" (Foucault, 1988, p. 19). Foucault describes technologies of the self as one of four major types of technologies, the others being technologies of production, of sign systems, and of power; these four types rarely function separately. In order to fulfill his ambition to develop a genealogy of the subject in Western civilization, Foucault insisted that he needed "to take into account not only techniques of domination, but also techniques of self. One has to show the interaction between these two types of techniques" (Foucault, 1985, p. 367).

3 In her genealogy of the "educated subject," Fendler (1998) poses the question: What is it impossible to think?" She seeks to "problematise what it has meant to be educated" (p. 40) by tracing some contrasting historical constructions of what has counted or not counted as "educated," of what matters as learning, and the kind of questions and ways of knowing that these constructions have made possible or impossible (Fendler, 1998).

4 I thank Kenneth Hultqvist for suggesting a helpful way to rethink my initial questions about the Foucault effect on Australian educational discourses, so that the formulation also enquires about the Australian effect on Foucault.

5 In his discussion of discourses about the child and modern childhood in Sweden, Hultqvist (1998) analyzes the discontinuities in discourses about children but also notes some continuities: the former child "shares some of the characteristics of the welfare child of the 1930s and 1940s. I would even say that the child is still part of our present" (p. 96). This is not to argue, he proceeds, that the present is simply a "repetition of the past" (p. 110). The present is always being constructed anew, even as it utilizes elements from the past. In a similar way, the shifting discourses about children's gendered subjectivity also register some ongoing anxieties about the responsibilities of schools to govern this identity, even if understandings about the meaning and formation of gender identity alter and are discontinuous.

6 Elsewhere I have explored how the pedagogies that flowed from these beliefs can be analyzed as particular "technologies of the self," ones that privileged vigilant self-monitoring in order to fulfill the new feminist norms of a nonsexist, nontraditional person (McLeod, 1998c). These were not simply ineffectual aspirations; rather they were regulatory and normative and it is this productive dimension that positions them as part of governmentality.

7 The field of poststructural research is large and diverse. Nevertheless, it is possible to identify certain trends and shifting—as well as overlapping—preoccupations and trajectories. While the brief discussion is in part autobiographical—a record of the debates and ideas that I have witnessed—it also attempts to represent more than simply one idiosyncratic version of how poststructuralist ideas have been put to work in educational discourses.

8 A historical account of poststructuralism in Australia would need to consider the issues raised by the concept of the "indigenous foreigner" and the relation of

Australia to western European and Anglo-American intellectual traditions. I note here a sample of some developments that I consider to be significant in tracing the trajectory of poststructuralist discourse in Australian educational research. Although poststructural ideas have been circulating in the social sciences since the 1970s, their impact has been most strongly felt in educational research since the late 1980s. In the 1970s, there was little research in education that explicitly declared itself to be poststructuralist. An exception was a much-cited and influential article by Jones and Williamson (1979) that developed an archaeology of the classroom in the context of mass schooling in nineteenth-century Britain. Analyzing the monitorial system and the role of schooling in governing unruly populations later become a favored topic for Foucauldian research on education (e.g., Ball, 1990; Hunter, 1994). Pursuing the lines of analysis developed in *Discipline and Punish*, this work sometimes led to fairly literal discussions about schooling and its disciplinary practices, modes of surveillance, and normalizing relation to social order (cf. Schrag, 1999). Into the 1980s there was a productive and influential tradition of cultural studies research (emanating, for example, from the Birmingham Centre for Contemporary Cultural Studies) that brought together a range of "new" theoretical insights to interpret education as a site of contemporary and historical cultural contest (e.g., Baron, Finn, Grant, Green, & Johnson, 1981; Hall, 1981). This work, straddling Gramsci, Althusser, and Foucault, attempted to work through, for example, the differences between the concepts of ideology and discourse, or the limits of Foucault's concept of power compared to a Gramscian notion of hegemony. These debates provided a backdrop for interpreting, for example, the effect of popular representations of schooling or for understanding the relationship of schooling to subjectivity (Baron et al.; Beechey & Donald, 1985) and were important in Australia. By the mid 1980s, poststructuralist ideas about subjectivity and discourses were gaining more widespread currency, and by the 1990s they had become relatively secure.

⁹ Hunter's work has influenced and been a part of range of a new scholarship in Australia; for example, Meredyth & Tyler (1993); Ian Hunter, "Personality as Vocation: The Political Rationality of the Humanities," in Ian Hunter, Denise Meredyth, Bruce Smith, & Geoff Stokes, *Accounting for the Humanities: The Language of Culture and the Logic of Government* (pp. 7–67), Griffith University, Brisbane: Institute for Cultural Policy Studies, 1991; see too the special issue of *Meanjin* (1992, Spring) for a series of essays on cultural policy studies, some of which extend Hunter's kind of analysis, for example, Denise Meredyth, "Changing Minds: Cultural Criticism and the Problem of Principle," pp. 491–504; and Ian Hunter, "The Humanities without Humanism," pp. 479–90. Hunter's work has also generated much criticism and debate. For example, Cherryholmes, Symes, Yates, & Hunter (1995); Wexler, Miller, Brown, & Dowling (1994–1995); and Apple (1995).

¹⁰ Popkewitz writes of the circulation of ideas across different domains in terms of the relations between "systems of reason and the actors who are authorised to speak" (Popkewitz, in press). He argues: "it is possible to think about correlating the images and narratives of policy and the sciences with the 'priests' (e.g. particular educational researchers) who bring the [indigenous] foreigner into national discourses and the groups with which the priests as well as the indigenous foreigner are associated, the resources used in playing the game, and the norms of regulation that join the local and the global" (Popkewitz, in press). In Australia, such a set of relations (between systems of reason—in this case poststructuralist discourses—and actors authorized to speak) has been crucial and, moreover, is characteristic of how feminists have worked with the policy reform process for some time.

[11] For further analysis of the popularity of poststructuralism in feminist educational research, see L. Yates (1993c, pp. 1–9).

[12] See Schrag (1999) for a discussion of the apparent homologies between Parsonian structural-functionalism and Foucauldian analysis of the purposes/effects of schooling derived from *Discipline and Punish*.

[13] Popkewitz and Brennan argue that "what is important for research is not a slavish cult of Foucaultian implementation studies but a continual problematization of the categorizations, foci, and methodological considerations to which he has given emphasis." One needs "to emphasize the need for rigorous questioning of the will to truth embodied in educational research in particular. In an arena that is centrally concerned with training in truth production, such an invitation may be difficult to accept" (Popkewitz & Brennan, 1998, pp. 29–31).

[14] I thank Lyn Yates for returning me to this essay.

References

Alcoff, L. (1988). Cultural feminism versus post-structuralism. *Signs: Journal of Women in Culture and Society, 13* (3), 405–36.

Alloway, N. (1995). *Foundation stones: The construction of gender in early childhood*. Carlton, Vic, Australia: Curriculum Corporation.

Alloway, N., & Gilbert, P. (1997). Boys and literacy: Lessons from Australia. *Gender and Education, 9* (1), 49–58.

Anyon, J. (1994). The retreat of Marxism and socialist feminism: Postmodern and poststructural theories in education. *Curriculum Inquiry, 24* (2), 115–33.

Apple, M. (1995). Review of *Rethinking the school: Subjectivity, bureaucracy, criticism*, by Ian Hunter. *Australian Journal of Education, 39* (1), 95–96.

Australian Education Council (1993). *National action plan for the education of girls 1993–97*. Melbourne: Curriculum Corporation.

Baker, B. (1998). "Childhood" in the emergence and spread of U.S. public schools. In T. S. Popkewitz & M. Brennan, M. (Eds.), *Foucault's challenge: Discourse, knowledge, and power in education* (pp. 117–43). New York: Teachers College Press.

Ball, S. (Ed.) (1990). *Foucault and education: Disciplines and knowledge*. London: Routledge.

Baron, S., Finn, D., Grant, N., Green, M., & Johnson, R. (1981). *Unpopular education: Schooling and social democracy in England since 1944*. London: Hutchinson, in association with the Birmingham Centre for Contemporary Cultural Studies.

Beck, U. (1992). *Risk society: Towards a new modernity*. London: Sage Publications.

Beechey, V., & Donald, J. (Eds.) (1985). *Subjectivity and social relations*. Milton Keynes: Open University Press.

Belenky, M. F., McVicker, B. C, Goldberger, M. R., & Tarule, J. M. (1986). *Women's ways of knowing: The development of self, voice, and mind*. New York: Basic Books.

Blair, M., Holland, J., & Sheldon, S. (Eds.) (1995). *Identity and diversity: Gender and the experience of education*. Clevedon, UK: Open University Press.

Butler, J. (1995). Contingent foundations. In S. Benhabib, J. Butler, C. Cornell, & N. Fraser, *Feminist contentions: A philosophical exchange*. New York: Routledge.

Cherryholmes, C. (1988). *Power and criticism: Poststructural investigations in education*. New York: Teachers College Press.

Cherryholmes, C., Symes, C., Yates, L., & Hunter, I. (1995). Review symposium: Rethinking the school with the help of Michel Foucault. *Australian Educational Researcher, 22* (1), 107–29.

Collins, C., Batten, M., Ainley, J., & Getty, C. (1996). *Gender and school education.* Canberra: Commonwealth Department of Education, Employment, Training and Youth Affairs.

Collins, C., Kenway, J., & McLeod, J. (2000). *Factors influencing educational performance of males and females at school and their initial destinations after leaving school.* Canberra: Commonwealth Department of Education, Training and Youth Affairs.

Commonwealth Schools Commission (1975). *Girls, school and society: Report by a study group to the schools commission.* Canberra.

Commonwealth Schools Commission (1984). *Girls and tomorrow: The challenge for schools.* Report of the Working Party on the Education of Girls. Canberra.

Commonwealth Schools Commission (1987). *The national policy for the education of girls in Australian schools.* Canberra.

Connell, R. W. (1983). The concept of role and what to do with it. In his *Which way is up: Essays on class, sex and culture* (pp. 189–200). Sydney: Allen & Unwin.

Connell, R. W. (1997). Teaching the boys: New research on masculinity, and gender strategies for schools. *Teachers College Record, 98* (2), 206–35.

Davies, B. (1989a). The discursive production of the male/female dualism in school settings. *Oxford Review of Education, 15* (3), 229–41.

Davies, B. (1989b). *Frogs and snails and feminist tales: Pre-school children and gender.* Sydney: Allen & Unwin.

Davies, B. (1993). *Shards of glass: Children reading and writing beyond gendered identities.* Sydney: Allen & Unwin.

Davies, B. (1997). Critical literacy in practice: Language lessons for and about boys. *Interpretations, 30* (2), 36–57.

Dean, M. (1994). *Critical and effective histories: Foucault's methods and historical sociology.* New York: Routledge.

Department of Education, Employment and Training (1992). *Femininity and reality: Factors that affect girls learning.* A Project of National Significance. Canberra.

Donald, J. (1992). *Sentimental education: Schooling, popular culture and liberty.* London: Verso.

Dussel, I. (1999, April). Foucault's conception of history: Reflections on the use(s) of genealogy. Paper presented at the annual meeting of the American Educational Research Association, Montreal, Canada.

Edwards, A. (1983). Sex roles: A problem for sociology and for women. *Australian and New Zealand Journal of Sociology, 19* (3), 385–412.

Eisenstein, H. (1991). *Gender shock: Practising feminism on two continents.* Sydney: Allen & Unwin.

Epstein, D., Elwood, J., Hey, V., & Maw, J. (Eds.) (1998). *Failing boys? Issues in gender and achievement.* Buckingham, UK: Open University Press.

Fendler, L. (1998). What is it impossible to think? A genealogy of the educated subject. In T. S. Popkewitz & M. Brennan (Eds.), *Foucault's challenge: Discourse, knowledge, and power in education* (pp. 39–63). New York: Teachers College Press.

Foucault, M. (1983). The subject and power. In H. L. Dreyfus and P. Rabinow, *Michel Foucault: Beyond structuralism and hermeneutics* (pp. 208–9). Chicago: University of Chicago Press.

Foucault, M. (1984a). Nietzsche, genealogy, history. In P. Rabinow (Ed.), *The Foucault reader* (pp. 76–100). New York: Pantheon Books.

Foucault, M. (1984b). *The history of sexuality: An introduction.* Trans. R. Hurley. Harmondsworth: Penguin.

Foucault, M. (1985). Sexuality and solitude. In M. Blonsky (Ed.), *On signs: A semiotic reader* (pp. 365–72). Oxford: Basil Blackwell.

Foucault, M. (1988). Technologies of the self. In L. Martin, H. Gutman, & P. Hutton (Eds.), *Technologies of the self: A seminar with Michel Foucault* (pp. 16–49). London: Tavistock Publications.

Fowler, R. (1983, September). Sexually-inclusive curriculum. *Victorian Teacher,* pp. 15–19.

Franzway, S., Court, D., & Connell, R. W. (1989). *Staking a claim: Feminism, bureaucracy and the state.* Sydney: Allen & Unwin.

Fraser, N. (1997) *Justice interruptus: Critical reflections on the "postsocialist" condition.* New York: Routledge.

Gilbert, P. (1996). *Talking about gender: Terminology used in the education of girls policy area and implications for policy priorities and programs.* Canberra: Department of Employment, Education and Training.

Gilbert, P. (1997). Gender and schooling in new times: The challenge of boys and literacy. *Australian Educational Researcher, 25* (1), 15–36.

Gilbert, P., & Taylor, S. (1989). *Fashioning the feminine: Girls, popular culture and schooling.* Sydney: Allen & Unwin.

Gilbert, R., & Gilbert, P. (1994). *Analysing gender and disadvantage: Theoretical perspectives.* A Gender Equity in Curriculum Reform Project, Department of Employment, Education and Training. Canberra.

Gilbert, R., & Gilbert, P. (1998). *Masculinity goes to school.* Sydney: Allen & Unwin.

Gilligan, C. (1977). In a different voice: Women's conceptions of self and morality. *Harvard Educational Review, 47* (4), 481–517.

Giroux, H. (1992). *Border crossings: Cultural workers and the politics of education.* New York: Routledge.

Gore, J. (1993) *The struggle for pedagogies: Critical and feminist discourses as regimes of truth.* New York: Routledge.

Hall, S. (1981). Cultural studies: Two paradigms. In T. Bennett (Ed.), *Culture, ideology and social process* (pp. 19–33). London: Open University Press.

Henriques, J., Hollway, W., Urwin, C., Venn, C., & Walkerdine, V. (1984). *Changing the subject: Psychology, social regulation and subjectivity.* London: Methuen.

Henry, M., & Taylor, S. (1999). *Conceptualisation, funding and monitoring programs relating to educational equity and disadvantage in Australian schools.* Unpublished report, University of Queensland, Brisbane, Australia.

Hultqvist, K. (1998). A history of the present on children's welfare in Sweden: From Frobel to present-day decentralization projects. In T. S. Popkewitz & M. Brennan (Eds.), *Foucault's challenge: Discourse, knowledge, and power in education* (pp. 92–116). New York: Teachers College Press, Columbia University.

Hunter, I. (1991). Personality as vocation: The political rationality of the humanities. In I. Hunter, D. Meredyth, B. Smith, & G. Stokes, *Accounting for the humanities: The language of culture and the logic of government* (pp. 7–67). Griffith University, Australia: Institute for Cultural Policy Studies.

Hunter, I. (1992, Spring). The humanities without humanism. *Meanjin, 3,* 479–90.

Hunter, I. (1993). Mind games and body techniques. *Southern Review, 26* (2), 172–85.

Hunter, I. (1994) *Rethinking the school: Subjectivity bureaucracy criticism.* Sydney: Allen & Unwin.

Hunter, I., Meredyth, D., Smith, B., & Stokes, G. (1991). *Accounting for the humanities: The language of culture and the logic of government.* Griffith University, Brisbane: Institute for Cultural Policy Studies.

Johnson, L. (1990, Autumn). Gender issues and education. *Australian Feminist Studies, 11,* 17–27.

Johnson, L. (1993). *The modern girl: Girlhood and growing up.* Sydney: Allen & Unwin.

Jones, K., & Williamson, K. (1979). The birth of the classroom. *Ideology and Consciousness, 5–6,* 59–110.

Kamler, B., Maclean, R., Reid, J-A., & Simpson, A. (1994). *Shaping up nicely: The formation of schoolgirls and schoolboys in the first month of school.* Canberra: Gender Equity and Curriculum Reform Project, DEET.

Kenway, J. (with Willis, S., Blackmore, J., & Rennie, L.) (1993). Learning from girls: What can girls teach feminist teachers? *Melbourne Studies in Education,* 63–77.

Kenway, J. (1997). Taking stock of gender reform policies for Australian schools: Past, present and future. *British Educational Research Journal, 23* (3), 329–44.

Kenway, J., & Willis, S. (with the Education of Girls Unit of South Australia) (1993). *Telling tales: Girls and schools changing their ways.* Canberra: Department of Education, Employment and Training.

Kenway, J., & Willis, S. (1995). *Critical visions: Rewriting the future of work, schooling and gender.* Canberra: Department of Employment, Education and Training.

Kenway, J., & Willis, S. (with Blackmore, J., & Rennie, L.) (1997). *Answering back: Girls, boys and feminism in schools.* Sydney: Allen & Unwin.

Lather, P. (1991). *Getting smart: Feminist research and pedagogy with/in the postmodern.* London: Routledge.

Lingard, B., & Douglas, P. (1999). *Men engaging feminisms: Pro-feminism, backlashes and schooling.* Buckingham, UK: Open University Press.

Luke, A., & Luke, C. (1990). School knowledge as simulation: Curriculum in postmodern conditions. *Discourse, 10* (2), 75–91.

Luke, C., & Gore., J. (Eds.) (1992). *Feminisms and critical pedagogy.* New York: Routledge.

Lyotard, J-F. (1984). *The postmodern condition: A report on knowledge.* Minneapolis: University of Minnesota Press.

Marshall, J. (1989). Foucault and education. *Australian Journal of Education, 33* (2), 99–113.

Martino, W. (1999). "Cool boys," "party animals," "squids" and "poofters": Interrogating the dynamics and politics of adolescent masculinities in school. *British Journal of the Sociology of Education, 20* (2), 239–63.

McInnes, S. (1996). *Girls, schools . . . and boys: Promoting gender equity through schools: Twenty years of gender equity policy development* (Report of the Social Policy Group Research Paper, number 24). Canberra: Department of the Parliamentary Library.

McLean, C. (1997). Engaging with boys' experiences of masculinity: Implications for gender reform. In J. Kenway (Ed.), *Will boys be boys? Boys' education in the context of gender reform* (pp. 13–16). Canberra: Australian Curriculum Studies Association.

McLeod, J. (1993). Impossible fictions? Utopian visions and feminist educational research. *Melbourne Studies in Education,* 107–17.

McLeod, J. (1996). *Regulating gender: Feminist truths and educational reform in Victoria since 1975.* Ph.D. thesis, La Trobe University.

McLeod, J. (1998a). Out of the comfort zone: Feminism after the backlash. *Discourse: studies in the cultural politics of education, 19* (3), 371–78.

McLeod, J. (1998b). Reforms, response and reality: Gender, schooling and feminism. In J. Allen (Ed.), *Sociology of education: Possibilities and practices* (pp. 141–67). Katoomba, NSW: Social Sciences Press.

McLeod, J. (1998c). The promise of freedom and the regulation of gender—feminist pedagogy in the 1970s. *Gender and Education, 10* (4), 431–45.

McNay, L. (1992). *Foucault and feminism.* Cambridge, UK: Polity Press.

Meanjin (1992, Spring). Special Issue, "Culture, Policy and Beyond."

Meredyth, D., & Tyler, D. (Eds.) (1993). *Child and citizen: Genealogies of schooling and subjectivity.* Griffith University, Australia: Institute for Cultural Policy Studies.

Middleton, S. (1998). *Disciplining sexuality: Foucault, life histories, and education.* New York: Teachers College Press, Columbia University.

Millet, K. (1972). *Sexual politics.* London: Abacus, Sphere Books.

Milligan, S., & Thomson, K., Ashendon, D. (1992). *Listening to girls: A report of the consultancy undertaken for the Australian Education Council Committee to review the national policy for the education of girls in Australian schools.* Carlton, Australia: Curriculum Corporation.

Ministerial Council on Education, Employment, Training and Youth Affairs (1997). *Gender equity: A framework for Australian schools.* Canberra.

Office of Schools Administration (1990). *A fair go for all: Guidelines for gender-inclusive curriculum.* Victoria: Ministry of Education.

O'Malley, P., Weir, L, & Spearing, C. (1997). Governmentality, criticism, politics. *Economy and Society, 26* (4), 501–17.

Peters, M. (1996). *Post-structuralism, politics and education.* Westport, CT: Bergin & Garvey.

Popkewitz, T. S. (1998a). The culture of redemption and the administration of freedom as research. *Review of Educational Research, 68* (1), 1–34.

Popkewitz, T. S. (1998b). *Struggling for the soul: The politics of schooling and the construction of the teacher.* New York: Teachers College Press.

Popkewitz, T. S. (in press). National imaginaries, the indigenous foreigner, and power: Comparative educational research. In J. Schriewer (Ed.), *Discourse formation in comparative education.* Berlin: Peter Lang Verlag.

Popkewitz, T. S., & Brennan, M. (Eds.) (1998). *Foucault's challenge: Discourse, knowledge, and power in education.* New York: Teachers College Press.

Pringle, R., & Watson, S. (1992). "Women's interests" and the post-structuralist state. In M. Barrett & A. Phillips (Eds.), *Destabilizing theory: Contemporary feminist debates* (pp. 53–73). Cambridge: Polity Press.

Roman, L. G., & Eyre, L. (Eds.) (1997). *Dangerous territories: Struggles for difference and equality in education.* New York: Routledge.

Rose, N. (1990). *Governing the soul: The shaping of the private self.* London: Routledge.

Schrag, F. (1999). Why Foucault now? *Journal of Curriculum Studies, 31* (4), 375–83.

Suggett, D. (1987). Inclusive curriculum: A gain or loss for girls? *Curriculum Perspectives, 7* (1), 69–74.

Tapper, M. (1993). Ressentiment and power; Some reflections on feminist practices. In P. Patton (Ed.), *Nietzsche, feminism and political theory* (pp. 130–43). Sydney: Allen & Unwin.

Tyler, D. (1993). "Going like a boy": Making up girls in the 1930s kindergarten. *Australian Historical Studies, 25* (100), 357–70.

Walkerdine, V. (1984). Developmental psychology and the child-centred pedagogy: The insertion of Piaget into early childhood development. In J. Henriques, W. Hollway, C. Urwin, C. Venn, & V. Walkerdine, *Changing the subject: Psychology, social regulation and subjectivity* (pp. 153–202). London: Methuen.

Walkerdine, V. (1990). *Schoolgirl fictions.* London: Verso.

Walkerdine, V. (1992). Progressive pedagogy and political struggle. In C. Luke & J. Gore (Eds.), *Feminisms and critical pedagogy* (pp.15–24). New York: Routledge.

Watson, S. (Ed.) (1990). *Playing the state: Australian feminist interventions.* Sydney: Allen & Unwin.

Wexler, P., Miller, J., Brown, A., & Dowling, P., (1994–1995). Governing the school [responses to Hunter's "Rethinking the School"]. *Arena, 4,* 161–200.

Yates, L. (1993a). Feminism and Australian state policy; Some questions for the 1990s. In M. Arnot & K. Weiler (Eds.), *Feminism and social justice in education: Intentional perspectives* (pp. 167–85). London: Falmer Press.

Yates, L. (1993b). *The education of girls: Policy, research and the question of gender.* Melbourne: ACER.

Yates, L. (1993c). Feminism and education: Writing in the '90s. *Melbourne Studies in Education,* pp. 1–9.

Yates, L. (1997). Gender equity and boys debate: What sort of challenge is it? *British Journal of the Sociology of Education, 18* (3), 337–47.

Yates, L. (1998). Constructing and deconstructing "girls" as a category of concern. In A. MacKinnnon, I. Elqvist-Saltzman, & A. Prentice (Eds.), *Education into the 21st century; Dangerous terrain for women?* (pp. 155–67). London: Falmer Press.

Yeatman, A. (1990). *Bureaucrats, technocrats, femocrats: Essays on the contemporary Australian state.* Sydney: Allen & Unwin.

Contributors

Marianne N. Bloch is a professor of education at the Department of Curriculum and Instruction, University of Wisconsin-Madison. Her research interests are related to historical and cross-national perspectives in early education, gender, work, and child care issues. Selected publications include *Historical Perspectives on the Aims and Effects of Early Education* (1987), *Re-conceptualizing the Early Childhood Curriculum* (1999), and *Governing the Good Parent, Teacher, and Child: Deconstructing the Discourses of Development* (in progress). She has also edited or is in the process of editing several books, including *The Ecological Context of Children's Play* (1989), *Women and Education in Sub-Saharan Africa* (1998), and *Restructuring the Governing Patterns of the Child, Education, and the Welfare State* (in process).

Rosa Nidia Buenfil-Burgos is a professor of education at the Departamento de Investigaciones Educativas, Centro de Investigación y Estudios Avanzados, and also a part-time lecturer at the Faculty of Philosophy, Universidad Nacional Autonoma de México. She is the author of three books about the educational discourse of the Mexican revolution and chapters, articles, and papers about philosophical debates on education and recent educational policies in Mexico in the context of globalization and postmodernity.

Gunilla Dahlberg is a professor of education at the Stockholm Institute of Education. She has published extensively in the field of early childhood and her work covers the critical analysis of the mentalities that govern childhood practices as well as children's learning. Her recent work includes *From the People's Home to the Enterprise of Reflection on the Constitution and Reconstitution of the Field of Early Childhood Pedagogy in Sweden* (2000), *Evaluation and Regulation. A Question of Empowerment* (with Gunnar Åsén) (1994), and *Beyond Quality in Early Childhood Education and Care* (with P. Moss and A. Pence) (1999).

Inés Dussel is a Ph.D. candidate at the University of Wisconsin-Madison and former professor and researcher at the University of Buenos Aires, Argentina, and FLACSO (Facultad Latinoamericana de Ciencias Sociales). She is coauthor of articles on contemporary educational policies and multiculturalism and author of books on the history of curriculum and the teaching of human rights and contemporary educational theories. She is the author of *La invención pedagógica del aula. Una genealogía de las formas de enseñar* (in press) and *Curriculum, Humanismo y Democracia en la Enseñanza Media (1863–1920)* (History of secondary school curriculum) (1997). She is also the winner of the special prize for educational books at the National Book Fair, sponsored by the Argentine Chamber for Books, Buenos Aires, 1997.

Lynn Fendler is a lecturer in educational policy studies and women's studies at the University of Wisconsin-Madison. Her research interests include the philosophy of education, critical theory, postmodern historical studies, and feminist theory. Her recent work includes the critical problematization of "reason" and the discursive construction of the educated subject in history. She is the author of *Making Trouble: Prediction, Agency and Intellectual Work* (1999), *What Is it Impossible to Think? A Genealogy of the Educated Subject* (1998), and *Postmodernism* (with Thomas and James E. Browne) (1997).

Kenneth Hultqvist is a professor of education at the Stockholm Institute of Education. He has published extensively on childhood and the political government of childhood. For the past two years he has been conducting a study on the mentalities that govern current strategies of school development in Sweden (during the period of 1960–1990). The project is funded by the Swedish Agency for Schools. His publications include *Förskolebarnet, en konstruktion för gemenskapen och den individuella frigörelsen* (The pre-school child, a construction for the community and the liberation of individuals) (1990), *Seendet och Seendets villkor, en bok om barns och ungas välfärd* (The scientific gaze and the conditions of seeing, a book about the welfare of children and youth) (1995), *Changing Rationales for Governing the Child: A Historical Perspective on the Emergence of the Child in the Context of Pre-School* (1997), and *A History of the Present on Children's Welfare in Sweden: From Fröbel to Present Day Decentralization Projects* (1998).

Chris Jenks is a professor of sociology and pro-warden (research) at Goldsmiths College, University of London. He has published extensively on the sociology of culture and the sociology of childhood. His most recent major works are *Childhood* (1996), *Theorizing Childhood* (1998), and *Durkheim and the Sociology of the Art* (with J. Smith) (2000).

Nancy Lesko is associate professor in the Department of Curriculum and Teaching, Teachers College, Columbia University, New York. She teaches in the areas of curriculum, gender studies, and youth studies. Recent publications include an edited collection, *Masculinities at School* (Sage, 2000), and a monograph, *Act Your Age! A Cultural Construction of Adolescence* (Routledge, 2001). Current projects include a study of service-learning curricula in secondary schools and an examination of the educational and community consequences of the U.S. Supreme Court decision to uphold homophobia in the Boy Scouts of America.

Julie McLeod is currently a postdoctoral research fellow in the Faculty of Education at Deakin University, Australia, where she also holds a lecturing position in women's studies. Her areas of research and publication include feminism and education, pedagogy, research methodology, and schooling and subjectivity. Her work has been published in a number of journals including *Gender and Education* and *Discourse*. For the past six years she has been conducting (with Professor Lyn Yates) a qualitative, longitudinal study of secondary students as they progress through each year of their schooling. "The 12 to 18 Project" is funded by the Australian Research Council. Julie is also completing a research project commissioned by the Commonwealth Department of Education, Training and Youth Affairs to investigate the factors influencing the educational performance and initial post-school destinations of males and females.

Thomas S. Popkewitz is a professor of education in the Department of Curriculum and Instruction at the University of Wisconsin-Madison. His books and articles cover a wide range of issues that are central to the field of education. His books include *A Political Sociology of Education* (1991), which was awarded the American Educational Studies Association Critics' Choice as an Outstanding Educational Study, *The Formation of School Subject: The Struggle for Creating an American Institution* (1987), *Changing Patterns of Power: Social Regulation and Teacher Education Reform* (1993), and *Struggling for the Soul* (1998).

Valerie Walkerdine is Foundation Professor of Critical Psychology and head of the Center for Critical Psychology at the University of Western Sydney, Nepean, Sydney, Australia. Her latest book is *Mass Hysteria: Critical Psychology and Media Studies* (with Lisa Blackman) (2000). She is currently directing a project on children and cyberspace funded by the Australian Research Council and has worked on issues of childhood for many years.

Mirian Jorge Warde is a teacher and coordinator of the Post-Graduate Program on Education: History, Politics, Society at Pontifical Catholic University-Sao Paulo/ Brazil and senior researcher on the relationship between culture and education in the nineteenth century and beginning of the twentieth century. She is the author of *O Banco Mundial e as pol'ticas educacionais* (1996), *Lorenzo Luzuriaga entrens* (1998), and *Para uma histria disciplinar: psicologia, criana e pedagogia* (1997).

Index